# Teach Yourself
# UNIX
## 4th Edition

# Teach Yourself
# UNIX
## 4th Edition

**Kevin Reichard and Eric Foster-Johnson**

 **IDG Books Worldwide, Inc.**
An International Data Group Company

Foster City, CA • Chicago, IL • Indianapolis, IN • New York, NY

**Teach Yourself UNIX, 4th Edition**

Published by
**IDG Books Worldwide, Inc.**
An International Data Group Company
919 E. Hillsdale Blvd., Suite 400
Foster City, CA 94404
www.idgbooks.com (IDG Books Worldwide Web site)

ISBN: 1-55828-588-1

Printed in the United States of America

10 9 8 7 6 5 4 3 2 1

4P/QY/QX/ZZ/IN

Distributed in the United States by IDG Books Worldwide, Inc.

Distributed by CDG Books Canada Inc. for Canada; by Transworld Publishers Limited in the United Kingdom; by IDG Norge Books for Norway; by IDG Sweden Books for Sweden; by IDG Books Australia Publishing Corporation Pty. Ltd. for Australia and New Zealand; by TransQuest Publishers Pte Ltd. for Singapore, Malaysia, Thailand, Indonesia, and Hong Kong; by Gotop Information Inc. for Taiwan; by ICG Muse, Inc. for Japan; by Norma Comunicaciones S.A. for Colombia; by Intersoft for South Africa; by Eyrolles for France; by International Thomson Publishing for Germany, Austria and Switzerland; by Distribuidora Cuspide for Argentina; by Livraria Cultura for Brazil; by Ediciones ZETA S.C.R. Ltda. for Peru; by WS Computer Publishing Corporation, Inc., for the Philippines; by Contemporanea de Ediciones for Venezuela; by Express Computer Distributors for the Caribbean and West Indies; by Micronesia Media Distributor, Inc. for Micronesia; by Grupo Editorial Norma S.A. for Guatemala; by Chips Computadoras S.A. de C.V. for Mexico; by Editorial Norma de Panama S.A. for Panama; by American Bookshops for Finland. Authorized Sales Agent: Anthony Rudkin Associates for the Middle East and North Africa.

For general information on IDG Books Worldwide's books in the U.S., please call our Consumer Customer Service department at 800-762-2974. For reseller information, including discounts and premium sales, please call our Reseller Customer Service department at 800-434-3422.

For information on where to purchase IDG Books Worldwide's books outside the U.S., please contact our International Sales department at 317-596-5530 or fax 317-596-5692.

For consumer information on foreign language translations, please contact our Customer Service department at 1-800-434-3422, fax 317-596-5692, or e-mail rights@idgbooks.com.

For information on licensing foreign or domestic rights, please phone +1-650-655-3109.

For sales inquiries and special prices for bulk quantities, please contact our Sales department at 650-655-3200 or write to the address above.

For information on using IDG Books Worldwide's books in the classroom or for ordering examination copies, please contact our Educational Sales department at 800-434-2086 or fax 317-596-5499.

For press review copies, author interviews, or other publicity information, please contact our Public Relations department at 650-655-3000 or fax 650-655-3299.

For authorization to photocopy items for corporate, personal, or educational use, please contact Copyright Clearance Center, 222 Rosewood Drive, Danvers, MA 01923, or fax 978-750-4470.

Library of Congress Cataloging-in-Publication Data
Reichard, Kevin.
    Teach Yourself UNIX / Kevin Reichard and Eric Foster-Johnson.
4th ed.
        p.  cm.
    Includes index.
    ISBN 1-55828-588-1
    1. Operating systems (Computers)   2. UNIX (Computer file)
I. Foster-Johnson, Eric.   II. Title.
QA76.76.O63R443    1999
005.4'32--dc21                                                                97–45826
                                                                                    CIP

# ABOUT IDG BOOKS WORLDWIDE

Welcome to the world of IDG Books Worldwide.

IDG Books Worldwide, Inc., is a subsidiary of International Data Group, the world's largest publisher of computer-related information and the leading global provider of information services on information technology. IDG was founded more than 30 years ago by Patrick J. McGovern and now employs more than 9,000 people worldwide. IDG publishes more than 290 computer publications in over 75 countries. More than 90 million people read one or more IDG publications each month.

Launched in 1990, IDG Books Worldwide is today the #1 publisher of best-selling computer books in the United States. We are proud to have received eight awards from the Computer Press Association in recognition of editorial excellence and three from Computer Currents' First Annual Readers' Choice Awards. Our best-selling ...*For Dummies*® series has more than 50 million copies in print with translations in 31 languages. IDG Books Worldwide, through a joint venture with IDG's Hi-Tech Beijing, became the first U.S. publisher to publish a computer book in the People's Republic of China. In record time, IDG Books Worldwide has become the first choice for millions of readers around the world who want to learn how to better manage their businesses.

Our mission is simple: Every one of our books is designed to bring extra value and skill-building instructions to the reader. Our books are written by experts who understand and care about our readers. The knowledge base of our editorial staff comes from years of experience in publishing, education, and journalism — experience we use to produce books to carry us into the new millennium. In short, we care about books, so we attract the best people. We devote special attention to details such as audience, interior design, use of icons, and illustrations. And because we use an efficient process of authoring, editing, and desktop publishing our books electronically, we can spend more time ensuring superior content and less time on the technicalities of making books.

You can count on our commitment to deliver high-quality books at competitive prices on topics you want to read about. At IDG Books Worldwide, we continue in the IDG tradition of delivering quality for more than 30 years. You'll find no better book on a subject than one from IDG Books Worldwide.

John Kilcullen
Chairman and CEO
IDG Books Worldwide, Inc.

Steven Berkowitz
President and Publisher
IDG Books Worldwide, Inc.

*Eighth Annual Computer Press Awards 1992*

*Ninth Annual Computer Press Awards 1993*

*Tenth Annual Computer Press Awards 1994*

*Eleventh Annual Computer Press Awards 1995*

IDG is the world's leading IT media, research and exposition company. Founded in 1964, IDG had 1997 revenues of $2.05 billion and has more than 9,000 employees worldwide. IDG offers the widest range of media options that reach IT buyers in 75 countries representing 95% of worldwide IT spending. IDG's diverse product and services portfolio spans six key areas including print publishing, online publishing, expositions and conferences, market research, education and training, and global marketing services. More than 90 million people read one or more of IDG's 290 magazines and newspapers, including IDG's leading global brands — Computerworld, PC World, Network World, Macworld and the Channel World family of publications. IDG Books Worldwide is one of the fastest-growing computer book publishers in the world, with more than 700 titles in 36 languages. The "...For Dummies®" series alone has more than 50 million copies in print. IDG offers online users the largest network of technology-specific Web sites around the world through IDG.net (http://www.idg.net), which comprises more than 225 targeted Web sites in 55 countries worldwide. International Data Corporation (IDC) is the world's largest provider of information technology data, analysis and consulting, with research centers in over 41 countries and more than 400 research analysts worldwide. IDG World Expo is a leading producer of more than 168 globally branded conferences and expositions in 35 countries including E3 (Electronic Entertainment Expo), Macworld Expo, ComNet, Windows World Expo, ICE (Internet Commerce Expo), Agenda, DEMO, and Spotlight. IDG's training subsidiary, ExecuTrain, is the world's largest computer training company, with more than 230 locations worldwide and 785 training courses. IDG Marketing Services helps industry-leading IT companies build international brand recognition by developing global integrated marketing programs via IDG's print, online and exposition products worldwide. Further information about the company can be found at www.idg.com. 1/24/99

# Credits

*Acquisitions Editor*
Debra Williams Cauley

*Development Editor*
Laura E. Brown

*Technical Editor*
Chris Stone

*Copy Editors*
Zoe Brymer
Timothy J. Borek

*Book Designers*
Daniel Ziegler Design
Cátálin Dulfu
Kurt Krames

*Production*
IDG Books Worldwide

*Proofreading and Indexing*
York Production Services

# About the Authors

**Kevin Reichard** is the author of 24 books for IDG Books Worldwide, including *Linux Configuration and Installation* and *UNIX in Plain English.* He's the Web Advisor columnist for Performance Computing.

**Eric Foster-Johnson** is a veteran programmer and computer book author. Faced with incompatible and problematic systems, his main goal is to ensure others don't experience the same pains he did. His books include *Cross-Platform Perl, Graphical Applications with Tcl and Tk*, and *UNIX Programming Tools*.

*To Norma and Katya, and many years together.*
*As always, for Sean.*

# Welcome to
# Teach Yourself

Welcome to *Teach Yourself*, a series read and trusted by millions for nearly a decade. Although you may have seen the *Teach Yourself* name on other books, ours is the original. In addition, no *Teach Yourself* series has ever delivered more on the promise of its name than this series. That's because IDG Books Worldwide recently transformed *Teach Yourself* into a new cutting-edge format that gives you all the information you need to learn quickly and easily.

Readers told us that they want to learn by doing and that they want to learn as much as they can in as short a time as possible. We listened to you and believe that our new task-by-task format and suite of learning tools deliver the book you need to successfully teach yourself any technology topic. Features such as our Personal Workbook, which lets you practice and reinforce the skills you've just learned, help ensure that you get full value out of the time you invest in your learning. Handy cross-references to related topics and online sites broaden your knowledge and give you control over the kind of information you want, when you want it.

## More Answers . . .

In designing the latest incarnation of this series, we started with the premise that people like you, who are beginning to intermediate computer users, want to take control of their own learning. To do this, you need the proper tools to find answers to questions so you can solve problems now.

In designing a series of books that provide such tools, we created a unique and concise visual format. The added bonus: *Teach Yourself* books pack more information into their pages than other books written on the same subjects. Skill for skill, you typically get much more information in a *Teach Yourself* book. In fact, *Teach Yourself* books, on average, cover twice the skills covered by other computer books — as many as 125 skills per book — so they're more likely to address your specific needs.

## ... In Less Time

We know you don't want to spend twice the time to get all this great information, so we provide lots of timesaving features:

E A modular task-by-task organization of information: Any task you want to perform is easy to find and includes simple-to-follow steps.

E A larger size than standard makes the book easy to read and convenient to use at a computer workstation. The large format also enables us to include many more code listings and illustrations.

E A Personal Workbook at the end of each chapter reinforces learning with extra practice, real-world applications for your learning, and questions and answers to test your knowledge.

E Cross-references appearing at the bottom of each task page refer you to related information, providing a path through the book for learning particular aspects of the software thoroughly.

E A Find It Online feature offers valuable ideas on where to go on the Internet to get more information or to download useful files.

E Take Note sidebars provide added-value information from our expert authors for more in-depth learning.

E An attractive, consistent organization of information helps you quickly find and learn the skills you need.

These *Teach Yourself* features are designed to help you learn the essential skills about a technology in the least amount of time, with the most benefit. We've placed these features consistently throughout the book, so you quickly learn where to go to find just the information you need — whether you work through the book from cover to cover or use it later to solve a new problem.

You will find a *Teach Yourself* book on almost any technology subject — from the Internet to Windows to Microsoft Office. Take control of your learning today, with IDG Books Worldwide's *Teach Yourself* series.

# Welcome to
# Teach Yourself

Go to this area if you want special tips, cautions, and notes that provide added insight into the current task.

Search through the task headings to find the topic you want right away. To learn a new skill, search the contents, chapter opener, or the extensive index to find what you need. Then find — at a glance — the clear task heading that matches it.

Learn the concepts behind the task at hand and, more important, learn how the task is relevant in the real world. Timesaving suggestions and advice show you how to make the most of each skill.

After you learn the task at hand, you may have more questions, or you may want to read about other tasks related to the topic. Use the cross-references to find different tasks to make your learning more efficient.

## Plucking Data from Tables

On a very rudimentary basis, you could use the basic UNIX commands as database-management tools to manage text files containing data.

Let's say you are managing a small workgroup, and you want to keep a small database of your workers. Using **vi** or **emacs**, you create a file that contains vital information about your employees, like the one shown in the first listing on the facing page.

The sample database is very simple: You list the name of the worker, his or her office telephone extension, login names, and the number of vacation days he or she has remaining this year. The columns of information are separated by tabs. (Using tabs to separate columns of data is important for many UNIX tools.) Databases like this are very common in UNIX, both for personal usage and for system administration.

From this workers file you can create many other lists. Say you want to create a file containing just the names and the phone numbers of the workers for the personnel office. You would do so using the cut command, specifying a file for output:

```
$ cut -f1,3 workers > workers_phone
```

The structure of this command is simple. You tell the shell to cut the first and third fields in the file **workers** and place it in the file **workers_phone**. You can specify one field, all but one field, or, as shown here, a range of fields:

```
$ cut -f1-3,5 workers > workers_phone2
```

You can also use **cut** to pluck information from a number of similarly structured files:

```
$ cut options filenames > output_file
```

The example file is highly structured, using tabs to separate columns. If another character is used to separate fields, you would need to specify the character using the **-d** option:

```
$ cut -d, -f1,3 workers.comma > workers_phone3
```

The character must be placed directly following the **-d** option. In this command, commas are specified as the separators between fields. To use a space as a separator, enclose it in single quotes:

```
$ cut -d' ' -f1,3 workers.single_space \
  > workers_phone4
```

If you don't include the quotes, the shell assumes that the space is part of the command and not related to the **-d** option.

Of course, not all UNIX files are going to be as highly structured as this example. In these cases, you can use specify a range of characters to be cut:

```
$ cut -c1-24 workers.space > workers_phone5
```

This tells **cut** to grab the first 24 characters in a line.

### TAKE NOTE

E **USE AWK FOR MORE SOPHISTICATED CUTS AND JOINS**

For more sophisticated text processing, you can use the advanced command **awk**. This command supports its own text-processing command language (also called AWK).

### CROSS-REFERENCE

Chapter 11 covers **vi** and **emacs**.

### FIND IT ONLINE

For more on **cmp**, see **docs.sun.com:80/ab2/ @DSCBrowse?reference=1.**

88

Use the Find It Online element to locate Internet resources that provide more background, take you on interesting side trips, and offer additional tools for mastering and using the skills you need. (Occasionally you'll find a handy shortcut here.)

The current chapter name and number always appear in the top right-hand corner of every task spread, so you always know exactly where you are in the book.

UNIX TOOLS
**Plucking Data from Tables**

CHAPTER
**3**

### Listing 3-20: A SAMPLE WORKERS FILE

```
$ cat workers
Eric      286    555-6674    erc       8
Geisha    280    555-4221    geisha    10
Kevin     279    555-1112    kevin     2
Tom       284    555-2121    spike     12
Tyler     281    555-2122    rot       4
Katya     282    555-2123    katya     4
```

▲ *Our simple employee database, containing names, office extensions, phone numbers, usernames, and number of vacation days remaining. A single tab character separates each field.*

### Listing 3-21: EXTRACTING NAMES AND PHONE NUMBERS

```
$ cut -f1,3 workers > workers_phone
$ cat workers_phone
Eric      555-6674
Geisha    555-4221
Kevin     555-1112
Tom       555-2121
Tyler     555-2122
Katya     555-2123
```

▲ *Selecting fields 1 and 3 from the **workers** file and sending the output to the file **workers_phone**.*

### Listing 3-22: EXTRACTING THE FIRST THREE FIELDS AND THE FIFTH FIELD

```
$ cut -f1-3,5 workers > workers_phone2
$ cat workers_phone2
Eric      286    555-6674    8
Geisha    280    555-4221    10
Kevin     279    555-1112    2
Tom       284    555-2121    12
Tyler     281    555-2122    4
Katya     282    555-2123    4
```

▲ *Selecting the first three and fifth fields from the **workers** file and sending the output to the file **workers_phone2**.*

### Listing 3-23: EXTRACTING DATA CONTAINING SPACES AS FIELD SEPARATORS

```
$ cut -d' ' -f1,3 workers.single_space >
workers_phone4
$ cat workers_phone4
Eric 555-6674
Geisha 555-4221
Kevin 555-1112
Tom 555-2121
Tyler 555-2122
Katya 555-2123
```

▲ *Using a single space as a delimiter with the **-d** option to the **cut** command. Note that this example works only on files using a single space as a field separator.*

### Listing 3-24: USING SPACES AS SEPARATORS

```
$ cat workers.space
Eric      286    555-6674    erc       8
Geisha    280    555-4221    geisha    10
Kevin     279    555-1112    kevin     2
Tom       284    555-2121    spike     12
Tyler     281    555-2122    rot       4
Katya     282    555-2123    katya     4
```

▲ *A similar data file that uses spaces as separators rather than tabs. The separator is important.*

### Listing 3-25: EXTRACTING CHARACTERS

```
$ cut -c1-24 workers.space > workers_phone5
$ cat workers_phone5
Eric      286    555-6674
Geisha    280    555-4221
Kevin     279    555-1112
Tom       284    555-2121
Tyler     281    555-2122
Katya     282    555-2123
```

▲ *The command **cut -c1-24** grabs the first 24 characters from the file **workers.space** and sends the output to the file **workers_phone5**. Note that this file uses spaces to separate fields.*

89

## Who This Book Is For

This book is written for you, a beginning to intermediate UNIX user who isn't afraid to take charge of his or her own learning experience. You don't want a lot of technical jargon; you *do* want to learn as much about UNIX technology as you can in a limited amount of time. You need a book that is straightforward, easy to follow, and logically organized, so you can find answers to your questions easily. And, you appreciate simple-to-use tools such as handy cross-references and visual step-by-step procedures that help you make the most of your learning. We have created the unique *Teach Yourself* format specifically to meet your needs.

Learn by example. Review the listings on the right-hand page of every task to understand the concepts more clearly and avoid errors and pitfalls.

# Personal Workbook

It's a well-known fact that much of what we learn is lost soon after we learn it if we don't reinforce our newly acquired skills with practice and repetition. That's why each *Teach Yourself* chapter ends with your own Personal Workbook. Here's where you can get extra practice, test your knowledge, and discover ideas for using what you've learned in the real world. There's even a Visual Quiz to help you remember your way around the topic's software environment.

## Feedback

Please let us know what you think about this book, and whether you have any suggestions for improvements. You can send questions and comments to the *Teach Yourself* editors on the IDG Books Worldwide Web site at **www.idgbooks.com**.

---

### Personal Workbook

**Q&A**

❶ Which command searches for text in files?

_____

_____

_____

❷ How could you find all occurrences of Bob Marley and Peter Tosh in a text file?

_____

_____

_____

❸ How would you search a text file for all instances of *Spacely* or *spacely*?

_____

_____

_____

❹ How would you sort a file numerically rather than alphabetically?

_____

_____

_____

❺ How do you store the output of **sort** in a file?

_____

_____

_____

❻ How would you split a file into chunks no larger than 60K?

_____

_____

_____

❼ How would you compare two sorted files to find out which lines are contained in both files and which are unique to a particular file?

_____

_____

_____

❽ Which command can you use to view text messages that may be hidden inside a program?

_____

_____

_____

ANSWERS: PAGE 346

96

After working through the tasks in each chapter, you can test your progress and reinforce your learning by answering the questions in the Q&A section. Then check your answers in the Personal Workbook Answers appendix at the back of the book.

Another practical way to reinforce your skills is to do additional exercises on the same skills you just learned without the benefit of the chapter's visual steps. If you struggle with any of these exercises, it's a good idea to refer to the chapter's tasks to be sure you've mastered them.

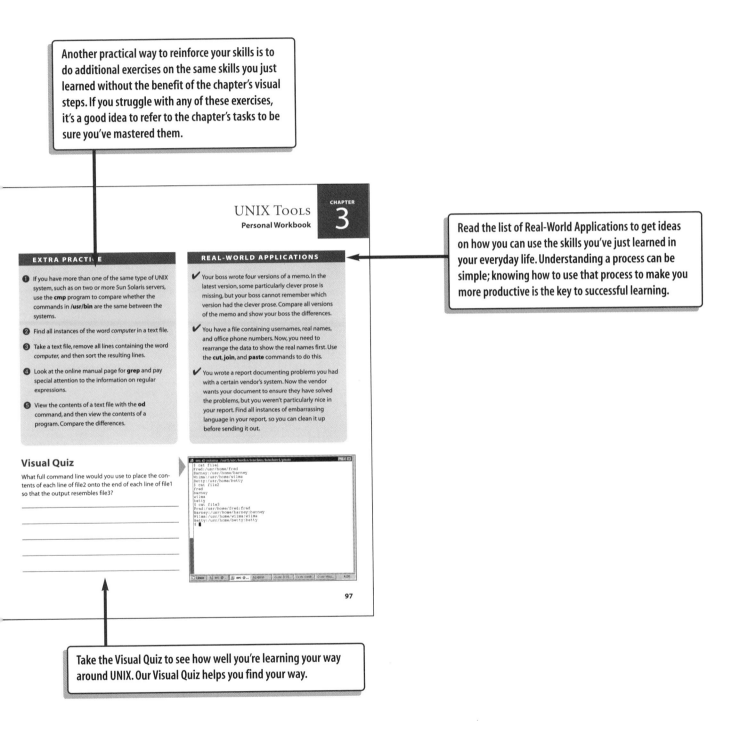

UNIX Tools
**Personal Workbook**

CHAPTER **3**

Read the list of Real-World Applications to get ideas on how you can use the skills you've just learned in your everyday life. Understanding a process can be simple; knowing how to use that process to make you more productive is the key to successful learning.

### EXTRA PRACTICE

❶ If you have more than one of the same type of UNIX system, such as on two or more Sun Solaris servers, use the **cmp** program to compare whether the commands in **/usr/bin** are the same between the systems.

❷ Find all instances of the word *computer* in a text file.

❸ Take a text file, remove all lines containing the word *computer*, and then sort the resulting lines.

❹ Look at the online manual page for **grep** and pay special attention to the information on regular expressions.

❺ View the contents of a text file with the **od** command, and then view the contents of a program. Compare the differences.

### REAL-WORLD APPLICATIONS

✔ Your boss wrote four versions of a memo. In the latest version, some particularly clever prose is missing, but your boss cannot remember which version had the clever prose. Compare all versions of the memo and show your boss the differences.

✔ You have a file containing usernames, real names, and office phone numbers. Now, you need to rearrange the data to show the real names first. Use the **cut**, **join**, and **paste** commands to do this.

✔ You wrote a report documenting problems you had with a certain vendor's system. Now the vendor wants your document to ensure they have solved the problems, but you weren't particularly nice in your report. Find all instances of embarrassing language in your report, so you can clean it up before sending it out.

## Visual Quiz

What full command line would you use to place the contents of each line of file2 onto the end of each line of file1 so that the output resembles file3?

_____

_____

_____

_____

_____

97

Take the Visual Quiz to see how well you're learning your way around UNIX. Our Visual Quiz helps you find your way.

# Contents

# CONTENTS

# CONTENTS

# Contents

# Contents

# CONTENTS

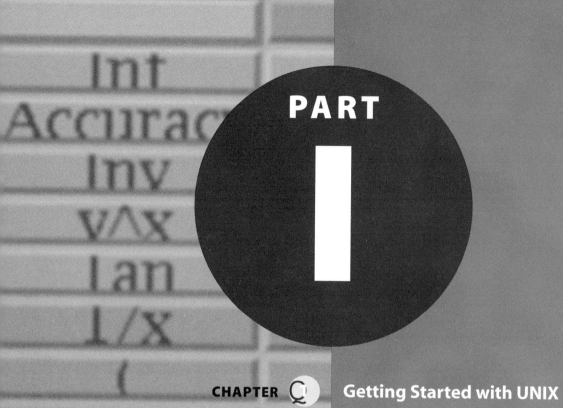

# PART

# 1

# UNIX from the Ground Up

Welcome to the UNIX operating system! This is where you begin your journey toward UNIX nirvana, beginning your path to total enlightenment via one of the most popular operating systems on the planet.

In this section, you learn the basics of UNIX. Chapter 1 begins with an overview of UNIX, explaining how the operating system works and how you interact with it.

Chapter 2 moves into the realm of specific tasks and covers what is arguably the most important aspect of UNIX — working with files and directories. Chapter 3 introduces the many tools that make up UNIX. Chapter 4 teaches you how to customize your own personal UNIX installation. In Chapter 5 you learn about the major UNIX shells — the C, Korn, and Bash shells — and how to further customize them to suit your needs.

Chapter 6 touches on another unique aspect of UNIX: how tasks are divided into processes and how UNIX manages these processes. Chapter 7 discusses the X Window System, the graphical interface used in most UNIX versions, as well as Linux and FreeBSD. X is implemented in many different ways — Motif, Common Desktop Environment, KDE, XFree86 — but all of these implementations work similarly.

# CHAPTER 1

**MASTER THESE SKILLS**

▶ Logging In a UNIX System

▶ Introducing Shells

▶ Using System Prompts

▶ Introducing UNIX Commands

▶ Changing Your Password

▶ Presenting Common UNIX Commands

▶ Introducing the Command Line

▶ Introducing Standard Input/Output

▶ Processing Pipes

▶ Running Commands in the Background

▶ Logging Off a UNIX System

# Getting Started with UNIX

This chapter covers the basics of a typical UNIX session. We begin with logging onto your UNIX system, and then guide you through some basic UNIX functions.

Because we believe the best way to learn something is to actually use it, we recommend you go through this chapter while using a UNIX, Linux, or FreeBSD system. To reach this beginning point is not quite as simple as it sounds, though. First of all, you need to learn about your system's configuration.

If you're using a multiuser system, you'll use a *terminal* to log in a UNIX system. UNIX can be running on virtually any kind of computer — anything from a PC to a super-computer. Approach the idea of a multiuser system somewhat abstractly — the actual computer may be located in your office, in another room, or (if you've connected via modem or local-area network) in another building or even another country. In this instance, you could be using a UNIX terminal with a character-based display, a bitmapped display (which allows for graphics), or a PC running the actual operating system and sharing it with other users.

If you're running on a single-user system, you'll probably be working via a keyboard and monitor that's attached directly to the computer. A Sun SPARCstation, FreeBSD, or Linux user falls into this category.

With UNIX, you need an *account* on a UNIX system. Every user must have an account, and not all accounts are equal: the *root user*— sometimes called the *superuser*— can do anything on the entire system. That includes having the power to set up an account for another user. With a multiuser system, the system administrator (the root user) must set up a user account and a password for you. When you actually login, as described later in this chapter, you use a name and password initially assigned by the system administrator.

If you're using a UNIX workstation and must set up your own user account, follow the documentation for your particular system regarding initial logins and setting up user accounts. Since these configurations are less frequent than large multiuser systems governed by a kind and benevolent system administrator, they aren't covered here.

# Logging In a UNIX System

You can't use a UNIX system if the system doesn't know you're there—which is why you must log in a UNIX system. This simple procedure tells the UNIX system who you are; the system responds with a request for a password for verification. If you're working on a computer system in your office, your system administrator will have given you a username and password. If you're installing a UNIX system, such as Linux or FreeBSD, you need to follow the onscreen directions on how to initially login a virgin system. Either way, logging in a UNIX system is a rather simple two-step process.

The system presents you with the following (or a variation on the following):

```
login:
```

Don't worry about whatever else is on the screen. Enter your *username* (also known as the *login name* or *logname*) and hit the **Enter** key.

After typing your login name, you are presented with an area for entering your password that should look something like this:

```
Password:
```

Enter your password. The terminal does not display what you type, preventing someone looking over your shoulder from stealing your password.

Every UNIX system is different in how it presents a password and login to the user. You may see a variey of messages after a successful login. If you're using a UNIX system running the X Window System, a screen with some windows and icons appears. If you're using

electronic-mail software, you may receive a message stating you have mail. If your login was unsuccessful, you are presented with something like this:

```
Login incorrect
login:
```

If you make a typing error, you can move back one space by pressing the **Backspace** (**BkSp**) key or **Ctrl-H** keys if you're using System V Release 4. If you're using an earlier or different version of UNIX, try the **Delete** (**Del**) or # (**Shift-3**) keys. You can also delete an entire line by typing the @ (**Shift-2**) character; when you do so, everything to the left of the cursor is deleted, and the cursor then appears at the beginning of the following line. Don't worry—whatever was contained on the earlier line is now part of the ether, and it won't come back to haunt you.

On many keyboards, the **Enter** key will be marked as Return. This book uses **Enter** and **Return** interchangeably. Also, whenever there's an instruction for you to give information to the UNIX system—whether it be a username, password, or command—the assumption throughout the rest of this book is that you're to press the **Return** or **Enter** key at the end of the input.

The opposite page shows examples of logins, including a *graphical* login, which may or may not be running under the X Window System (it doesn't really matter if it is or not). At this point in your UNIX journey, your only concern is entering your password and username to gain access to the system.

*Continued*

**CROSS-REFERENCE**

Check out Appendix B for information on the introductory UNIX text, *UNIX: The Basics*, second edition, MIS Press, 1998.

**FIND IT ONLINE**

Discover the rich history behind the UNIX operating system, as seen at **www.amdahl.com/internet/ events/unix25.html**.

### ▶ ON THE NETWORK?

We're already throwing around terms like *multiuser* and *local-area network* rather loosely. UNIX purists argue users should know the difference between running off a network and working on a local machine connected to a network. When you're working on a multiuser system, you're working on a machine that derives its computing power from a central UNIX server; when you enter a command, that command is actually executed on the central server and the results are sent back to you. Conversely, if you're working on a local machine, you enter the command and the command is executed locally; access to the server occurs only when a specific functionality is needed.

## Listing 1-1: LOGGING ONTO LINUX

```
Welcome to Linux 2.0.33.
gilbert login: reichard
Password: not displayed
```

▲ *This login session features Linux 2.0.33. The password does not appear onscreen.*

## Listing 1-2: LOGGING ONTO A GENERIC UNIX SYSTEM V RELEASE 4 SYSTEM

```
login: reichard
Password: not displayed
UNIX System V Release 4.0
Systemid
Copyright (c) 1984, 1986, 1987, 1988 AT&T
All Rights Reserved
Last login: Fri Jun 12 10:45:21 on term/12
```

▲ *In this example, the terminal displays the time, date, and location of the last login.*

## Listing 1-3: LOGGING ONTO AN OLDER SUN UNIX SYSTEM V RELEASE 4 SYSTEM

```
UNIX(r) System V Release 4.0 (bigcorp)

login: reichard
Password: not displayed
Last login: Sun Dec 1 12:35:51 from remote
Sun Microsystems Inc.    SunOS 5.3
You've got mail.
$
```

▲ *The terminal displays the time, date, and location of the last login, as well as alerting the user to mail. The user is immediately provided a system prompt for entering commands.*

# BigCorp. System

**login:** reichard

**Password:**

❶ *Enter your login name and press the **Enter** key.*
❷ *This places your cursor in the password field, where you enter your password.*

In the previous spread, you logged in the UNIX system from a local connection. Some UNIX systems allow you to login remotely—that is, over telephone lines from a location outside of your office. In this case, you need a computer—whether it be a UNIX workstation or PC—configured to call into a remote system with a modem. A modem is a piece of hardware that allows computers to communicate via telephone lines.

## Think Globally, Work Locally

Your system administrators will know if you can remotely login your UNIX system from home or on the road. They should also be able to recommend the appropriate software. For instance, you need terminal-emulation software to remotely login a UNIX system from a PC or compatible. There are freely available versions, as well as commercial packages; again, your system administrators will know which software you need, as well as which settings to use.

Settings? You need to make sure your local system and the remote UNIX system are communicating with the same language, so to speak. For instance, you need to choose your terminal type. A popular terminal type when logging in remotely is VT100, which makes it a safe choice—the VT100 is recognized by virtually every UNIX system, so using it will almost always ensure a successful session. (Once you've logged in, you may need to tell the remote UNIX system what terminal type you're using. This is done by setting the TERM variable.)

After making the proper connection to the remote UNIX system, you are presented with a truncated login prompt, usually listing the name of the operating system and a login prompt.

It's surprising to UNIX beginners that something as straightforward as logging in a system can be fraught with danger and suspense. However, the typical UNIX system is built to maximize security—and the first step when addressing security is making sure unauthorized users are denied access to the system. Hence, UNIX can be a little vague when it denies you access to the system.

That's why a message such as "login denied" doesn't tell you what was wrong with your login—the login or the password. This vagueness is designed to keep potential troublemakers at bay.

There are a few things that could be thwarting your login:

▶ **You inadvertently changed the case of a character.** With UNIX, case counts—a lesson you'll learn over and over again. Entering *Reichard* instead of *reichard* will cause the system to choke on your username. This is an area that frequently frustrates new users.

▶ **You entered a typo when typing the username or password.** Typos happen. When you're entering a username or password, you could have accidentally mistyped a character. In this case, you can use the **Backspace** (**BkSp**) key to go back and erase the offending character. Or you can be lazy and enter the incorrect information, knowing the system will ask you to login again.

**CROSS-REFERENCE**
Chapter 8 illustrates more about electronic mail.

**FIND IT ONLINE**
A good guide to shopping for a 56K modem can be found at **www.sirius.com/~rmoss/.**

▶ **The system could be slow.** If you enter the login information and nothing happens, don't panic — there are times when the system will slow down to a crawl, especially when many people are performing the same task (such as logging in the system at the beginning of the workday). If you get no immediate response from the system, don't worry. If, however, you don't get a response after several minutes, check with your system administrator to make sure the system is functioning properly.

If you know that you've entered the correct information and are still told the login information is incorrect, check with your system administrator or check your system's documentation.

## Dealing with System Administrators

The system administrator is god of the UNIX system, so it's always a good thing to make friends with your system administrator. If you're working in a corporate setting, the system administrator is the person who sets up the system and makes sure it runs properly. They're the ones who can fix any problems you may encounter, so your successful UNIX experience may rely on their willingness to help you.

If you're working on a single-user UNIX system, such as Linux or FreeBSD, *you're* the system administrator. Congratulations! We suggest you check out a text that covers Linux usage from the system-administration level, such as *Linux Configuration and*

*Installation*, fourth edition, M&T Books (1998). You don't need to know all the ins and outs of system administration when you work with a single-user UNIX, but you do need to know the basics.

**TAKE NOTE**

▶ **SECURITY RULES**

Many things in the UNIX operating system were designed with security in mind. UNIX is designed to support a great number of users, any one of whom could cause serious problems to the system if they managed to destroy valuable files. So when the system doesn't let you do something, you need to ask yourself these two questions: Did I enter the command or information correctly? Did I try doing something that I wasn't allowed to do?

▶ **SHOPPING FOR A MODEM**

Prices for modems are falling rapidly — high-quality 56Kbps (kilobits per second) modems can be found for $100 or so. When buying a modem, you should look for as much speed as possible, within your price parameters.

▶ **KEYBOARD FOLLIES**

When it comes to keyboard combinations, you'll notice throughout this book that we tend to give several methods for doing the same thing. In the early days of UNIX, different UNIX vendors created different keyboards that were specially manufactured for different purposes. Because there were vast differences between these keyboards, UNIX was designed to work on a lowest-common denominator basis, giving users several methods to do the same thing.

# Introducing Shells

A shell is a program like any other UNIX program. However, it's charged with a very important and unique responsibility: It translates your instructions to the UNIX system in a way the UNIX system can handle. It facilitates all aspects of your UNIX usage — telling the system where to find specific files, where your home directory is, and how to deal with your presence as a user in general.

UNIX features several shells. For the most part, you want to stick with the shell your system administrator has chosen, since that allows a certain level of conformity amongst the users. Other users on single-user workstations and PCs have a little more freedom when it comes to choosing a shell.

When you login your UNIX system, you're immediately thrust into your login shell. This information is usually contained in the file **/etc/passwd**, as is login information for all the users on your system. (Obviously, this file is a tool for your system administrator, not for your frequent usage.) This file is organized by user, with each line containing the basic information regarding every user: name, login ID, and so on. The final field in your line lists the shell you want to run after logging in.

There are infrequently used shells available in the public domain, such as **wksh** (the windowing Korn shell), **zsh** (the Z Shell), and **pdksh** (public-domain Korn shell). If you want more information about these shells, check with your system administrator or system documentation.

Based on the information contained in the **/etc/passwd** file, the UNIX system launches your shell, with information contained in the **.profile** file (for C shell users, the **.login** and **.cshrc** files). As a new UNIX user, one of the most useful aspects of your shell is its flexibility. You can customize everything associated with the shell.

## TAKE NOTE

### ▶ INVESTIGATING YOUR PERSONAL SHELL

You can find out what shell you're using via the command line. We're getting ahead of ourselves a little here, since you've not officially learned about the command line. Just follow the directions here: enter a command (echo $SHELL) at the command prompt (represented here by $, although you may see something different on your screen):

```
$ echo $SHELL
sh
```

The response should be **sh**, **csh**, **ksh**, or something else ending in **sh**; here it is **sh**. Typically, shells are stored in the **/usr/bin** directory on a UNIX system. To see what shells are available on your system, type the following command line:

```
$ ls /usr/bin/*sh
/usr/bin/csh    /usr/bin/ksh
/usr/bin/sh
```

If the response to the previous command line is:

```
*sh: No such file or directory exists
```

it means the shell files are stored somewhere else on your UNIX system.

**CROSS-REFERENCE**

Learn more about shell maintenance in Chapters 4 and 5.

**FIND IT ONLINE**

You can learn about the Bourne Again Shell at the Free Software Foundation Web site, **www.fsf.org**.

## Table 1-1: THE MOST POPULAR UNIX SHELLS

| Filename | Full Name | Description |
| --- | --- | --- |
| **sh** | The Bourne Shell | This is the shell that shipped with the original System V release of UNIX in 1979, and it has remained largely unchanged since then. It's named after its developer, Stephen Bourne. |
| **ksh** | The Korn Shell | Developed by David Korn at Bell Labs, the Korn shell builds upon the functionality of the Bourne shell by adding useful features first introduced in the C shell (such as job history and aliases). In addition, scripts and programs written for the Bourne shell can be used without alternation in the Korn shell. Because of this feature, coverage in the book of these shells will be lumped together. |
| **csh** | The C Shell | Developed by Bill Joy (a founder of Sun Microsystems, Inc.) while he was working on the release of Berkeley UNIX (also known as BSD), the C shell improves upon the Bourne shell with the introduction of job history, aliases, and other features. The C shell is different enough from the Bourne and Korn shells to warrant its own coverage throughout this book. |
| **jsh** | The Job Shell | An extension of the Bourne shell, the job shell features specialized tools for handling multiple jobs. |
| **bash** | The Bourne Again Shell | Developed by the Free Software Foundation, the Bourne Again shell also builds upon the Bourne shell by adding useful features found in both the C shell and the Korn shell. |
| **zsh** | The Z Shell | This shell closely resembles the Korn shell but adds programmable command completion, history, and built-in spelling correction. |
| **tcsh** | Public-Domain C Shell | As the name says, this is a public-domain C shell. It adds filename completion and command-line editing. |
| **ash** | The Adventure Shell | We think the name is cool; that's really our only reason for mentioning it here, since it's very unlikely that you'll ever use it. Because this shell isn't the most *stable* of shells, running it is often an adventure. |

# Using System Prompts

If your login is successful, you are presented with something like this: $ or %. Appearing either on its own or within a window of some sort. This is called the *prompt*. As you might expect, the $ prompts you for commands. If you're coming from the DOS world, the $ is the equivalent of the **C:>** prompt.

Of course, *exactly* what you see after logging in will depend on your system and how it's configured. UNIX allows you to insert virtually anything within a command prompt, including the current directory and the current date. UNIX features two ways of interacting with users: *graphical interface* and *text-based display*. And they couldn't be more dissimilar, as you can see in the two figures on the opposite page. On the top is a text-based display; on the bottom is a graphical display.

A text-based display uses the standard alphabetic characters to interact with you. No windows appear on the screen, and essentially you're always doing one thing at a time. Older systems feature text-based displays. When you're done with a task, the screen scrolls up or clears, presenting you with a prompt that will appear by itself on the screen (usually near the bottom of existing text).

In contrast, a graphical interface uses graphics, icons, and windows to present a more appealing face. To run a program, double-click an icon, or enter a standard UNIX command in a window. The most popular graphical interface for UNIX is the *X Window System*, a freely available interface developed at MIT and currently administered by the Open Group. *Motif*, a specific implementation of X developed originally at the Open Software Foundation and now maintained by the Open Group, is widely used, as is the *Common Desktop Environment*, which is based on Motif and included by commercial vendors such as Sun Microsystems, Hewlett-Packard, and IBM as part of their UNIX workstations.

In the case of an X environment, the prompt appears in its own window, which is usually labeled **xterm**.

No matter which interface is featured on your UNIX system, you still need to know about system prompts and why they're important. In essence, the system prompt is the shell's way of saying, "OK, you can enter a command whenever you're ready." The $ prompt is used by the Korn and Bourne shells, while % is used by the C shell. For now, it's important that you know that the shell in use determines your prompt.

Since the Bourne and Korn shells are so popular amongst UNIX users, we use the $ prompt in our examples. However, we give the C shell equivalents to commands if they differ from the Korn and Bourne shell commands. (Please note that you are not to type in the $ or the % when entering commands.) If you were the root user, your prompt would be: #

*Continued*

**CROSS-REFERENCE**

Chapter 7 describes more about the X Window System and Motif.

**FIND IT ONLINE**

Useful information about the X Window System and Motif can be found at **www.opengroup.org**.

## TAKE NOTE

### ▶ CHANGING YOUR PROMPT

The shell controls almost every aspect of your UNIX usage. To show this, we explain how you can alter your prompt. For instance, you may want to change your prompt to appear more like the DOS prompt. In this case, you would enter the following command:

```
$ PS1="> "
```

This changes the string **$** to the string **>**, with a space at the end. The space is so that the commands you type don't abut the prompt. The quotation marks won't appear on the screen; only the characters between them. (In UNIX commands, characters to be displayed on a screen are bracketed by quotation marks.) You can run the **PS1** command whenever you want; it affects only your account, so you can personalize the string to whatever extent tickles your fancy. For instance, if you have a task to perform at a specific time in the day, you could run a command like the following:

```
PS1="Call Dr. Johnson at 3 > "
```

Your prompt would be:

```
Call Dr. Johnson at 3 >
```

A C shell user would use the following command to change a prompt:

```
% set prompt = "Call Dr. Johnson at 3 > "
```

### ▶ PUTTING LIPSTICK ON AN OLD MULE

For most of the commands explained throughout this book, it doesn't matter if you're using a text interface or a graphical interface. For instance, several examples in this book will be illustrated when run in an **xterm** window. The return from these commands would be the same, no matter if they're run in an **xterm** window under X or on a straight text-based terminal.

### Listing 1-4: USING A TEXT-BASED INTERFACE

```
bash# ls
Info        adm        etc      info
man         share      X11      bin
g++include  interviews openwin  spool
X11R6       dict       games    lib
preserve    src        X386     doc
include     local      sbin      tmp
bash#
```

▲ *A text-based interface allows you to do one thing at a time on the screen. The **ls** command generates a contents directory.*

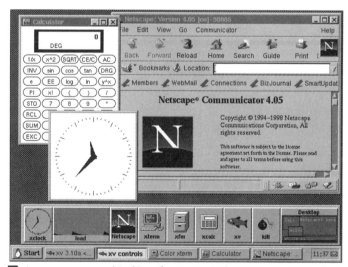

■ *In contrast, a graphical interface uses windows to represent tasks. You can view the contents of a directory while doing other things, such as watching the clock.*

# Using System Prompts
*Continued*

Should you be looking at switching to a different shell? Probably not. Most users won't get into the advanced features found in most shells. We find that most users are using the Korn or Bourne Again shells, and in our experience these shells serve the needs of virtually every user.

The Bourne Again shell is distributed free of charge by the Free Software Foundation, and it's an increasingly popular shell in the UNIX world. It's the default shell in most Linux distributions, and it encapsulates many of the cool features found in the Korn and C shells, while adding some cool features of its own, such as filename completion and command-line editing. You can compile the source code on your own after reading Chapter 10 or be really nice to your system administrator in the hopes of having it installed on your UNIX system.

However, be warned that in many cases, you won't have the opportunity to change your shell, as your system administrator may dictate a specific shell in order to maintain uniformity across the entire network.

If you make an error while typing a command, you can use the **Backspace** (**BkSp**) or **Ctrl-H** keys to erase the previous character — if you're using System V Release 4 or something compatible (such as Linux or FreeBSD). Some systems use the **Delete** (**Del**) key — it all depends on your setup. If you're using an older version of UNIX, or just want to use something other than **Backspace** or **Ctrl-H**, use the UNIX command # (**Shift-3**) to cancel the last character. Using # to erase a character is somewhat awkward; the character is still displayed on your terminal, and if you suffer through a lot of typing errors, you must divine a command sequence containing many instances of #.

If you really can't figure out which key is used to delete characters (or if you don't like the system-chosen key), you can change the key used to delete characters. This is an old tradition harking back to the days when few users had compatible terminals. UNIX allows you to redefine most keys, and here we explain how to change the **Delete** key.

To change the **Delete** character key, use the **stty erase** command. You type **stty**, then a space, the word **erase**, space and then press the key you want, such as **Del**:

```
$ stty erase [Del]
```

In this case, [**Del**] refers to the physical act of pressing the **Delete** key. You could do that with any key. Of course, you don't want to spend too much time redefining keys — most of the time the keyboards on your keyboard should work just fine the way they are.

**CROSS-REFERENCE**

Chapter 2 gives more information about the **ls** command.

**FIND IT ONLINE**

Information about XFree86 — the version of X used on PCs — can be found at **www.xfree86.org**.

## Correcting Your Errors

If you make several errors and want to erase the entire line, type the @ character (**Shift-2**). This presents you with a new prompt:

```
$ PS1="Clla Dr. Jhohnsen at 3@
```

If you're a Korn shell user, use the **Escape** (**Esc**) key instead of the @ key to erase a line:

```
$ PS1="Clla Dr. Jhohnsen at 3/
```

These failed commands will still be displayed on your screen, even though the computer ignored them. Why? In the old days of UNIXdom, most terminals were unable to use a backspace on lines — especially if the terminals were teletype or typewriter terminals that wrote everything to paper, not to a VDT screen. In UNIX, there is an almost obsessive need to maintain compatibility with older systems and mindsets, so things such as backspacing characters and bitmapped graphics have been slow to gain wide acceptance.

## Keyboard Follies

If you're coming from a PC environment, you're used to having virtually the same keyboard, with a few exceptions, on every PC you sit down and use. This is also the same if you're using newer equipment in the UNIX world, where most new workstations use some sort of keyboard based on a PC keyboard.

If you're working with an older UNIX system, you may run into a keyboard that contains fewer keys than PC keyboards or other newer UNIX workstations. There's no rhyme or reason to these other keyboards. You can be assured that they contain the basic keys that you need to do your work. However, you may need to check with your system administrator if you see a key mentioned in the text that doesn't correspond to anything on your keyboard.

**TAKE NOTE**

**THE BASH BROTHERS**

The source code for the Bourne Again shell can be found at **prep.ai.mit.edu/pub/gnu/**. Be warned, however, that there's precious little documentation that covers the Bourne Again shell from the Free Software Foundation, and unless you know about compiling source code on a UNIX system — a skill you will master in Chapter 10 — you don't want to waste a lot of time with downloading **bash** source code.

# Introducing UNIX Commands

**S**tty and **ls**, both used in the previous section, are examples of UNIX *commands*. In this instance, you're telling the shell to run a program called **stty**, which actually changes the information stored regarding your system prompt.

UNIX features literally hundreds of commands—too many for us to cover individually in a beginning tutorial book. Some commands are used frequently; for instance, you can use the **date** command to get the current date and time. Some commands are specific to UNIX versions, such as the Slackware Linux distribution of Linux, a UNIX work-alike meant for PCs. If you're a System V Release 4 user you have access to virtually every UNIX command from every UNIX version.

For instance, depending on your version of UNIX, you may have to use UNIX commands to read news items distributed over the entire system. If you're working on a multiuser system, a message of the day (MOTD) may follow a successful login. This is merely a text file generated by the system administrator and sent to every user, usually detailing important facts like system shutdowns for maintenance. The ability to distribute information electronically to a wide range of users is a great feature of UNIX; an electronic message is certainly more efficient (and environmentally healthy) than having to distribute memos to every employee.

Some system administrators may choose not to send a message of the day and instead use UNIX's

**news** command to distribute information. If this is the case in your system, you may find a message like this after you log on:

```
TYPE "news" to READ news
```

To read the news, you type:

```
$ news
```

The command **news** runs the news program, which displays text files containing news items. These may include notices about the computer system, or they may detail important company-wide information.

Don't worry if your system doesn't use the **news** command. Often important messages are carried to users via electronic mail. If you had new mail, you'd be told so after you logged on the system.

With UNIX you can add *arguments* and *options* to most commands. Let's say you want to read all the news items, including those you've previously read. You can add an option to the news command, allowing you to read all news items:

```
$ news -a
```

where *-a* tells the system to display all news items. This is an option; all options are letters preceded by a minus sign. Most options are merely mnemonic shortcuts for the full names of options. In this case, we could have typed the following command and option to display all items:

```
$ news -all
```

**CROSS-REFERENCE**

See "Presenting Common UNIX Commands" later in this chapter to learn more about the **man** command.

**FIND IT ONLINE**

You can learn more about FreeBSD at **www.freebsd.org.**

When you combine a command and any options, you're creating a *command line*. Essentially, a command line is all the information you pass after the prompt. At its simplest, a command line can feature only a single command; at its most complicated, it can feature several commands, each providing input and output to one another.

This command and option displays the current news items:

```
$ news —n
```

A list of the current news items will appear:

```
$ news —n
news: vacations vi
```

One-word descriptions of the news items are displayed. In this case the new news items describe changes in the company policy and changes concerning vi, the text editor.

To retrieve the news items about vacations, type:

```
$ news vacations
```

To stop a command, simply press the **Delete** (**Del**), **Ctrl-C**, **Ctrl-D**, or **Break** key. Your system prompt will then appear. **Ctrl-D** means end of file in UNIX. In UNIX, everything is a file — a fact you'll hear time and time again in this book. Even terminal input is a file, and so to stop a command, you tell the system to end a file. Use what works on your system.

## TAKE NOTE

### ▶ INCONSISTENCY RULES

Not all UNIX programs accept the same options. And those that do accept the same options (-*a*, for example) don't always mean the same thing to every command that accepts -*a*. This is one reason why UNIX has long been considered cryptic — there's a lot to memorize.

### ▶ NO NEWS IS GOOD NEWS

The **news** command illustrates something about UNIX that's not always good: Commands aren't always implemented across UNIX platforms, either licensed UNIX platforms or UNIX work-alikes, such as Linux or FreeBSD. You won't find the **news** command on a Linux system, but you will find it on a larger network that may rely on news items for system-wide news. Whether or not the **news** command is included on your system is really beside the point of this coverage; the point is, you can add options and arguments to augment commands.

### ▶ DOUBLING UP

Some commands, most notably those produced by the Free Software Foundation and used in the Linux and FreeBSD operating systems, use two hyphens instead of one for options and arguments; you'll see this when you read online-manual pages for individual commands with the **man** command. We have no idea why they use two hyphens instead of one.

# Changing Your Password

If you're logging onto an account set up by a system administrator, you may have to enter a new password to replace the original password provided by the system administrator. (In fact, some system administrators require you to enter a new password.) This process should look like the following:

```
login: reichard
Password:
Your password has expired.
Choose a new one.
Old password:
New password:
Re-enter new password:
```

Remember that the terminal does not display the passwords for security reasons.

Changing your password is a matter of using the **passwd** command. The process is simple: After you've logged onto your system, you run a command — **passwd** — that confirms your old password and asks for the new one.

Since security is so important on so many UNIX systems, there are a variety of tools that enhance security while not impacting too heavily on users. One such tool is the **lock** command, which is found in many, but not all, versions of UNIX. (An X Window version, **xlock**, is also available.) The **lock** command does only one thing: Locks your keyboard until you enter your password, as in the following:

```
$ lock
Password:
Sorry
Password:
```

If the correct password isn't entered, then the lock command fails to release control of the keyboard. If the correct password isn't entered in a certain number of tries, then the lock command logs you off of the system automatically. This is a handy tool to use when you're leaving your chair for a few minutes and want to make sure there's no tampering with the system done through your account.

Some UNIX systems may force you to choose new passwords every so often. The system administrator sets the password time limits. With the introduction of Release 4, you can view the status of your password by adding the *-s* command-line parameter to the **passwd** command.

The information returned by the **passwd** command is rather terse. Some other versions of UNIX return more information — mainly, they explain what the heck the numbers mean:

```
$ passwd -s
reichard  PW  06/15/91  10  40  7
name
passwd status
date last changed
min days between changes
max days between changes
days before user will be warned to change
password
```

The final six status lines directly relate to the second line. In our example, *name* equals *reichard*, *passwd status* equals *PW*, *date last changed* equals *6/15/91*, *min days between changes* equals *10*, *max days between changes* equals *40*, and *days before user will be*

**CROSS-REFERENCE**

Learn more about the command line and how it works in Chapter 4.

**SHORTCUT**

Not every version of UNIX uses the same mechanism for changing passwords; use **man passwd** on your system.

18

*warned to change password* equals *7*. These parameters are set up by the system administrator, so your system may not display all six status lines.

*Continued*

▶ **MORE NAGGING ABOUT SECURITY**

Do a search for "UNIX security" on any Web search engine and you'll retrieve hundreds of thousands of documents that cover the subject in some sort. UNIX is implemented in situations where security concerns are paramount, which is why you encounter such measures when you're trying to do something like change your password. Don't worry — no one is out to get you.

▶ **PASSWORDS ARE FOREVER**

Make sure you remember your password. When you enter a password, it's encrypted and saved in a specific file within the UNIX system. If you forget your password, you're effectively barred from the system, as system administrators lack the ability to unencrypt this file and decipher your password. In this case, the system administrator will need to create an entirely new account for you.

▶ **PASSWORDS AND ADMINISTRATORS**

It's important to note that system administrators set up time limits to prevent frequent password changes — in other words, you're stuck with a password for a certain amount of time. If you try to change your password and find that the system won't accept the change, it could be that you're prohibited from changing your password for a given amount of time.

**Listing 1-5: USING THE PASSWD COMMAND**

```
darkstar:~# passwd
Changing password for root
Enter the new password
(minimum of 5, maximum of 8 characters)
Please use a combination of upper and
lowercase letters and numbers.
New password:
```

▲ *Use the **passwd** command for entering new passwords.*

**Listing 1-6: RESUBMITTING THE NEW PASSWORD**

```
darkstar:~# passwd
Changing password for root
Enter the new password
(minimum of 5, maximum of 8 characters)
Please use a combination of upper and
lowercase letters and numbers.
New password:
Re-enter new password:
Password changed.
darkstar:~#
```

▲ *You are asked to resubmit the new password when using the **passwd** command.*

# Changing Your Password

*Continued*

This is not a perfect world, and so computer systems with more than one user must be set up with security features to prevent unauthorized usage. Most new users will be assigned passwords by their system administrator. This is done mainly for convenience and security reasons; when your system administrator sets up your account, it's convenient at that time to enter a password that is known to be secure (in other words, it probably will appear to be total gibberish to you). However, there may be times when you need to choose your own password. Here are a few guidelines for login name and password selection:

▶ Your login name must be more than two characters long, and normally not more than eight. It must begin with a lowercase letter. In our cases, we've chosen different paths with our logins: **reichard** and **erc**. Few Reichards exist in Minnesota (our home state), but Minnesota is the Land of 10,000 Johnsons and almost as many Erics. Subsequently, it was feasible to use **reichard** as Kevin's login name, and **erc** is distinctive enough to be remembered.

▶ Use a password longer than six characters. The shorter the password, the more likely it is to be divined randomly.

▶ A password should contain two alphabetic characters and one numeric or special character. It cannot contain any spaces. (Some versions of UNIX won't let you use special nonalphabetic characters in your password.

These are generally older systems. Newer systems recognize the need for more distinctive passwords, which are harder for hackers to break.)

▶ Don't use a password based on personal information. For instance, don't use your spouse's name, your middle name, your job title or your Social Security number as a password.

▶ Don't use simple, easily guessed words such as **guest, sun, hp,** or **password**.

▶ Don't use a word that can be found in a dictionary. Hackers have been known to enter words from a computer-based dictionary as passwords, hoping that a random word was selected as a password.

▶ Don't make your password too complicated. If you can't memorize your password, you'll be more likely to leave a copy on a piece of paper near your computer. Therefore, you should use a combination of easily remembered parts. For instance, your favorite book may be *Valley of the Dolls*, and your favorite color is puce. You can't use **puce** as a password (too short) or **valley** (no numerals), but a password of **pucevalley1** would certainly thwart any would-be hackers.

▶ Never display your password next to your computer terminal. You're just asking for trouble.

**CROSS-REFERENCE**

Find out about permissions and how to track them in Chapter 2.

**FIND IT ONLINE**

To learn more about Beyond the Valley of the Dolls — the Russ Meyers masterpiece — see **sashimi.wwa. com/~jjf/bvd.html**.

## TAKE NOTE

▶ ### A QUICK TIP FOR CHOOSING A PASSWORD

Some users try a neat technique for choosing their passwords. First, choose a word or phrase that means something to you, like **consume** (it's the American way). Next, look at the keyboard. For your real password, use the keys to the upper left of the keys for the word. Using this technique, **consume** becomes **f0je8k4**. Use **f0je8k4** as your real password. Yes, **f0je8k4** is impossible to remember, but **consume** isn't. So you need to remember the algorithm — the method used to generate the password as well as your word, **consume**. We find this technique not only generates the special characters that are hard to guess, but makes for easy-to-remember passwords.

▶ ### YET MORE NAGGING ABOUT SECURITY

We can't stress enough, how important it is that you take your password seriously. The password is the first line of defense against system intruders. If these intruders get into a UNIX system, they can cause you personal harm by deleting files or sending abusive e-mail under your name. (Yes, this certainly does happen!) And if an intruder is in the system they can potentially do even more damage by deleting or altering important system files. So play it safe and be sure to use your password wisely.

### Table 1-2: PASSWD COMMAND OPTIONS

| | |
|---|---|
| -s | Displays current password information: |
| *user* | Username |
| *status* | Password status; **NP** (no password), **PS** (password), or **LK** (locked) |
| *mm/dd/yy* | Date when last changed |
| *min* | Minimum number of days before password must be changed |
| *max* | Maximum number of days before password must be changed |
| *notice* | Number of days before you are given notice that your password must be changed |

### Table 1-3: PRIVILEGED USER OPTIONS

| Option | Description |
|---|---|
| **-a** | Displays password information for all users |
| **-d** | Stops prompting user for password |
| **-f** | Forces user to change password |
| **-l** | Locks user password |
| **-n** | Sets number of days that must pass before user can change password |
| **-w** | Sets number of days before user is warned that the password expires |
| **-x** | Sets number of days before password expires |

# Presenting Common UNIX Commands

This section lists some widely used commands that will illustrate some important concepts that make UNIX so unique and useful. Go ahead and type these commands into your system; they won't do any damage (even if you misuse them), and you'll certainly learn about using UNIX through them.

## The Write Command

The **write** command allows you to send messages to other users over the UNIX network. Let's say you wanted to send a message to Eric over the network. After checking his status with the **who** command, shown on the opposite page, you decide to initiate the message. Do so with:

```
$ write erc
```

This command causes a message to pop up on his terminal and rings his computer's bell. (Most modern UNIX systems don't really have a bell, of course, but the tradition in UNIX dictates that the sound from a speaker be referred to as the bell.) If Eric wants to participate, he sends the following:

```
$ write reader
```

where your login name is *reader*. You can then send messages back and forth over the network. When you are done sending messages, type **o-o** (*over and out*), and then type **Ctrl-D** or **Del** to stop the program. **Ctrl-D** is the standard UNIX end-of-file marker. Remember when we stated that everything in UNIX

is a file? In this case, what you type using the **write** command is also treated as a file. You give the end-of-file marker (**Ctrl-D**) to terminate the file and, therefore, the **write** command.

## The Talk Command

If you're using System V Release 4 or FreeBSD, you have an improved version of **write** available to you, called **talk**. The **talk** command allows a chat session between two users, but in an easier-to-use format. With **talk**, a screen is divided into two halves, with your messages displayed in the top half and your chat partner's messages displayed in the bottom half. To start the **talk** command, type:

```
$ talk erc
```

Eric will see a message like the following:

```
Message from Talk_Daemon@systemid at 14:15
talk: connection requested by
reader@systemid
talk: respond with: talk reader@systemid
```

where your login name is *reader* and your system's name is *systemid*. If Eric wants to chat, he can respond by typing:

```
$ talk reader@systemid
```

At this point your screen is divided into halves. As with the **write** command, type **o-o** to signal that the conversation is over. To stop the program, press the **Del** key.

**CROSS-REFERENCE**

See "Introducing the Command Line" later in this chapter to learn about redirecting output.

**FIND IT ONLINE**

See **www.bsd.org/unixcmds.html** for a basic UNIX command summary.

## The Cal Command

The **cal** command displays the current month's calendar:

```
$ cal
```

If you want to see a calendar for an entire year, type the command plus the year:

```
$ cal 1999
```

The entire year will whip by, month by month. To stop the entire year from scrolling by, type **Ctrl-S**; to start it again, type **Ctrl-Q**. To stop the output, type **Ctrl-D**. (You can use these commands at any point in UNIX usage to stop and start the scrolling of text.)

*Continued*

---

**TAKE NOTE**

▶ **HAPPY ENDINGS**

The **Del** key and the end-of-file marker (**Ctrl-D**) can be used with almost every UNIX command. This is an important thing to note: There will be times when a command will fly out of control, impervious to your input. In these cases, you'll want to try using **Del** or **Ctrl-D** to end the command. It's not a pretty way to end a command, and since the command is killed at the instant the end-of-file marker is issued, you have the chance of losing some data.

---

**Listing 1-7: USING THE WHO COMMAND**

```
$ who
oper       term/10     Jun 14 12:32
reichard   term/08     Jun 14 08:12
erc        term/07     Jun 14 18:01
```

▲ The **who** command allows you to see who else is logged onto the system. This tells you the users on the system, their terminal ID numbers, and when they logged onto the system. If you're working on a UNIX system at a large corporation, the results from this command can be on the voluminous side; if this information is important to you, then you should learn how to redirect the output.

**Listing 1-8: USING THE CAL COMMAND**

```
darkstar:~#cal
      December 1998
Su Mo Tu We Th Fr Sa
       1  2  3  4  5
 6  7  8  9 10 11 12
13 14 15 16 17 18 19
20 21 22 23 24 25 26
27 28 29 30 31
```

▲ The **cal** command displays a calendar of the current month.

**Listing 1-9: GETTING NOVEMBER'S CALENDAR**

```
$ cal 11 1999
```

▲ To view a month within the current year, type the month's number plus the year. If you only type 11, for instance, you will get the calendar for all of 11 A.D., not the month of November. Also, the calendar is based on British/American convention. Try cal 1752 to see the jump to the Gregorian calendar.

# Presenting Common UNIX Commands *Continued*

Let's say Eric is in the middle of some very important work and doesn't want to chat over the network using the **write** or **talk** commands. The **mesg** command allows him to turn away your requests for idle chatter:

```
$ mesg n
```

The following appears on your terminal:

```
Permission denied
```

If Eric changes his mind and was open to receiving messages from other users, he would type:

```
$ mesg y
```

If Eric wasn't sure about his status, he could type:

```
$ mesg
is y
```

This short answer tells us that Eric does allow other users to talk to him.

## The Finger Command

In larger systems, you may get a far longer list than the one used in our **who** example, and the identities of some of the users may not be clear to you. To get more information about specific users, use the **finger** command, as shown on the opposite page.

If you want to know about everyone currently logged onto the system, type:

```
$ finger
```

Again, the output from this command can be on the voluminous side for a larger corporation.

## The Man Command

The **man** command is used in terminal mode, while **xman** is used under X. Both display the online-manual pages associated with UNIX commands. They are the exact pages from the printed documentation. It's not quite like an online-help system; the **man** pages tend to be very tersely written, they apply only to commands and not to common UNIX terms or operations (for instance, there's no **man** page covering the basics of electronic mail), and they tend to be technical in nature. For instance, to get the **man** pages for the **man** command — sort of like help on help — type:

```
$ man man
```

The online-manual pages show UNIX at its best and worst simultaneously. It's great that the entire manual is online. It's terrible that the online manual is obtuse, as you'll soon find out. Personally, we find **man** pages to be an advanced topic and more of interest to programmers looking for information about obtuse or poorly documented subjects. However, they can be handy if you're looking for the exact syntax of a command or if you're looking for the arguments associated with a command. If you do need to know the syntax for a command, the online **man** pages can prove invaluable. But, you'll have to learn how to decipher them. Don't say you weren't warned.

**CROSS-REFERENCE**

The **finger** command can also be used on the Internet. See Chapter 9.

**FIND IT ONLINE**

All Linux online-manual pages can be found at **www.linux.org**.

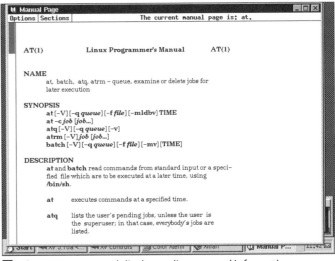

■ *The xman command displays online-manual information.*

## Listing 1-10: USING THE FINGER COMMAND

```
$ finger erc
Login name: erc In real life: Eric F.
Johnson
(612) 555-5555
Directory:/home/erc
Shell:/usr/bin/ksh
Last login Thurs Jun 11 12:14:32 on term/07
Project: X Window Programming
erc       term/07    Jun 13 18:01
```

▲ *The finger command in this instance gives you more information about **erc**'s identity. Using the **finger** command with an argument (erc) gives you information about the user, whether they're logged onto the system or not.*

## Listing 1-11: USING THE FINGER COMMAND

```
darkstar:~# finger
Login  Name  Tty  Idle  Login Time    Office
root          1    28    Dec 21 10:07
root          p0         Dec 21 11:41 (:0.0)
darkstar:~#
```

▲ *When run without a specific user, the **finger** command returns information about everyone on the network.*

# Introducing the Command Line

We've broadly hinted so far that UNIX commands have a number of parts. First, there's the command itself, such as **ls** for listing files or **man** for the online manuals. And, we've also talked about command syntax, options, and parameters. In this section, we'll explain what all the fuss is about.

Most UNIX commands sport a number of options that change the way the command behaves. For example, we've seen that the **ls** command prints out information on more files with the –a option (think *all*). **Ls** also prints out more information on each file with the –f (think *full*). The **ls** command alone lists the files in the current directory. The –F options show special characters at the end of file names to help tell you the type of each file (/ for directory names, I for pipes, and * for executables). All these options make minor variations to the basics of the **ls** command. **Ls** still lists files — it's purpose in life — but you can control how it lists files with options.

Commands can also take parameters. While options tell a command how to do its work, parameters tell a command what to work on. Continuing with our **ls** example, you can pass the name of a file, a directory, or a number of files and directories to **ls**, telling **ls** to only list information on those files and directories.

Most UNIX commands take the name of files as parameters. These parameters tell the command which files to work on. For example, a backup command would take the names of files to back up. The **rm** command gets a list of files to delete, and so on.

Together, the options and the parameters are often called arguments. These arguments are often used to redirect input and output for commands.

Input and output? Redirection? (Repeat the mantra: *Everything in UNIX is a file. Everything in UNIX is a file . . . .*)

Let's go back to the earlier days of UNIX, when computers weren't quite so powerful and interaction with the shell not as easy as plunking down a few commands at a prompt. Tasks were processed by the computer one at a time, and so programmers/users (in those days, the two were synonymous) needed a way to combine commands and tasks into a more workable order, not requiring interaction with the computer at every step. The notion of batch files — files that contain a series of commands executed sequentially — evolved from this period.

Creative UNIX designers took the notion of combined commands a step further, creating an infrastructure for directing the output of one program as the input of another program. And even though today's computers are overwhelmingly more powerful than the early UNIX-based computers, this redirection of input and output, along with the related notion of piping, are still very handy tools — perhaps the handiest tools your shell has to offer.

**CROSS-REFERENCE**
You'll learn more about the ls command in Chapter 2.

**FIND IT ONLINE**
Yes, there's even a UNIX Web site devoted to shell humor: **http://www.cs.virginia.edu/~bah6f/ funnies/unixcmds.html.**

▶ **LONG COMMAND LINES**

You can pass a lot of file names and other parameters on the UNIX command line. With DOS, you're typically limited to 127 characters. With UNIX, if there is a limit, it will be much greater. Consequently, you'll see a lot of long command lines for UNIX commands.

▶ **EXTRA OPTIONS WITH GNU UTILITIES**

The GNU utilities, used heavily on Linux, typically include extra options beyond the normally large UNIX set. Furthermore, you'll often see options with two dashes instead of the normal one dash. For example, –h is a common option for displaying help on a command (but –h does not mean help for every command, so watch out). GNU utilities usually add a --help option (with two leading dashes).

▶ **DECIPHERING ERROR MESSAGES**

If you make a mistake, don't expect UNIX to spend a lot of time explaining why something failed. Some commands will fail because the command doesn't actually exist or exists in a place that UNIX can't find. Some commands will be launched and then keep processing without accepting any more input from you. This might occur when UNIX tries to access a peripheral that can't be accessed; we can't tell you how many times we've been frustrated when making a dial-up connection to the Internet and having a command hang when the modem is turned off. (Of course, the system doesn't tell us that the modem is turned off; it just throws up another command line and uses some processing power trying to dial the powerless modem.) The lesson: Don't expect a UNIX system to give you a lot of detail when a command fails.

**Listing 1-12: OPTIONS FOR COMMANDS**

```
$ ls -aF
./        barney*   fred*    wilma1
../       foo       wilma    wilma2
```

▲ *Options tell a command how to do its work. In this case, the –a and –F options (combined into –aF) tell the **ls** command to display information on all files, and insert special characters based on the type of the file (/ for directory names, | for pipes, and * for executables).*

**Listing 1-13: PARAMETERS FOR COMMANDS**

```
$ ls /usr/local/bin
ghostview   nedit      tkrat
nc          netscape   vreg
```

▲ *Here, **/usr/local/bin** is a parameter to the **ls** command. Parameters tell a command what to work on. The **ls** command normally lists the files in the current directory. Here, we tell **ls** to list the files in a different directory, **/usr/local/bin** (a location for locally-installed commands).*

**Listing 1-14: FILE NAME PARAMETERS**

```
$ ls fred barney wilma*
barney   fred   wilma   wilma1   wilma2
```

▲ *Here we tell **ls** that we are only interested in information on the files fred and barney, along with any file starting with wilma, hence wilma*.*

# Introducing Standard Input/Output

As you can see, providing input to the shell via the command line can sometimes be complicated. We're going to increase the complexity now with a discussion of standard input and output (I/O), or redirection, via the command line.

UNIX is unique in its treatment of virtually every aspect of the computer as a file of some sort. Here we bring the abstraction (mantra time!) into a more tangible, but not necessarily less complex, subject.

With standard input/output, you can take the output of one program, turn it into the input for another program, and then display or print the results of the operation — which is presented as a single command with many components. (That's why it was important for you to learn how to parse UNIX commands. There is a rhyme and reason to our approach to UNIX.)

Why is this important? Because the standard UNIX model involves input from the keyboard and output to a file. For instance, the command line:

```
$ cat > spacely
```

creates a file named **spacely**, which consists of input from your keyboard. Also, the command:

```
$ cat > spacely
```

appended the file **spacely** with input from the keyboard. These are both examples of *standard input*.

Standard input can come from your keyboard, another command, or a file, while output can be directed to a file, your screen, or another command. In UNIX, the default output for almost every command is to print to your screen; the variance comes when you want to output to a file or to a printer. These procedures are governed by input/output commands, as shown in Table 1-4 on the opposite page.

These commands are not limited to usage with files; you could direct output to a printer, for instance. Let's use each of these input/output commands, using the by-now-familiar **ls** and **cat** commands, as shown in Table 1-5.

The input/output tools can be used in conjunction with any commands, programs, or arguments. A particularly handy usage for standard input/output is in shell programming. You can also use standard input/output in the same command, using the same style:

```
$ command < infilename > outfilename
```

Any command employing standard input/output must begin with a command. While it would be more logical (and sequential) to use a command structure like:

```
$ infilename > command < outfilename
```

your system will choke on it. And the last thing we want to do as a UNIX beginner is have the system choke, right?

**CROSS-REFERENCE**
Learn more about the **cat** command in Chapter 2.

**FIND IT ONLINE**
Information about cats of a different stripe — the New Britain Rock Cats — can be found at **www.minorleaguebaseball.com/teams/new-britain/**.

## Twice as Nice

These two commands:

```
$ cat < filename
```

and

```
$ cat filename
```

create the same result: a display of filename on your monitor. The only difference is in the process: The former is treated as a single step by the UNIX shell, while the latter as a two-step process, with **cat** taking **filename** as an argument.

**TAKE NOTE**

**MAKING MISTAKES**

You really need to think things through when using redirection. It's very easy to write information to a bad file, and it's even easier to write a good file to the name of an existing file.

Let's say that you want to send the results of a command to a file named **grab**. You may not be very specific about your location in the file system and forget that there's already a file named **grab** in the destination directory. In this case, when you run the redirection command, you end up deleting the existing **grab** with the contents of your new file.

By default, Linux will not overwrite the contents of an existing file when using redirection commands.

**Table 1-4: STANDARD INPUT/OUTPUT COMMANDS**

| Command | Usage | Meaning |
|---|---|---|
| > | command > filename | Send output of command to filename. |
| < | command < filename | Input from filename to be used by command. |
| >> | command >> filename | Output of command to be appended to filename. |

**Table 1-5: SHELL INPUT/OUTPUT EXAMPLES**

| Command | Result |
|---|---|
| ls > filename | The current directory listing is sent to the file filename. If filename does not exist, the shell will create it. If filename does exist, the new data generated by ls will replace the existing data. |
| cat < filename | The cat program displays the file filename on your monitor. |
| ls >> filename | The current directory listing is appended to the file filename. |
| ls \| lp | The current directory listing is sent to the printer **lp**. |

# Processing Pipes

Pipes take the notion of input/output a step further. It is also an area of particular interest to programmers, since the idea of pipes plays a large role in UNIX programming.

When you set up a *pipe*, you specify that the output from one command should be the input to another command. So what's the difference between a pipe and redirection? Redirection always sends output to a file, while a pipe sends output to another command. You can think of a pipe as a temporary file that holds the output of the first command in anticipation of the second command.

Usage of the pipe command is simple:

```
$ command1 | command2
```

The end result is referred to as a *pipeline* (naturally). In our example, the shell places the output of ***command1*** as the input of ***command2***. There are no limitations to the number of pipes on a command line.

Put more simply: The shell sees the entire command line and divides the task into four steps:

- ▶ The first command is run.
- ▶ The output from the first command is then sent to the second command.
- ▶ The second command is run, using the input from the first command.
- ▶ The output from the second command is then sent to standard output, which is usually the screen.

So why use a pipe instead of merely stringing together two commands on the same command line? Because stringing together two commands doesn't actually link the two commands — it merely runs them sequentially. When you put together two commands in the form of a pipeline, you're using the output from one command as input for another command. This fits the UNIX philosophy to a tee: it breaks tasks into discrete elements that can be handled with multiple commands.

For instance, a pipe can be set up to accept input from your keyboard. Let's look at an example memo, erc.memo:

```
The proposal by Spacely Sprockets is simply
unacceptable and does not fit with our
long-term corporate interests. Nuke it.
```

After creating the memo and storing it, Eric notices that there's no salutation on the memo. Before printing it, he wants to add his boss's name to the memo so it looks more professional. He could use the **cat** command to tell the shell to print the file **erc.memo** only after Eric had the chance to add a salutation — an action he can take directly from the keyboard. The command line would be:

```
$ cat - erc.memo | lp
Dear Boss:
Ctrl-D
```

In this case, the hyphen (-) tells the shell to accept standard input from the keyboard, place it at the beginning of the file **erc.memo**, and then print the file.

**CROSS-REFERENCE**

Find out how to run commands in the background in the next task.

**SHORTCUT**

Check out **man troff** to see how pipes are used in text processing.

The printed file would appear as follows:

```
Dear Boss:
The proposal by Spacely Sprockets is simply
unacceptable and does not fit with our
long-term corporate interests. Nuke it.
```

The shell proscribes no limits on the number of pipelines on a command line. A pipeline like the following would be acceptable:

```
$ ls *.c | xargs grep arg | lp
```

This pipeline searches for all files ending in *.c* in the current subdirectory, searches these files for the string *arg*, and then prints out all the lines containing *arg*.

Since there are no limits to the size of a pipeline, longer pipelines can be confusing and harder for you to identify. The shell allows you to divide a long pipeline into several easier-to-read components. The above command could be written as follows:

```
$ ls *.c |
> xargs grep arg |
> lp
```

Are we mixing redirection commands with pipe commands? No. In this instance, the > tells us that the shell is waiting for additional input from the user. The > is a secondary prompt, or **PS2**. Since your initial command line ended with the pipe command, the shell correctly assumes that there's more input coming; otherwise, you'd be generating an error with the incorrect use of a pipe command.

**TAKE NOTE**

▶ **HANDLING ERROR MESSAGES**

The shell uses standard input and output to send you error messages; technically speaking, they are known in UNIX parlance as *standard error*. Standard error is sent to the screen by default — the most logical place for it, as you want to know immediately why a command failed. As you might expect, UNIX uses this mechanism to tell you that your commands cannot be carried out, as well as *why* they cannot be carried out.

Error messages are generated under a variety of circumstances: When you try to delete a file and you only have read permission, for instance, the shell tells you that you can't delete the file. Similar errors are generated if a pipe or redirection command cannot be carried out.

Since the default with most UNIX commands is sending output to your screen, it makes sense that all error messages related to commands are sent to your screen. However, this shell goes a step further and sends all error messages to the screen, even those related to file operations that don't normally generate any response. Let's say you were looking for all files ending in the string *.c*, but there were no files ending in *.c* in the current directory. Instead of getting a printed page full of lines containing the string *arg*, you'd get the following:

```
$ ls *.c | grep arg | lp
ls: *.c not found
```

Without this response, you'd never know exactly why your command line failed — alternatives in the absence of such a specific response includes the **grep** command or the printer failing.

# Running Commands in the Background

UNIX is a multiuser, multitasking operating system. So far we've been concentrating on its multiuser capabilities, with our discussions of logging on the system and sending messages to other users. Here we discuss its multitasking capabilities.

Multitasking is a fancy way of saying that UNIX can do more than one thing at a time. We humans are multitasking, to a degree; most of us can walk and chew bubble gum at the same time, for instance. When you run a command in the background, the shell assigns the command a job number and prompts you for another command. This way, you can still be running multiple commands at the same time.

This command runs in the background:

```
$ find / -name 1999.report -print &
```

This tells the shell to search for the file **1999.report**, beginning at the top of the file structure with the root directory and moving downward, and alerting us when the file is found. The ampersand (**&**) tells the shell to perform this task in the background.

What would happen if you didn't run this command in the background? Nothing serious, really. You'd be reduced to waiting while the system processed your command. In this case of the **find** command, you might be waiting a long time for the command to process — it takes a long time to run through an entire UNIX file system, especially on a large multiuser system that may have many gigabytes of online storage. On the other hand, if you were to run the command in the background, you could do your other work while you wait for the **find** command to display its findings to the screen.

Any command can be run in the background. Some tasks, such as **find** and **troff**, should almost always be run in the background, because these commands can take a long time to execute. However, if you're using the X Window System as your main interface, you don't need to run many commands explicitly in the background, since you can easily change between tasks by switching between windows.

What if your background command takes an exceptionally long time to execute and you want to log off the system? If you're working at the end of the day or know you'll be pulled away during your computing session, you can start a command line with the **nohup** (*no hang up*) command. When you log out, the command is suspended and restarted the next time you login the system. Use it as follows:

```
$ nohup find / -name 1999.report -print >
results &
```

The command won't actually be running when you log off the UNIX system. Instead, the state of the command — information about what directories have been searched, in the case of the **find** command listed here — will be saved to disk and then relaunched the next time you login the system. You don't really save any time by running a command under the **nohup** command, but you do gain the flexibility of running a command and then not having to worry about interrupting the command when you log off the system.

**CROSS-REFERENCE**

See Chapter 6 for more information on foreground and background commands.

**SHORTCUT**

More information about **nohup** can be seen in its manual page.

You can also run a series of commands in the background. As you'll recall from earlier in this chapter, the following command line was used as an example of two commands that were run sequentially from the same command line:

```
$ calendar; vi
```

In this case, the **calendar** command would be run first, followed by the **vi** command. Both of these commands would run in the foreground, tying up your machine until the command line was complete.

You can run two or more commands sequentially on the same command line in the background by adding the ampersand (**&**) to the command line. However, there's a trick to doing so — the commands must be enclosed in parentheses, making sure that the ampersand (**&**) applies to the contents of the parentheses, not just to the last command in the sequence. The resulting command line would look something like this:

```
$ (calendar; vi) &
```

**TAKE NOTE**

▶ **REDIRECTING RESULTS TO A FILE**

Note that we redirected the results of the **find** command to a file. If you don't specify this output, it will go to the file **nohup.out**. Since you'll never remember to look in the file **nohup.out**, it will effectively be lost.

▶ **SCHEDULING EVENTS**

Several other commands exist that are more appropriate if you need to schedule events at times that you're not logged on to the UNIX system. The **at** command schedules an individual command to be run once at a specific time. The **crontab** command runs a regular schedule of commands. Neither may be available to the average user, so check with your system administrator about your options should you want the ability to schedule events.

▶ **ROOTING OUT POSEURS**

The Free Software Foundation version of the **find** command and the mainstream version of the **find** command don't work in exactly the same manner. The FSF version, used in Linux and FreeBSD, doesn't require the use of the *–print* argument to the command in order to print out the results of the search. When you're reading a book about Linux, you can tell if the author really knows about Linux or if they're just a poseur by the treatment of the *–print* option and whether or not it is included in examples.

# Logging Off a UNIX System

When you're ready to leave your terminal — whether it's to go to lunch or go home at the end of the day — it's a good idea to log off the system. Why? Security, mainly. If you leave your terminal and are still logged in, someone else could come in and tamper with your information, like deleting or reading your private files. In many large, multiuser sites, security must be on the minds of every user — as we've told you time and time again throughout the course of this chapter.

If you are in this situation, tell the system that you're leaving by logging off and then turn off your monitor. If you're using a UNIX workstation, a PC running UNIX, or a UNIX variant, logoff your UNIX system and then decide whether or not you want to power down your workstation or PC. Most of the time you won't want to power down your workstation or PC. If you're in a situation where a system administrator is available for advice, check with him or her regarding the best way to handle your computer or terminal at the end of the workday.

That's why logging off the system is also a better idea than merely turning off your terminal. Although most recent UNIX systems are smart enough to recognize that a powered-down terminal means to log off a user, many older systems — or those with PCs running as terminals — do not. It's a waste of system resources to keep your account active when you're not at your terminal. This is a case where it's important to know which type of UNIX system you're

using — you sure as heck don't want to just cut the power to an expensive UNIX workstation or PC.

To log off the system, type:

```
$ exit
login:
```

if you're a Bourne or Korn shell user.

If you're a C shell user, **exit** will work, or you can type:

```
% logout
```

These commands should work on virtually every UNIX system. If they don't work in your situation, try one of the following:

```
logoff
bye
```

This leads us to a rule for PC UNIX users: Don't be so fast to shut down PC UNIX systems. UNIX, by and large, is geared for running continuously; you don't need to turn off the computer every time you're done with a PC UNIX computing session. It's better just to turn off the monitor and let the CPU run in most circumstances.

There are some exceptions. If you're connected to the Internet and are storing some sensitive data on your PC, you may want to power down the PC after your work is finished — it's impossible for someone to hack into your system via the Internet if its power is off, no matter how clever a hacker is. If you're not sure about the next time you'll be using the PC, go ahead and shut it down, especially if it's a single-user machine.

**CROSS-REFERENCE**

Chapter 6 deals with tasks and how to manage them.

**SHORTCUT**

Check out **man shutdown** to see how your system shuts down.

Again, everything comes back to the omnipotent system administrator. Do whatever your system administrator tells you regarding logging off your system.

If you're working on a large multiuser system, your act of logging off the system doesn't do anything more than tell the computer that you're not connected. If you're working with just a monitor and your keyboard, turning off a switch merely turns off the power to the monitor and doesn't really affect the UNIX system.

On a larger multiuser system, the actual box containing the UNIX operating system is in another part of the building. It's designed to be on all the time, which means that no one but the system administrator (or a trusted associate) actually cuts the power to the UNIX system. On a large system, actually cutting off the power is an involved process under the hood of the UNIX system, which is why it's not done too often. In any case, shutting down a larger multiuser UNIX system will never be your responsibility.

## TAKE NOTE

### ► CORRALLING LOST PROCESSES

There may be times when you try to log off the system, but you're unable to do so. UNIX enables you to do more than one thing at a given time, and you have started a task, only to forget about it in the course of your daily computing activities. In these cases, the system will let you know that there are some unfinished tasks with an error message like "There are stopped jobs." In this case, you need to track down the job and deal with it.

### ► MR. SPOCK WOULD BE PROUD

If you do want to shut down a Linux system, you can always give it the Vulcan death grip: **Ctrl-Alt-Delete**. PC users will recognize that this reboots a PC. However, in the case of Linux, the keyboard combination is intercepted by the Linux system and an orderly shutdown occurs. If there are other users on the system, they will be warned that the system is shutting down and that they should save their work immediately. When the system powers down and then restarts, you can merely turn off the power to the PC, pour yourself a nice dry martini and consider it a day well spent learning the Linux — and by extension — the UNIX operating system.

# Personal Workbook

## Q&A

**1** Why is an account important in your UNIX usage?

_____

_____

_____

**2** Which two important pieces of information do you need to enter when you login a UNIX system?

_____

_____

_____

**3** Name the three standard elements of a command line?

_____

_____

_____

**4** In standard input/output, where does input come from?

_____

_____

_____

**5** In standard input/output, where does output go?

_____

_____

_____

**6** In a pipe, what are you redirecting from a command? Where is it being redirected?

_____

_____

_____

**7** What's the difference between running commands in the foreground and in the background?

_____

_____

_____

**8** How do you logoff a UNIX system?

_____

_____

_____

**ANSWERS: PAGE 345**

## EXTRA PRACTICE

1. Find out what other shells are on your system.

2. Eliminate portions of a command line using *both* the **Backspace** and **Delete** keys.

3. Run two commands — **cal** and **date** — on the same command line.

4. Change your system prompt to *Emperor of All*.

5. Redirect the output of the **man** page to a file called **myman**.

6. Read the online-manual page for the **ls** command.

## REAL-WORLD APPLICATIONS

✔ You're heading to the local coffee shop for a skinny latte, but you don't want your mischievous cubicle mate to play with your system. Use the **lock** command to prevent anyone from playing with your system while you're gone.

✔ Your mischievous cubicle mate has seen you enter your password and used it to login the system as you, creating a series of embarrassing e-mail messages involving tequila, sheep, and Woodrow Wilson. Change your password so this doesn't happen again.

✔ You realize that a coworker has given you a shell script that won't work on your shell. Change your shell to another shell, such as the Bourne shell, that will run the script properly.

## Visual Quiz

There are four separate applications displayed in this X window. Can you name them?

_____

_____

_____

_____

_____

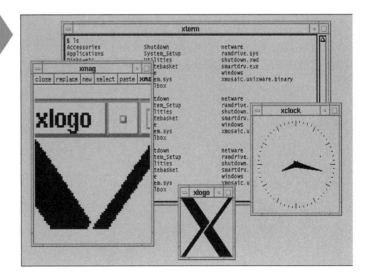

# CHAPTER 2

# File and Directory Basics

Everything in the UNIX operating system can be represented by a file. A letter you write, a program, your computer, a disk drive — all of these physical entities can be represented by the abstract file, organized into directories and subdirectories.

We find that for a true beginner the idea of files is not quite as simple or as clear-cut as computer veterans think. We also find that some veteran computer users don't know as much about files as they think they do — especially in a discussion of UNIX file basics. Finally, we find that we don't know as much about files as we think we do, and that something as simple as permissions trips us up more often than it should.

Exactly what is a file? It's a way to organize data under a single name. On a disk, a file is nothing more than the sum of bits of data scattered across the disk. It's up to the operating system to organize this data in terms of files and directories, and it's up to you to manipulate these files and directories via related commands. Almost every command in UNIX can be related to working with files, but the commands reviewed in this chapter are directly related to the manipulation of files.

This chapter covers the basics of UNIX files, how they are stored, and where you can find them. In many ways this could be the most important chapter in this book if you're a true UNIX beginner. Working directly with files is one of the greatest strengths of the UNIX operating system, but to harness this extensive power, you must be thoroughly grounded in file basics.

The length and level of detail in this chapter is indicative of the importance of files and directories in UNIX. In order to master UNIX, you need to master files and directories. That doesn't mean that you need to know the technical details about how files are physically written to disk, but you do need to know how UNIX organizes files.

# Introducing Filenames

In the UNIX operating system, *everything* is represented by a file—and we mean *everything*. Your documents, software, floppy and hard disks, monitor, and keyboard are all represented by a file. Let's say you create a report for your boss. You use a text editor (itself comprising several files) to create a document, which is stored on your hard disk as a file. When you print that report, you're printing it on a printer that is also represented within the operating system by a file.

Simply put, a file is a computer structure to store information. Stored in the electronic format that a computer can use—in bits. A bit is either 0 or 1; when strung together, these bits comprise the characters that you and I recognize. There are eight bits in a byte, 1,024 bytes in a kilobyte, and 1,048,576 bytes in a megabyte. It's from this basic level of computing that we get much of the truly bad humor flowing through the computer world (puns on byte, etc.).

Of course, you don't need to keep track of all 1,048,576 bytes in your one-megabyte document—that's what UNIX is for. You merely need to create the file using a UNIX command (such as **cat**) or an application (a word processor, a spreadsheet, a database manager, a desktop-publishing program, etc.) and then name it.

Every file has a *filename*. A filename is up to 14 characters in length (generally speaking, anyway; System V Release 4 allows unlimited length of filenames, but if the first 14 characters in two separate files match, Release 4 considers them to have the same filename). Other versions of UNIX, such as BSD and Linux, allow for much longer filenames—as many as 1,024 characters (not that you'll need all of them, of course). If you're used to working with DOS or Macintosh computers, there are some similarities between them and UNIX when it comes to filenames, but there are also some important differences.

There's no absolute freedom in UNIX, and the earlier you learn that fact the better. So you might as well know that there are some rules regarding filenames—you can't just name a file **1234566** and expect your operating system to be happy with it.

## Some UNIX Filename Ground Rules

Thus, here are a few UNIX rules and guidelines concerning filenames:

▶ A filename can be only one word, as opposed to the multiple words that comprise Macintosh and Windows 95 filenames. You can use periods (.) or underscores (_) to connect multiple words in a filename. Using our earlier example of creating a report for your boss, you could properly call the name of your report **boss_report**. However, the following filename is improper and will be rejected by UNIX:

```
boss report
```

**CROSS-REFERENCE**
Discover why hyphens can be a problem when used in a filename later in this chapter.

**FIND IT ONLINE**
More information about UNIX filenames can be found at **www.cis.ohio-state.edu/rsrg/sce/reference/unix/filenames.html**.

▶ If you're a DOS user, you're used to working with a filename of eight characters followed by a three-character suffix, known as a file extension. (Unless you're a Windows 95 user, which allows long filenames on the surface, but writes short filenames to disk — a most confusing and unfortunate circumstance.) In this case, the period denotes the end of the filename. You can follow the same model in UNIX, if you're so inclined, but with a major difference — you can place the period at any point in a UNIX filename, because the period is merely another character and doesn't denote the end of a filename. For this same reason you could place multiple periods in a filename.

▶ Putting the previous point to the test, let's say that you're creating many reports for your boss. You could end all their filenames with a **.report** suffix: **boss.report**, **daily.report**, **weekly.report**, **monthly.report**, and so on. Or, you could put a date at the end of a filename: **report.61298**, **report.61398**, and so on. You could go a step further and insert multiple periods in a filename: **Kevin.memo.612**, **Kevin.mail.614**, and so on. These touches allow you to keep better track of filenames; the more descriptive the filename, the less likely you are to lose a file containing important information.

▶ As you've already been told several times in this book, case counts in UNIX. You can use uppercase letters and lowercase letters in a UNIX filename (as opposed to DOS, which doesn't distinguish case within a filename). **Boss_report**, **Boss_Report**, and **boss_report** would be three different filenames in the UNIX operating system. At times, this case sensitivity becomes a pain, particularly if you plan on tackling programming later in your computer usage.

**TAKE NOTE**

▶ **BAD CHARACTERS**

There are some characters you shouldn't use in a UNIX filename. Technically, you could use these characters in a filename, but more likely than not, you will run into some problems if you use them. (You'll see further evidence of this later in this chapter.) In addition, you should not use spaces or tabs in a filename. The banned characters are:

```
! @ # $ % ^ & ( ) [ ] ' "
? \ | ; < > ` + - ..
```

▶ **A WORST-CASE SCENARIO**

UNIX, while having the reputation of being difficult to work with, is actually pretty lax when it comes to filenames — too lax, probably. UNIX will take a bad filename and actually use it, not telling you at the time that you're headed for problems down the road. Don't say you weren't warned when hours of hard work is rendered inaccessible by a bad filename that came back to bite you in the butt.

# Analyzing Common Filename Extensions

When naming files on a UNIX system certain conventions exist. Though they aren't necessary in UNIX, the three-character extensions forced by DOS have become an unofficial standard in the UNIX world for denoting the contents of files. The tables on the opposite page list some common filename extensions and what they mean. When possible, use these extensions on your own files.

There are practical reasons to using these extensions whenever possible. In terms of file system maintenance, it's easier to manage files that do the same thing if they have the same extension. If you're a programmer and working on a large programming project, it's easier to deal with a large number of source-code files if they all end with .c — in this case, you can copy or remove all the source-code files with a single command line, rather than listing the contents of a directory and dealing with each file on an individual basis.

In addition, there are applications that are designed to associate behaviors with specific filename extensions. For instance, the Midnight Commander (a popular file-management program that's part of most Linux distributions) can launch a specific application when presented with a filename extension. In this case, an extension of .txt can be associated with a text editor such as **vi** or **emacs**. When you double-click a file ending in .txt from within Midnight Commander, it automatically launches the associated application already containing the file.

It also makes sense to use common filename extensions when you're sharing your work with others. Let's say that you're creating a small application and giving it away to the rest of the world. If you're anticipating that it might be used widely by others in the UNIX world, you'll want to compress and archive it using the **gzip** and **tar** commands, since these are the standards in the UNIX world. In this case, you'd have a file that ends in **tar.gz**, which means that any other UNIX system with the **tar** command (in practical terms, every other UNIX system) knows how to handle the file. But if you arbitrarily decide to use your own filename extension (say, **.tarredzipped**), the other **tar** commands won't know how to deal with your file. This will frustrate other users and ensure that your claims of programming brilliance will forever be ignored by the rest of the world.

## TAKE NOTE

### TEMPORARY INSANITY

You may occasionally run across endings with .tmp. Some UNIX applications need to temporarily store data somewhere on the file system, and so they store them in temporary files (which are usually erased by the originating application after they have served their purpose). These files usually end in tmp or else have tmp somewhere in the filename. Generally speaking, you shouldn't mess with these files if you find them in your home directory.

## CROSS-REFERENCE

See Chapter 10 to find out about filename extensions for programming.

## FIND IT ONLINE

More information about **gzip** can be found at
**www.di.uoa.gr/~admin/English/Tools/Gzip.html**.

## Table 2-1: COMMON FILENAME EXTENSIONS FOR TEXT FILES

| Extension | Meaning |
| --- | --- |
| **.txt** | Text file, generated (probably) by a text editor such as **vi** or **emacs**. |
| **.mm** | Text files formatted with the Memorandum Macros. |
| **.ms** | Text files formatted with the ms macros package, a text processor. |
| **.xx** or **.tex** | Text files formatted with TeX. |

## Table 2-2: COMMON FILENAME EXTENSIONS FOR COMPRESSED FILES

| Extension | Meaning |
| --- | --- |
| **.z** | File compressed with the UNIX **pack** command. |
| **.Z** | File compressed with the UNIX **compress** command. |
| **.tar** | File(s) archived with the UNIX **tar** command. |
| **.gz** | File(s) compressed with the **gzip** command (a compression program from the Free Software Foundation not found with every version of UNIX). |
| **.zip** | File(s) compressed using the **zip** format. |
| **.uu** | File encoded using the **uuencode** command. |
| **.bz2** | File(s) compressed using the **bzip** command. |

## Table 2-3: COMMON FILENAME EXTENSIONS FOR GRAPHICS FILES

| Extension | Meaning |
| --- | --- |
| **.gif** | File formatted in Graphics Information Format (GIF), used often in Web pages. |
| **.jpg** | File formatted in the JPEG file format, used often in Web pages. |
| **.ps** | File formatted in the PostScript page format. |
| **.xwd** | File formatted in the X Window screen-dump format. |

## Table 2-4: COMMON FILENAME EXTENSIONS FOR PROGRAMMING FILES

| Extension | Meaning |
| --- | --- |
| **.a** | Library file, like a DOS .lib file. |
| **.c** | C-language source code. |
| **.h** | Header file. |
| **.o** | Object file. |

## Table 2-5: COMMON FILENAME EXTENSIONS FOR SHELL SCRIPTS

| Extension | Meaning |
| --- | --- |
| **.csh** | C-shell script. |
| **.sh** | Bourne, Korn, or Bash script. |

# Reviewing File Types

In UNIX, everything is a file. (Gee, that sounds familiar, doesn't it?) Here we discuss the four different file types, how to find out the file type of a specific file, and why file types are important in your UNIX usage. The four major file types are:

- ▶ Ordinary files
- ▶ Directories
- ▶ Links
- ▶ Special device files

We've mentioned each type of file so far in this chapter (except symbolic links), though not explicitly by name.

## Ordinary Files

An *ordinary file* is, well, fairly ordinary. Most of the files that you create and edit using applications are ordinary files. There are four kinds of ordinary files, the first of which is *text files* (sometimes called English files). These files contain ASCII characters. ASCII characters are numerical representations of regular letters and numerals. They are not tied to any specific operating system or computer type, so an ASCII file created in a UNIX text editor could be read by a PC or Macintosh word processor. These are the most ordinary of ordinary files.

*Data files* are a step up from text files; in addition to ASCII characters, data files will usually contain instructions on how those characters are to be treated by an application. For instance, a letter created in a text-processing application will contain not only the characters in the text of the letter but instructions about how the characters are arranged on the page (margins, etc.), the typefaces of the characters, and other miscellaneous information. *Command files* (also known as shell scripts) are ASCII files that provide commands to your shell. *Executable files* are written in binary code and are created by programmers.

## Directories

We've already mentioned *directories*; these are files that contain all pertinent information regarding a directory: a listing of files and subdirectories, file type, and more.

## Links

A *link* is actually a second name for an existing file. Why have two names? Remember that UNIX is a multiuser operating system, which means that it supports more than one user. Often more than one user will want access to the same file. Instead of creating two files (with separate changes from separate users — the start of a logistical nightmare), UNIX allows two users to share one file, and changes made by either user are reflected in the one file. (An added bonus is that only one file need be present on the hard disk, freeing valuable disk space.)

**CROSS-REFERENCE**

See "Navigating the UNIX Directory Structure" later in this chapter to learn more about directories.

**FIND IT ONLINE**

Information about UNIX files and directories can be found at **riceinfo.rice.edu/Computer/Documents/Unix/UNIX1/unix1.html**.

Modern UNIX goes a step further with the introduction of *symbolic links*, files that contain the name of another file. Symbolic links address some of the limitations inherent in linked files, such as the inability to link files on different but networked computers.

Links are best left to system administrators and programmers, whose business it is to set up these links. As a user, you should consider links to be a topic to be avoided, for the most part. (However, because this book is devoted to full disclosure of the UNIX operating system, there will be an extended discussion of links and the **ln** command later in this chapter.)

## Special Device Files

Finally, we have *special device files*, which represent physical aspects of a computer system. You can't read these files, nor can you change them; they're used by the operating system to communicate with your hardware, such as printers and terminals.

You won't directly use these special device files very often, and in some ways it's better to put them out of your mind. We come back to that nasty topic of abstraction again, and a special device file is perhaps the ultimate in abstractions; an electronic file that represents a physical device such as a printer. When you want to print a file, you should think

through the process directly — to print a file, you must send the file to the printer — and leave it at that, unless you're truly into abstractions. (As many computer people are, we should hasten to add.) Your knowledge of special device files need extend only to knowing what files represent the cool laserprinter down the hall.

> **TAKE NOTE**
>
> ▶ **DETERMINING FILE TYPES**
>
> The **ls** command and its *-l* (that's a lowercase *L*, not the number *one*; it's shorthand for *long*) option is used to list a file's type. We cover this command later in this chapter, but for now you can go ahead and use this command line: **ls –l** along with a specific filename. A long listing for the file will appear, and directly after the permissions section will be a character that's associated with a specific file type: - (ordinary file), **d** (directory), or **l** (link). There are also a few obscure file types that may be returned: **b** (special block file), **c** (special character file), or **p** (named pipe special file). You won't run across these three too often.

# Introducing Directories

The UNIX operating system oversees how files are organized and stored on electronic media of some sort, which can be floppy disks, hard disks (sometimes called hard drives or fixed disks), CD-ROM drives, or tape drives. The operating system takes care of the dirty details, such as where the parts of a file are physically stored on a disk. While you don't need to know where each individual bit is stored on a disk, you do need to know where the operating system stored the file. This leads us to the concept of *directories* and how you use them.

A directory on a hard disk can be thought of as a file folder containing files. (If you're a Macintosh user, you certainly recognize the concept.) Essentially, a directory is a special file that contains the names of other files. The idea is to place similar documents into the same directory so they are easier to find; for instance, the aforementioned reports to your boss could be contained in a directory named **Reports**. Correspondence from colleagues sent via electronic mail could be stored in a directory named **Mail**.

There can also be directories within directories; these are called *subdirectories*. You can have as many subdirectories as your heart desires. In a way, every directory in UNIX is really a subdirectory; think of your hard disk as one large directory, with everything contained within organized into subdirectories. In this manner, you could envision your computer's hard disk as a file cabinet, your top-level directories as drawers, the subdirectories as file folders, and the actual files as pieces of paper. (As we warned you earlier, a certain amount of abstraction is needed to tackle not only the UNIX operating system but computing in general.) The term *subdirectory* is relative; any directory you're working in is the *current directory* or *working directory* and any directory under that is termed a subdirectory. In the end, everything is a subdirectory, save the root directory, which is at the top of the directory hierarchy.

## Using Your File System

There is one very important concept regarding directories that is essential to your UNIX usage: that the sum of all the directories is called a *file system*.

In the real world — that is, the physical world — a computer doesn't store data in a sequential pattern that matches the abstract model of a file system. That is, the contents of the root directory aren't always stored at the beginning of a hard disk, followed by the immediate subdirectories of the root directory. In reality, data can be stored anywhere on a hard disk, which is why you hear hard disks churning away when you perform a simple task, such as opening or saving a file.

When you call up the contents of your file system, you may be calling data from more than one physical disk or CD-ROM. The Windows/DOS and

**CROSS-REFERENCE**

See Table 2-7 for an overview of the major directories in a UNIX file system.

**FIND IT ONLINE**

More information about directories can be found at **www.cit.ac.nz/smac/os100/unix01.htm**.

Macintosh worlds use partitions and allow access to only one physical device at a time. Here, you call the contents of one hard disk, then physically change your location to another hard disk or CD-ROM drive, and then continue with your chores.

This isn't so in the UNIX world. All storage available to you — whether it be multiple physical disks, CD-ROM drives, or tape devices — appear in one large homogenous listing. You often aren't told that you're calling data from a CD-ROM or tape drive (although you certainly can run into problems if you accidentally try to call data from these devices). The point is simple: You shouldn't need to know about the identity of a storage device to call data from it.

Many system administrators go to great lengths to make sure that you don't know about the physical layout of your file system, if you're working on a large network. You don't need to know that part of your directory structure is stored on a local machine and the other portion is stored on a network server at the other end of the building. If you have that sort of knowledge, you'd be tempted to worry more about where you're storing your data and not spending enough time focusing on your work.

## TAKE NOTE

### ▶ NEATNESS COUNTS

Organization is a hard habit to teach in a computer book, but we can't stress enough that you take your file organization seriously. Files are like rabbits; they tend to breed quickly and in great numbers, and unless you keep a tight control over them they'll end up wandering away and disappearing. Throwing all your files into a single directory is a logistical nightmare; you'll be scrolling through directory lists all day and lose track of older files. (In addition, you'll make your hard disk work awfully hard to list all those files.) By creating several subdirectories to organize similar files, you'll be saving yourself a lot of time For instance, we find it handy to keep reports in a directory called **reports**, memos in a directory called **memos**, and so on.

### ▶ CAPITALIZATION COUNTS

The rules regarding capitalization and filenames also applies to directories: UNIX would consider **Reports**, **reports**, and **REportS** three different directory names.

### ▶ LOCATING YOUR CURRENT POSITION

If you start moving between directories, it's possible to forget exactly where you are on the directory tree. To print out the current working directory, use the **pwd** (for *print working directory*) command:

```
$ pwd
/users/data/1999
$
```

# Navigating the UNIX Directory Structure

Flash back to your childhood when you created a family tree in elementary school. Your great-grandparents were at the top of the tree, followed by your grandparents, parents, and finally your generation at the bottom. The tree got wider nearer the bottom, reflecting the greater number of persons in succeeding generations.

You could think of the UNIX file structure as a family tree of sorts. Technically speaking, the UNIX file system is called a *hierarchical* file system. At the top of the tree is the root directory, usually represented by a slash (/). The figure on the opposite page illustrates a typical UNIX file system.

There's no limit on the number of directories and subdirectories within UNIX; this figure is perhaps atypical because of the relatively small number of directories and files. If you were working on a large network supporting hundreds or thousands of users, you'd see a much larger number of directories.

When you start looking through UNIX directory structures, you'll find that there is usually a method to the file madness, and that the same method is used in most UNIX systems. Over time, many conventions have developed regarding UNIX file systems.

Most of you have little choice in how your directories are structured; if you're working on a large file system, your system administrator handled all of these details. However, if you're using a single-user workstation or a PC-based UNIX variant, we recommend that you organize your own directory in a

similar fashion (these are usually the defaults in any Linux or FreeBSD system). It's simply easier to store programs in a **bin** directory, device files in a **dev** directory, and miscellaneous system files in an **etc** directory, and it's also where applications expect to find information.

When you login your UNIX system, you are placed immediately by the system into your *home directory*. This directory has been set up to store all your files; it's represented by a tilde character (~) at a shell prompt. From your home directory you move up, down, and through the file structure. In our example file structure on the opposite page, we use the example of **home** as a home directory, although it's never actually called **home**; usually it's given your login name as a name. You can change this default by editing your **.profile** file, but this is an action that you probably won't want to attempt.

## TAKE NOTE

### WORKING IN TWO DIMENSIONS

When you're logged in a UNIX system, you're always said to be located in your *current directory*. You, as a user, can exist only in one directory at one time. If you've configured your shell correctly you'll be told the name of your current directory at all times. This location is also relative to the other directories in your file system.

**CROSS-REFERENCE**
Learn more about changing your home directory in Chapter 4.

**FIND IT ONLINE**
Some frequently used commands can be found at www.nmt.edu/tcc/help/unix/unix_cmd.html.

## Table 2-6: THE MAJOR DIRECTORIES IN A UNIX FILE SYSTEM

| Directory | Meaning |
|---|---|
| **adm** | Administration files. |
| **bin** | This directory contains most of the standard UNIX programs and utilities. The term bin is short for *binary*. |
| **dev** | This directory contains device files. We discussed device files earlier in this chapter. |
| **etc** | Essentially, this directory contains everything but device files and program files — in short, a lot of miscellaneous files. Most system administrators use this directory to store system configurations, as well as user profiles. Most of these files are accessible only to the system administrator. You'll rarely need to modify these files. |
| **include** | Programming header, or include files are stored here. |
| **lib** | Programming libraries. |
| **local** | Files added at your site. The name local separates these files from the files that come with UNIX. Under local, you'll often find subdirectories like bin, for local programs; and lib, for local libraries. |
| **man** | Some versions of UNIX place online-manual pages (which you learned about in Chapter 1) in a separate directory. |
| **src** | An abbreviation for source, src holds source code for programs. |
| **share** | Files that can be shared between systems. |
| **tmp** | This temporary directory is used by the system for temporary storage of working files. Many programs will temporarily store working files in this directory and then delete the files when the chore is completed. Management of the contents of this directory is best left up to system administrators. |
| **usr** | This directory also contains commands. |
| **var** | This directory contains system definitions. |

# Parsing Pathnames

Two files with the same name cannot exist in the same directory. But two files with the same name can exist if they are stored in different directories. But wait — didn't we earlier warn against giving files the same filenames? We did. And in the example given, the files don't have the same name, despite initial appearances. When we described filenames earlier in the chapter, we weren't telling you the entire story. By including a description of the location of the file in the directory structure, you can create many files named **Kevin.report**, as long as they're placed in different directories. These different **Kevin.reports** are distinguished by their pathnames. In our example, the pathnames for the two **Kevin.report** files are

```
/users/home/data/Kevin.report
```

and

```
/users/kevin/data/Kevin.report
```

These are called *full pathnames* because they provide an exact description of the file's location in the directory structure. These descriptions can get very long, so watch your typing carefully — it's a real drag retyping long full pathnames after you discover the system wouldn't accept your original pathname because of a typo in the middle.

How do we decipher a pathname? In our example pathname of **/users/home/data/Kevin.report**, the initial slash (/) refers to the root directory, as we mentioned above. The following slashes separate the names of subdirectories within subdirectories. The final slash denotes the actual filename. In our example, the directory **users** is a subdirectory of the root directory, **home** is a subdirectory of users, and **Kevin.report** is a file within the data subdirectory.

Many UNIX tools help you avoid typing long pathnames. A *relative pathname* is just that — a pathname that's shortened in relationship to your present directory position. Because you're always entered into your home directory when you initially login your UNIX system, you can specify a pathname relative to your home directory. From your home directory location of **home**, you could specify **data/Kevin.report** — which would be as valid as **/users/home/data/Kevin.report**. To specify a directory from your home directory, use a tilde (~) character, for example, **~/data/Kevin.report** is stored in the data subdirectory of your home directory.

To change your current directory, use the **cd** (*change directory*) command. There are relatively few restrictions on this command, but lots of options. In all common situations you'll have two parts to a command — using the **cd** command to move to another directory, while an option tells the **cd** command what to work upon. Here are common usages of this command.

▶ To move to the root directory use:
```
$ cd /
```

▶ To move up one level in the directory tree to the parent directory of your current directory, use the **cd** command followed by two dots:
```
$ cd ..
```

**CROSS-REFERENCE**

Learn how to copy files later in this chapter, in the section entitled "Copying Files and Directories."

**FIND IT ONLINE**

More information about creating directories can be found at **www.nmt.edu/tcc/help/unix/fund.html**.

▶ If you want to move to another directory, you can combine the **cd** command with the pathname:

```
$ cd /users/kevin/junk
```

▶ To move to the previous directory (if you're a Korn-shell user, anyway), use:

```
$ cd -
```

▶ If you want to return to your home directory, use **cd** by itself:

```
$ cd
```

Despite sharing the same name, there are some differences between the DOS **CD** command and the UNIX **cd** command. With DOS, you get the name of the current directory when you invoke **CD** (since it's DOS shorthand for *current directory*):

```
C:> CD
curdir
```

where *curdir* is the current directory. In UNIX, using **cd** by itself will place you into your home directory (which is always designated with a tilde character). However, the UNIX and DOS versions of **cd** work similarly when presented with parameters like double dots (**..**) and pathnames.

DOS also uses a backslash character (\) instead of the forward slash (/) that UNIX uses. (If this looks familiar, it should; the World Wide Web is based on the same forward-slash tool used in UNIX, as the Web is heavily based on UNIX conventions.) In addition, DOS does not require a space after **CD**; UNIX does.

---

**TAKE NOTE**

▶ **RELATIVE PATHNAMES**

If your current directory is **users**, you can use a single dot (**.**) to specify its position relative to other pathnames. If you have a subdirectory named personnel, and within it a subdirectory named **1998**, you could use **./personnel/1998** as its relative pathname. If you want to specify the parent directory of the current directory, use double dots (**..**) in a relative pathname.

▶ **USING SUBDIRECTORIES**

Let's say you want to move out of your home directory and use another directory as your current directory. You may want to have your home directory contain many subdirectories, each containing different types of work data (financial reports, personnel files, etc.). We recommend creating a subdirectory for each type of work data and then using UNIX commands to navigate between the directories, according to the work being done.

▶ **SUBDIRECTORIES AND PERMISSIONS**

When you create a subdirectory, you automatically have permission to store files in it. However, you don't automatically have permission to write to every subdirectory in a system, and if you didn't create a subdirectory maintained by another person, you may not have permission to read or write files from it.

# Listing Files with the ls Command

On a base level, the **ls** command combined with an argument of some sort will list the contents of your current directory. The **ls** command by itself will list the entire contents of a directory without differentiating between files and subdirectories:

```
$ ls
data        expenses    figures     financials
misc        newdata     personnel
$
```

As you can tell, the files and directories are listed in alphabetical order in columnar form.

The utility of the plain **ls** command is limited, as you don't know the difference between files and directories. Plus, the **ls** command does not list any hidden files. In UNIX, any files beginning with a period (.) are *hidden files*. These files are used by the operating system for standard housekeeping tasks; the **.profile** file stores details about your particular configuration, while other hidden files are used by programs like your electronic-mail program. This is why it's very important to know about the various, useful arguments for **ls**, as illustrated in this three-step process:

▶ If you want to view the contents of a subdirectory, use the **ls** command with the name of the subdirectory as an argument. In this instance, we're asking for the contents of the subdirectory **data**:

```
$ ls data
1999.proj  Kevin.report  stats
```

▶ To determine if a given file is within your current directory, use the **ls** command with the name of the file as the argument:

```
$ ls newdata
newdata
```

▶ If the file is not found, you get the following message:

```
$ ls god
god not found
```

▶ You can also use the **ls** command to view hidden files (mentioned above). Use **ls** with the *-a* (for *all*) option:

```
$ ls -a
.           .profile    misc
..          data        newdata
.mailrc     financials  personnel
```

▶ The command line also lists the current (.) and parent (..) directories as well as the two hidden files (**.mailrc** and **.profile**).

Our examples so far have used directories with only a few files. Most directories will contain many, many files (at least ours do), and it can be hard to find files in a long list without any logical organization. Using the *-F* option brings some order to a confusing directory:

```
$ ls -F
data/       misc/       personnel/
financials/ newdata
```

The -*F* option tells ls to provide us with details about each listing. This directory contains four subdirectories, as noted by the slashes (/) following the

**CROSS-REFERENCE**
Learn about changing your **.profile** file in Chapter 4.

**FIND IT ONLINE**
More information about **ls** can be found at
**www.gnu.org/software/fileutils/fileutils.html**.

filename. Also contained is an ordinary file, **newdata**. If this directory contained symbolic file links, they would have been denoted by an @ symbol following the filename. Executable files have an asterisk (*) after the filename.

If you want to display the contents of a directory in one column, use the *-1* (the number one) option:

```
$ ls -1
data
financials
personnel
misc
newdata
```

Of course, **ls** isn't the only tool for displaying files on a UNIX system. Almost every version of UNIX comes with a *file manager*, a graphical tool that usually runs under the X Window System or the Common Desktop Environment. The opposite figure shows a generic file manager that ships with the version of X adapted for PCs.

## A Linux Ls: Dir

The folks at the Free Software Foundation are pretty smart. If you're using an operating system that relies on GNU commands— Linux or FreeBSD for example— you can use the **dir** command to list the contents of a directory. The **dir** command works the same way as the **ls** command, and you don't need to monkey around with aliases to use it.

In fact, on all levels the FSF version of **ls** works a lot better than the generic UNIX version. Even though **ls** is designed to work in a text environment, the GNU **ls** works in color and denotes different file types in different colors. In addition, **ls** clearly tells

you what's a directory and what's a file by attaching a symbol to the end of a directory.

*Continued*

TAKE NOTE

### WHY LS MAY FAIL

Your version of **ls** may not support the *-1* option, since it's not uniformly implemented in the UNIX world.

### LS IN DIFFERENT DIMENSIONS

You can think of the **ls** command as being the equivalent of the DOS **DIR** command. In fact, we usually set up an alias for the **ls** command in the form of **dir**, so that we don't need to think about what operating system we're using to use the same command to do the same thing.

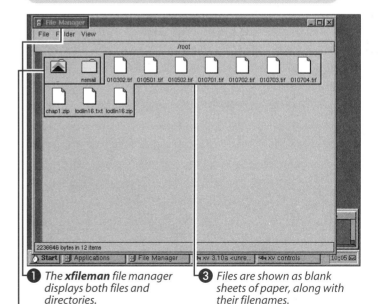

① The **xfileman** file manager displays both files and directories.

② The directories are shown as file folders, storing directories.

③ Files are shown as blank sheets of paper, along with their filenames.

# Listing Files with the ls Command

*Continued*

The **ls** command obviously works better in a directory with relatively little content. If you're working with a directory containing many files and directories, use the -*x* option to sort the entries in alphabetical order across the screen:

```
$ ls -x
1timer        6.21.proposal
Notes         UNIXBOOK
a1            data
financials    misc
newdata       personnel
```

As you can probably divine from this directory listing, there's a structure to the UNIX **ls -x** command line: ASCII order. (Remember that everything in computing has a numerical basis, and that ASCII characters are merely representations of numerical values.) In ASCII, numerals are listed first, followed by uppercase letters and lowercase letters.

These options can be combined. For instance, you could merge entries horizontally:

```
$ ls -xF
1timer        6.21.proposal
Notes         UNIXBOOK
a1            data/
financials/   misc/
newdata       personnel
```

The -*t* option to **ls** lists files in order of time (most recent first) instead of alphabetically. If you forget which file you modified last, you can use **ls -t** to help find it.

You can list all the files in a directory, as well as all the files in any subdirectories, using the -*R* (short for *recursive*) option:

```
$ ls -R
1timer        UNIXBOOK
6.21.proposal a1
Notes         data

./Letters
6.21.letter 6.22.letter letter.kevin
```

This lists the contents of the current directory (**1timer**, **6.21.proposal**, **UNIXBOOK**, **Notes**, **a1**, and **data**), as well as the contents of the subdirectory **Letters** (**6.21.letter**, **6.22.letter**, and **letter.kevin**).

## Using the -t Option with Ls

The -*t* option lists files based on the last time they were upgraded, with the most recently changed files listed first:

```
$ ls -t
6.21.proposal  UNIXBOOK  1timer
a1             Notes     data
```

## Using the -l Option with Ls

So far we've worked with the short version of the **ls** command, which provides filenames only. If we want complete information about filenames, we can use the -*l* option (short for *long* format) with the **ls** command.

Using this option in our home directory, we'd see a listing like the following (this has been abbreviated for space):

**CROSS-REFERENCE**

Learn about permissions in the next section.

**FIND IT ONLINE**

More information about **ls** can be found at
www.mcsr.olemiss.edu/unixhelp/DOStoUNIX.html.

```
$ ls -l
total 32
-rwxrwxrwx  1  user  group1  27  Feb  2
09:20  1timer
drwxr--r--  6  user  group1  347  Jun 21
14:41  data
-rwx------  3  user  group1  995  Dec 25
00:41  personnel
```

The listing starts with a summary of the disk space used by the directory, in *blocks*. (A block is normally 4,096 bytes, but some systems use different block sizes, depending on what type of file system you have.) Most of the remaining information in this listing is self-evident, but is better explained when read right-to-left (backwards). The first column lists the files and directories in alphabetical order. The second column lists the date and time the entries were created. The third column lists the size (in bytes) of the entries. The fourth column lists the group that the entry belongs to (we discuss the concept of groups in the next section). The fifth column lists the owner of the file (denoted by your login name, user).

The sixth column is the *link count*, which lists how many files are symbolically linked to the file (in the case of the **personnel** file, there are three linked copies), or, in the case of directories, how many subdirectories are contained within it plus two (one for the directory itself and one for the parent directory; in this case there are four actual subdirectories).

In the final (but first overall) column, we see a series of seemingly illogical characters. The first character in the column lists the type of file (earlier in this chapter we covered file types), which are summarized in Table 2-8.

For our present needs, the most important file types are directory (**d**), symbolic link (**l**) and ordinary file (-). Most of the files you use regularly will fall into these three types.

The rest of the characters in that column have to do with permissions, which is an involved subject worthy of extended coverage.

---

**TAKE NOTE**

▶ **WATCH THAT CASE**

As always, case counts with UNIX. The *-R* option and the *-r* option do two different things when combined with the **ls** command.

---

**Table 2-7: FILE TYPES ASSOCIATED WITH THE -L OPTION**

| Symbol | Meaning |
|--------|---------|
| -      | Ordinary file. |
| b      | Special block file. |
| c      | Special character file. |
| d      | Directory. |

# Begging for Permissions

In a multiuser operating system, the needs of a potentially very large number of users coupled with the diverse security needs of some users, means that there needs to be safeguards as to who can read and write files, as well as run certain programs.

UNIX handles this elementary security through *permissions*. For files, there are three levels of permissions: read permission means that you can read the file, write permission means that you can change the file, and execute permission means that you can run the file as a program.

Permissions can also be applied to directories: Read permission means that you can list the contents of a directory, write permission means that you can make or delete files and/or directories within the directory, and execute permission means that you can make that directory your current directory via the **cd** command.

Let's look at a line we first introduced in the previous section, when we used the **ls** command to list the contents of a directory:

```
-rwx------  3  user  group1 995 Dec 25
00:41  personnel
```

The first nine characters in our example apply different permissions to the various files and subdirectories. When reading this column (the first character denotes the file type, the final nine denote the permissions), you must divide the nine permissions characters into three clusters of three characters: The first cluster of three refers to permissions granted to the owner of the entry, the second cluster of three refers to the permissions granted to the group that the entry belongs to, and the third cluster of three refers to the permissions granted to all users.

Bear with us; permissions are better understood when illustrated by an example. Using the first file listing:

```
-rwxrwxrwx  1  user  group1   27 Feb  2
09:20  1timer
```

we can see that the permissions associated with this file is *rwxrwxrwx*. The owner can read (*r*), write (*w*), and execute (*x*) the file. Anyone in the group **group1** can read (*r*), write (*w*), and execute (*x*) the file. In fact, all users can read (*r*), write (*w*), and execute (*x*) the file.

However, things are different in this second listing:

```
drwxr--r--  6  user  group1 347 Jun 21
14:41  data
```

the permissions associated with this directory are *rwxr---r--*. The owner of this directory can read (*r*), write (*w*), and execute (*x*) the directory. Members of the group, as well as all users, can read (*r*) the directory, but cannot write (-) the directory or make the directory a current directory (-). All users can only read (*r*) the file.

The permissions are even more restrictive with a final **personnel** file:

```
-rwx------  3  user  group1 995 Dec 25
00:41  personnel
```

In this instance, with such an obviously sensitive personnel file, the user has decided to deny access to

---

**CROSS-REFERENCE**

Learn more about the **grep** command in Chapter 3.

**FIND IT ONLINE**

Check out ftp.freebsd.org for information about FREEBSD UNIX.

everyone else. The user can read (*r*), write (*w*), and execute (*x*) the file. No one else can read (-), write (-), or execute (-) the file. This sort of restriction is common within the UNIX system and indeed forms the basic level of security.

## Group? What Group?

As mentioned earlier, everyone on a UNIX system is assigned to a group, and you can be assigned to more than one group. When you login a UNIX system, you're automatically placed in your primary group, which can be found listed in the **/etc/passwd** file.

If you don't know what groups you're assigned to, you can use the **groups** command to get this information:

```
$ groups
group1
secret
```

This tells you that you're a member of the **group1** and **secret** groups. (It's always cool to belong to a secret group.) Information about the groups and their members can be found in the **/etc/group** file, which you can read; however, on a large system, this file can be extremely long, so you're best off using a command like **grep** if you want to see more about the groups you belong to:

```
$ grep kevin /etc/groups
group1:114:geisha,kevin,spike
secret:446:eric,geisha,kevin,tom
```

From this, we can see the members of each group, as well as the group IDs (114 for group1, 446 for

secret). This information is important if you want to switch groups during the course of your normal work; if you're logged in as a member of **group1**, you won't have access to group permissions of the secret files.

---

**TAKE NOTE**

▶ **THE IN CROWD**

Everyone on a UNIX system is assigned to a group when their accounts are set up by the system administrator, and you can belong to several groups. This normally is nothing you need to worry about.

▶ **GROUP LOVE**

Who sets up groups? Basically, anyone with the permission to set up a group. System administrators often set up groups on a system-wide basis: accountants belong to the accounting group and so on. Past that, anyone with the permission to edit the **/etc/group** file has the ability to set up and maintain groups. In addition, some UNIX packages — mostly groupware and World Wide Web packages — also impose their own permissions and group privileges on other users. As always: When in doubt, chat up your system administrator.

▶ **CHANGING GROUPS**

You can change groups at any point in your work (provided you're a member of the new group), with the **newgrp** command:

```
$ newgrp secret
```

# Changing Permissions with chmod

The method of listing permissions covered so far in this chapter — the *symbolic form* — is one of two ways the UNIX system tracks permissions. The other method, the numeric form, comes in very handy when changing permissions with the **chmod** command.

As you'd expect, the numeric form uses numerals to track permissions. This is done in a very quirky way, however, and is probably more complicated than it need be, forcing you to add up three different sets of numbers in determining who has what permissions. Note that the actual types of permissions — owners, groups, and all users having read, write, and execute permissions — have not changed; only the way of listing them.

The numeric form uses modes to list permissions. A mode is an octal number in one of the forms listed in the table on the opposite page. You get the numeric form by adding together the numbers and then combining the number with the **chmod** command (short for *change mode*). Let's go back to an example from earlier in this chapter, shown on the top of the facing page.

If we translate the example to numeric form, the result would be 744. How did we arrive at that? We explain how on the opposite page, in the top table. In essence, all you do is add the numerical values associated with each level of permission. A file that's open to the entire world (meaning they can read, write, and execute the file) would have a value of 777; a file that's totally inaccessible would have a value of 000.

When you want to change the permissions, you combine the numerals representing the desired permissions with the **chmod** command. Here are two examples of how this works:

▶ To change the permissions for the aforementioned data file, giving the entire world permission to read, write, and execute the file, you'd use a command line like:

```
$ chmod 777 data
```

▶ To change the permissions to where only the owner has the ability to read, write, and execute the file data, you'd use the following command line:

```
$ chmod 700 data
```

You can also use the *symbolic* method when setting permissions, but this method is a little trickier than using the numeric method. With the numeric method, you're setting the new permissions absolutely; it doesn't matter what the existing permissions are. With the symbolic method, you're setting the new permissions relative to the old permissions. Also, you're embarking on some slightly different terminology when it comes to permissions when you use the symbolic method, as you'll see in the following example of the **chmod** command used with the symbolic method:

```
$ chmod u+x data
```

**CROSS-REFERENCE**
Appendix C covers basic UNIX commands

**FIND IT ONLINE**
See **consult.ml.org/˜trockij/mon** for mon, a UNIX system monitoring package.

This might appear to be confusing at first, but it really isn't. When using this symbolic method, **chmod** changes permissions relative to the old one, and does so through a syntax that adds or subtracts permissions for the user (who's been called the owner of the file so far in this discussion), the group, and others (the world). Breaking down the *u+x* portion of the previous command line yields the following information:

▶ The **u** refers to the user, or the owner of the file. From this we know that the permissions are being set for the owner.

▶ The **+** refers to the process of adding a permission to the current permissions. If a minus sign (-) were used here, a permission would be subtracted from the current permissions.

▶ The **x** means that the addition to the permissions should be the ability to execute the file.

Let's use an example. You can give every user access to a file with the following command line:

```
$ chmod ugo+rwx
```

You can specify multiple permissions on a command line with the **chmod** command, provided the individual permissions are separated with a comma:

```
$ chmod u+x,go-w data
```

This command line takes away (-) the ability to write (*w*) to the file from the group (*g*) and others (*o*).

*Continued*

---

**TAKE NOTE**

▶ **DECIPHERING PERMISSIONS**

The following numerals have the corresponding permissions:

| | |
|---|---|
| 400 | Owner has read permission. |
| 200 | Owner has write permission. |
| 100 | Owner has execute permission. |
| 040 | Group has read permission. |
| 020 | Group has write permission. |
| 010 | Group has execute permission. |
| 004 | All users have read permission. |
| 002 | All users have write permission. |
| 001 | All users have execute permission. |

### Listing 2-1: PERMISSIONS: EXAMPLE ONE

```
drwxr--r-- 6 user group1 347 Jun 21 14:41
data
```

▲ *This permission line has a numeric total of 744.*

### Listing 2-2: PERMISSIONS: EXAMPLE TWO

```
drwxrwxr-- 6 user group2 347 Jan 30 11:14
data
```

▲ *This permission line has a numeric total of 774.*

### Listing 2-3: PERMISSIONS: EXAMPLE THREE

```
drwxrwxrw- 6 user group1 347 Jun 21 14:41
data
```

▲ *This permission line has a numeric total of 776.*

# Changing Permissions with chmod *Continued*

You can do all sorts of changing with the **chmod** command. Here are three examples:

▶ To change the permissions so that the owner has the ability to read, write, and execute the file, with members of the group also having the ability to read, write, and execute the file, use the following command line:

```
$ chmod 770 data
```

▶ To change the permissions so that the owner has the ability to read, write, and execute the file, with members of the group and the world having the ability to read the file, use the following command line:

```
$ chmod 744 data
```

▶ You can also change the permissions of the contents of an entire directory with **chmod**, by using it with the *-R* option. The following command line makes the entire contents of the **letters** directory readable for only the owner of the directory:

```
$ chmod -R 700 letters
```

A full listing of the symbols possible with the **chmod** command can be found in the table at the bottom of the facing page.

When you create a file or directory, default permissions are automatically assigned to the file or directory. Most of the time, the default permissions will be acceptable. However, you may find that you want to change these defaults. To do so, use the **umask** (short for *user-mask*) command. When run without any options, the **umask** command returns the default permissions:

```
$ umask
744
```

This is a pretty expansive set of permissions (and not usually the default; this is being used purely as an example, and it's more that likely this won't be your default). Most of the time the **umask** command will be used to make permissions more restrictive, therefore, the following example will change the permissions to give full permission to the owner and the group, but not to the world:

```
$ umask 007
```

Wait a second — 007? Yes. In yet another glaring inconsistency within the UNIX system, the **umask** command changes permissions relative to a baseline of 777. Therefore, your input of 007 to the **umask** command is actually subtracted from the baseline 777, yielding a final permission of 770 — which gives full permissions to the owner and the group, but no permissions to the world. After running the previous command line, you can check the new permissions like this:

```
$ umask
770
```

When you create a file, you're automatically the owner of the file (unless you change that file with the **umask** command, explained in the previous section).

**CROSS-REFERENCE**

Learn more about the **cp** command in relation to copying and creating files and directories later in this chapter.

**FIND IT ONLINE**

Check out **www.linux.org** for information on Linux.

When you copy a file with the **cp** command, you become the owner of the copied file.

At some point, you'll want to change the ownership of a file; for instance, Eric may be working on a mondo report (called, appropriately enough, **mondo_report**) on the state of the accounting department, but after Eric is laid off, Kevin has to take over the preparation of the report. Using the **cp** command is one way of changing the ownership, but this works only if Kevin has permission to read the file. (Eric, distrusting Kevin, has made sure this isn't so. Isn't the cutthroat world of high finance fascinating?)

In this case, the system administrator — logged in as the root user — can use the **chown** command to change the ownership of the **mondo_report** file, specifying the name of the file and the new owner:

```
$ chown kevin mondo_report
```

In fact, the root user could make Kevin the owner of all the files in Eric's directory, by adding the *-R* option (short for *recursive*) to the **chown** command:

```
$ chown -R kevin Reports
```

## Setting the Sticky Bit

Messing with the directory, as opposed to individual files, has always been a way for malicious computer users to get around the permissions associated with individual files. Because this has been a concern for many system administrators, newer versions of UNIX add the ability to make a directory impregnable to everyone but the owner of the directory and the root

user. To do this, you set the *sticky bit* of the directory with the **chmod** command, as follows:

```
$ chmod +t letters
```

This command line refuses everyone (except the owner and the root user) the ability to move or remove files in a directory, no matter what permissions are set with individual files.

---

**TAKE NOTE**

▶ **MORE LIMITATIONS**

The *-R* option to the **chmod** command is not supported on all versions of UNIX.

---

**Table 2-8: SYMBOLS USED WITH THE CHMOD COMMAND**

| Symbol | Meaning |
|--------|---------|
| u | User (or the owner of the file) |
| g | Group |
| o | Other (or the world) |
| + | Adds a permission to the existing permissions |
| - | Takes away a permission from the existing permissions |
| r | Reads the file |
| w | Writes to the file |
| x | Executes the file |
| t | Sets the "sticky bit" on a directory |

# Moving Files and Directories

You may want to move a file from one directory to another in many instances. For example, you may want to move older files to an archival directory, or you may want to move previous versions of existing files.

The **mv** command allows for the movement of files in UNIX. Let's say you want to move the file **1999.reports**, located in your current directory, to the **misc** subdirectory (remember, this subdirectory's full pathname is **/users/home/misc**). The following accomplishes the task:

```
$ mv 1999.reports /users/home/misc
```

The process and syntax are simple: After invoking the **mv** command, designate the file to be moved and then the destination, which can be a directory, a sub-directory in relation to the current directory (remember what we said on the subject earlier in this chapter), or another filename. When moving a file, you can also rename it. (There's no separate command for renaming a file—an unfortunate oversight on the part of UNIX designers.) If you want to rename a file and leave it in the current directory, use the **mv** command, followed by the current filename and then the new filename:

```
$ mv 1999.reports newname
```

To rename a file and move it to a new directory simultaneously, use the **mv** command, followed by the current filename, then designate the new directory and filename (in this case, **newinfo**):

```
$ mv 1999.reports /users/kevin/newinfo
```

This process is very quick and is not slowed down by the size of the file (or files) being moved. Why? When you move a file, you're not actually moving the physical information contained in the record, but rather you're moving the record of the file as maintained by the operating system. In the introduction we detailed how one of the roles of the operating system was to maintain a current listing of all the directories on a hard disk. When you move a file—as well as copy or rename it—you're merely editing that listing, not manipulating the actual file. Note that if you cross disk partitions or cross hard disks, UNIX may have to copy the file contents to the new location.

To make sure that the file was actually moved, you can use the familiar **ls** command:

```
$ ls /users/home/misc/1999.reports
1999.reports
```

## Problem Characters and Removing Them

Earlier in this chapter you were warned about avoiding specific characters, such as - and ?, when naming files. We now explain the reasons behind the warning, at the least the reason why you shouldn't use a hyphen (-) in a filename.

The UNIX shell uses the hyphen to tell it that the following characters are used to slightly alter the command preceding it. As you know from reading Chapter 1, this is known as an option to the

---

**CROSS-REFERENCE**

Chapter 6 covers multitasking and processess.

**FIND IT ONLINE**

For Linux information, refer to **ftp.linux.org**.

command, which is why the hyphen is reserved for use by the shell. However, UNIX (to an extent, anyway) assumes that you know what you're doing, and so if you create a file whose name begins with a hyphen, such as **-letter**, the system will let you go right ahead and do it.

You will experience untold grief after doing so, however. You can't move the file using the **mv** command, as the shell assumes that **-letter** is an option to the **mv** command (like *-i*). You can't remove the file using standard removal commands, and you can't edit the filename using the **cat** command or the standard redirection commands. The same thing is true of other UNIX commands covered later in this chapter.

So what you do you? You can get around it in a few ways. If recall, this chapter covered pathnames, and how some pathnames include the directories above the current directory. Using this knowledge, you can trick the shell into ignoring the hyphen because it's buried in a pathname. For instance, the following command line would tell the shell to stay in the current directory and then move a file named **-letter** into a new directory:

```
$ mv ./-letter /users/eric/memos
```

This method will work with any UNIX command.

Another method is to use one of the X Window file managers, such as **xfm**. With a file manager, you can override any weird filenames and problems by pointing and clicking the file to be deleted. Using **xfm**, for instance, you would first select the file, then press on the right mouse button and select **Delete** from the resulting pop-up menu.

## TAKE NOTE

▶ **OVERWRITING YOUR OWN WORK**

Make sure that there is no existing file named **newinfo** in the **/users/kevin** subdirectory. When you move a file, UNIX does not ask for a confirmation of any sort. If there's an existing file with the same name as your new file, the old file will be wiped out and replaced by the new, renamed file.

▶ **AVOIDING DISASTERS WITH A SIMPLE OPTION**

If you're using System V Release 4 or BSD UNIX, you can avoid problems like this with the *-i* option. With it, you'll be asked if you want to overwrite an existing file:

```
$ mv -i 1999.reports
/users/kevin/newinfo
mv: overwrite newinfo ?
```

If you want to overwrite newinfo, type y. If you do not want to overwrite newinfo, type *n* or hit any other key. Only a positive response by you will overwrite the file; any other response will stop the operation.

▶ **LINUX TO THE RESCUE**

The default in Linux is never to overwrite an existing file without first checking with you; in other words, the *-i* option to the **mv** command is always enabled. This saves you from yourself.

▶ **MOVING DIRECTORIES**

You can use the **mv** command to move directories and contents, including files and subdirectories, provided you're using System V Release 4. Let's say you want to move the **/users/home/misc** directory (with all its files and subdirectories) to the **/users/kevin** directory. Use the following:

```
$ mv /users/home/misc/users/kevin
```

# Copying and Creating Files and Directories

Copying files is also a rather routine function — you may want to make a copy of a file for backup purposes, or you may want to use a copy of an existing file as the basis of a new document. These tasks are accomplished with the **cp** command, which is used similarly to the **mv** command — you designate the file to be copied, followed by its destination:

```
$ cp 1999.report /users/kevin
```

This copies the file **1999.report** to the **/users/kevin** subdirectory.

As with the **mv** command, you can use **cp** to give a new filename to the copied file:

```
$ cp 1999.report
/users/kevin/1999.report.bk
```

This copies the file **1999.report** to the **/users/kevin** subdirectory and renames it **1999.report.bk** (we've used the **.bk** suffix to denote a backup file; you can use your own verbiage, obviously).

As with the **mv** command, imprudent use of the **cp** command could lead you to overwrite existing files when copying other files. For instance, in our above example, you should make sure that there is not a file named **1999.report.bk** already existing in the **/users/kevin** subdirectory; if there is, your actions would cause it to be wiped out with a copy of the file **1992.report**.

We suggest that you create many directories as a tool for file management, using the directory for storage of similar files. The process is simple:

▶ Create the new directory.
▶ Check if the directory was actually created, using the **ls** command.

This is illustrated in the following example:

```
$ mkdir newdirect
$ ls
newdirect
```

In this case, the **mkdir** command creates a new directory, **newdirect**, as a subdirectory within the current directory. You can also use **mkdir** to create directories within directories other than the current directory:

```
$ mkdir /users/kevin/newdirect
```

This creates **newdirect** as a subdirectory with the **/users/kevin** directory, even though **/users/kevin** may not be your current directory.

You can also use **mkdir** to create multiple subdirectories within the current directory:

```
$ mkdir memos letters
```

Finally, you can use **mkdir** to create a directory and a subdirectory, when using the *-p* option:

```
$ mkdir -p /memos/letters
```

As we noted earlier in this chapter, UNIX allows you to link files. Remember that UNIX is a multiuser operating system, which means that it supports more than one user. Often more than one user will want access to the same file — a very common occurrence within many company departmental situations. Instead of creating two files (with separate changes

**CROSS-REFERENCE**
Appendix C lists basic UNIX commands.

**FIND IT ONLINE**
For more on working with directories, see
www.mathcs.duq.edu/unixhelp/tasks/index.html.

from separate users — the start of a logistical nightmare), UNIX allows two users to share one file, and changes made by either user are reflected in one file. Also, only one file need be present on the hard disk, freeing valuable disk space.

In addition, there's the potential for creating future harm if you create an ill-conceived link. Therefore, approach links with caution.

Let's say Kevin wanted to share information with Eric, contained in Kevin's home directory, **/users/kevin**, under the filename **addresses**. We want to link the file to a file created in Eric's home directory, **/users/eric**. We do so with the **ln** command, working out of Kevin's home directory:

```
$ ln addresses /users/eric/addresses
```

In other words, the syntax is:

```
$ ln originalfile targetfile
```

Even though there are two directory entries for the file addresses (in the **/users/eric** and **/users/kevin** directories), there exists only one actual file, in the **/users/kevin** directory.

Here we use **addresses** to denote the linked files. However, both linked files do not necessarily need to share the same name. If you remove this linked file later, it will not affect the original file.

System V Release 4 introduces the notion of symbolic links, which can link files from other file systems. Use the **-s** option to the **ln** command:

```
$ ln -s /othersystem/data/numbers
numbers.link
```

This creates a linked file named **numbers.link** in your current subdirectory; the file is linked to the file numbers in the **/othersystem/data** directory on the other file system. In other words, the syntax is:

```
$ ln -s originalfile targetfile
```

---

**TAKE NOTE**

▶ **DOS PARALLELS**

The DOS **COPY** command works similarly to the UNIX **cp** command, at least on a base level. To copy a file in DOS, you'd use the following:

```
C:>COPY 1999.REP \USERS\KEVIN
```

▶ **MORE DOS PARALLELS**

DOS uses the same command, **MKDIR**, to create new directories:

```
C:>MKDIR \USERS\KEVIN\NWDIRECT
```

▶ **PREVENTING DISASTER**

If you're using System V Release 4 or BSD UNIX, use the *-i* option to make sure the copied file doesn't wipe out an existing file:

```
$ cp -i 1999.report
/users/kevin/1999.report.bk
cp: overwrite 1999.report.bk ?
```

If you do want to overwrite the existing file, type y. If you do not want to overwrite the existing file, type n or hit any other key.

You can use the cp command to copy the entire contents of a directory, including all files and subdirectories, provided you're using System V Release 4:

```
$ cp -r /users/data /users/kevin
```

# Deleting Files and Directories

Unwanted files can clog up a hard disk, slowing it down and making your file-management chores unnecessarily complicated. It's good to regularly go through your subdirectories and remove unneeded files.

Do so with the **rm** (for *remove*) command:

```
$ rm 1999.report
```

UNIX will not confirm that a file was removed, nor will it confirm the actual operation, asking you if you do indeed want to remove the file. If you want to remove multiple files, merely list them in the command:

```
$ rm 1999.report 1998.report
```

You can remove many files at one time by using a wildcard; we cover wildcards later in this chapter. If you're worried about removing the wrong files, use the *-i* option, which will ask you on a file-by-file basis, for every file, whether or not you want to delete each file:

```
$ rm —i 1999.report 1998.report
1999.report: ?
1998.report: ?
```

At each **?** prompt, type **y** to delete the file, **n** to keep the file.

## Removing Directories

There are two ways to remove directories under UNIX. Both require a little planning. The UNIX command **rmdir** will remove an empty directory, containing no files or subdirectories:

```
$ rmdir users
```

where **users** is an empty directory. If **users** contains files or subdirectories, UNIX will interrupt the operation with an error message. Also, you cannot use **rmdir** to remove your current directory; you must be in another directory to perform this action. To successfully remove a directory with the **rmdir** command, first remove all the files in the directory with the **rm** command, and then remove each subdirectory with the **rmdir** command.

## Repenting For Your Mistakes

If you accidentally delete a file, there are some steps you can take to mitigate the damage. When you use the **rm** command, you're erasing the record of a file by the operating system and allowing the hard-disk space previously occupied by the file for use by other files. You are not actually erasing the file contents.

Therefore, it should theoretically be possible to restore the file by restoring the record of it in the operating system. This is how utilities can restore deleted files: They restore the record of the file in the operating system. However, these utilities work best if they're used immediately after a file was accidentally erased. Since the operating system is free to write the contents of a new file to the space vacated by the deleted file, it's possible that portions of the old file may not exist after some time — which means that

**CROSS-REFERENCE**
Appendix A lists Usenet newsgroups covering UNIX.

**FIND IT ONLINE**
For more on the command line, see **www.mathcs. duq.edu/unixhelp/commanz/cmd2.html.**

the entire file cannot be restored. So, it's dangerous to rely on utilities to restore deleted files.

The best way to avoid damage through inadvertently deleted files is by making frequent backups of your work. If you're working on a large UNIX system, your system administrator should be making frequent backups of the entire system. If you accidentally erase the file **1992.report**, you should be able to ask your system administrator to copy an old version of the file for present use. How frequently the system is backed up depends on the system administrator's policies.

If you're working on a UNIX workstation and are storing files locally (as opposed to the file server), you're on your own. If you are sporadic in your backup efforts, you run the danger of not having a recent backup. We advocate regular backups; if you're on a network with a large file server, you can copy important files frequently to the server (remembering to remove them when they become unnecessary); if your workstation features a tape drive, you should frequently back up to tape on a weekly basis, if possible. (We find that Friday afternoons are perfectly suited to making backups.)

We also strongly recommend you use the **-i** option with **rm**, so that you get asked whether or not to delete every file you pass to **rm**. Linux users don't need to use the **-i** option, however; that option is the default in the GNU version of the **rm** command that ships with all Linux distributions.

## TAKE NOTE

▶ **WALKING ON A WIRE**

An alternative method to using multiple command lines to delete the contents of a directory, including all files and subdirectories — though a decidedly more dangerous method — is through the combination of the **rm** with the **-r** option:

```
$ rm -r users
```

This will remove all the contents of the directory **users** (including files and subdirectories). It won't confirm *anything* with you before deleting the directories and files, however, so use this command with caution.

▶ **LOOKING AT SOME DOS EQUIVALENTS**

There are two ways to remove a file under DOS that work very similarly to the **rm** command: **DELETE** (**DEL** for short) or **ERASE**:

```
C:>DEL 1999.REP
```

or

```
C:>ERASE 1999.REP
```

Like UNIX, DOS does not tell you when a file is removed, nor does it ask you to confirm a file erasure. In addition, DOS does not allow you to remove a directory and all its files in one fell swoop. Instead, you must delete all the files in a directory either individually or using the following command line:

```
C:>DEL *.*
All files in the directory will be
erased! Proceed? <y/n>
```

After deleting the files in the directory, you can then go ahead and delete the directory itself:

```
C:>RMDIR \USERS\DATA
```

# Working with Wildcards

So far our discussion has centered about the manipulation of single files and directories. UNIX provides an amazingly powerful tool, called *wildcards*, which allows you to manipulate multiple files at one time, with a single command. Wildcards are a kind of shorthand that allows you to specify similar files without having to type multiple names. Wildcards allow you to search for files even if you don't remember the exact name.

There are three types of UNIX wildcards: *, ? and [...]. In every instance in this chapter where we've used single filenames, you could use a wildcard. Let's say you wanted to find all files in your directory ending with the string **report**. You could use the **ls** command in conjunction with a wildcard:

```
$ ls *report
1998.report      1999.report
kevin.report     kevin.report
```

These four files represent the number of files in the current directory ending in the string **report**.

The asterisk wildcard is used to match any number of characters in a string (including zero characters). It can be used anywhere in the string. To list the files beginning with the string **report**, you would use **ls** along with the following wildcard:

```
$ ls report*
report.new      report.old      reports.old
reporters.note
```

To list the files with the string **report** somewhere in the filename, use

```
$ ls *report*
```

```
1998.report      1999.report      eric.report
kevin.report
newreport98      newreport99      oldreport98
oldreport99
report.new       report.old       reports.old
reporters.note
```

Note that we've received a list of files that both end and begin with **report**, as well as the files with report in the middle. As we said, the * wildcard can be used to match any number of characters in a string. In this case, the wildcard matched zero characters.

You can combine the * and ? wildcards as in:

```
$ ls ?report*
1report1998      2report      3report99
```

to return the filenames of all files beginning with a single character followed by the string **report** and ending with any number of characters. Conversely, the ? wildcard is used to match a single character in a string:

```
$ ls report?
report1      report2      report3      report4
```

In our example, the **ls** command did not return **report.1999** as a match. That's because five characters follow the string **report**, and we only asked for one. As with the asterisk wildcard, the ? wildcard can appear anywhere in a string.

The final wildcard option is denoted by brackets. Here you can ask UNIX to match specified characters:

```
$ ls report199[89]
```

**CROSS-REFERENCE**

Chapter 6 covers multitasking and processes.

**FIND IT ONLINE**

See **www.faqs.org/faqs/by-newsgroup/comp/comp.unix.shell.html** for frequently asked questions about shells.

```
report1999
```

This becomes especially useful when looking for files and you're not entirely sure of the case (remember, UNIX distinguishes between uppercase and lowercase characters):

```
$ ls report.[Ee]rc
report.Erc      report.erc
```

You can also use a hyphen to denote a range of characters between brackets:

```
$ ls report[a-d]
reporta     reportb     reportc     reportd
```

This command did not return the filename **reporte**, because it did not fall in the range of characters defined within the brackets.

Even though we've used the ls command in our examples, wildcards can be used with any UNIX command — **rm**, **mv**, **cp**, and so on.

DOS/Windows wildcards are similar to UNIX wildcards. However, DOS wildcards are surprisingly limited. Only the * and **?** wildcards are supported and they can be used in limited circumstances — either at the beginning or end of filenames, or only as a substitute for the entire suffix. The following would be an acceptable DOS command:

```
C:>dir *.c
```

but not the following:

```
C:>dir *.C*
```

If you're a Macintosh user, then the notion of wildcards will be as foreign as Sanskrit. One of the great failures of the Macintosh operating system is the lack of wildcards for file manipulation.

---

### TAKE NOTE

▶ **THE MORAL OF OUR STORY IS...**

The moral of this section on wildcards is simple: thoughtful file organization will save you tons of time in the future. Instead of giving your files haphazard or cutesy names, take the time to think through your work and name your files accordingly. For instance, if you place the string **report** or **rep** in every report file you create, it will be a lot easier to locate these files in the future thanks to wildcards.

▶ **TAKING GREAT CARE WITH WILDCARDS**

It's very easy to make a typing error when entering a command — and in the case of wildcards and file removals, a typo can be disastrous. Let's say you want to remove all the files in your current directory ending in 1998. The command is simple:

```
$ rm *1998
```

But, if you're sloppy or inattentive, you could easy type a command that is slightly different:

```
$ rm * 1998
```

In this case, UNIX will ignore the *1998* and concentrate on the wildcard when removing files — in other words, all your files in the current directory will be removed. You can use the **-i** option to **rm**, described above, to help limit the effects of a misinformed **rm** command.

# Finding Files

Even though we've lectured you about the necessity of good file organization, it's inevitable that you'll lose track of a file — and usually the more important the file the more likely you are to lose track of it.

UNIX features a wonderful command, **find**, that helps you locate the wayward file. Let's say you've misplaced a file named **1999.data**. If you're truly masochistic, you can use the following command to find it:

```
$ find / -name 1992.data -print
```

Why do we call this a masochistic maneuver? Because UNIX does exactly as you tell it. In this case, we told it to start its search from the top of the directory structure (remember, the root directory is indicated by the slash character). We told it to look for a file named **1999.data** (using the **-name** option) and then tell us the results via the **-print** option. If you don't specify the **-print** option, UNIX will search for the file but fail to tell you the results. (There are valid reasons for this seeming incongruity, mostly concerning pipes. But it's nothing you need to know.)

In this case, UNIX searches for the file **1999.data** in every directory and subdirectory in the entire system. If you're working on a large, multiuser system with hundreds of megabytes of storage space, it can take quite a while to find this file. Especially given the fact that **1999.data** is not exactly a distinctive filename and that there's a very good chance another user may have appropriated the same name. Even on a single-user system with 300 or 600 megabytes of hard-disk space, the search can take too long.

It's best to use the **find** command with some limitations, such as specific directories. Let's say we know the file **1999.data** is located somewhere in the **/users** directory. We use the following to narrow the search criteria:

```
$ find /users -name 1999.data -print
/users/home/data/1999.data
/users/kevin/data/1999/1999.data
```

Let's say you don't remember the exact name of the file; you know that you created it sometime in the 1990s but don't remember the exact year. Since you're an organized user and denote all your files with the year as a prefix, you could use a wildcard to search for all files beginning with the string *199*:

```
$ find -name "199*" -print
```

As we mentioned earlier, it's best to use the **find** command with some constraints; after all, it takes a long time to chug through a large hard disk.

However, there will be times when you can't avoid searching for a file across the entire hard disk. Remember: UNIX is a multitasking operating system, which means it can perform more than one task at a time. Under these circumstances, you may want to run the **find** command in the background; this allows you to perform other task in the foreground while UNIX looks for the file.

**CROSS-REFERENCE**

See Chapters 4, 5, and 9 for more on UNIX shells.

**FIND IT ONLINE**

More information about shells can be found at www.ee.siue.edu/HELP/std_unix.html.

To search for the command **1999.report** in the background, end the command with an ampersand:

```
$ find / -name 1999.report -print &
```

This tells UNIX to search for the file **1999.report**, beginning at the top of the file structure with the root directory and moving downward, and alerting you when the file is found. The ampersand (&) tells UNIX to perform this task in the background.

However, you may not want to be alerted when the file is found, particularly if there are potentially many instances of the file. To print the results to a file instead of to your screen, insert the > symbol as well as a filename in the command:

```
$ find / -name 1999.report -print > results
&
```

This directs the output of the search to the file **results**. In general, the > command will direct the output of a command to a file; we use the > command many times throughout the course of this book.

Table 2-12 lists a number of options to the **find** command that you'll find useful.

---

**TAKE NOTE**

▶ **PROPER QUOTATIONS**

When using the **-name** option, be sure to enclose your search string in quotes. UNIX is rather quirky on this point and perhaps overly complex. The reason for this is that the shell would expand the **199*** to mean the name of every file in the current directory that starts with **199** — which is most definitely not what you intended.

▶ **PONDERING PRINTING**

If you're using the **find** command under Linux, you don't need to include the **–print** option. That's because virtually every Linux implementation uses the GNU version of the **find** command, which assumes that the **–print** option is wanted at all times — which it is.

---

**Table 2-9: OPTIONS TO THE FIND COMMAND**

| Option | Outcome |
| --- | --- |
| **-group** *groupname* | Limits search to files owned by a specific *groupname*. |
| **-type** *t* | Limits search to a specific file type: **c** (character), **d** (directory), **l** (link), or **s** (symbolic link). |
| **-user** *username* | Limits search to files owned by a specific *username*. |

# Viewing Files from the Command Line

At times, you may want to view the contents of a file, but don't want to go to the fuss of running a text editor. UNIX provides a number of relevant commands. To merely display the contents of a file containing ASCII text, use the **cat** (short for *concatenate*) command:

```
$ cat kevin.memo
The proposal by Spacely Sprockets is simply
unacceptable and does not fit with our
long-term
corporate interests. Nuke it.
```

In this instance, the screen is the default output for the **cat** command. This means that the results of your command are displayed on your screen, unless you specify otherwise. This refers back to the UNIX philosophy as defined at the beginning of this chapter: Everything in UNIX can be represented as a file, and in this case the unsaid assumption is that the output of the **cat** command is output to the screen.

However, this means you can direct the output of the **cat** command to other outputs, such as other files (this is also how UNIX manages to print files). For instance, you can send the output of the **cat** command to another file (creating a very simple backup procedure for single files):

```
$ cat kevin.memo > eric.memo.bak
```

The system creates the file eric.memo.bak if it doesn't exist. If it does, **cat** will overwrite the file with the new data — once again, we see that UNIX will trample existing files unless you, the user, take some safeguards.

You can also use cat to create ASCII files, if you're not inclined toward using a text editor. This command creates a file named spacely and sends output from your keyboard into that file, one line at a time:

```
$ cat > spacely
```

## File Types and the File Command

The commands here are meant for text files. However, you may not be sure that a file is a text file and suitable for viewing. If you're not sure what format a file is, use the **file** command to see what the file's type is. The **file** command looks through a file and returns information about the file. Some UNIX files contain a magic number that identifies the type of the file, its purpose, and its originator. The use of magic numbers isn't total in the UNIX world (check the file **/etc/magic** to see what file types your system can spot), but in most cases you'll find that the **file** command works quite well when identifying these mystery files.

To use the **file** command, enter it on a command line, along with the mystery file:

```
$ file mysteryfile
```

If **mysteryfile** is a binary program, file will return information relating to your machine (such as *sparc* if the file is compiled to run on your Sun SPARCstation), how it's compiled (dynamically linked), and the "pure" file type (in this case, the file would be an executable). However, if the file is a program file and the **file** command can't figure out exactly what it contains, you'll be told that the file is ***data***.

**CROSS-REFERENCE**

See Chapter 7 to find out about some X Window tools for viewing files.

**FIND IT ONLINE**

View the **bash** frequently-asked questions list www.faqs.org/faqs/unix-faq/shell/bash/.

When you're typing a file using the **cat** command, there are a few rules to follow:

- ▶ At the end of every line, hit the **Enter** key.
- ▶ You can move around the current line with the **Backspace** key. However, you cannot move from line to line.
- ▶ When you're finished typing into the file, type **Ctrl-D**.

The **cat** command may be adequate for viewing short files, but it is awkward for viewing long files. The **pg** command allows you to view files one page at a time. In many ways **pg** invokes a primitive text editor — not quite as advanced as something such as **vi** or **emacs**, but powerful enough for rudimentary work.

Starting **pg** is simple:

```
$ pg spacely
```

This displays the first page of the file **spacely** on your screen, then prompts you for a subsequent command:

- ▶ To display the next page, type **Enter**.
- ▶ To move back one page, type - (the hyphen key).
- ▶ To move ahead or back a given number of pages, use plus (+) or minus (-) and the number of pages to be moved.
- ▶ To move ahead one-half of a page, type **d**.
- ▶ To search for a string of text, bracket the string between slashes:

  ```
  /eric/
  ```

**TAKE NOTE**

▶ **CAT TAILS**

You can also use **cat** to add data to the end of an existing file. If you want to add information to the file **spacely**, use the following:

```
$ cat >> spacely
```

and begin typing.

▶ **MORE AND LESS, MORE OR LESS**

Two of the more useful commands for viewing files are **more** and **less**. Both present a file one page at a time. Many UNIX users argue that both are easier to use than **pg**. The **less** command isn't found in all UNIX versions, although it is common in the Linux world.

Using **more** is pretty simple: you press the **spacebar** to go ahead one page, and **q** to quit.

```
$ more long_file
```

The **less** command adds a slew of useful options; check out the online-manual pages for more information.

▶ **HEADS AND TAILS**

You may not want to scroll through an entire document to get to the end, or you may just want to quickly check out the beginning of a file. Use the **head** and **tail** commands in these instances. To view the first 10 lines of the file **data**, use the following:

```
$ head data
```

To view the last 10 lines of the file **data**, use the following:

```
$ tail data
```

To view a specific number of lines at the beginning or end of a file, combine **head** or **tail** with a numerical argument.

# Printing Files

Our final topic relating to files and directories concerns printing. If you're a system administrator, printing can be a complex area filled with arcane printer types and configurations. But for the user, printing documents in UNIX is a relatively simple matter that revolves around three commands: **lp**, **lpstat**, and **cancel**.

Depending on your version of UNIX, you'll use the **lp** (System V) or **lpr** (System V Release 4 and BSD UNIX) commands to print a file:

```
$ lp filename
```

or

```
$ lpr filename
```

After running the commands, the system lists the printer and generates an ID number, for you to check the status of the printing request.

Using wildcards, you could print several files at once:

```
$ lpr file*
```

In this instance, all files that begin with the string file are being printed.

There may be more than one printer on a UNIX network . UNIX allows for a system default, which is the printer used by the system unless specified otherwise. Printer names may not be immediately clear to you (sometimes lazy system administrators use numbers instead of names like laser1 which provide clearer information to users), so if you have access to multiple printers on your network, ask your system administrator for a complete and clear listing.

If you want to send a file to a printer that is not the default printer, use the **-d** option along with the printer's name:

```
$ lpr -d pslaser filename
```

This sends the file *filename* to the printer **pslaser**.

On a large multiuser system, there may be several users wanting immediate access to a printer. UNIX manages these multiple requests by setting up a print queue to the printer. Printer requests are handled in the order they appear. The print requests are then spooled, kept in memory by UNIX, and acted upon later.

Some systems use **lp** for the print command, instead of **lpr**. In such a case, to print out a file named 1999.report, you'd use the following command:

```
% lp 1999.report
```

As mentioned, print requests may not be performed immediately. If there are many files to be printed, you may want to monitor the print requests; after all, printers do go down, and UNIX does not provide error messages should a printer run out of paper or suffer a paper jam.

Use the **lpstat** command to view the current status of print requests:

```
$ lpstat
sysdot-141    kevin        2121   Jun 28
10:29 on sysdot
```

**CROSS-REFERENCE**
You can change your default by editing your **.profile** file, a topic we cover in Chapter 4.

**FIND IT ONLINE**
More information about printing and Linux can be found at **metalab.unc.edu/pub/Linux/docs/ HOWTO/Printing-HOWTO**.

```
laser1-198    erc        19002    Jun 28
10:31 on laser1
laser1-124    erc         5543    Jun 28
10:35
laser1-136    kevin       1992    Jun 28
10:36
```

Using the first line as the guide, we can divine the printer (**sysdot**), the document ID (**141**), the user ID (**kevin**), the size of the file in bytes (**2121**), the date (**June 28**), the time (**10:29**), and whether the file is printing (denoted by the **on** notation; if the file was not printing, there would be no **on** notation). We can also see from this output that there are multiple print requests from both Kevin and Eric to the laser printer, and that Kevin and Eric should both be patient because Eric has sent a large file to the laser printer.

Under X Window, many applications use the standard **lp** command under the hood. For instance, printing under **emacs** involves a call to the **lp** command. Similarly, if you select Print from the File menu under Netscape Navigator, you are presented with a dialog box that looks like the Print dialog box found in the Windows and Macintosh versions of Netscape Navigator. This would include several printing options, including letter size, orientation, and the order pages are to be printed. Upon closer examination, however, you'll see that the Print dialog box uses the **lpr** command by default as the printing mechanism. Netscape Navigator will handle many of the printing details, but ultimately it relies on the standard **lpr** print command.

## TAKE NOTE

### ► CANCELING PRINT REQUESTS

Cancel print requests with the **cancel** command:

```
$ cancel laser1-124
request "laser1-124" canceled
```

BSD UNIX users would use the **lprm** command:

```
$ lprm laser1-124
```

### ► HITTING A MOVING TARGET

How UNIX actually prints files can be a confusing notion to some users — and rightfully so. When you send a file to be printed, you're not really sending the actual file, you're sending a request for the system to print a particular file when it is ready. Since printer requests can be spooled, the system may take a few minutes or more to get ready. Generally speaking, if you change the file — by editing it, renaming it, or deleting it — and then save the file to disk, the system will print the changed file or, in the case of renamed or deleted files, not be able to complete the print request.

This isn't universally true in the UNIX world, unfortunately. BSD UNIX does it the opposite way, printing the file as it existed when you made the **lp/lpr** command.

### ► WORKING WITH CHANGING FILES

If you're using System V Release 4 and are planning on changing a file immediately after sending to the printer, use the **-c** (*copy*) option in your command:

```
$ lp -c filename
```

The system makes a copy of the file **filename** and uses the copy for printing.

# Personal Workbook

## Q&A

**1** Is **boss report** a valid filename under UNIX?

_____

_____

_____

**2** What kind of file typically has a filename extension of .txt?

_____

_____

_____

**3** What's the difference between an ordinary file and a link?

_____

_____

_____

**4** Which command is used to return the name of your current working directory?

_____

_____

_____

**5** Which command is used to change your current directory?

_____

_____

_____

**6** Which command is used to delete a directory?

_____

_____

_____

**7** Which character do you add to a command line to run a command in the background?

_____

_____

_____

**8** Which command do you use to send a file to the printer?

_____

_____

_____

ANSWERS:PAGE 345

## EXTRA PRACTICE

**1** Copy a file — any file — from your current directory to another directory.

**2** Use the tilde (~) character to change your current directory to your home directory.

**3** List the contents of your home directory.

**4** Create a new subdirectory called **work**.

**5** Create a file named **test** using the **cat** command and then use three different commands to view it.

**6** Use the **find** command to find the **test** command that you just created.

## REAL-WORLD APPLICATIONS

✔ Use the appropriate UNIX commands to create subdirectories for each of the different projects you work on.

✔ You realize that by mistake you placed a period at the beginning of a filename, which makes it hidden. Your mission is two-fold: using the **ls** command and the appropriate option to view a listing for the file, and then using the **cp** command to copy the file to a new filename.

✔ You stored some important information some months ago in a file called **financials**. However, with a report due to your boss in an hour, you realize with some panic that the file is not in your home directory. You do a search of the UNIX file system using the **find** command to see if you accidentally stored the **financials** file in another subdirectory.

## Visual Quiz

This window displays the contents of an average directory. Using the information in this chapter, which UNIX variant is being used?

_____

_____

_____

_____

_____

```
Color xterm                                          _ □ X
darkstar:~# dir
010302.tif    010701.tif    010704.tif    lodlin16.zip
010501.tif    010702.tif    chap1.zip     nsmail/
010502.tif    010703.tif    lodlin16.txt
darkstar:~#

 Start   Color xterm    xv 3.10a <unregistered>   xv controls    10:47
```

# CHAPTER 3

# UNIX Tools

**M**uch of the hidden power of the UNIX operating system lies within the various utilities summoned from the command line. These tools can be used by themselves or in conjunction with other commands to create even more powerful combinations.

The name UNIX itself comes from the concept of doing one thing well. The designers of UNIX worked on an earlier project called Multics, an operating system that was supposed to perform many tasks at once. The goal for UNIX was to scale down expectations and concentrate on single-purpose tools.

UNIX consists of many small tools that work together. Sticking to simple roots, most UNIX commands can take input from the command line or from a file as part of input redirection. They then feed their output to the screen, but the output can also be redirected, as mentioned in Chapter 1. This may seem primitive, but it enables many tools to function together in new ways.

Many of the commands discussed in this chapter can work with other commands in this fashion. By using pipes (discussed in Chapter 1), you can take the output of one command and make it the input of the next command.

To send the output of one command to another, use the following syntax:

```
$ first_command | second_command
```

Here, *second_command* takes as its input the data output by *first_command*.

To send the output to a file instead of a command, use the > redirection symbol:

```
$ command > output_file
```

Here the data output by *command* gets sent to the file *output_file* instead of to the screen. You can do the same with input, reading in the data from a file:

```
$ command < input_file
```

These techniques work with many UNIX commands and enable you to build more powerful tools from the rich set already available.

Although UNIX originally may have been small and simple, recent versions sport hundreds of tools, most of which appear in **/usr/bin** or **/bin**. This chapter covers some of the more important tools that you will use.

# Searching for Text with the grep Family

All of us, at one time or another, have discovered that we've forgotten the location of a particular nugget of data just when we needed it. Instead of manually searching through the hundreds of files on a system, you can invoke three UNIX tools for finding what you're looking for: **grep**, **egrep** and **fgrep**. All three work similarly.

The **grep** command searches for text in either a single file or in any number of files you specify. It goes through the file and returns the lines containing your specified text, which can be a single word or longer.

To have **grep** search through the file **erc.memo.712** for the word *Spacely*, enter the following:

```
$ grep Spacely erc.memo.712
This proposal from Spacely Sprockets is a
farce
```

In this instance, **grep** is used to search for a single word. To have **grep** search for a phrase containing a space, you must enclose the phrase in quotation marks, as shown on the facing page.

If you can't remember the exact file containing the words *Spacely Sprockets*, use wildcards in the file-names to have **grep** search through some or all of the files in the current directory.

When searching, **grep** distinguishes between uppercase and lowercase characters, unless told otherwise. To tell **grep** to ignore case, use the **-i** option.

If you don't want **grep** to list the lines of text matching your specified string, use the **-l** option to list only the matching files:

```
$ grep -l "Spacely Sprockets" *
```

```
erc.memo
erc.memo.712
```

The **egrep** command, short for extended grep, not only supports all the functions of **grep**, it goes a step further by allowing searches for multiple strings. For instance, say you want to search for every instance of multiple companies that have been the recipients of your correspondence. Do so by invoking **egrep** followed by a list of the names of the companies separated by pipe symbols and surrounded by quotation marks, as shown on the facing page.

The **fgrep** command (shorthand for fast grep) works similarly to **egrep**, but instead of using a pipe command and quotation marks to specify the text, each item must be placed on its own line, as shown in the last listing on the facing page.

Many systems provide a **fgrep** command that acts just as **grep** does, only faster and with limited options. Consult your system manuals to determine what your version of **fgrep** does.

The **grep**, **egrep**, and **fgrep** commands are designed to search text files. Working with binary files may show results you didn't anticipate and will likely lead to garbage output.

The following example file is used for searching in the listings on the facing page:

```
$ cat erc.memo.712
Dear Mr. King:
This proposal from Spacely Sprockets is a
farce and an insult to the intelligence of
every worker here.
—Eric
```

**CROSS-REFERENCE**

Appendix B lists books useful for finding out more about regular expressions.

**FIND IT ONLINE**

You can download the source code to **grep**, **egrep**, and **fgrep** from **www.gnu.org**.

## TAKE NOTE

▶ **RULES WHEN WORKING WITH GREP**

▶ The **grep** program searches one line at a time. If, in our examples, *Spacely* and *Sprockets* had appeared on two different lines, **grep** would not have reported a match.

▶ When searching, **grep** looks for strings of text and does not limit itself to whole words. A search for the word *town* could return lines containing the words *townspeople*, *downtown*, and *town*.

▶ You can use **grep** with wildcards to search for patterns, called *regular expressions*. Let's say you want to look for all instances of *Spacely Sprockets*, but you're familiar with **grep's** rules, and you know if the two words appear on different lines, **grep** would ignore them. In this case, you could use a wildcard search to return all instances of words beginning with *Sp*:

```
$ grep "Sp*" *
```

▶ Here, wildcards (denoted by the asterisks) are used to search for two different things. The first instance tells **grep** to search for any word beginning with *Sp*; the second wildcard tells **grep** to search through all the files in the current directory. The online manual entry for **grep** explains regular expressions in more detail.

▶ You may want to search files for lines not containing a certain string. To use **grep** as an "anti-search" tool, include the **-v** option, as shown in Listing 3-2.

### Listing 3-1: SEARCHING FOR A STRING WITH SPACES

```
$ grep "Spacely Sprockets" erc.memo.712
This proposal from Spacely Sprockets is a
farce
```

▲ *If you want to search for text that includes at least one space, you need to enclose the entire text string with quotes.*

### Listing 3-2: USING GREP AS AN ANTISEARCH TOOL

```
$ grep -v Spacely erc.memo.712
Dear Mr. King:
and an insult to the intelligence of every
worker here.
—Eric
```

▲ *The –v option turns **grep** into an antisearch tool. It responds with all lines that do not have the search string, in this case, Spacely.*

### Listing 3-3: LOOKING FOR MULTIPLE PATTERNS WITH EGREP

```
$ egrep "Spacely Sprockets|Jetson
Enterprises" *
erc.memo.712: This proposal from Spacely
Sprockets
erc.memo.714: As a representative of Jetson
Enterprises
```

▲ *The **egrep** command enables you to search for multiple strings in one command.*

### Listing 3-4: USING FREGP

```
$ fgrep "Spacely Sprockets
Jetson Enterprises" *
erc.memo.712: This proposal from Spacely
Sprockets
erc.memo.714: As a representative of Jetson
Enterprises
```

▲ *When using **fgrep**, place each search pattern on a separate line.*

# Sorting Files with the sort Command

At times you'll want to arrange the contents of a file in a specific order. Whether it be comparing files in alphabetic order or setting up a database in numerical order, sorting a file can be a great productivity enhancer. UNIX features a particularly useful tool for sorting files, named (predictably enough) **sort**.

To use an example, say you want to sort a list of city names that you entered in no particular order into a file named **AL_Central**. You discover this disorder after reading through the file using the **cat** command, as shown in the first listing on the facing page.

Let's also say you're from Detroit and don't like the fact that Minnesota is first in the **AL_Central** file. You could sort the file to make things more to your liking, as shown on the facing page.

The **sort** command reports only to the screen; the actual file remains unchanged. Thus, in the example, Minnesota remains in first place in the file **AL_Central**. If you want to save the results of a sort in another file, you would name both the originating and destination file on the command line:

```
$ sort AL_Central > AL_Central.sort1
```

The results of this sort are not shown on the screen because the > redirection symbol is used to denote a destination file. Use the **cat** command to view the resulting file, **AL_Central.sort1**.

You cannot use redirection to sort a file and have it retain the same name. Instead, use the **-o** option:

```
$ sort -o AL_Central AL_Central
```

You could use **sort** to sort and combine more than one file:

```
$ sort AL_Central AL_West AL_East >
AL_Baseball
```

## Comparing Sorted Files

You can use **comm** to compare two sorted files. This command displays the results in multiple columns, as shown on the facing page.

The output from **comm** arrives in three columns: The first column contains lines unique to the first file, the second column contains lines unique to the second file, and the third column contains lines occurring in both files. In this example, *Chicago* appears in both files.

Saving the results of **comm** is a matter of directing the output to a file:

```
$ comm AL_Central NL_Central >
baseball.sort
```

In this example, Chicago appears in both files. To eliminate such redundancies when sorting multiple files, use the **-u** (for unique) option:

```
$ comm -u AL_Central NL_Central >
baseball.sort
```

*Continued*

**TAKE NOTE**

▶ **SYSTEM DIFFERENCES WITH COMM**

Some versions of **comm**, such as DEC UNIX 4.0 and HP-UX 10.20, don't support the **-u** option. If you're using UNIX System V Release 4, **comm** should support the **-u** option.

**CROSS-REFERENCE**

Chapter 1 covers output redirection. Chapter 2 covers the **cat** command.

**FIND IT ONLINE**

You can find baseball scores and more information at **tsn.sportingnews.com/baseball/**.

## Listing 3-5: SAMPLE AL_CENTRAL FILE

```
$ cat AL_Central
Minnesota
Detroit
Kansas City
Chicago
Cleveland
```

▲ Displaying the sample data file, **AL_Central**, with **cat**.

## Listing 3-6: SORTING THE AL_CENTRAL FILE

```
$ sort AL_Central
Chicago
Cleveland
Detroit
Kansas City
Minnesota
```

▲ Sorting the AL_Central file with the sort command.

## Listing 3-7: SENDING THE OUTPUT OF A SORT TO THE FILE ITSELF

```
$ sort AL_Central -o AL_Central
$ cat AL_Central
Chicago
Cleveland
Detroit
Kansas City
Minnesota
```

▲ You can use the **-o** option to send the output back to the original file. This modifies the original file, of course. You can place the **–o** filename option before or after the file to sort.

## Listing 3-8: A SECOND SAMPLE DATA FILE

```
$ cat NL_Central
Cincinnati
Houston
Chicago
Milwaukee
St. Louis
Pittsburgh
```

▲ The **NL_Central** file, displayed with **cat**.

## Listing 3-9: SORTING TWO FILES TOGETHER

```
$ sort AL_Central NL_Central
Chicago
Chicago
Cincinnati
Cleveland
Detroit
Houston
Kansas City
Milwaukee
Minnesota
Pittsburgh
St. Louis
```

▲ Sorting two files together. Notice that Chicago is duplicated.

# Sorting Files with the sort Command *Continued*

So far you've seen the default **sort** command, which arranges the lines in a file in alphabetical order. But regular alphabetic order need not be the focus of every sort. Let's say you maintain a file, **debts**, with the names of all the people who owed you money and the exact amounts owed. The first listing on the facing page shows the contents of this file.

To sort a file numerically, use the **-n** option.

Why use the numerical sort? Compare the numeric and alphabetic sorts on the facing page. The alphabetic sort sorts on the leading text, but in alphabetic (ASCII) order. Thus, 12 comes after 1 and before 3.

With a numeric sort, the leading data is compared numerically, resulting in output that shows the values ascending.

Of course, in a file full of debtors, you'd want to list the largest debts first. The **-r** option enables you to sort a file in reverse order. The facing page shows the **-r** option combined with the **-n** option.

Let's say you wanted to sort the list of debtors by name instead of debt. You accomplish this by using the **+1** option to tell **sort** to skip a column, as shown on the facing page.

You can tell **sort** to skip as many columns as you want. A column is defined by a tab between the data fields. For example, a tab appears between 23 and Geisha.

## Combining Sort with Other Commands

You've seen how **sort** is useful on its own and how it adheres to the UNIX philosophy of each tool performing one task. Thus, **sort** is well-placed to be combined with other UNIX commands to create new tools. Using the capability to pipe the output of one command into another command, you can create new commands such as the following:

```
$ sort document.txt | uniq >
unique_lines.txt
```

This command sorts the file **document.txt.** The sorted output gets passed to the **uniq** command, which removes duplicate lines. (This is why the data must be sorted first.) Once the command is finished, you end up with a file, **unique_lines.txt**, that contains all unique lines from the file **document.txt**.

> **TAKE NOTE**
>
> ▶ **UNIX WORKS WELL WITH TEXT FILES**
> Notice that the examples with **sort** all use text files as a means of storing data. UNIX provides many tools that work with text files, which has led to many people storing their data in text files rather than databases. This is not a catch-all solution (or else Oracle and other database firms would be out of business), but it works well for many small collections of data.

**CROSS-REFERENCE**

Chapter 1 covers pipes.

**FIND IT ONLINE**

You can find more on sorting at **docs.sun.com:80/ab2**.

## Listing 3-10: A SAMPLE FILE FOR NUMERIC SORTING

```
$ cat debts
3        Spike
12       Eric
23       Geisha
1        Kevin
32       Halloween
4        Chiaro
```

▲ *A file of people who owe money. It is important that the columns are separated by Tab characters, not spaces.*

## LISTING 3-11: SORTING NUMERICALLY

```
$ sort -n debts
1        Kevin
3        Spike
4        Chiaro
12       Eric
23       Geisha
32       Halloween
```

▲ *Sorting the **debts** file in numeric order.*

## Listing 3-12: SORTING ALPHABETICALLY

```
$ sort debts
1        Kevin
12       Eric
23       Geisha
3        Spike
32       Halloween
4        Chiaro
```

▲ *Sorting the **debts** file in alphabetic order. Compare this listing with the previous listing to see the differences. The **-r** option tells **sort** to work in reverse order.*

## Listing 3-13: SORTING NUMERICALLY IN REVERSE ORDER

```
$ sort -rn debts
32       Halloween
23       Geisha
12       Eric
4        Chiaro
3        Spike
1        Kevin
```

▲ *You can combine options. In this case, **-rn** sorts in reverse numeric order.*

## Listing 3-14: SORTING ON A DIFFERENT COLUMN

```
$   sort +1 debts
4        Chiaro
12       Eric
23       Geisha
32       Halloween
1        Kevin
3        Spike
```

▲ *Sorting the **debts** file on the second column of data, rather than the first column. This is done by skipping one column with the **+1** option.*

# Comparing Files

We've mentioned previously that the number of files generated by UNIX tends to increase exponentially over the course of time. Many new files are created during the course of updating older files. And, knowing human nature, you may not have been perfectly meticulous in your file-management duties. The end result may be a set of files that are similar, but contain small differences as a result of editing and revisions.

UNIX contains several tools that compare files, including **cmp**, **comm**, **diff**, and **dircmp**. Of these, **cmp** and **diff** are most often used. (We described **comm** earlier, in the section "Sorting Files with the Sort Command.")

The **cmp** command compares two files and tells you if the files are different; if they are, **cmp** reports the first instance of a difference. The command does not report *all* differences between the files, and **cmp** will report nothing back to you if the files are the same. After you sneak a peek at two files (using the **cat** command), you can see how **cmp** works in the third listing on the facing page.

In the third listing, **cmp** reports that the two files differ in the sixth character of the document, located in line 1. And indeed they do — the salutation has changed. Using **cmp** is the simplest and quickest way to compare two files, but it only tells you if the files are different. You don't know to what extent the files are different, nor do you know how they are different.

The **diff** command, on the other hand, compares two files, tells you if the files are different, and cites each difference. Using the same two files as before, Listing 3-7 on the facing page shows how **diff** works.

As you can see, **diff** reports back significantly more information than does **cmp**. Lines beginning with < are found only in the first file, whereas lines beginning with > are found only in the second file. A dashed line separates two lines that appear in the same place in the differing files. Numerals and characters indicate exactly where and how differences occur. For example, 1c1 means that a change (c) exists between line 1 of the first file (as indicated by the first 1) and line 1 of the second file (as indicated by the second 1). Characters that were deleted from one version are noted by a **d**, whereas an **a** means that a line was appended to a file. The rigid format of this output is used to advantage by other programs such as **patch** (which uses the output of **diff -c**, an option that provides more context information about the differences).

> ### TAKE NOTE

> #### PATCH AS PATCH CAN

> The **patch** utility uses the output of **diff** to update a file to a newer version. The **patch** command uses the data from **diff** and determines what changes are necessary to update one file to match a later version. This is often used to update free software packages you download from the Internet.

**CROSS-REFERENCE**

Chapter 14 describes how to compile software you download from the Internet.

**FIND IT ONLINE**

The graphical file comparison tool **tkxcd** is available at www.doitnow.com/~quillan/john/tkxcd/.

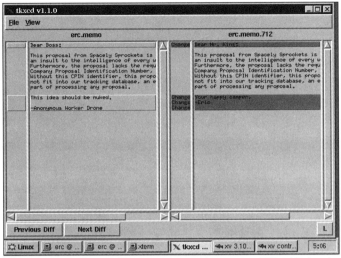

Comparing the two files erc.memo and erc.memo.712 with tkxcd.
Note the highlighted changes in erc.memo.712.

## Listing 3-15: USING CMP TO COMPARE FILES

```
$ cmp erc.memo erc.memo.712
erc.memo erc.memo.712 differ: char 6, line 1
```

▲ The **cmp** command only tells you if files are different.

## Listing 3-16: COMPARING EXACT MATCHES WITH CMP

```
$ cmp erc.memo erc.memo
```

▲ The **cmp** command returns nothing if the files are the same.

## Listing 3-17: USING DIFF TO COMPARE FILES

```
$ diff erc.memo erc.memo.712
1c1
< Dear Boss:
—
> Dear Mr. King:
11,13c11,12
< This idea should be nuked.
<
< -Anonymous Worker Drone
—
> Your happy camper,
> -Eric
```

▲ The **diff** command reports all differences detected.

## Listing 3-18: COMPARING EXACT MATCHES WITH DIFF

```
$ diff erc.memo erc.memo
```

▲ The **diff** command reports nothing if the two files match exactly.

## Listing 3-19: USING PATCH TO UPDATE FILES

```
$ patch < patch_file
```

▲ Runs the **patch** command using the data stored in the **patch_file**. This command will modify files in the current directory, as indicated in the **patch_file**.

# Plucking Data from Tables

On a very rudimentary basis, you could use the basic UNIX commands as database-management tools to manage text files containing data.

Let's say you are managing a small workgroup, and you want to keep a small database of your workers. Using **vi** or **emacs**, you create a file that contains vital information about your employees, like the one shown in the first listing on the facing page.

The sample database is very simple: You list the name of the worker, his or her office telephone extension, login names, and the number of vacation days he or she has remaining this year. The columns of information are separated by tabs. (Using tabs to separate columns of data is important for many UNIX tools.) Databases like this are very common in UNIX, both for personal usage and for system administration.

From this workers file you can create many other lists. Say you want to create a file containing just the names and the phone numbers of the workers for the personnel office. You would do so using the cut command, specifying a file for output:

```
$ cut -f1,3 workers > workers_phone
```

The structure of this command is simple. You tell the shell to cut the first and third fields in the file **workers** and place it in the file **workers_phone**. You can specify one field, all but one field, or, as shown here, a range of fields:

```
$ cut -f1-3,5 workers > workers_phone2
```

You can also use **cut** to pluck information from a number of similarly structured files:

```
$ cut options filenames > output_file
```

The example file is highly structured, using tabs to separate columns. If another character is used to separate fields, you would need to specify the character using the **-d** option:

```
$ cut -d, -f1,3 workers.comma > workers_phone3
```

The character must be placed directly following the **-d** option. In this command, commas are specified as the separators between fields. To use a space as a separator, enclose it in single quotes:

```
$ cut -d' ' -f1,3 workers.single_space \
  > workers_phone4
```

If you don't include the quotes, the shell assumes that the space is part of the command and not related to the **-d** option.

Of course, not all UNIX files are going to be as highly structured as this example. In these cases, you can use specify a range of characters to be cut:

```
$ cut -c1-24 workers.space > workers_phone5
```

This tells **cut** to grab the first 24 characters in a line.

---

**TAKE NOTE**

**USE AWK FOR MORE SOPHISTICATED CUTS AND JOINS**

For more sophisticated text processing, you can use the advanced command **awk**. This command supports its own text-processing command language (also called AWK).

---

**CROSS-REFERENCE**

Chapter 11 covers **vi** and **emacs**.

**FIND IT ONLINE**

For more on **cmp**, see docs.sun.com:80/ab2/ @DSCBrowse?reference=1.

## Listing 3-20: A SAMPLE WORKERS FILE

```
$ cat workers
Eric     286    555-6674    erc      8
Geisha   280    555-4221    geisha   10
Kevin    279    555-1112    kevin    2
Tom      284    555-2121    spike    12
Tyler    281    555-2122    rot      4
Katya    282    555-2123    katya    4
```

▲ *Our simple employee database, containing names, office extensions, phone numbers, usernames, and number of vacation days remaining. A single tab character separates each field.*

## Listing 3-21: EXTRACTING NAMES AND PHONE NUMBERS

```
$ cut -f1,3 workers > workers_phone
$ cat workers_phone
Eric     555-6674
Geisha   555-4221
Kevin    555-1112
Tom      555-2121
Tyler    555-2122
Katya    555-2123
```

▲ *Selecting fields 1 and 3 from the **workers** file and sending the output to the file **workers_phone**.*

## Listing 3-22: EXTRACTING THE FIRST THREE FIELDS AND THE FIFTH FIELD

```
$ cut -f1-3,5 workers > workers_phone2
$ cat workers_phone2
Eric     286    555-6674    8
Geisha   280    555-4221    10
Kevin    279    555-1112    2
Tom      284    555-2121    12
Tyler    281    555-2122    4
Katya    282    555-2123    4
```

▲ *Selecting the first three and fifth fields from the **workers** file and sending the output to the file **workers_phone2**.*

## Listing 3-23: EXTRACTING DATA CONTAINING SPACES AS FIELD SEPARATORS

```
$ cut -d' ' -f1,3 workers.single_space >
workers_phone4
$ cat workers_phone4
Eric 555-6674
Geisha 555-4221
Kevin 555-1112
Tom 555-2121
Tyler 555-2122
Katya 555-2123
```

▲ *Using a single space as a delimiter with the **-d** option to the **cut** command. Note that this example works only on files using a single space as a field separator.*

## Listing 3-24: USING SPACES AS SEPARATORS

```
$ cat workers.space
Eric     286    555-6674    erc      8
Geisha   280    555-4221    geisha   10
Kevin    279    555-1112    kevin    2
Tom      284    555-2121    spike    12
Tyler    281    555-2122    rot      4
Katya    282    555-2123    katya    4
```

▲ *A similar data file that uses spaces as separators rather than tabs. The separator is important.*

## Listing 3-25: EXTRACTING CHARACTERS

```
$ cut -c1-24 workers.space > workers_phone5
$ cat workers_phone5
Eric     286    555-6674
Geisha   280    555-4221
Kevin    279    555-1112
Tom      284    555-2121
Tyler    281    555-2122
Katya    282    555-2123
```

▲ *The command **cut -c1-24** grabs the first 24 characters from the file **workers.space** and sends the output to the file **workers_phone5**. Note that this file uses spaces to separate fields.*

# Merging Files

The **cut** command helps you extract data from files. UNIX also provides specialized commands to merge data: **paste** and **join**. The **paste** command joins two or more files line by line; that is, the first line in the second file is pasted to the first line of the first file. With text files, the results of this command would look pretty silly; but with files full of columns and tables, this command can be useful. Using **paste** is easy — simply specify the files to be pasted together along with a file to contain the pasted data:

```
$ paste file1 file2 > file.paste
```

As with **cut**, you can specify the character that was used to separate fields:

```
$ paste -d, file1 file2 > file.paste2
```

The character must be placed directly following the **-d** option. In the preceding example, **paste** has been instructed to use commas as the separators between fields. This works best if each of the input files has a column of data.

You can combine **cut** with **paste** to form new files or to rearrange existing files. Let's say you want to change the order of your employee database. Instead of retyping the entire file, you could cut the phone-number column from the file, rearrange the remaining lines, and then paste the whole shebang to a new file:

```
$ cut -f1-2,4-5 workers > newworkers
$ cut -f3 workers > newworkers.2
$ paste newworkers newworkers.2 > workers.2
```

The facing page shows all the steps leading to the **workers.2** file.

A better way of merging files, provided that the files contain one common field, is through the join command. Continuing with the example of worker-based files, let's say you maintain two separate files of employee information and want to join them. This process is illustrated on the facing page.

By default, the **join** command works only when the first fields of each file match and are sorted identically. However, you can join files based on fields other than the first in each of the files. The following command joins two files based on the second and fourth columns:

```
$ join -j1 2 -j2 4 workers.3 workers.4 >
workers.5
```

This syntax is somewhat confusing. Here the **-j** option joins the second column of the first file (**-j1 2**) to the fourth column of the second file (**-j2 4**). The files are specified *after* the command and options.

As with **cut** and **paste**, you can specify field separators.

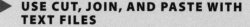

## TAKE NOTE

### USE CUT, JOIN, AND PASTE WITH TEXT FILES

As you've probably guessed by now, the **cut**, **join**, and **paste** commands are meant for text files. Don't try these on spreadsheet files or other binary files.

**CROSS-REFERENCE**

Chapter 2 covers the **cat** command.

**FIND IT ONLINE**

The emacs text editor also helps with merging files. See **www.gnu.org/software/emacs/emacs.html**.

## Listing 3-26: USING THE PASTE COMMAND

```
$ paste file1 file2 > file.paste
$ cat file.paste
Eric      erc
Geisha    geisha
Katya     katya
Kevin     kevin
Tom       spike
Tyler     rot
Zowie     zow
```

▲ *Pasting two files together. A tab separates the data from each input file.*

## Listing 3-27: SPECIFYING A FIELD SEPARATOR

```
$ paste -d, file1 file2 > file.paste2
$ cat file.paste2
Eric,erc
Geisha,geisha
Katya,katya
Kevin,kevin
Tom,spike
Tyler,rot
Zowie,zow
```

▲ *Using a comma as a separator with the **paste** command.*

## Listing 3-28: A SAMPLE WORKERS FILE

```
$ cat workers
Eric      286    555-6674    erc        8
Geisha    280    555-4221    geisha     10
Kevin     279    555-1112    kevin      2
Tom       284    555-2121    spike      12
Tyler     281    555-2122    rot        4
Katya     282    555-2123    katya      4
Zowie     283    555-2124    zow        7
```

▲ *This employee database is used in the following examples.*

## Listing 3-29: USING PASTE TO REORDER FIELDS IN A FILE

```
$ cut -f1-2,4-5 workers > newworkers
$ cat newworkers
Eric      286    erc       8
Geisha    280    geisha    10
Kevin     279    kevin     2
Tom       284    spike     12
Tyler     281    rot       4
Katya     282    katya     4
Zowie     283    zow       7
```

```
$ cut -f3 workers > newworkers.2
$ cat newworkers.2
555-6674
555-4221
555-1112
555-2121
555-2122
555-2123
555-2124
```

```
$ paste newworkers newworkers.2 > workers.2
$ cat workers.2
Eric      286    erc       8     555-6674
Geisha    280    geisha    10    555-4221
Kevin     279    kevin     2     555-1112
Tom       284    spike     12    555-2121
Tyler     281    rot       4     555-2122
Katya     282    katya     4     555-2123
Zowie     283    zow       7     555-2124
```

▲ *These commands result in a new data file, **workers.2**, which contains the original data but with the fields in a different order.*

# Splitting Files

Some text editors and e-mail systems choke on very large files. Even if they do load, large files, such as UNIX log files, can be a real pain to work with because they tend to slow down the system. Just calling up a really large file in a text editor may take minutes. To help with all this, you can use the **split** command to break up files into more manageable chunks.

The **split** command splits an ASCII text file into smaller files. The basic syntax is as follows:

```
$ split filename prefix
```

This command splits up the file *filename* into smaller files, each at most 1,000 lines long (the default of **split**). The original file remains intact. The **split** command creates a number of new files — how many depends on the size of the original file. These new files follow a logical naming scheme: The first file created will be *prefix.aa*, the second *prefix.ab*, and so on. An alternative naming scheme is *prefixaa*, *prefixab*, and so on. If you omit the prefix, the filenames will be **xaa, xab,** and so on.

The **split** command breaks up one file into multiple files but maintains the original data. To restore the original data, you can combine these files together using the **cat** command. For example:

```
$ cat filename.* > filename
```

The default naming scheme for the split files follows an alphabetical order.

When splitting files, if you want files of a size other than 1000 lines long, you can use the *-number* option. For example:

```
$ split -200 filename
```

This command creates files 200 lines long.

You can also use the **-l** option for the same effect. For example:

```
$ split -l 200 filename
```

If you want to restrict the size of the output files to a particular number of bytes rather than number of lines, use the **-b** option (for bytes):

```
$ split -b bytes filename
```

The **-b** option can be modified by units to make things easier. The available units are **b** for 512-byte blocks, **k** for 1 kilobyte, and **m** for 1 megabyte. For example, the following command splits a file into files containing up to 2 megabytes each:

```
$ split -b 2m filename
```

---

### TAKE NOTE

#### DON'T USE SPLIT WITH BINARY FILES

As with **cut**, **paste**, and **join**, the **split** command works with lines of text. This command uses a very simple algorithm to determine where lines end — usually based on the fact that UNIX treats a new-line character (ASCII 10) as the end of a line. In a binary file, then, every byte with a value of 10 could be detected as an end-of-line marker. Furthermore, there may be megabytes of data before the first 10 is discovered, making for wildly skewed output files. In general, don't use **split** with binary files.

---

### CROSS-REFERENCE
Chapter 11 covers the **wc** command.

### FIND IT ONLINE
You can get the source code for many of these utilities at **ftp://prep.ai.mit.edu/pub/gnu/**.

## Listing 3-30: EXAMINING A LARGE FILE

```
$ ls -l testfile.uu
-rw-r--r-- 1 erc users 543427 Jul 22 13:38
testfile.uu
```

▲ Start with a large file.

## Listing 3-31: SPLITTING THE FILE

```
$ split testfile.uu
$ ls -l x*
-rw-r—r-- 1 erc users 61957 Jul22 13:39 xaa
-rw-r—r-- 1 erc users 62000 Jul22 13:39 xab
-rw-r—r-- 1 erc users 62000 Jul22 13:39 xac
-rw-r—r-- 1 erc users 62000 Jul22 13:39 xad
-rw-r—r-- 1 erc users 62000 Jul22 13:39 xae
-rw-r—r-- 1 erc users 62000 Jul22 13:39 xaf
-rw-r—r-- 1 erc users 62000 Jul22 13:39 xag
-rw-r—r-- 1 erc users 62000 Jul22 13:39 xah
-rw-r—r-- 1 erc users 47470 Jul22 13:39 xai
```

▲ This version of **split** makes files starting with the letter x. The large file became nine smaller files.

## Listing 3-32: VERIFYING THAT SPLIT WORKED PROPERLY

```
$ cat x* > testfile2.uu
$ cmp testfile.uu testfile2.uu
```

▲ The **cat** command rebuilds the file. The **cmp** command verifies that data has not been lost by splitting the file.

## Listing 3-33: CHECKING THE SIZE AND NUMBER OF LINES OF EACH COMPONENT

```
$ wc testfileab
    1000    1000    62000 testfileab
```

▲ The **wc** (word count) command indicates how many lines are in an output file.

## Listing 3-34: VERIFYING THE SPLIT

```
$ wc xaa
    331     334    20480 xaa
```

▲ You can use **wc** to verify that **split** broke up the file into proper-sized chunks.

## Listing 3-35: SPLITTING INTO 200-LINE FILES

```
$ split -l 200 testfile.uu
$ ls -l
total 1148
-rw-r—r-- 1 erc users 543427 Sep29 19:14
testfile.uu
-rw-r--r-- 1 erc users 12357 Sep29 19:18 xaa
-rw-r--r-- 1 erc users 12400 Sep29 19:18 xab
-rw-r--r-- 1 erc users 12400 Sep29 19:18 xac
-rw-r--r-- 1 erc users 12400 Sep29 19:18 xad
-rw-r--r-- 1 erc users 12400 Sep29 19:18 xae
-rw-r--r-- 1 erc users 12400 Sep29 19:18 xaf
-rw-r--r-- 1 erc users 12400 Sep29 19:18 xag
-rw-r--r-- 1 erc users 12400 Sep29 19:18 xah
-rw-r--r-- 1 erc users 12400 Sep29 19:18 xai
-rw-r--r-- 1 erc users 12400 Sep29 19:18 xaj
-rw-r--r-- 1 erc users 12400 Sep29 19:18 xak
-rw-r--r-- 1 erc users 12400 Sep29 19:18 xal
-rw-r--r-- 1 erc users 12400 Sep29 19:18 xam
-rw-r--r-- 1 erc users 10270 Sep29 19:18 xan
```

▲ The -l option controls the number of lines in each output file, here set to 200 lines.

## Listing 3-36: VERIFYING THE SPLIT

```
$ wc xab
    200     200    12400 xab
```

▲ You can use **wc** to verify that **split** broke up the file into proper-sized chunks.

# Viewing Files with Strings and od

Much of UNIX revolves around manipulating text files. Configuration data, such as usernames and passwords (encrypted, of course) are stored in text files, such as **/etc/passwd**. Many of the plethora of UNIX commands work on text files. For example, **cat** concatenates text files. However, all files aren't made up entirely of printable text. In many cases, you have to deal with binary files.

UNIX offers a few commands to help you see the contents of binary files. The **strings** command, for example, is especially useful for software developers. The **strings** command prints out the text it can find in a binary file, such as a program. For example, most programs contain some text, such as instructions for how to use the commands themselves. Graphical programs may contain lots of text (but then again, this text may be stored in a separate file or files).

The first listing on the facing page shows an example of using **strings** to see the text buried within the Bourne shell, **/bin/sh.** There will be a lot of output, so you probably want to pipe it to **more**. Many of the text names are C function names used in programming. Other text strings include error messages, as well as basic commands such as *else*. The listing shows a sample of the text.

You can often find out the version of a program by using the data from **strings** and hunting for interesting text, such as *Revision*.

Sometimes you need to see the exact contents of a binary file byte by byte. That's where **od** comes in. This odd-named command performs an octal dump of a file, translating each byte in the file to octal format.

The basic syntax is as follows:

```
$ od filename
```

If the file is long, you probably want to pipe the output to **more**.

The **-c** option, shown in the command line that follows, displays the data as text characters, using special codes such as **\t** for a tab and **\n** for a linefeed character:

```
$ od -c filename | more
```

In addition to octal format — the default — **od** can display the results in hexadecimal format with the **-x** option and in decimal format with the **-d** option. A related command called **xd** defaults to hexadecimal mode.

The facing page shows three examples of how to use **od**. In general, we've found the hexadecimal (**-x**) and ASCII modes (**-c**) to work the best.

## TAKE NOTE

### NEWER VERSIONS OF OD

Newer versions of **od** support **-A** and **-t** options to better control the output. Most versions also support the command-line options shown here as well, so we stuck to the least common denominator.

**CROSS-REFERENCE**

Chapter 2 covers **cat**.

**FIND IT ONLINE**

You can get the source code for many of these utilities at **ftp://prep.ai.mit.edu/pub/gnu/**.

## Listing 3-37: USING STRINGS TO VIEW TEXT IN BINARY FILES

```
$ strings /bin/sh | more
parser stack overflow
Now at end of input.
parse error
unexpected EOF while looking for `%c'
case
elif
else
then
getwd: cannot access parent directories
Stopped
Running
Done
strcpy
libtermcap.so.2
```

▲ *Partial output of using **strings** on **/bin/sh**, the Bourne shell.*

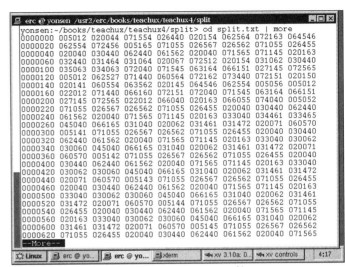

■ *Using **od** in its default octal mode on a text file.*

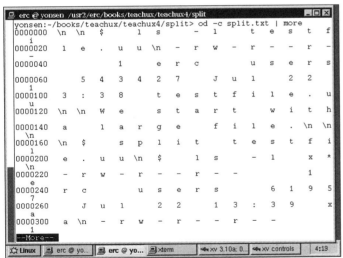

■ *Using **od** with the **–c** option (ASCII mode) on a text file shows you every byte in the file.*

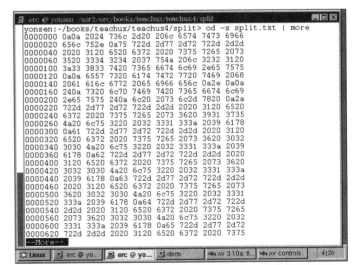

■ *The hexadecimal and ASCII modes are the most useful.*

# Personal Workbook

## Q&A

**1** Which command searches for text in files?

_____

_____

_____

**2** How could you find all occurrences of Bob Marley and Peter Tosh in a text file?

_____

_____

_____

**3** How would you search a text file for all instances of _Spacely_ or _spacely_?

_____

_____

_____

**4** How would you sort a file numerically rather than alphabetically?

_____

_____

_____

**5** How do you store the output of **sort** in a file?

_____

_____

_____

**6** How would you split a file into chunks no larger than 60K?

_____

_____

_____

**7** How would you compare two sorted files to find out which lines are contained in both files and which are unique to a particular file?

_____

_____

_____

**8** Which command can you use to view text messages that may be hidden inside a program?

_____

_____

_____

ANSWERS: PAGE 346

## EXTRA PRACTICE

**1** If you have more than one of the same type of UNIX system, such as on two or more Sun Solaris servers, use the **cmp** program to compare whether the commands in **/usr/bin** are the same between the systems.

**2** Find all instances of the word *computer* in a text file.

**3** Take a text file, remove all lines containing the word *computer,* and then sort the resulting lines.

**4** Look at the online manual page for **grep** and pay special attention to the information on regular expressions.

**5** View the contents of a text file with the **od** command, and then view the contents of a program. Compare the differences.

## REAL-WORLD APPLICATIONS

✔ Your boss wrote four versions of a memo. In the latest version, some particularly clever prose is missing, but your boss cannot remember which version had the clever prose. Compare all versions of the memo and show your boss the differences.

✔ You have a file containing usernames, real names, and office phone numbers. Now, you need to rearrange the data to show the real names first. Use the **cut**, **join**, and **paste** commands to do this.

✔ You wrote a report documenting problems you had with a certain vendor's system. Now the vendor wants your document to ensure they have solved the problems, but you weren't particularly nice in your report. Find all instances of embarrassing language in your report, so you can clean it up before sending it out.

## Visual Quiz

What full command line would you use to place the contents of each line of file2 onto the end of each line of file1 so that the output resembles file3?

_____

_____

_____

_____

_____

```
erc @ yonsen /usr2/erc/books/teachux/teachux4/paste
$ cat file1
Fred:/usr/home/fred
Barney:/usr/home/barney
Wilma:/usr/home/wilma
Betty:/usr/home/betty
$ cat file2
fred
barney
wilma
betty
$ cat file3
Fred:/usr/home/fred:fred
Barney:/usr/home/barney:barney
Wilma:/usr/home/wilma:wilma
Betty:/usr/home/betty:betty
$ 
```

CHAPTER **4**

# Learning About Your Environment

Assuming you've been following along up to this point, we've shown you various commands that you need for basic system usage and accomplishing limited tasks. Now it becomes important for you to learn how these commands are actually carried out by the UNIX operating system, which requires a little abstraction on your part.

When you type **ls** to see a list of your files, you're not *really* directly telling the operating system to list the files in your directory. Instead, you're asking the shell to tell the operating system to carry out your request for a listing of files in your directory. The shell is the component of the UNIX operating system that interacts directly with you, the user. As we noted in Chapter 1, different shells are available to you: the C shell, the System V job shell, the Korn shell, and the Bourne shell, among others. These all are used by UNIX to execute your commands.

The shell also supports built-in commands and handles wildcards (for example, *.*txt*, which includes the wildcard *, refers to all files ending in .*txt*). The shell contains a programming language, as well, to automate your tasks. We're not about to turn you into a programmer, but we do share a few helpful shortcuts to streamline your daily tasks.

And, perhaps more importantly, your shell determines your *environment*: information that affects your daily usage and configuration. This chapter covers the environment provided by your shell and how you can modify that environment to make yourself more productive.

If you go back to your high school–level algebra, you may remember the notion of *variables*. Notice the following line:

`z=x+y`

In this case, *x*, *y*, and *z* are all variables. That is, what *x*, *y*, or *z* stands for can change depending on input.

UNIX uses variables in a similar sense; it enables the user to define information with both a name and a value that may change over the course of time. They allow a level of abstraction for tasks such as defining the text editor you prefer or specifying where your e-mail gets stored.

# Using Various Variables

UNIX makes extensive use of variables — also called *environment variables* — to hold your system's configuration as well as your personal preferences. Your shell and other UNIX programs can make use of these variables. Many UNIX variables have become standard parts of the environment and help describe things like your choice of text editors (EDITOR), the terminal type you've logged in on (TERM), and so on.

When you initially login a UNIX system, many of the variables (like the prompt variables and the HOME variable) have been set by the system automatically. However, many others, like the TERM variable, have not. Configuring these variables is up to you; you've already started this (in a previous chapter) by changing your prompt. The structure is simple:

```
$ VARIABLENAME=VARIABLEVALUE
```

Here, *VARIABLENAME* is the name of the variable and *VARIABLEVALUE* the value of the variable. To change your TERM (terminal) variable to the very common vt100 value, type the following:

```
$ TERM=vt100
```

To generate a list of your current shell variables, use the command **set,** as shown on the facing page.

C shell users should use the command **setenv** or **env**.

Most users will have additional variables, as most mail programs set up variables for sorting and storing electronic-mail messages.

Here are a few additional rules to remember:

▶ As with everything else in UNIX, case counts. DATA, Data, and data would represent three different variables. The first character of a variable must be an underscore ( _ ) or a letter (uppercase or lowercase); subsequent characters can be letters, numerals, or underscores.

▶ To use a variable on a command line, you must preface it with a dollar sign ($). This tells the shell that you're invoking a variable — that is, you want the value held in the variable and not a command-line argument.

▶ If you want to view a variable at any time, use the **echo** command along with the name of the variable.

In the C shell, setting an environment variable requires the use of the **setenv** command; with the Korn and Bourne shells, you merely need to separate the elements of the variable with an equal sign (=). Here's how to set the C shell in the **.login** file:

```
% setenv SHELL /bin/csh
```

---

### TAKE NOTE

#### ▶ HANDLING MULTIPLE VALUES IN AN ENVIRONMENT VARIABLE

Most UNIX environment variables that hold multiple values, such as a set of directories, use colons to separate each directory name. This is different from the semicolon used in Windows. For example:

```
CDPATH=:/users/home/:/users/kevin
```

---

**CROSS-REFERENCE**
The X Window System is covered in Chapter 7.

**FIND IT ONLINE**
Answers to frequently asked questions about UNIX shells are available at **www.faqs.org/faqs/ by-newsgroup/comp/comp.unix.shell.html**.

# Learning About Your Environment

## Using Various Variables

### Table 4-1: COMMON SHELL VARIABLES

| Variable | Meaning |
| --- | --- |
| CDPATH | Directories searched via the **cd** command |
| DISPLAY | Where X Window programs should display |
| EDITOR | Your desired text editor, usually **vi** or **emacs** |
| HOME | The full name of your login directory |
| LOGNAME | Your login name |
| MAIL | The full name of the directory containing your electronic mail |
| MANPATH | The directories searched by the **man** command for online manuals |
| PATH | The directories where the shell searches for programs |
| PS1 | Primary shell prompt (Korn shell) |
| PS2 | Secondary shell prompt (Korn shell) |
| SHELL | Your current shell |
| TERM | Your terminal type. This determines how your UNIX system interprets keyboard input and sends output to your screen |
| TZ | Your current time zone, usually in terms of Universal (Greenwich) time |
| USER | Your login name, like LOGNAME in the preceding example |

### Listing 4-1: SETTING ENVIRONMENT VARIABLES IN THE BASH AND KORN SHELLS

```
$ TERM=vt100
```

▲ Use the equal sign, =, to set variable values in the Bash and Korn shells.

### Listing 4-2: QUERYING THE ENVIRONMENT FOR KORN SHELL USERS

```
$ set
DISPLAY=yonsen:0.0
FCEDIT=/usr/bin/ed
GROUP=users
HOME=/usr/home/erc
LOGNAME=erc
MAIL=/usr/spool/mail/erc
MAILCHECK=600
MANPATH=/usr/man:/usr/local/man:/usr/local
/share/man:
/usr/local/xemacs/man:/usr/dt/man:/usr/dt
/share/man
PATH=/usr/home/erc/bin:/usr/bin/X11:
/usr/local/bin:/usr/local/share/bin:/usr/sb
in:/sbin:
.:/bin:/usr/bin:/usr/bin/X11:/usr/ucb:/usr/dt
/bin
PRINTER=post
PS1='$ '
PS2='> '
PS3='#? '
PS4='+ '
PWD=/usr/home/erc
RANDOM=30173
SHELL=/usr/local/bin/tcsh
TERM=vt100
TMOUT=0
USER=erc
WINDOWID=16777229
```

▲ For Korn shell users, the **set** command lists the variables set in your environment.

### Listing 4-3: SETTING ENVIRONMENT VARIABLES IN THE C SHELL

```
$ setenv TERM vt100
```

▲ With the C shell, use the **setenv** command to set environment variables.

**101**

# Setting Your Own Shell Variables

You aren't limited to the variables defined by the system; you could set up your own variables and refer back to them. This process is called *assigning variables* in UNIX parlance. If this seems like a dubious proposition at best, think again, and think of a variable not as something connected with algebra and programming, but rather as a macro of sorts that enables you to substitute a variable for a long filename or command line.

You can assign a variable at any point in a UNIX computing session. To use an example, let's say you're working on a giant data research project, and you want to save all files to the directory **/users/kevin/data/2001stuff**. That's quite a lot to type every time you want to call or save a file. In this instance, assigning a variable to store this long pathname would definitely be a good idea. Do so by typing the following:

```
$ DATA="/users/kevin/data/2001stuff"
```

Any text string to be saved as a variable must be enclosed in quotation marks. If you want to list all files in the subdirectory **/users/kevin/data/2001stuff**, you would type the following:

```
$ ls $DATA
```

When you create a variable, it is available for use by the shell but not necessarily to your UNIX applications. Similarly, if you change a shell variable, it may not be available to other applications. In these instances, you want to explicitly tell the shell to export its variables to all programs. Do so with the **export** command:

```
$ export DATA
```

You can export multiple variables with the same command. You can also combine **export** with the setting of the initial value of the variable.

If you're planning on exporting every variable you assign, you can use the **set** command with the **-a** option to tell the shell to automatically do so:

```
$ set -a
```

After a variable serves its purpose, it's a good idea to remove it, using the **unset** command. The following command removes the variable DATA:

```
$ unset DATA
```

In this instance, the use of a dollar sign before the variable name would be inappropriate, as the dollar sign means to extract the value of the variable. Here, we want to operate on the variable itself, not the value it holds.

A path is the series of directories that the shell searches to find a command. For example, when you use the **ls** command, the shell looks through a predefined series of directories in search of the file that makes up the **ls** command — a file named **ls**.

You generally want your PATH to include **/usr/bin** and **/bin**, where most UNIX commands are stored. Use a colon to separate the directories.

Two of the most important environment variables are PATH (path with the C shell), and MANPATH.

*Continued*

**CROSS-REFERENCE**

Chapter 2 covers file and directory commands.

**FIND IT ONLINE**

For more information on shell differences, see **www.faqs.org/faqs/unix-faq/shell/shell-differences/**.

## TAKE NOTE

▶ **COMMAND NOT FOUND ERRORS**

If you run a command and get an error message saying that it was not found the command may exist, but its directory may not be in your PATH. (The command may also not be available on your system.)

### Listing 4-4: SHOWING VALUES WITH ECHO

```
$ DATA="/users/kevin/data/2001stuff"
$ echo $DATA
/users/kevin/data/2001stuff
```

▲ The **echo** command reports values of variables — in this case, the DATA variable.

### Listing 4-5: USING GREP TO ACCESS VARIABLES

```
$ set | grep DATA
DATA=/users/kevin/data/2001stuff
```

▲ The **set** command lists all the environment variables. You can pipe the output to **grep** to search for a particular name.

### Listing 4-6: GREP MAY RETURN MORE THAN YOU EXPECT

```
$ set | grep DATA
DATA=/users/kevin/data/2001stuff
DTDATABASESEARCHPATH=/usr2/erc/.dt/types,
/etc/dt/appconfig/types/%L,/etc/dt/appconfi
g/types/C,
/usr/dt/appconfig/types/%L,/usr/dt/appconfi
g/types/C
```

▲ You may get more output than you expect from **grep**.

### Listing 4-7: REFINING YOUR SEARCH

```
$ set | grep ^DATA
DATA=/users/kevin/data/2001stuff
```

▲ You can refine your searches with **grep** using regular expressions. Here, **^DATA** means search for items beginning with the letters DATA.

### Listing 4-8: YOU NEED TO EXPORT VARIABLES IN THE KORN AND BASH SHELLS

```
$ DATA="/users/kevin/data/2001stuff"
$ echo $DATA
/users/kevin/data/2001stuff
$ bash
bash$ echo $DATA

bash$
```

▲ Unless you export variables in the Korn and Bash shells, you won't be able to access variable values within other commands (in this example, running another shell).

### Listing 4-9: SETENV EXPORTS VARIABLES

```
% setenv DATA /users/kevin/data/2001stuff
% echo $DATA
% bash
bash$ echo $DATA
/users/kevin/data/2001stuff
bash$ exit
%
```

▲ In the C shell, **setenv** exports the variables for you, so you can access the values within commands you run from the shell.

# Setting Your Own Shell Variables
*Continued*

Most of your environment variables are set in the startup files run by your shell, such as the **.profile** file. The table on the facing page lists which files pertain to which shells.

When the C shell first starts up, it looks for a file named **.login** in your home directory. Any commands in this file are executed. The C shell also looks for a file named **.cshrc**, also in your home directory. Any commands in this file get executed, too.

The difference between the **.login** and **.cshrc** files is simple: The **.login** file is read only when a user logs on the system, whereas the **.cshrc** file is read every time the user starts a shell or otherwise accesses a new C shell. (Note that on login, the **.cshrc** file is normally read in first, before the **.login** file. When you log out, **csh** executes the **.logout** file, if you have one.)

For example, you may want to place important variables in the **.cshrc** file, to make sure you or another application don't inadvertently change an important setting. The C shell accomplishes this by setting environmental variables, aliases, and other system defaults in this file through various commands.

The Korn shell supports the same environment variables as the Bourne shell, plus three important ones: ENV, HISTSIZE, and VISUAL. These are usually all defined in your **.profile** file.

When you log in, the C shell runs the commands in a file named **.login.** The Korn shell acts similarly but runs the commands in a file named **.profile**.

The ENV environment variable defines where the Korn shell can find an environment file at startup. This file, usually called **ksh_env**, is analogous to the C shell's **.cshrc** file and is found in your home directory. However, the Korn shell does not assume any default position, so you must define the location in your **.profile** file. To tell the Korn shell to look for this file in your HOME directory, use this command:

```
$ ENV=$HOME
```

The table on the facing page lists the startup files used by the C, Korn, and Bash shells. The Bash shell was designed to include features from both the C and Korn shells. When you log in, Bash looks in your home directory for a file named **.bash_profile, .bash_login, or .profile**, in that order, executing the commands in the first one found. When you log out, Bash executes the commands in **.bash_logout,** if the file exists.

If the shell is not a login shell, that is, if you launched this shell from another (such as in **xterm** shell windows), then Bash executes a file named **.bashrc** if it exists in your directory.

**CROSS-REFERENCE**
Chapter 7 covers **xterm** and the X Window System.

**FIND IT ONLINE**
You can get the source code for Bash at **ftp://prep.ai.mit.edu/pub/gnu/**.

## Table 4-2: START-UP FILES BY SHELL

| Shell | Login File | Start-Up File | Logout File |
|-------|-----------|---------------|-------------|
| bash | **.bash_profile**, or <br> **.bash_login**, or <br> **.profile** | **.bashrc** (if not login shell) | **.bash_logout** |
| csh | **.login** | **.cshrc** | **.logout** |
| ksh | **.profile** | $ENV | None |
| sh | **.profile** | None | None |
| tcsh | **.login** | **.tcshrc** or **.cshrc** | **.logout** |

## Listing 4-10: A .PROFILE FILE

```
PATH=$HOME/bin:/usr/local/xemacs/bin/alpha-dec-osf3.2:/usr/local/bin:/usr/bin/X11:
/usr/local/share/bin:/usr/sbin:${PATH:-/usr/bin:.}
export PATH
PS1="`hostname`> "
MAIL=/usr/spool/mail/$USER
ENV=$HOME/.kshrc
MANPATH=/usr/man:/usr/local/man:/usr/local/share/man:/usr/local/xemacs/man

EDITOR=xemacs

export MAIL EDITOR ENV LPDEST LESS MANPATH

#
# Set our term type based on login device
#
if [ x`tty` = "x/dev/tty01" ] ; then
        TERM=vt220
fi

export TERM

# end of .profile
```

▲ *A sample Korn shell* ***.profile*** *file.*

# Defining Your Terminal

Originally, users who wanted to access UNIX systems logged in through what we now know as dumb ASCII terminals. This concept of terminals remains part of UNIX, albeit with ancient roots. Whenever you log in, whether it be via a workstation's graphic screen, a **telnet** network login, or from a terminal, UNIX always assumes you have some sort of terminal device — highly abstracted, of course.

There are 70 or so options of the **stty** command specifically designed for terminal configuration . Some of the options are highly technical and applicable in very specific situations (such as the options for turning on and off flow control), whereas others have wide application.

For example, you can use the **stty** command to erase characters from the screen when you use the Backspace key (the default is to leave the characters on the screen):

```
$ stty echoe
```

One of the most useful functions of **stty** is fixing the Backspace key. If you press **Backspace** and it doesn't delete a character — you instead see garbage — try the following command:

```
$ stty erase Backspace
```

Press the **Backspace** key instead of typing the word *Backspace*. End the command by pressing the **Enter** key.

If you run into any problems, however, there are some things you can do.

The first thing, should you have access to a command prompt, is to merely log off the system and then login again immediately. This usually solves the problem, but it doesn't address the whole issue of what's causing the craziness in the first place.

An alternative for BSD UNIX and Linux users is to try the following command line:

```
$ clear
```

This calls upon the **/etc/termcap** database in an attempt to solve the display problem.

System V users can use a similar command that draws upon a similar database, **terminfo**, as shown in the following command line:

```
$ tput clear
```

There's one final thing to try: using the **stty** command to pass along some tried-and-true generic values to the terminal. These **stty** settings go by the name of (appropriately enough) **sane**, as in the following command:

```
$ stty sane
```

## TAKE NOTE

### CTRL-J ACTS AS THE ENTER KEY

If your terminal is really screwed up, you need to use Ctrl-J at the end of a line, instead of hitting the Return or Enter key.

**CROSS-REFERENCE**

Chapter 10 covers **telnet**.

**FIND IT ONLINE**

You can get replacements for terminals from NCD, at **www.ncd.com**.

## Listing 4-11: THE STTY COMMAND

```
$  stty
#2 disc;speed 9600 baud; -parity hupcl
brkint -inpck -istrip icrnl -ixany onlcr
echo echoe -echok
```

▲ *The **stty** command with no options lists the current settings in a brief form.*

## Listing 4-12: THE STTY –A COMMAND

```
$  stty -a
#2 disc;speed 9600 baud; 28 rows; 80
columns
erase = ^H; werase = ^W; kill = ^U; intr =
^C; quit = ^\; susp = ^Z
dsusp = ^Y; eof = ^D; eol = <undef>; eol2 =
<undef>; stop = ^S
start = ^Q; lnext = ^V; discard = ^O;
reprint = ^R; status = <undef>
time = 0; min = 1
-parenb -parodd cs8 -cstopb hupcl cread -
clocal -crtscts
-ignbrk brkint -ignpar -parmrk -inpck -
istrip -inlcr -igncr icrnl -iuclc
ixon -ixany -ixoff imaxbel
isig icanon -xcase echo echoe -echok -
echonl -noflsh -mdmbuf -nohang
-tostop echoctl -echoprt echoke -altwerase
iexten -nokerninfo
opost -olcuc onlcr -ocrnl -onocr -onlret -
ofill -ofdel tabs -onoeot
```

▲ *The **stty -a** option expands the listing of the current options.*

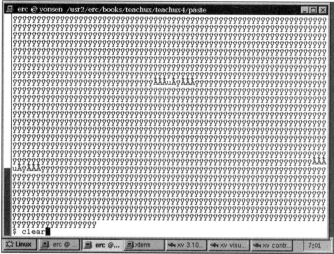

■ *If your terminal has too much data, you can use the **clear** command. If you, for example, try to use the **cat** command on a binary file, you may end up with a messed-up terminal. If your system does not support the **clear** command, try **tput clear**.*

■ *After issuing the **clear** command (or **tput clear**), your terminal should show just the prompt.*

# Customizing Commands

In Chapter 1 we introduced the command line and how to use it to run basic commands. The command line is your gateway to the shell; using the shell easily and efficiently means grasping the meaning of some of the additional command-line options and concepts. We've used the term *command* rather loosely to this point to refer to anything typed at a command prompt. For our purposes here, we distinguish between executables (programs) and what is typed into a command line. The two, though similar, are not synonymous.

For instance, the difference is demonstrated adequately in a discussion of multiple commands. You aren't limited to only one command on the command line. It is possible to run more than one command as long as they are separated by semicolons (;). In this instance, you are telling the shell to run more than one command (or, as in our next example, more than one program) on the command line:

```
$ cal; ls
```

This command tells the shell to run the programs (here we are referring to actual programs) **cal** and **ls**. In this case, the shell runs the **cal** command first, followed by the **ls** command. Both of these commands will run in the foreground, tying up the shell until all the commands complete.

You can run two or more commands sequentially in the background by adding the ampersand, &, to the command line. But there's a trick: You must surround the commands with parentheses, as follows:

```
$ (cal; ls) &
```

If you don't surround the commands with parentheses, the ampersand will apply only to the last command, **ls** in this case.

## Command Substitution

One of the ways you can customize your command line is via command substitution. A command substitution inserts the output of one program into your command line. In the example that follows, we use *date* both as a string for use by the **echo** command and as input for the **echo** command. Because the **echo** command merely echoes input from the command prompt, neither example does a whole lot, but they adequately illustrate the difference:

```
$ echo date
date
$ echo `date`
Sat Jul 25 12:27:48 CST 1999
```

One of the nastiest names you can give a file is **-r**. When you try to remove such a file, the **rm** command will interpret the **-r** as a command-line option. To get around this, you can use the following simple syntax:

```
$ rm ./-r
```
*Continued*

---

**TAKE NOTE**

► **USE ACCENT MARKS FOR COMMAND SUBSTITUTION**

Note that commands used in command substitution are enclosed with accent marks, not single quotation marks. The accent mark is usually found on the left-most part of the number line on most keyboards.

---

**CROSS-REFERENCE**

File and directory commands are covered in Chapter 2.

**FIND IT ONLINE**

Information on 21st century computing issues is available at **www.nist.gov/y2k/**.

## Listing 4-13: COMBINING COMMANDS IN THE FOREGROUND

```
$ cal 1 2010; ls
      January 2010
Su Mo Tu We Th Fr Sa
                1  2
 3  4  5  6  7  8  9
10 11 12 13 14 15 16
17 18 19 20 21 22 23
24 25 26 27 28 29 30
31
cal.txt.swp  file1        workers.comma
cut.txt      file2
workers.single_space
debts         newworkers    workers.space
diff.txt      newworkers.2  workers_phone
erc.memo      paste.txt     workers_phone2
erc.memo.712  sort.txt      workers_phone5
file.paste    workers       workers_phoneCO
file.paste2   workers.2     workers_phoneSP
```

▲ *Running both the **cal 1 2010** and the **ls** command on the same command line.*

## Listing 4-14: PWD WITH THE C SHELL

```
% pwd
/usr2/erc/books/teachux/teachux4/sort
% echo `pwd`
/usr2/erc/books/teachux/teachux4/sort
% echo $cwd
/usr2/erc/books/teachux/teachux4/sort*
```

▲ *Using command-line substitution with the C shell. Note that for some commands, such as **pwd**, the shell provides an environment variable as well, **cwd** in this case. (The C shell also supports the **PWD** variable.)*

## Listing 4-15: COMBINING COMMANDS IN THE BACKGROUND

```
$  (cal 1 2010; ls) &
[2] 258
$       January 2010
Su Mo Tu We Th Fr Sa
                1  2
 3  4  5  6  7  8  9
10 11 12 13 14 15 16
17 18 19 20 21 22 23
24 25 26 27 28 29 30
31
cal.txt       file1
workers.single_space
cal.txt.swp   file2         workers.space
cut.txt       newworkers    workers_phone
debts         newworkers.2  workers_phone2
diff.txt      paste.txt     workers_phone5
erc.memo      sort.txt      workers_phoneCO
erc.memo.712  workers       workers_phoneSP
file.paste    workers.2
file.paste2   workers.comma

[2]  Done  ( cal 1 2010; ls -F )
$
```

▲ *Running both commands in the background. The shell's prompt can mess up the output.*

## Listing 4-16: WHICH AND FILE COMMANDS WITH BASH

```
$ which bash
/usr/local/bin/bash
$ file `which bash`
/bin/bash: ELF 32-bit LSB executable,
Intel 80386, version 1, dynamically linked,
stripped
```

▲ *Using command substitution to make the output of one command a parameter for another command.*

# Customizing Commands

*Continued*

## Parsing a UNIX command

Let's begin by examining the way your shell responds to a typical command line. The shell goes through a lot of activity before actually responding to your instructions. You don't need to know exactly what the shell does before it carries out your command; you merely need to know the proper methods of structuring these commands.

Analyzing these structures is called *parsing* a UNIX command, or breaking it into its various components. When the shell parses a command, it assumes spaces separate the components such as the name of the command and any options. The shell can also use tabs or multiple spaces to distinguish between parameters. (Technically speaking, these are *interfield separators* that can be changed by the user. We can't think of a good reason why anyone would want to use anything other than spaces or tabs to distinguish between parameters, so it's highly unlikely you'll want to change your interfield separators.)

The shell doesn't respond sequentially to the separate components in a command. Instead, the shell runs through all aspects of the command (substituting for wildcards, examining variables, and so on). After the shell fully parses the command, it then executes the command. Knowing how the shell parses commands can help you when you work with UNIX.

Let's start with the use of specific marks in UNIX: the prime or accent (`), the apostrophe ('), and the

quotation mark ("). Each is used in a different situation, but sometimes they can be used interchangeably—as in the case of apostrophes and quotation marks when separating parameters. Anything contained in a set of apostrophes or quotation marks is regarded by the shell as a single parameter or argument. For instance, look at the first example on the facing page.

Most of the time quotation marks are used to tell the shell not to do things: not to expand an asterisk (*) out to names of files on disk, not to use an exclamation mark (!) for **csh**'s history mechanism, not to use the dollar sign ($) to signify the value of a variable, and so on. For example, what happens if you accidentally create a file named **report***? (We say accidentally because you never want to use a * in a filename.) If you have a number of report files, such as **report1, report.2000, report.1999**, and so on, what do you think the following command will do?

```
$ rm report*
```

The above command *will* remove the file **report***, but it will do so by taking the Genghis Khan approach: It will delete *all* files that begin with *report*, including **report1, report.1999**, and **report.2000**. We suspect you wouldn't want that. So, to delete a file named **report***, use quotation marks, as shown here, to tell the shell not to expand the * :

```
$ rm "report*"
```

**CROSS-REFERENCE**

Chapter 7 covers the **xterm** program, used in the examples.

**FIND IT ONLINE**

Frequently asked UNIX questions are answered at **www.cis.ohio-state.edu/hypertext/faq/usenet/ unix-faq/faq/top.html**.

```
 erc @ yonsen  /usr2/erc/books/teachux/teachux4/paste        _ □ ×
$
$
$
$ ls kevin eric
eric    kevin
$
$
$ ls "kevin eric"
ls: kevin eric: No such file or directory
$
$
$ ls 'kevin eric'
ls: kevin eric: No such file or directory
$
$
$ xterm -title "This is my title with spaces" &
[2] 556
$
$
$ ■




  Linux   erc @ ...   erc @...   xterm    xv 3.10...   xv visu...   xv contr...   7:11
```

■ *You can combine parameters using single (') or double (") quotes. This allows a space in a parameter.*

```
 erc @ yonsen  /usr2/erc/books/teachux/teachux4/paste        _ □ ×
$
$
$
$ ls report*
report.1999    report.date    report1        report_header
report.2000    report.header  report4
$
$
$ rm -i report*
rm: remove 'report.1999'? y
rm: remove 'report.2000'? n
rm: remove 'report.date'? n
rm: remove 'report.header'? n
rm: remove 'report1'? n
rm: remove 'report4'? n
rm: remove 'report_header'? n
$
$
$ ls report*
report.2000    report.header  report4
report.date    report1        report_header
$ ■

  Linux   erc @ ...   erc @...   xterm    xv 3.10...   xv visu...   xv contr...   7:14
```

■ *You can use the -i option with the **rm** command to prompt you when deleting files, especially files with difficult names like **report***.*

```
 erc @ yonsen  /usr2/erc/books/teachux/teachux4/paste        _ □ ×
$
$
$ ls report*
report*        report.date    report1        report_header
report.2000    report.header  report4
$
$
$ rm "report*"
$
$
$ ls report*
report.2000    report.header  report4
report.date    report1        report_header
$ ■




  Linux   erc @ ...   erc @...   xterm    xv 3.10...   xv visu...   xv contr...   7:16
```

■ *You can also place the text report* within quotation marks when deleting a file named **report*** (which is a very bad filename to use).*

```
 erc @ yonsen  /usr2/erc/books/teachux/teachux4/paste        _ □ ×
$
$ ls report*
report*        report.date    report1        report_header
report.2000    report.header  report4
$
$
$ rm 'report*'
$
$
$ ls report*
report.2000    report.header  report4
report.date    report1        report_header
$ ■




  Linux   erc @ ...   erc @...   xterm    xv 3.10...   xv visu...   xv contr...   7:18
```

■ *Single quotes work just as well as double quotes.*

# Personal Workbook

## Q&A

**1** How can you view the value held in a shell variable?

_____

_____

_____

**2** What is the EDITOR environment variable for?

_____

_____

_____

**3** What does the PS1 environment variable hold?

_____

_____

_____

**4** Which startup files set up the environment for C shell users?

_____

_____

_____

**5** Which command should you use to set variables in the C shell? How about the Korn shell?

_____

_____

_____

**6** What is held in the PATH variable?

_____

_____

_____

**7** What does the TERM environment variable signify?

_____

_____

_____

**8** How can you run two or more commands from the same command line?

_____

_____

_____

ANSWERS: PAGE 346

## EXTRA PRACTICE

**1** List all the variables in your environment.

**2** Create a file named **-r** and then remove it. (This is a more common problem than you'd think.)

**3** Add **/sbin** and **/usr/sbin** to your PATH.

**4** Set up your environment to name the **emacs** text editor as your editor of choice.

**5** Change to the **/usr/local/src** directory and list the files there, placing the output in your home directory in a file names **local.src**, all from one command line in the background.

**6** Create the command line necessary to copy a file named **data\*** but not files starting with *data*, such as **data.2000**?

## REAL-WORLD APPLICATIONS

✔ You've been reading risque messages from the Internet or playing a text-based game on your terminal and your boss has entered the room. Quickly remove all the text from your terminal's screen.

✔ You log onto a system, and as you use the Backspace key to fix your commands, you find out that the Backspace key doesn't work. Fix this problem.

✔ Users at your site are complaining about the long and difficult to type directory names used for the location of the company's application data. Set up a variable to hold the directory name, **/usr/application/version1-30.a2beta/WunderWord2.03_0005.p1.trial15**.

## Visual Quiz

From the files listed here, guess which shell this user runs.

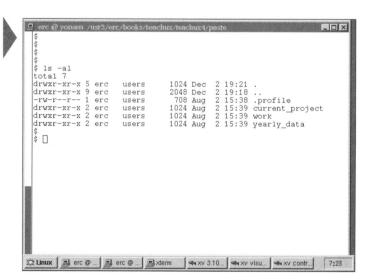

113

**CHAPTER**

# 5

# The C, Korn, and Bash Shells

All the commands discussed so far are launched by a *shell*—the UNIX command-line interpreter. The shell reads in the text you type and then executes the commands when you press the **Enter** key, controlling most of your interaction with UNIX. Shells go even further than this, though, and provide special built-in commands, aliases, and the means to group commands in a *shell script*—a text file containing shell commands.

Unlike Windows or Digital Equipment's VMS operating system, UNIX separates the command shell from the operating system. This key feature of UNIX has led to the development of many shells. These shells include the Bourne shell (named after Steven Bourne), one of the oldest UNIX shells. The Bourne shell program is **sh**, and this is the shell most often used for writing shell scripts. Other shells include the C shell, **csh**, the Korn shell, **ksh**, and the Bourne Again Shell, **bash**.

If you're a newcomer to UNIX, you may not be aware of which shell you're running, which means you may be missing out on the advantages of using the shell that best fits your needs.

The name of the default shell should be stored in the SHELL environment variable, which you can check with the **echo** command:

```
% echo $SHELL
/bin/csh
```

You should see a response that includes **sh, csh, bash,** or **ksh**.

Because UNIX provides so many choices for command shells, you may want to experiment with **csh, ksh, bash,** or other shells. To start a shell, type in the name of the shell as a command. For example, if your default shell is **ksh**, but you want to try the C shell (**csh**), enter the following command:

```
$ csh
```

Now, you can test out **csh** commands. When you're done, issue the **exit** command:

```
% exit
```

The **exit** command causes the current shell (**csh** in this example) to quit and returns you to the previous shell (**ksh** in this example). All these shells accept **exit** as the command to quit the program.

# Working with the C Shell

The C shell's roots can be traced back to Bill Joy's stint at Berkeley when he was developing the Berkeley UNIX System. The C shell, **csh**, provides a syntax aimed at C programmers, hence the name.

A few variants of the C shell exist, most notably the T C shell, or **tcsh**. In general, **tcsh** acts like **csh** on steroids. Most **csh** commands work exactly the same in **tcsh**. In fact, on Linux, **csh** is really **tcsh**.

The C shell is highly configurable due to its series of *toggles*, settings you can turn on or off from the command line or in the startup **.cshrc** or **.login** files. Table 5-1, on the facing page, lists the commonly used toggles.

One of the most useful toggles, in our experience, is the **noclobber** toggle: The listing on the facing page shows what happens if you have the set **noclobber** option on and how you can override it if it is on.

## Filename Completion

UNIX is full of long filenames and directory names that you often have to type in. Filename completion helps with this task. After you turn this feature on with the **set filec** toggle, type in a few letters of a filename — just enough to uniquely identify the file — press **Esc**, and **csh** will try to complete the name for you.

For example, if you want to remove a file named **2000.annual.financial.report**, you could type in the following command:

```
rm 2000.ann
```

Next, press the **Esc** key, and **csh** should complete the filename, as shown here:

```
rm 2000.annual.financial.report
```

If you use the **tcsh** shell, you should press the **Tab** key instead of **Esc**.

If there are other files that start with *2000.ann*, you have not fully identified the file, and **csh** will beep at you.

The C shell also completes commands such as **emacs**.

The T C shell extends the C shell's capability to complete filenames by adding a space after a filename and a / after a directory name. You can disable this feature by adding the following line to your **.cshrc** file (or **.tcshrc** file):

```
unset addsuffix
```

The T C shell also completes environment variables, which start with a *$*, and user home directory names, which start with a tilde and a portion of the username.

*Continued*

---

### TAKE NOTE

#### ESCAPE VERSUS TAB

Remember that **csh** uses the **Esc** key for filename completion and **tcsh** uses the **Tab** key. In most other respects, **tcsh** acts as a compatible replacement for **csh**.

---

### CROSS-REFERENCE

Chapter 4 covers the **.cshrc** and **.login csh** startup files.

### FIND IT ONLINE

You can find frequently asked questions on UNIX shells at **www.faqs.org/faqs/bynewsgroup/comp/comp.unix.shell.html**.

## Changing Your Shell Permanently

A system administrator sets up your default shell. Your administrator may not be amused if you try to change things on your own. So, after discussing things with your system administrator, try the **chsh** command (short for *change shell*), which changes the default login shell. The syntax follows:

chsh *username new_default_shell*

　For example:

chsh eric /bin/bash

　Some versions of **chsh** prompt you for the new shell. To determine what version of **chsh** you have, use the **man** command.

　Some versions of BSD UNIX provide a **chpass** command instead of **chsh**. In this case, you can call **chpass** as follows:

chpass -s /bin/bash

### Table 5-1: COMMON C SHELL TOGGLES

| Toggle | Purpose |
| --- | --- |
| **set ignoreeof** | Tells the shell not to log you off with the command **Ctrl-D**. |
| **set noclobber** | Protects you from accidentally writing over an existing file. |
| **set filec** | Turns on filename completion. |
| **set autologout= number** | Sets *number* to 0 to turn off the annoying automatic log off feature. (Said feature logs you off if you don't type in any commands for a set time period, the default being 60 minutes.) |

### Listing 5-1: TESTING THE NOCLOBBER MODE

```
% cat file1 > file2
file2: file exists
```

▲ With **noclobber** set, the C shell helps protect files from accidental clobbering.

### Listing 5-2: OVERRIDING THE NOCLOBBER MODE

```
% cat file1 >! file2
```

▲ To override the **noclobber** mode, use an exclamation point, as shown here.

### Listing 5-3: TESTING FILENAME COMPLETION WITH TCSH

```
% ls /usr/loc Tab
% ls /usr/local/ Tab
% ls /usr/local/apa Tab
% ls /usr/local/apache/
% ls /usr/local/apache/htd Tab
% ls /usr/local/apache/htdocs
```

▲ Using **tcsh**, press the Tab key to expand filenames. (Don't type the word **Tab**). The shell will show the expanded name, as shown here.

### Listing 5-4: CHECKING YOUR SHELL WITH TCSH

```
% echo $SHELL
% /bin/tcsh
```

▲ Using **tcsh**, you should see your shell listed when you echo the **SHELL** environment variable. Another common location for **tcsh** is in **/usr/local/bin**.

# Working with the C Shell

*Continued*

The **tcsh** variant of **csh** enables you to edit previous commands (as do **ksh** and **bash**). Like **ksh** and **bash,** **tcsh** provides two sets of editing commands, based on the two popular UNIX editors, **emacs** and **vi**.

In both **emacs** and **vi** modes, **Ctrl-P** displays the previous command. **Ctrl-N** displays the next command (once you've gone to a few previous commands). Both of these display part of the command history, discussed later in this chapter.

**Ctrl-C** cancels the current command and clears the command line in both editing modes.

To enter **emacs** editing mode, use the **bindkey -e** command:

```
% bindkey -e
```

In **emacs** editing mode, you can type in editing commands at any time, as **emacs** commands all require the **Esc** key or the **Ctrl** (Control) key. Table 5-2, on the facing page, lists the commands to move about the command line in **emacs** editing mode.

Two of the handiest commands are **Esc-p** and **Esc-n**. **Esc-p** searches backward, and **Esc-n** searches forward. What you do is enter text that is in a command in the history list and then type **Esc-p** or **Esc-n**. You'll then see the first command in the history that matches, going in the given direction.

For example, if one of the previous commands was a change of directory, you can search for the **cd** command by typing **cd** and then **Esc-p**. When found, **tcsh** fills in the command.

The **emacs** edit mode also provides a number of commands for deleting text on the command line, as listed in Table 5-3, on the facing page.

To enter **vi** editing mode, use the **bindkey -v** command:

```
% bindkey -v
```

Unlike **emacs**, the **vi** text editor is a **modal editor**. You're either in insert mode or command mode. Which commands you can use depend on the mode you're in.

By default, you start in insert mode, otherwise you wouldn't be able to enter commands at all. In insert mode, you can use the same movement commands as the **emacs** mode uses, described in the first table on the facing page.

To change to command mode, press the **Esc** key. In command mode, everything you type is considered a command.

---

### TAKE NOTE

#### ▶ DISCOVERING KEY BINDINGS

The **bindkey** command by itself lists the current key bindings. In the output, ∧ symbolizes the Ctrl key, ∧[ the Esc key, and ∧? the Delete key. Therefore ∧**A** means Ctrl-A, ∧**[[A** means Escape-[A, and ∧**[∧?** means Escape-Delete. (Escape-[A is really the up arrow key for most terminals.)

#### ▶ THE HOME DIRECTORY

The C shell (as well as the Korn shell), provides a quick shorthand for the path to your home directory. The tilde symbol (~) can replace the pathname of your home directory. Thus you could use ~/dir to name a subdirectory (dir) in your home directory.

---

**CROSS-REFERENCE**

Chapter 11 covers **vi** and **emacs**.

**FIND IT ONLINE**

The T C shell is available at **ftp://ftp.cdrom.com/ pub/linux/slackware_source/a/tcsh/.**

## Table 5-2: EMACS EDIT MODE MOVEMENT COMMANDS

| Command | Usage |
|---|---|
| Ctrl-A | Move cursor to beginning of line. |
| Ctrl-B | Move cursor one character to the left (back). |
| Ctrl-C | Cancel command and clear command line. |
| Esc-b | Move cursor back one word. |
| Ctrl-E | Move cursor to end of line. |
| Ctrl-F | Move cursor one character to the right. |
| Esc-f | Move cursor forward one word. |
| Up arrow | Move to previous command in history. (Not supported in **ksh**.) |
| Down arrow | Move to next command in history. (Not supported in **ksh**.) |
| Left arrow | Move cursor one character to the left. (Not supported in **ksh**.) |
| Right arrow | Move cursor one character to the right. (Not supported in **ksh**.) |

## Table 5-3: EMACS EDIT MODE DELETION COMMANDS

| Command | Usage |
|---|---|
| Delete | Delete character to left of cursor. |
| Esc Delete | Delete word to left. |
| Esc Ctrl-H | Delete word to left. |
| Ctrl-D | Delete character to right of cursor. |
| Esc-d | Delete word. |
| Ctl-H | Delete character to left of cursor. |
| Ctrl-K | Delete from cursor to end of command line. |
| Ctrl-U | Delete entire command line. |

### Listing 5-5: USING CTRL-P TO VIEW COMMAND HISTORY

```
echo $DISPLAY
cd /home/erc/books/teachux4
```

▲ *If you type **Ctrl-P** a few times, you might see these commands.*

### Listing 5-6: LISTING CURRENT KEY BINDINGS

```
% bindkey
"^@"            -> set-mark-command
"^A"            -> beginning-of-line
"^B"            -> backward-char
"^C"            -> tty-sigintr
"^E"            -> end-of-line
"^F"            -> forward-char
"^H"            ->  backward-delete-char
"^P"            ->  up-history
"^T"            ->  transpose-chars
"^U"            ->  kill-whole-line
"^[[A"          -> up-history
"^[^?"          -> backward-delete-word
Arrow key bindings
down            -> down-history
up              -> up-history
left            -> backward-char
right           -> forward-char
...
```

▲ *Highly edited output of the **bindkey** command, showing the current key bindings.*

# Corralling the Korn Shell

In response to the C shell, AT&T, at the time the developer of UNIX, created the Korn shell, **ksh**. The Korn shell, named for David Korn, took many of the advances in the C shell (**csh**) and migrated these advances back to the original Bourne shell (**sh**) syntax. Because the Korn shell is based on the Bourne shell, most Bourne shell scripts can be used without adjustment under the Korn shell. The Korn shell also added a new feature: command-line editing. This shell is popular on most commercial versions of UNIX.

Like **csh, ksh** provides the capability to complete long filenames if you type in enough characters to uniquely identify the file. In **ksh**, type **Esc-\** (Escape and backslash) for **ksh** to fill in the rest of a filename you start to enter.

When set on, the VISUAL variable enables you to edit a command line with a **vi**-style text editor. This is a very handy feature: If you make a typographical error in the middle of a long command, you can merely use a cursor to scroll back to the typo and correct the typo. Let's say you want to edit the file **chap5.doc**, but you mistakenly typed the following at the command prompt:

```
$ vi cjap5.doc
```

To correct the error, press **Esc** to move into editing mode. Use either your cursor key or the **vi** command (**b**) to move back one word, type over with the correct characters, and then hit the **Enter** key. (The cursor can be anywhere in the command line; it doesn't have to be at the end of the line for you to hit the **Enter** key.)

To set this feature in your environment file, enter the following line:

```
set -o vi
```

You can also set the VISUAL environment variable to the value **vi**:

```
VISUAL=vi
```

The **Esc** key changes from **vi** insert mode to **vi** command mode, which acts the same as the **vi** command mode in **tcsh**. Arrow keys, though, don't work in **vi** mode in **ksh**.

To use **emacs** editing commands, you can run either of the following commands:

```
set -o emacs
```

or

```
VISUAL=emacs
```

In **emacs** editing mode, **ksh** acts very much like **tcsh**, and supports the commands listed in Tables 5-2 and 5-3. On some systems, though, **Ctrl-U** repeats the next command four times instead of deleting text. Arrow keys normally don't work in **emacs** mode in **ksh**.

---

**TAKE NOTE**

**FREE VERSIONS OF THE KORN SHELL**

The Korn shell is a commercial product and so isn't available on all versions of UNIX. A free version called **pdksh** is available on the Internet. In addition, Bash, covered in the next task, was designed partially as a replacement for **ksh**.

---

**CROSS-REFERENCE**

Chapter 4 covers more on **ksh**.

**FIND IT ONLINE**

The source code for **pdksh** is available at
ftp://ftp.cs.mun.ca/pub/pdksh/.

## Weight Watchers

The following command limits the size of a file to 15 megabytes:

```
$ ulimit -f 15000
```

The Korn shell measures input from this command line in terms of thousands of bytes. Thus, 15,000 thousand bytes equals 15 megabytes.

For the C shell, use the **limit** command. The following C shell command would limit the size of any file to 15 megabytes:

```
$ limit filesize 15m
```

### Listing 5-7: USING VI EDIT MODE

```
$ set —o vi
$ ls /usr/loc Esc \
$ ls /usr/local
$ ls /usr/local/apa Esc \
$ ls /usr/local/apache/
$ ls /usr/local/apache/htd Esc \
$ ls /usr/local/apache/htdocs/
index.html    manual
```

▲ Using **ksh**, press the **Esc** and backslash (\) keys to expand filenames. The shell will show the expanded name, as shown here. Press **Enter** to end the command.

### Listing 5-8: EDITING COMMANDS IN VI MODE

```
$ set —o vi
$ vi cjap5.doc Esc
$ vi chap5.doc Enter
```

▲ After typing in the filename incorrectly, press **Esc** to enter **vi** editing mode. Next, press the **h** key to move the cursor back one character. Press the **h** key seven times until the cursor is over the letter j — the incorrect letter. Now, use the **r** (replace) command to replace the letter j. Type the command **r** and then the letter **h**. When the command looks right, press **Enter** to execute the command.

## Table 5-4: VI COMMANDS IN COMMAND MODE

| Command | Usage |
| --- | --- |
| **Space** | Move cursor right one character. |
| **A** | Append text at end of line. |
| **a** | Append text after cursor. |
| **b** | Move cursor back one word. |
| **e** | Move cursor to end of word. |
| **h** | Move cursor left one character. |
| **I** | Insert text before beginning of line. |
| **i** | Insert text at cursor. |
| **j** | Move to next command in history. |
| **k** | Move to previous command in history. |
| **l** | Move cursor right one character. |
| **R** | Replace existing text, starting at cursor. |
| **w** | Move cursor forward one word. |
| **0** | Move cursor to beginning of line. |
| **^** | Move cursor to beginning of line. |
| **$** | Move cursor to end of line. |
| **Up arrow** | Move to previous command in history. |
| **Down arrow** | Move to next command in history. |
| **Left arrow** | Move cursor one character to the left. |
| **Right arrow** | Move cursor one character to the right. |
| **x** | Delete character under cursor. |
| **Nx** | Delete N characters, N being a number you specify. |
| **D** | Delete from cursor to end of line. |
| **dd** | Delete entire line. |
| **dw** | Delete word. |
| **Ndw** | Delete N words, N being a number you specify. |

# Corralling the Korn Shell
*Continued*

As we said earlier, the Korn shell borrows from the C shell, including the following toggles:

▶ **Ignoreeof**, used to prevent you from accidentally logging off the system by typing **Ctrl-D**. The Korn shell equivalent command is as follows:

```
$ set -o ignoreeof
```

▶ **Noclobber**, used to prevent you from overwriting existing files by accident. The Korn shell equivalent command is as follows:

```
$ set -o noclobber
```

One important difference exists between the C shell and Korn shell: Instead of using the exclamation point to override the **noclobber** command, the Korn shell uses the pipe character:

```
% cat file1 >| file2
```

The Korn shell acts like the C shell and enables you to use a tilde symbol (~) to replace the pathname of your home directory. Thus you could use:

```
$ mv filename ~/subdirect
```

instead of:

```
$ mv filename $HOME/subdirect
```

In this case, *~/subdirect* refers to a subdirectory of your home directory.

You could also use the tilde (~) symbol to save files to someone else's home directory. For instance, the following would move a file to Eric's home directory, assuming Eric has the username *eric*:

```
$ mv filename ~eric
```

You can extend this to naming subdirectories of another user's home directory. For example:

```
$ cp ~eric/bin/adduser bin
```

This command copies a file named **adduser**, located in the **bin** subdirectory of user eric's home directory, to your **bin**, which we assume is a subdirectory in the example.

Finally, the Korn shell, unlike the C shell, enables you to move between directories by using the hyphen (-) option with the **cd** command:

```
$ cd -
```

With the Common Desktop Environment, or CDE, you may have an extended Korn shell called **dtksh**, short for *desktop Korn shell*. **dtksh** supports all the commands of **ksh**, and adds the capability to create windows with buttons, menus, and other widgets based on X and Motif functions built into the scripting language.

---

**TAKE NOTE**

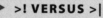

### >! VERSUS >|

The C shell uses **>!** and the Korn shell uses **>|** to override the **noclobber** mode; the similarity sometimes makes it hard to distinguish the two.

---

**CROSS-REFERENCE**

Chapter 7 covers Motif and the CDE.

**FIND IT ONLINE**

For more on the Common Desktop Environment, see **www.opengroup.org/**.

## Listing 5-9: CREATING A WINDOW WITH DTKSH

```
#!/usr/dt/bin/dtksh
# Sets up a small user interface for
# launching xterm windows.
launch_window()
{
exec /usr/bin/X11/xterm -n $1 &
}
# Set up X connection.
XtInitialize TOPLEVEL TestWindow Dtksh
"$0$@"
XmCreateRowColumn RC $TOPLEVEL rc

# Create pushbuttons for major sites.
XtCreateManagedWidget PB1 button1
XmPushButton $RC
XtSetValues $PB1 labelString:"Seattle"
XtAddCallback $PB1 activateCallback
"launch_window Seattle"

XtCreateManagedWidget PB3 button3
XmPushButton $RC
XtSetValues $PB3 labelString:"Portland"
XtAddCallback $PB3 activateCallback
"launch_window Portland"

# Create a pushbutton to exit.
XtCreateManagedWidget PB4 button4
XmPushButton $RC
XtSetValues $PB4 labelString:"Exit"
XtAddCallback $PB4 activateCallback "exit"
# Make all the windows appear.
XtManageChild $RC
XtRealizeWidget $TOPLEVEL
XSync $(XtDisplay "-" $TOPLEVEL) False
XtMainLoop
```

▲ *The script used to create the window shown in the figure. The top three buttons launch the* **xterm** *program. The final button quits the script.*

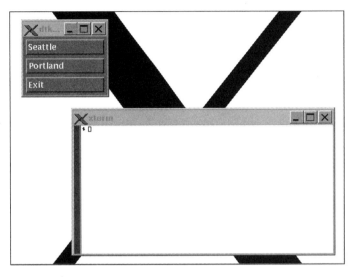

▲ *An X Window user interface created by a* **dtksh** *script.*

## Listing 5-10: TURNING ON IGNOREEOF

```
$ set -o ignoreeof
$ Ctrl-D
Use 'exit' to terminate this shell
```

▲ *When you turn on the* **ignoreeof** *mode,* **ksh** *will complain with an error message (such as "Use 'exit' to terminate this shell") if you type* **Ctrl-D** *(hold down the* **Ctrl** *key and type d), the UNIX end-of-file marker. Without this mode set,* **ksh** *will exit if you type* **Ctrl-D** *at the prompt.*

## Listing 5-11: OVERRIDING NOCLOBBER MODE

```
$ set -o noclobber
$ cat env.txt > clob.txt
ksh: clob.txt: file already exists
$ cat env.txt >| clob.txt
```

▲ *When you turn on the* **noclobber** *mode,* **ksh** *will complain with an error message like the one shown here if you try to overwrite a file by accident. To override the* **nocobber** *mode, use >| in place of > for the file redirection.*

# Executing the Bash Shell

Although many UNIX shells, and indeed, most of UNIX itself, have existed in free versions, the Korn shell, a commercial product, was not originally available for free. To help offset this, the free software GNU project wrote the Bourne Again Shell, called **bash**, a pun on the original Bourne shell. The Bash shell is in many ways similar to the Korn shell. Bash brings over many of the advances of the C shell to the Bourne shell syntax, much the same as the Korn shell. Bash also provides command-line editing.

You'll find Bash very similar to the Korn shell, so most of the material covered in the section on **ksh** works for **bash**, too. For example, Bash supports the use of the tilde character, ~, to represent your home directory. Thus, you can use commands like the following to refer to files and subdirectories in your home directory:

```
$ mv filename ~/subdirect
```

The command moves the file *filename* into a subdirectory, *subdirect*, in your home directory.

The reason there are so many similarities between Bash and the Korn shell is because Bash was originally designed as a freeware alternative to **ksh**. The sections that follow briefly describe what you can expect from Bash and differences between Bash and other shells.

## Filename Completion

Bash supports filename completion, as you'd expect of a modern shell. Bash uses a **Tab** for filename completion, as does **tcsh**. In addition, you can use **Esc-/** for filename completion.

Bash extends the filename completion to include **Esc-~** (Escape and tilde) for username completion and **Esc-$** for variable completion.

## Command-Line Editing in Bash

Bash also supports command-line editing and provides **vi** and **emacs** editing modes. To use **emacs** editing, issue the following command:

```
set -o emacs
```

To use **vi** editing instead, issue the following command:

```
set -o vi
```

These are the same as the Korn shell commands for setting the editing mode.

In **emacs** mode, **bash** works the way **tcsh** does in **emacs** mode with a few exceptions. The **Esc-n** and **Esc-p** commands do not search in **bash** as they do in **tcsh**, (which is unfortunate, as these commands are very handy).

In **vi** mode, **bash** works the same way **tcsh** does in **vi** mode.

All in all, **bash** is very similar to **ksh** and works well in environments where you typically don't have **ksh**, such as Linux. Tables 5-5 through 5-7 compare **bash, csh, tcsh,** and **ksh** to help you separate the features.

---

**CROSS-REFERENCE**

The section on **tcsh** earlier in this chapter covers the **emacs** edit mode commands.

**FIND IT ONLINE**

You can get the source code for Bash at **ftp://prep.ai. mit.edu/pub/gnu/**.

## TAKE NOTE

▶ **FORWARD AND BACKWARD SLASHES**

Bash command-line completion uses **Esc** with a forward slash, /. The Korn shell in **vi** editing mode uses **Esc** with a backward slash, \, for command-line completion.

### Table 5-5: SETTING EDIT MODES

| Shell | Set vi Mode | Set emacs Mode |
|-------|-------------|----------------|
| bash | set -o vi | set -o emacs |
| csh | Not applicable | Not applicable |
| ksh | set -o vi | set -o emacs |
| tcsh | bindkey -v | bindkey -e |

### Table 5-6: COMPARING SHELL CAPABILITIES

| Function | bash | csh | ksh | sh | tcsh |
|----------|------|-----|-----|-----|------|
| Compatible with Bourne Shell scripts | Yes | No | Yes | Yes | No |
| Alias support | Yes | Yes | Yes | No | Yes |
| Command-line editing | Yes | No | Yes | No | Yes |
| Filename completion | Yes | Yes | Yes | No | Yes |
| History support | Yes | Yes | Yes | No | Yes |

### Table 5-7: FILENAME COMPLETION FOR SHELLS

| Shell | Filenames | List All Possible Files | Usernames | Shell Variables |
|-------|-----------|-------------------------|-----------|-----------------|
| bash | Tab, Esc-/ | Esc-? | Esc-~ | Esc-$ |
| csh | Esc | Ctrl-D | Not applicable | Not applicable |
| ksh (emacs mode) | Esc-Esc | Esc-= | Not applicable | Not applicable |
| ksh (vi mode) | Esc-\ | Esc-= | Not applicable | Not applicable |
| tcsh | Tab | Ctrl-D | Not applicable | Not applicable |

# Mastering Command History

Because UNIX commands tend to get long, most shells have special features that help you get by with less typing (the creators of UNIX were well known for their aversion to typing, which led to short command names such as **cp** instead of copy). The most helpful feature is called a command history. A *command history* is a list of previous commands you've entered and a means of selecting those commands for re-execution, saving you a lot of typing. (You'll be surprised how many commands you run again and again.)

This is useful for a number of reasons. You may have saved a file earlier in your session and now can't locate it; it's easier and quicker to use the **history** command to locate the command where you actually saved the file, as compared to using the slower **find** command to search the entire file system. You may repeatedly use the same command followed by the **history** command to cut down on the number of keystrokes you have to make.

## The C Shell and Command History

The C shell will maintain a listing, or history, of your previous commands, which you can access via the **history** command:

```
% history
ls
```

In this example, we list the current directory previous to using the **history** command. The shell maintains a history of only the most recent command unless you use the **set history** command, as shown in the following line:

```
% set history=32
```

Here we are telling the C shell to keep a record of the 32 most recent commands. (We do this in our **.cshrc** file and recommend you do the same.)

After you have told the C shell to maintain a longer history, the **history** command will list your previous commands — up to the number of commands you specified in the **set history** command. The first listing on the facing page shows an example of this. In the first two listings on the facing page, you'll notice that the commands are numbered. You can use these numbers to set up substitute commands. For example, you may need to go back and read the **.login** file using the **vi** text editor. You can rerun a specific command from the command history by specifying the number of the command in the history list on the command line, as shown here:

```
% !3
```

Obviously our examples won't result in you saving enough keystrokes to avoid carpal-tunnel syndrome. However, in cases where your commands are rather long and involved (as in instances where long pathnames or particularly complicated pipe commands are used), the **history** command can significantly cut down on your keystrokes.

The facing page shows some of the handiest parts of the **csh** history facility.

*Continued*

**CROSS-REFERENCE**

Chapter 11 covers the **vi** text editor.

**FIND IT ONLINE**

For more on C shell command history, see **www.mathcs.duq.edu/unixhelp/shell/ csh_hist.html.**

---

**TAKE NOTE**

▶ **VIEWING A TRUNCATED HISTORY LISTING**

If you want to see a truncated list of recent command lines, you can combine the **history** command with a number, as shown below.

---

## Listing 5-12: USING THE HISTORY COMMAND

```
% history
 1 ls
 2 ls -a
 3 vi .login
 4 vi .cshrc
 5 ls
```

▲ This example shows the **csh** command history with five previous commands. If hundreds of commands had been issued prior to the **history** command, you would get a listing of the 32 most recent commands.

## Listing 5-13: VIEWING A TRUNCATED HISTORY LISTING

```
% history 10
    59   11:40    nc tclwin.htm
    60   12:08    telnet yonsen
    61   12:23    ftp yonsen
    62   12:24    telnet yonsen m
    63   12:47    telnet yonsen
    64   13:21    alias
    65   13:22    xcd ~/erc
    66   13:22    nc ch5.txt
    67   13:23    vi ~/.cshrc
    68   13:25    alias
```

▲ To see a truncated history listing, use the **history** command with a number that lists how many previous commands you want to see.

## Listing 5-14: USING THE ! NOTATION TO RUN PREVIOUS COMMANDS

```
% !vi
vi .login
```

❶ To go back to the last instance of a particular command, use **!vi** to re-execute the last command that started with the text **vi**.

❷ The C shell responds with the full text of the command.

## Listing 5-15: RERUNNING THE LAST COMMAND

```
% !!
vi .login
```

▲ You can rerun the previous command by using the **!!** command.

## Listing 5-16: RERUNNING COMMANDS BY THE NUMBERS

```
% history
 1 ls
 2 ls -a
 3 vi .login
 4 vi .cshrc
 5 ls
% !3
vi .login
```

▲ You can rerun a command from the history list using !number, where number is the number of the command within the history — in this case, a command to edit the file **.login** with the **vi** command.

## Listing 5-17: USING !$

```
% mv *.htm public_html
% mv *.shtml !$
mv *.shtml public_html
```

▲ The C shell replaces **!$** with the last argument to the previous command. Here, the C shell replaces the **!$** with **public_html** and responds with the full text of the command.

## The Korn Shell and History

The Korn shell features command history similar to that of the C shell, though there are some differences. For instance, the C shell uses the **set history** command to set the number of commands to maintain in the history list. The Korn shell, on the other hand, uses the **HISTSIZE** environment variable:

```
HISTSIZE=32
```

The **r** command re-executes the last command in the history file. Unlike the C shell, the Korn shell shares the history file between all running copies of **ksh**. Thus, **r** may not execute the command you expect if you have multiple windows all running **ksh**.

The Korn shell also gives you a lot of flexibility with the **r** command. For instance, you can run the command line you ran five commands ago with the **r –5** command. To rerun the last command starting with *vi*, you can use the **r vi** command.

The **fc** command provides something closer to the C shell's history commands (**fc** is short for *fix command*). The basic command, **fc -l,** presents a list of previous commands, like the history command in **csh**. See the listing on the facing page for an example of this.

The **fc** command by itself calls up your text editor to edit the previous command. When you exit the text editor, **ksh** runs the command. If you pass a number to the **fc** command, **fc** calls up the text editor to edit the command associated with that number. (You these numbers and a list of associated commands using the **fc -l** command, described previously.) For example, **fc 5** calls up the editor with the fifth command in the history. If you pass part of a command to **fc**, such as **fc cp**, **fc** calls up the editor with the most recent command that starts with *cp*.

Table 5-8 compares the C shell and the Korn shell history mechanisms.

## The Bash Shell and History

Bash acts like a combination of the C shell and the Korn shell where history is concerned. Like the C shell, the **history**, !!, !*number* and !*partial_text* commands work with the history list. The **history** command lists the commands in your history. You can use !*number* to rerun the command with that number in the history. In addition, you can use !*partial_text* to rerun the first command in the history that matches the partial text.

Like the Korn shell, **fc –l** lists the command history. The **fc** command enables you to edit commands. Unlike **ksh**, though, **bash** does not support the **r** command, which repeats the last command.

> ### TAKE NOTE
>
> #### ▶ BORROWING FROM THE C SHELL
> Both the Korn and Bash shell history mechanism borrow heavily from that of the C shell, discussed earlier in the chapter.

**CROSS-REFERENCE**
Chapter 11 covers the **vi** text editor.

**FIND IT ONLINE**
For more on Korn shell command history, see **www.mathcs.duq.edu/unixhelp/shell/ksh_hist.html.**

## Table 5-8: SHELL HISTORY COMMANDS

| Shell | List Previous Commands | Run Last | Run by Text | Run from Number |
|-------|------------------------|----------|-------------|-----------------|
| bash | history, fc -l | !! | ! *partial_text* | !*number* |
| csh | history | !! | ! *partial_text* | !*number* |
| ksh | fc –l | r | **r** *partial_text* | **r** *number* |
| tcsh | history | !! | !*partial_text* | !*number* |

### Listing 5-18: LISTING COMMAND HISTORY

```
$ fc -l
1 ls
2 fc -l
3 which ksh
4 which emacs
5 which nedit
6 which nedit
7 which nedit
8 fc -l
```

▲ The **fc -l** command in the Korn shell shows the history of previous commands. The number of commands displayed is controlled by the **HISTSIZE** environment variable.

### Listing 5-19: RE-EXECUTING PREVIOUS COMMANDS

```
$ vi ~/.profile
$ r
vi ~/.profile
$ ls
chap5.doc     chap7.doc
$ r vi
vi ~/.profile
```

▲ The Korn shell **r** command re-executes previous commands. In both cases, the **r** and **r vi** commands will re-execute the command **vi ~/.profile**.

### Listing 5-20: GETTING THE COMMAND HISTORY IN BASH

```
$ history
    32  alias lsf='ls -CF'
    33  alias
    34  exit
    35  alias -p
    36  alias lsf='ls -CF'
    37  alias -p
    38  unalias lsf
    39  alias -p
    40  exit
    41  bindkey
    42  exit
    43  history
```

▲ The Bash shell supports the history command like the C shell. Bash also supports **fc -l** command to display the command history, acting like the Korn shell.

# Setting Up Aliases

When does a command not mean what it says? When it's an *alias*. The C, Korn, and Bash shells enable you to define one command to do the same thing as another potentially complicated command. Aliases are useful for automating long, obscure UNIX commands with one simple command you can type in at the prompt.

The basic C shell syntax is as follows:

```
alias alias_name actual_command
```

The first listing on the facing page shows some example aliases, including **dir** for **ls** with the **–alx** option. This means that when you type in the **dir** command (we're showing our DOS roots) the C shell will really execute the **ls –alx** command, which provides a long listing of files.

Aliases can be a little tricky. For example, say you have defined **rm** in such a way as to include the **–i** option so that you are prompted first before a file is actually deleted. This is very useful, but introduces a problem: You now have no means of directly running the real **rm** command. Each time you type **rm** in the C shell, you get the alias, **rm –i**. The way around this is to use the full path to the command to execute the original (**/bin/rm**) and not the alias (**rm -i**).

If this bothers you, you can remove an alias setting with the **unalias** command:

```
% unalias rm
```

In addition, if you want to run the real command—as opposed to the alias—you can preface it with a backslash. In this instance, to run the real **rm** command, your command line would look like this:

```
% \rm
```

Though the Korn and C shells are very similar in their approach to aliases, they differ in a few areas. For instance, the C shell syntax to set an alias won't work with the Korn shell. The Korn shell uses an equal sign as part of the command line to denote the alias and what it stands for. You must also enclose the real command within single quotes, as shown here:

```
alias dir='ls -alx'
```

To make the Korn shell work even more like the C shell, set up the following alias in your **.profile** file:

```
alias history=fc -l
```

Bash aliases are like Korn shell aliases and take the following format:

```
alias new_name=command
```

In most cases, Bash acts the same way the Korn shell does when working with aliases.

---

**TAKE NOTE**

**ALIASES FOR KSH, CSH, AND BASH**

Both the Korn and C shells use the **alias** command to list aliases. Bash uses **alias -p** to list the current aliases.

---

**CROSS-REFERENCE**

Chapter 4 covers the shell start-up files, such as **.cshrc.**

**FIND IT ONLINE**

For more on shell aliases, see **www.mathcs.duq.edu/ unixhelp/shell/alias.html.**

## Listing 5-21: EXAMPLE CSH ALIASES

```
alias   dir    ls -alx
alias   lsf    ls -CF
alias   ll     ls -l
alias   rm     rm -i
alias   mail   mailx
alias   df     df -k
alias   h      history
alias   ens    enscript -2 -j -Ecpp
alias   nc     nc -noask

# Handle typos.
alias   maek   make
alias   emcas  emacs
alias   gmaek  gmake
```

▲ *Example aliases using the **csh** syntax suitable for the **.cshrc** file.*

## Listing 5-22: LISTING CURRENT ALIASES

```
% alias
dir     (ls -CF)
emcas   emacs
ens     (enscript -2 -j -Ecpp -f Courier5)
gmaek   gmake
h       historylsf    (ls -CF)
ll      (ls -l)
maek    make
mail    mailx
nc      (nc -noask)
rm      (rm -i)
```

▲ *To get a list of your existing aliases in the C shell, use the **alias** command.*

## Listing 5-23: CREATING A SHORT ALIAS FOR A LONG COMMAND

```
$ alias ens='enscript -2 -j -Ecpp -f
Courier5'
```

▲ *The **ens** alias is an example of using a short simple name for a much larger command, the options of which are easy to forget. This example sets up a Korn shell alias.*

## Listing 5-24: USING ALIASES TO MAKE SHELLS WORK MORE ALIKE

```
$ alias history='fc -l'
$ history
1       rwho
2       who
3       uptime
4       ls
5       ls -l
6       dir
7       ping www.idgbooks.com
8       vi example1
9       ls -l example1
10      chmod u+x example1
11      ls -l example1
12      example1
13      vi example2
14      ls -l example2
10      chmod u+x example2
11      ls -l example2
12      example2
13      ps -ef
14      ps -ef | grep erc
15      alias history='fc -l'
16      history
```

▲ *The history alias makes the Korn shell act more like **csh**.*

**131**

# Personal Workbook

## Q&A

**1** How can you find out what shell you are running?

_____

_____

_____

**2** You work with data files that have very long names. What can you use to avoid so much typing when you work with these files?

_____

_____

_____

**3** Does the C shell support **vi** or **emacs** command-line editing?

_____

_____

_____

**4** How do you turn on **vi** command-line editing mode in the Korn shell?

_____

_____

_____

**5** Which shell enables you to create graphical applications?

_____

_____

_____

**6** How do you control the number of commands stored in the command history in the C shell? In the Korn shell?

_____

_____

_____

**7** How do you turn on filename completion in the C shell?

_____

_____

_____

**8** How do you re-execute the last command in the Korn shell? In the C shell?

_____

_____

_____

**ANSWERS: PAGE 347**

## EXTRA PRACTICE

**1** Re-execute the same command at least three ways using the C shell.

**2** Experiment with command-line editing in your shell, if this feature is supported.

**3** You've deleted a number of files by accident and don't want this to happen ever again. Create a C shell alias to help avoid this problem.

**4** Glance through the online manual page for your shell to see one of the longest UNIX manual entries.

**5** List all the available shells on your system. Common locations include **/bin, /usr/bin, and /usr/local/bin**.

**6** Take a different shell than the one you normally use for a test drive. Try out some of the features and see if you'd like to switch.

## REAL-WORLD APPLICATIONS

✔ You use the Korn shell for your default shell, but now you need to work on a UNIX server (perhaps a Linux server) that doesn't include the **ksh** program. Name the options you have to make your work on the new system match your old system as closely as possible.

✔ Your boss always wants you to do "more, better, faster." Your latest assignment is to copy all the Web files ending in *.html*, *.shtml*, and *.cgi* from the current directory to the **public_html** directory. Do this from **csh** or **tcsh** and eliminate as many keystrokes as possible to meet the expectations of your boss.

✔ You use the C shell for your daily work but realize **tcsh** gives you more power in a compatible package. Download **tcsh** and try it out. (Hint: Chapter 10 covers downloading and Chapter 14 covers compiling freeware.)

## Visual Quiz

Which edit mode is active in this shell, **vi** or **emacs**?

_____

_____

_____

_____

_____

_____

```
xterm                                            _ □ X
yonsen:~> bindkey -v
yonsen:~> whoami
erc
yonsen:~> set ignoreeof
yonsen:~> history
     1  17:10    clear
     2  17:10    whoami
     3  17:10    date
     4  17:10    ls
     5  17:10    clear
     6  17:10    bindkey -v
     7  17:10    whoami
     8  17:10    set ignoreeof
     9  17:10    history
yonsen:~> □
```

```
Linux    erc @ yo...   xterm    xterm    xv 3.10a <...   xv controls   5:11
```

**133**

# CHAPTER 6

MASTER
THESE
SKILLS

▶ **Mastering Multitasking**

▶ **Killing Processes**

▶ **Processing in Real Time**

# Multitasking and Processes

So far, our discussion has centered around a practical approach to the UNIX operating system. We've shown you how to use UNIX's commands to automate your daily tasks. For the most part, we've avoided discussions of concepts and abstractions unless they were related directly to the task at hand. The strategy has served us well.

However, this approach takes you as a user only so far. Yes, you can perform your daily work without delving into the depths of UNIXdom. Yes, you could go along for many years without learning about processes, daemons, and signals. But this approach, while ideal for beginning computer users and those getting their feet wet in UNIX, is too limiting for the truly ambitious UNIX user. You've learned how things work; now we take a little side journey to introduce why things work the way they do.

Many forests have been felled in the production of books detailing the concepts underlying the UNIX operating system. Entire academic and research careers have been devoted to conceptually advancing the UNIX operating system. Since UNIX has developed in such a seemingly haphazard fashion, different people bring different conceptual frameworks to UNIX.

Still, there are a few concepts that make UNIX what it is. Most discussions of UNIX tend to downplay or sidestep UNIX's multitasking capabilities, on the assumption that the topic is too advanced (or too esoteric) for most users. Most discussions tell you how to run commands in the background and leave it at that.

And for most UNIX beginners, however, even the concept of background tasks can be daunting. PC and Macintosh users have no experience with true multitasking; sure, Windows and the Macintosh operating system can load more than one application at a time and make it appear that both are running, but they don't handle multiple tasks in the same manner that UNIX does. And if you're a true beginner, the entire notion of multitasking is odd.

However, the more you know, the more efficiently you can complete your work, and multitasking is a way for you to work more efficiently. Hence, this chapter.

# Mastering Multitasking

**M**ultitasking is a fancy computer-speak way of saying that the operating system can do more than one thing at a time. While this may seem like a simple matter, it's really not; personal computer users have been screaming for a multitasking operating system for (seemingly) years (though, ironically, they for the most part ignore OS/2, which handles multitasking in much the same manner as UNIX).

UNIX documentation doesn't actually often use the term *multitasking* (even though the rest of the computer world uses it); instead, UNIX is said to be *multiprocessing*—the same thing described differently. When you run a UNIX command, such as **ls** or **cat**, you're running a *process*. When you boot the UNIX operating system, you are actually launching a series of processes without consciously doing so. (If you use a graphical user interface like the X Window System, you're launching many, many processes.) On a large multiuser system, there may be literally thousands of processes running at a given time.

UNIX organizes processes (as it does almost everything else) in hierarchical fashion: Processes beget other processes, with one process at the top of the pyramid. When a process launches another process, it uses a system call entitled a *fork*, which creates the new process.

When you boot a UNIX system, the first process (process 0) launches a program called **init**, which then launches other processes. **Init** is the mother of all UNIX processes—or, as referred to in UNIXdom, **init** is a parent to other processes, which in turn can act as parents to additional processes, called *child processes*. It is, ultimately, the ancestor of all processes running on the system.

To see what processes are running on your system, use the **ps** command, as shown in the two figures on the opposite page.

## Swapping Files

Processes compete with each other for computing resources. Running programs in the background, as described earlier, is a way for the UNIX user to allocate resources efficiently. Such allocation is necessary to keep the system from bogging down, especially a large multiuser system with less-than-adequate resources. If there are more processes running than can fit in your system's random-access memory (RAM), then UNIX uses a hard disk as extended RAM in an action called *swapping* to disk. However, hard disks are much slower than RAM, so swapping to disk is not the most desirable of solutions; many experts advise the purchase of UNIX systems with huge amounts of RAM. UNIX workstations with hundreds and hundreds of megabytes of RAM are not uncommon these days, especially those systems dealing with graphics.

---

**CROSS-REFERENCE**

Review the section on running commands in the background in Chapter 2.

**FIND IT ONLINE**

More information about workstations can be found at **www.performancecomputing.com**.

# MULTITASKING AND PROCESSES

## Mastering Multitasking

### Listing 6-1: A BASIC PROCESSES LISTING

```
gilbert:~# ps
PID       TTY       STAT      TIME      COMMAND
 97        1         S        0:00      —bash
 98        2         S        0:00      /sbin/agetty 38400 tty2 linux
 99        3         S        0:00      /sbin/agetty 38400 tty3 linux
100        4         S        0:00      /sbin/agetty 38400 tty4 linux
101        5         S        0:00      /sbin/agetty 38400 tty5 linux
102        6         S        0:00      /sbin/agetty 38400 tty6 linux
119        1         R        0:00      ps
```

▲ *To see what processes are running on your system, use the **ps** command. The most important information is the process identification, or PID. When the kernel launches a new process, it assigns an ID number to the process. The fourth field covers the time the processes have run.*

### Listing 6-2: MORE PROCESSES INFORMATION

```
gilbert:~# ps -l
 FLAGS UID PID PPID PRI NI SIZE RSS WCHAN       STA TTY TIME COMMAND
   100   0  97    1  19  0 1136 616 wait4        S    1 0:00 —bash
   100   0  98    1   4  0  816 292 complement_  S    2 0:00 /sbin/agetty 38400 tty2
   100   0  99    1   4  0  816 292 complement_  S    3 0:00 /sbin/agetty 38400 tty3
   100   0 100    1   5  0  816 292 complement_  S    4 0:00 /sbin/agetty 38400 tty4
   100   0 101    1   5  0  816 292 complement_  S    5 0:00 /sbin/agetty 38400 tty5
   100   0 102    1   5  0  816 292 complement_  S    6 0:00 /sbin/agetty 38400 tty6
100100   0 125   97  19  0 1024 376              R    1 0:00 ps -l
```

▲ *This is the **ps** command run in the long form (with the **-l** option). This lists all information about every process. Some versions of UNIX use the **–f** option instead of the **-l** option for listing information in the long form.*

# Killing Processes

When we described the shell and its importance in running programs for you, we were referring to the shell acting as the parent and managing other child processes. Unless you tell it otherwise (by issuing the **kill** command), the shell waits while you run a child and returns with a prompt after the child process is finished, or dies. If a child process dies but this fact is not acknowledged by the parent, the child process becomes a zombie. What macabre imagery!

It's up to the operating system to keep track of these parents and children, making sure that processes don't collide. This means scheduling processes to within a fraction of a second, ensuring that all processes have access to precious CPU time. It's also up to the operating system, through the **init** program, to manage child processes that have been abandoned by their parents. These abandoned processes are called *orphans*. (Family values obviously play an important a role in the UNIX operating system, as they do in the Republican Party.)

Though we have mockingly referred to the high level of abstraction associated with the UNIX operating system, using names such as parent, orphan, zombie, and child to describe the various stages of processes is a very useful thing; it helps both users and programmers visualize very intangible actions.

In the previous task we referred to the importance of the PID number. This number is important because it allows you to manipulate the process via the ID number. For example, there are times when you may want to kill a process because it's using too many precious system resources or not performing in the manner that you anticipated. If the process is running in the foreground, you can press the **Delete** or **Break** keys (depending on your keyboard) to stop the process. (If **Delete** or **Break** don't work, try **Ctrl-C** or **Ctrl-D**.)

## TAKE NOTE

### ▶ USING THE KILL COMMAND

If a process is running in the background or has been launched by another user at another terminal, you must kill the process via the **kill** command using the PID returned by the **ps** command or other commands:

```
$ kill PID
```

This sends a *signal* to the process, telling it to cease and desist. Most processes don't know what to do when they receive a signal, so they commit suicide. Not all processes respond to the straight **kill** command; for instance, shells ignore a **kill** command with no options. To kill a shell or other particularly stubborn processes, use **kill** with the **-9** option:

```
$ kill -9 PID
```

This sends an unconditional kill signal to the process. If you have many processes to kill, you can wipe them all out with:

```
$ kill 0
```

This kills all of the processes in a current process group, which oversees all processes created by a common ancestor, usually the shell.

**CROSS-REFERENCE**
Chapter 1 covers common UNIX commands.

**FIND IT ONLINE**
The Republican National Committee's Web site is at **www.rnc.org**. The Democratic Party's home page is at **www.democrats.org**.

## Listing 6-3: PROCESSES: BERKELEY UNIX USERS

```
gilbert:~# ps -aux
USER       PID  %CPU %MEM   SIZE    RSS TTY STAT START    TIME COMMAND
bin         67  0.0  0.4    824    312  ?  S    15:42    0:00 /usr/sbin/rpc.portmap
nobody      92  0.0  0.9   1056    584  ?  S    15:42    0:00 /usr/sbin/httpd
nobody      93  0.0  0.9   1056    584  ?  S    15:42    0:00 /usr/sbin/httpd
nobody      94  0.0  0.9   1056    584  ?  S    15:42    0:00 /usr/sbin/httpd
nobody      95  0.0  0.9   1056    584  ?  S    15:42    0:00 /usr/sbin/httpd
nobody      96  0.0  0.9   1056    584  ?  S    15:42    0:00 /usr/sbin/httpd
root         1  0.1  0.5    828    356  ?  S    15:41    0:03 init
root         2  0.0  0.0      0      0  ?  SW   15:41    0:00 (kflushd)
root         3  0.0  0.0      0      0  ?  SW<  15:41    0:00 (kswapd)
root         4  0.0  0.0      0      0  ?  SW   15:41    0:00 (nfsiod)
root         5  0.0  0.0      0      0  ?  SW   15:41    0:00 (nfsiod)
root         6  0.0  0.0      0      0  ?  SW   15:41    0:00 (nfsiod)
root         7  0.0  0.0      0      0  ?  SW   15:41    0:00 (nfsiod)
```

▲ Use the **–aux** option if your version of UNIX is based on Berkeley UNIX or Linux.

## Listing 6-4: PROCESSES: SYSTEM-WIDE INFORMATION

```
gilbert:~# ps -ef
PID TTY STAT TIME COMMAND
 97   1 S    0:00 -bash TERM=linux HZ=100 HOME=/root SHELL=/bin/bash PATH=/usr
135   1 R    0:00  \_ ps -ef LESSOPEN=|lesspipe.sh %s ignoreeof=10 HOSTNAME=da
 98   2 S    0:00 /sbin/agetty 38400 tty2 linux HOME=/ TERM=linux BOOT_IMAGE=L
 99   3 S    0:00 /sbin/agetty 38400 tty3 linux HOME=/ TERM=linux BOOT_IMAGE=L
100   4 S    0:00 /sbin/agetty 38400 tty4 linux HOME=/ TERM=linux BOOT_IMAGE=L
101   5 S    0:00 /sbin/agetty 38400 tty5 linux HOME=/ TERM=linux BOOT_IMAGE=L
102   6 S    0:00 /sbin/agetty 38400 tty6 linux HOME=/ TERM=linux BOOT_IMAGE=L
```

▲ To get a fuller view of the whole system — as opposed to your individual machine — you can use **ps -ef**.

# Processing in Real Time

As the UNIX operating system keeps track of many processes, it must set priorities; after all, computing resources are typically a finite resource. Yes, we'd all love to have the power of a Cray supercomputer for our tasks, but we make do with our underpowered multiuser systems, and some tasks are simply more important than other tasks when it comes to your attention. If a job doesn't require input from you, go ahead and run it in the background. This means that the process will run out of sight (and out of mind, too often), popping up only when the command is completed. While the command runs in the background, you're free to work on other tasks with other commands.

As you learned earlier in this book, running a process in the background is a matter of adding an ampersand (&) to the end of the command line:

```
$ command options &
```

For instance, you should run CPU-intensive commands, such as **sort**, in the background. There's no reason for you to interact with the **sort** command as it goes through large files; your role in the process is to issue the command and then stay out of the way. The **sort** command requires no input from you, and it doesn't write to the screen as it performs the sort. The same goes for programmers who need to compile programs; their damage is done when creating the source code, not when compiling the code.

The temptation, of course, is to assume that all commands can be run in the background. Yet this isn't true; as a matter of fact, there's a rather limited number of commands that you should run in the background. For instance, any command that relies on continued input from you, such as text editors and anything to do with electronic mail, shouldn't be run in the background.

Almost every version of UNIX contains support for real-time processes, which ensures that a given process will be executed at a given time, no matter what other processes are running. This is a radical departure from previous versions of UNIX, which used various algorithms to allocate system resources more equally. With real-time processes, the system does not interrupt a process for any reason until the process is completed.

Using real-time processes is important in many fields, including multimedia (music and sounds won't be interrupted with pauses), factory automation, and medical computing. If you're interested in learning more about real-time processes, check the System V Release 4 documentation listed in Appendix B.

## TAKE NOTE

### USING THE JOB SHELL

The job shell, **jsh**, may not be the most frequently used shell, but it does a credible job at allowing you tight control over multiple jobs. This is a situation where knowledge of processes is important; otherwise, the many nifty features of **jsh** would be lost on you. We show how to use the job shell on the opposite page.

## CROSS-REFERENCE

Chapter 7 covers working with shell windows.

## FIND IT ONLINE

More information about LynxOS, a real-time operating system that works like UNIX, is at **www.lynx.com/**.

# Job Control (jsh)

Starting **jsh** enables Job Control. This means every command the user enters at the terminal is a job. All jobs run in the foreground, background or are classified as stopped. Foreground jobs have read and write access to the controlling terminal. Background jobs do not have read access, but do have conditional write access to the controlling terminal. Stopped jobs are in a suspended state.

The following Job Control commands manipulate jobs:

```
bg [%jobid ...]
```

This command resumes a stopped job in the background. If %jobid is omitted, the current job moves to the background.

```
fg [%jobid ...]
```

This command resumes a stopped job in the foreground and moves a background job into the foreground. Omitting %jobid causes the current job to move to the foreground.

```
jobs %jobid
```

Here jobid refers to the job number. If %jobid is omitted, all stopped or background jobs are reported.

There are two common options for the jobs command. The **–l** option displays the working directory and process group ID number of each job. The **–p** option lists each job's process group ID.

## Listing 6-5: DECIPHERING JOBS

```
$ jobs
[1]   +   Running        sort AL_West > AL &
[2]   -   Suspended      sort AL_East > AL &
```

▲ *The job shell allows you to get a decipherable list of current jobs. Job number one is currently running, while job number two is suspended.*

## Listing 6-6: KILLING A JOB

```
$ kill %1
```

▲ *Under the job shell, you can kill a job with the ever-popular **kill** command, but you must combine the job number with a percentage sign (%). In our example, we are killing job number one.*

## Listing 6-7: STOPPING A JOB AND STARTING IT IN THE FOREGROUND

```
$ stop %1
$ fg %1
```

▲ *The job shell also allows you to stop (suspend) a job. You have the option of starting the command again in either the foreground or in the background. Here, we are starting job number one in the foreground.*

## Listing 6-8: STOPPING A JOB AND STARTING IT IN THE BACKGROUND

```
$ stop %1
$ bg %1
```

▲ *Here, we've stopped job number one. We're now starting the job again in the background.*

# Personal Workbook

## Q&A

**1** How do you generate a short list of processes on your system?

_____

_____

**2** How do you generate a long list of processes on your system?

_____

_____

_____

**3** How do you generate a long list of processes on the entire UNIX network?

_____

_____

_____

**4** How do you kill a process?

_____

_____

_____

**5** How do you kill a process that refuses to be killed?

_____

_____

_____

**6** Why are real-time processes important?

_____

_____

_____

**7** How do you stop a process when using the job shell?

_____

_____

_____

**8** How do you relaunch the same process when using the job shell?

_____

_____

ANSWERS: PAGE 348

## EXTRA PRACTICE

**1** Figure out what processes are running on your local system.

**2** Figure out what processes are running on the entire network.

**3** Use the **kill** command to kill the **vi** text editor.

**4** Figure out if the job shell is available on your system.

**5** Launch the **sort** command in background mode.

**6** Use the job shell for a day, if it's available on your system.

## REAL-WORLD APPLICATIONS

✔ You've been working on an application and discover to your horror that a bug or two or three is crippling the application. Find the offending process and kill it.

✔ You need to sort a huge database in preparation for a mass mailing. Run the **sort** command in the background.

✔ A badly coded game ends up spawning several child processes that do nothing — not even respond to the **kill** command. Use the proper option to kill these processes.

✔ You're implementing a multimedia kiosk running under X and UNIX. Because you want to make sure that sufficient resources are allocated to the multimedia application, use the job shell to run the application.

## Visual Quiz

Find the process that launches the shell in this listing.

_____

_____

_____

_____

_____

_____

```
erc @ yonsen  /usr2/erc/books/teachux/teachux4                    _ □ X
gilbert:~#
gilbert:~# ps -l
FLAGS UID  PID PPID PRI NI SIZE RSS WCHAN        STA TTY TIME COMMAND
   100 0  97   1 19  0 1136 616 wait4         S   1 0:00 ~Vbash
   100 0  98   1  4  0  816 292 complement_  S   2 0:00 /sbin/agetty
38400 tty2
   100 0  99   1  4  0  816 292 complement_  S   3 0:00 /sbin/agetty
38400 tty3
   100 0 100   1  5  0  816 292 complement_  S   4 0:00 /sbin/agetty
38400 tty4
   100 0 101   1  5  0  816 292 complement_  S   5 0:00 /sbin/agetty
38400 tty5
   100 0 102   1  5  0  816 292 complement_  S   6 0:00 /sbin/agetty
38400 tty6
100100 0 125 97 19  0 1024 376                R   1 0:00 ps -l
gilbert:~# □
```

```
☆ Linux  │ 🖳 erc @ yo...│ 🖳 erc @ yo...│ 🖳 erc @ yo...│ ◄xv 3.10a <...│ ◄xv controls │ 3:58 ✉
```

# CHAPTER 7

# The X Window System

Even the concept of the X Window System confuses most new users. Is it a UNIX shell? No. Is it the all-singing, all-dancing graphical system that will cure all of your computing woes? Not yet. Is it a standard? Yes, although some vendors — most notably workstation giant Sun Microsystems — have been brought into the X fold kicking and screaming. Is it a workable business-oriented environment? Yes, but only just.

X is complex, confusing, and bloated, but it's also a graphical windowing system. X provides multiple windows (run by multiple applications) on a graphics monitor — the bare bones building blocks of a graphical user interface (or GUI, to use a popular and trendy term).

X, as a graphical user interface, provides two immediate benefits for you, the UNIX user:

▶ First, X allows you to use more of your display, because you can access every dot on the monitor, instead of just 24 lines by 80 characters in text mode. Graphics monitors have dramatically dropped in price over the last few years, so that most users can take advantage of X's capabilities.

▶ Second, a graphical user interface eases your transition to UNIX and speeds up your daily work. Several studies clearly indicate a well-designed graphical interface reduces corporate training time and increases worker productivity.

Just about every modern UNIX software package, from the **xmahjongg** game to the WYSIWYG Applix Words word processor, runs under a graphical interface. Unlike the cryptic dot commands required for **troff**, Applix Words provides a friendly menu-driven graphical interface, as does Corel WordPerfect, FrameMaker, and almost every other X-based package. All of these programs run on top of the X Window System.

Never refer to X as *X Windows*. X partisans are extremely picky about the name, which is the *X Window System*, *X*, or *X11*. The 11 in X11 refers to eleventh version of the X protocol. Only X10 and X11 were ever released to the general public. The current version of X is X11R6.4, X11 Release 6.4. New releases of X with minor changes come out every year or two.

# Going Graphics

The X Window System provides the basics for graphical windowing in a way that is portable to most UNIX platforms. What makes X special is that this graphical interface runs on just about every UNIX platform, as well as on VMS, DOS, Windows, AmigaDOS, and MacOS. X is not the only modern attempt at providing a graphical user interface — Microsoft Windows and the MacOS are two well-known graphical interfaces. So why use X?

▶ **Flexibility**. X allows you to layer any number of graphical user interfaces on top of the underlying window system. You can run programs sporting any interface you desire. Few other windowing systems offer this flexibility.

▶ **Portability**. X programs run on a wide variety of computer systems. If your company or university owns UNIX workstations from a number of vendors — a very common occurrence — the knowledge you gain learning X will aid you on any of these platforms.

▶ **Network transparency**. X programs can compute across a network. X divides computing into two parts, based on a client-server relationship. This relationship can be rather confusing, but it offers the ability to efficiently distribute applications over a network. (We cover this in more depth later.)

▶ **Because it's there**. If you're using UNIX (which we assume you are, or you wouldn't have read this far) and running a graphical windowing system, you're running X. So, if you want to learn how to get the most out of your system, it would be advantageous for you to learn X.

▶ **Accessibility to UNIX applications from PCs**. Using software from companies such as Hummingbird, you can run X applications on UNIX and display the interface on Windows PCs. Many sites place PC systems on the desktop and use UNIX servers. X emulation software for Windows allows you to make the most of this arrangement.

## The Common Desktop Environment

Because X mandates no user interface style, a mishmash of interfaces exist, and there are periodic attempts to unify the whole GUI mess. The Common Desktop Environment, or CDE, is an attempt to unify the UNIX world on a common user interface and set of productivity applications. A product of the Open Group, CDE is based on the Motif user interface, which is very similar to the Windows style. The first figure on the facing page shows a typical CDE screen. Most commercial UNIX systems include the CDE.

The CDE provides a front panel, normally located at the bottom of the screen. From this panel, you can launch a number of common productivity applications that come with the Common Desktop Environment. The facing page also shows other X displays, from non-CDE systems, to show the wide variety of X.

**CROSS-REFERENCE**

Chapter 10 covers networking.

**FIND IT ONLINE**

For CDE information, see **www.opengroup.org/**.

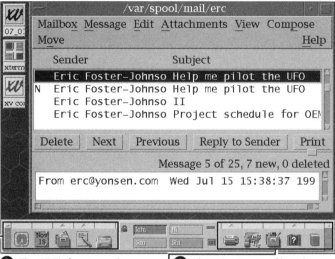

❶ The CDE's front panel launches applications. These icons tell time, manage the calendar and files, edit text, and read e-mail.

❷ These icons print files, change fonts and colors, launch applications, get help and delete files.

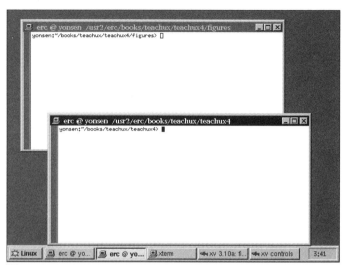

■ The fvwm95 window manager presents a look similar to Windows. The two **xterm** programs allow you to enter UNIX commands.

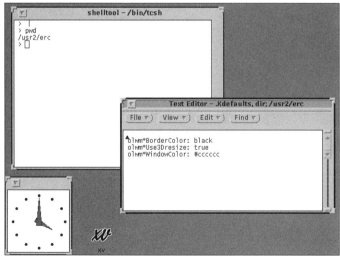

■ An Open Look interface includes a clock program, shelltool shell window, and the textedit text editor.

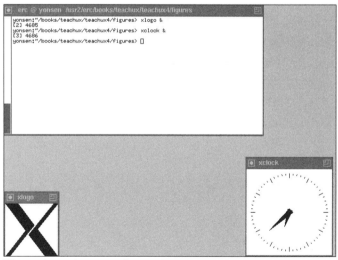

■ Here's another X interface, with no fancy name, using only default X applications, such as the **xterm** shell window, xclock time-displaying program, X logo, and twm window manager.

# Working with the X Server

In the micro worlds, a *server* is usually a hardware device (an AS/400, a Novell file server, and so on) running at the center of a network, distributing data and processing power to networked workstations and terminals. Because other systems on your network have access to your display, the X server cannot be thought of in the same way as a file server on a local-area network. With X, the role of the server (sometimes called a *display server*) is reversed. The server is a program that runs on your local machine and controls and draws all output to the display. Your local machine, whether it's a PC running SCO UnixWare or a Sun SPARC workstation running the Common Desktop Environment, is called a *display*. The server draws the images on your physical monitor, tracks input via the keyboard and pointing device (usually a mouse), and updates windows appropriately.

The server also acts as a traffic cop between clients running on local or remote systems and the local system. Clients are application programs that perform specific tasks. (In X, the terms *clients* and *applications* are used interchangeably.) Because X is a networked environment, the client and the server don't necessarily compute on the same machine (although they can and do in a number of situations). That's how X features distributed processing. For example, a personal computer running SCO UnixWare can call upon the processing power of a more-powerful Hewlett-Packard host within a network, displaying the results of the Hewlett-Packard's computations on the PC's monitor. In this case, the client is actually running on the remote Hewlett-Packard, not your local machine — thus distributing the processing across the network. The idea is simple: The actual computing should take place on the machine with the most computing power on a network, not necessarily at the computer that a user happens to be using.

## X Terminals

This distributed capability led to a whole new type of device, an X terminal. An X terminal includes a monitor, keyboard, mouse, network connection, and a dedicated computer that runs the X server software. Designed to replace ASCII terminals — the so-called green screens — X terminals allow you to display X applications. In recent years, X terminals have metamorphosed into Network Computers by adding the Java run-time engine to the dedicated computer inside the X terminal, in an attempt to revive the industry.

---

**TAKE NOTE**

**DON'T CONFUSE X TERMINAL WITH XTERM**

An *X terminal* is a hardware device that allows you to access X. An **xterm** is a program that provides a UNIX shell window. The names are very similar, but the meaning quite different.

---

**CROSS-REFERENCE**

Chapter 4 covers more on terminals

**FIND IT ONLINE**

X terminal vendors include Network Computing Devices (NCD), located at **www.ncd.com/**, and Tektronix, located at **www.tek.com/**.

■ *An X server includes a monitor, keyboard, and pointing device — usually a mouse.*

■ *X servers can support more than one monitor with the same keyboard and mouse, though this is rare.*

■ *Each separate keyboard, monitor, and mouse running X forms its own X server.*

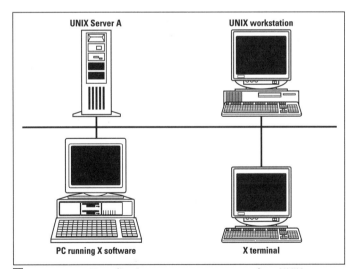

■ *You can run X applications on one system — such as UNIX Server A — and display the results on another such as a PC running X emulation software.*

# Introducing Window Managers

Most X users run a window manager to help control their display. A *window manager* is a program that controls the placement of windows and the look of window title bars. Unlike Windows and MacOS systems, X does not lock in the look of the windowing system. X provides the building blocks for a graphical interface. You are free to use any window manager you like.

Window managers exist primarily to help you organize your display. You can move windows about under most window managers by moving the mouse pointer over the title bar, holding down the left mouse button, and dragging the window to its new location with the mouse.

Because X separates the window manager from the underlying windowing system, this leads to two types of user interfaces: the interface provided by the application and the interface provided by the window manager.

This sounds more confusing than it is. The window manager controls the title bar, so the same application can appear differently under different window managers. For example, the first three figures on the facing page show the **xcalc** mathematical calculator program running under three different window managers: The **mwm** (Motif), **olwm** (Open Look), and **fvwm95** (Windows 95-like) window managers. (Most window managers have *wm* in the name of the program.)

In all cases, the application, **xcalc**, remains the same, but the window manager's title bar changes.

But, **xcalc**, no matter what window manager is running, is still **xcalc** and, because X doesn't mandate a particular window manager, there are quite a few choices.

The second interface change stems from the fact that X doesn't specify any user interface standards. The last figure on the facing page shows a calculator written to a different user interface style, **dtcalc**, part of the Common Desktop Environment, or CDE.

Compare **xcalc** with **dtcalc**. Both programs are simple desktop calculators, but both interfaces look quite different. This is both the freedom and bane of the X Window System. You can layer any user interface you want on top of X, but there are few standards.

Window managers differ — that's the freedom provided by X — but most follow similar conventions. The next section covers those conventions.

## TAKE NOTE

### WHAT IS MOTIF?

Motif is a user interface style that appears very much like Windows, but with more three-dimensional bevels than Windows. Motif is also a programming library used to create applications that comply with the Motif interface style. Finally, Motif includes a window manager (that follows the Motif style). This tends to be confusing because you can run a Motif window manager with Open Look applications, so it's not an all-or-nothing deal. Open Look applications tend to have rounded-corner buttons, while Motif applications use square corner buttons. Both Open Look and Motif use a lot of 3D bevels.

## CROSS-REFERENCE

The task on Basic X Applications in this chapter introduces more standard applications in addition to **xcalc**.

## FIND IT ONLINE

A list of virtually all X window managers is available at **www.PLiG.org/xwinman/**.

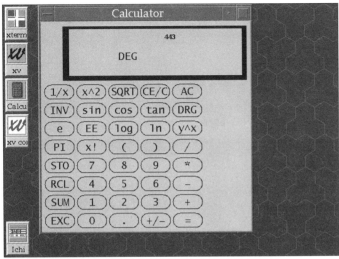

■ *The **xcalc** program under the Motif window manager.*

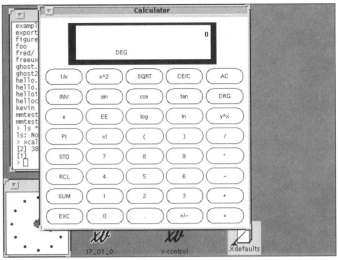

■ *The **xcalc** program shows a different title bar when run under the Open Look window manager.*

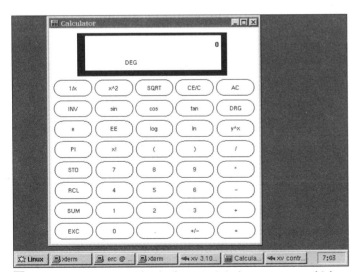

■ *The **xcalc** program under the **fvwm95** window manager, which presents a Windows look and feel.*

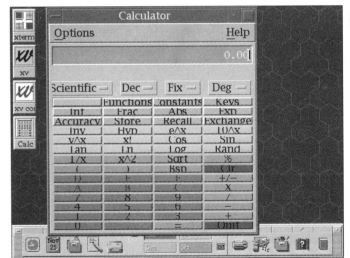

■ *A different calculator program, **dtcalc**, running under the **dtwm** window manager on a CDE system.*

# Manipulating Windows

To work with windows in X, you need to know some of the basics about how windows operate. Most window managers place a title bar on the top of each application window, as shown in the upper-left hand figure on the facing page. This figure shows the various elements — called *decorations* — placed by the window manager on top of most application windows.

While window managers can differ greatly, most follow a Motif or Windows style. Common elements such as a title bar help identify the window, and special controls on the title bar. Usually, you can minimize (also called iconify) or maximize (zoom to full screen) windows. Some window managers, particularly those displaying a Windows 95/98 look, include a close button on the title bar. With the close button, you can exit the application if it only has one window, or close the window if the application has many windows on the display.

Most window managers allow you to change the size of a window from the resize handles, normally found on all four corners of the window. By positioning the pointer over the corner and dragging, you can resize the window. As the mouse goes over the resize handles, the pointer changes to an arrow against a right angle, mimicking the angle of the corner of the window.

An icon represents a running program that has its windows shrunk in order to clear up clutter on the screen. Double-clicking an icon usually brings the window back to its normal size.

The X style for icons tends to be quite different than modern versions of Windows, where icons on the desktop typically represent a shortcut for launching a program, not a program that is already running.

In X, windows are said to have *focus* (or sometimes *input focus* or *keyboard focus*), which is a fancy way of stating that you can type into or manipulate a window. Only one window at a time can have focus and this window usually has a title bar with a distinctive color.

With most window managers, you need to explicitly set the focus by moving the pointer over a window and clicking the left mouse button. This is called a *click-to-type* interface. If you click a window that's partially obscured by another window, giving it the focus will move the obscured window on top of the previously obscuring window. (This sounds much more complicated than it really is. Trust us.) Don't worry if you have a window partially obscuring another; the obscured window is still fully functional and running a program.

## TAKE NOTE

### CLICK-TO-TYPE VERSUS FOCUS FOLLOWS MOUSE

Many X window managers provide the option to set the keyboard focus to follow the mouse pointer, which means that the window immediately underneath the pointer has the focus. (Yes, it is a tad odd to be thinking of these two-dimensional interfaces in three-dimensional terms.) Most window managers can be configured to enable this.

**CROSS REFERENCE**
Appendix B lists books that provide more information about the X Window System and keyboard focus.

**FIND IT ONLINE**
More information on X is available at **www.pconline .com/~erc/motif.htm**.

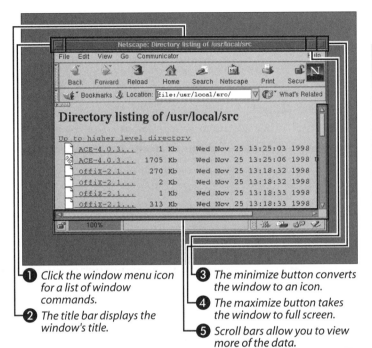

**1** Click the window menu icon for a list of window commands.

**2** The title bar displays the window's title.

**3** The minimize button converts the window to an icon.

**4** The maximize button takes the window to full screen.

**5** Scroll bars allow you to view more of the data.

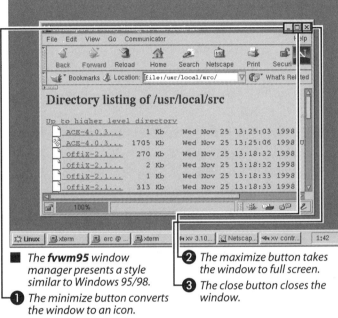

■ The **fvwm95** window manager presents a style similar to Windows 95/98.

**1** The minimize button converts the window to an icon.

**2** The maximize button takes the window to full screen.

**3** The close button closes the window.

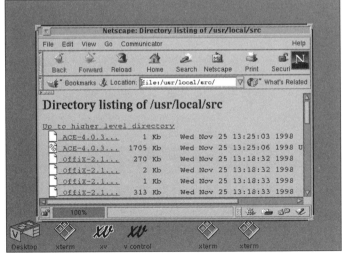

■ The **olwm** window manager presents an Open Look style. Right-click the main icon to see a menu of window commands. Left-click the main button to convert the window to an icon.

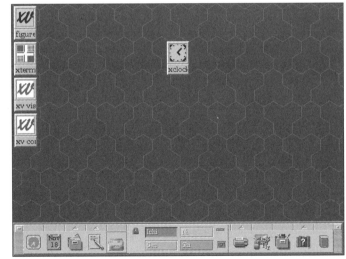

■ The **xclock** icon appears in the middle of the display. You can save a lot of space by minimizing or iconifying programs.

# Launching X

Before you can run an X application, you need to start the X server. The X server takes control of a display — the keyboard, a pointing device (usually a mouse), and at least one video monitor, sometimes more in multi-headed systems.

An X server alone isn't worth much — all you get is a cross-hatch pattern and an X cursor. You also need to start a number of X applications, including a window manager, when you start up the X server. The applications are important; the X server merely provides the infrastructure.

Many UNIX systems ship with X preconfigured to start up. If you're this lucky, then by all means stick with that method. Otherwise, you can start the X server with the **xinit** or the **startx** commands. Of course, if you're already running X, that is, if you see a graphics display in front of you, you don't need to run **xinit**, as this (or the equivalent on your system) has already been done for you.

Normally, **xinit** can run without any arguments:

```
$ xinit
```

The **xinit** command starts the X server, a program named, appropriately enough, **X**, that's normally stored in **/usr/bin/X11**. After starting the X server, **xinit** executes the programs listed in the file **.xinitrc**, which is located in your home directory, much like the **.profile** or **.login** files used by **ksh** and **csh**. This usually includes a graphical clock, at least one **xterm**, and a window manager, such as **twm**, **olwm**, or **mwm**.

In addition to **xinit**, many systems supply a shell script called **startx**. There's no great mystery to **startx** — it merely calls the **xinit** command under the hood. Most PC UNIX systems use **startx** to launch the X server.

Another means of starting X is called XDM, short for *X Display Manager*. Running **xdm** will get you an X Window login screen shown in the third figure on the facing page.

Setting up **xdm** is an advanced topic that should only be attempted by experienced UNIX and X users. An easy change to make, though, is modifying the greeting you see at the top of the login window. Edit the **/usr/lib/X11/xdm/Xresources** file to change this.

With many systems, setting up XDM is taken care of. For example, any Common Desktop Environment system, such as Sun Solaris, Hewlett-Packard HP-UX, or IBM AIX system, should already be running the CDE version of **xdm**, called **dtlogin.**

The basic thing to remember is that if you log in and get an X display, you're already done and probably don't want to take the chance of misconfiguring your system.

---

**TAKE NOTE**

► **X MAY ALREADY BE SET UP**

If you use workstations from Sun, Hewlett-Packard, IBM, Digital Equipment, or Silicon Graphics, X is likely to be set up to launch automatically.

---

**CROSS-REFERENCE**

See Appendix B for a number of X books that can help you with configuring **xdm**.

**FIND IT ONLINE**

For more information on setting up XDM, see **www.gaijin.com/X/**.

X without a **.xinitrc** file to specify applications to launch.

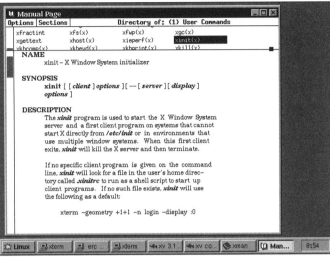

Viewing the online manual entry for **xinit** with the **xman** command.

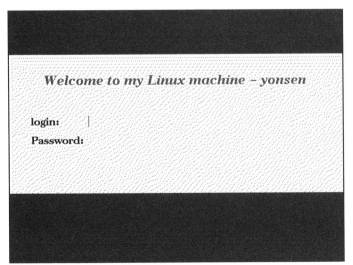

The **xdm** login window.

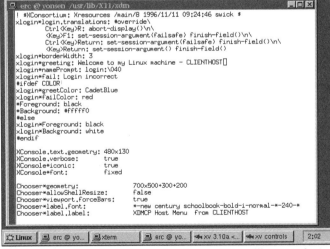

To change the **xdm** login greeting, type: **edit/usr/lib/X11/xdm/ Xresources file**. Change the **xlogin*greeting** entry to contain the new text, in this case, **Welcome to my Linux machine** — CLIENTHOST. **Xdm** replaces the term CLIENTHOST with the name of the system, **yonsen** in this case.

# Configuring X and the .xinitrc File

Typically, when you start X, you want a number of applications to start up. The techniques for customizing the set of applications you see when X starts up follow the same techniques for users who launch X via **xinit**, **startx**, or **XDM**. Common Desktop Environment users should work with the style manager.

When X starts up from **xinit** or **startx**, it looks for a file named **.xinitrc** in your home directory. That file is a shell script and it contains commands to launch all the applications you want. So, to change what runs when X starts, simply edit this file.

If you haven't customized this file before, chances are you don't have a **.xinitrc** file in your home directory. In that case, copy the system master file into your home directory and name the copy **.xinitrc**. The system master file is normally stored at **/usr/lib/X11/xinit/xinitrc**. It's important to copy this master file, since there may be system-specific commands that set up your X environment.

Normally, at the end of the **.xinitrc** file, you specify the applications you want to launch. (The beginning part may have special setup commands for your system which you want to leave alone.) Because **.xinitrc** is a shell script, all the programs it launches, except the last, should be run in the background, with an ampersand (&) trailing the command.

When **.xinitrc** terminates, **xinit** kills the X server. This, in essence, is how you stop X.

If you run every program in **.xinitrc** in the background, then **.xinitrc** will quickly terminate, and so will your X server. To avoid this, run the last program in **.xinitrc** in the foreground, like the example **.xinitrc** file shown here:

```
xterm -geometry 80x24+100+0 &
xclock -geometry 100x100+0+10 &
exec twm
```

This example launches an **xterm** shell window, an **xclock** clock and then runs the window manager, **twm**, in the foreground. The **–geometry** options, explained in the section on Passing X Command-Line Parameters, sets the window's size and position. There are two main reasons for using a window manager as the last program in the **.xinitrc** file. First, you want a window manager running during your entire X session. Second, most window managers provide a menu choice that allows you to exit. This menu choice is an easier (and easier to remember) way to quit X than typing **exit** in an **xterm** window, or using **kill** to terminate the X server. Using the previous example, exiting the window manager also exits **X**.

## TAKE NOTE

### XDM STARTUP

When you log in, **xdm** runs the commands in a file named **.xsession** in your home directory, instead of **.xinitrc**. The concepts that apply to **.xinitrc** also apply to **.xsession**; only the name changes. The system master session file is normally located at **/usr/lib/X11/xdm/Xsession**. Copy this file to your home directory, name it **.xsession**, and edit away.

## CROSS-REFERENCE
Chapter 13 covers shell scripts.

## FIND IT ONLINE
Information on setting up your **.xinitrc** file is available at **www.gaijin.com/X/**.

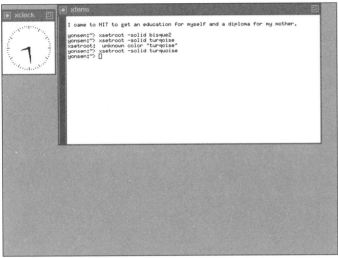

The X startup file discussed in the text, launching the **twm** window manager:

```
xterm -geometry 80x24+100+0 &
xclock -geometry 100x100+0+10 &
exec twm
```

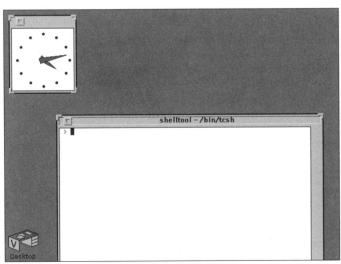

An X startup file that runs the Open Look Window manager, **olwm**:

```
shelltool -geometry 500x300+100+200 &
clock -geometry 120x120+10+10 &
exec olwm
```

Open Look applications typically don't accept **-geom;** instead you must use **-geometry**.

## Listing 7-1: VIEWING A SAMPLE .XINITRC FILE

```
#!/bin/sh
userresources=$HOME/.Xresources
usermodmap=$HOME/.Xmodmap
sysresources=/usr/X11R6/lib/X11/xinit
/.Xresources
sysmodmap=/usr/X11R6/lib/X11/xinit/.Xmodmap

# merge in defaults and keymaps

if [ -f $sysresources ]; then
    xrdb -merge $sysresources
fi

if [ -f $sysmodmap ]; then
    xmodmap $sysmodmap
fi

if [ -f $userresources ]; then
    xrdb -merge $userresources
fi

if [ -f $usermodmap ]; then
    xmodmap $usermodmap
fi

# Start our initial X clients.
xterm -ls -geom 80x40+100+200 &
oclock -geometry 120x120+900+10 &

# Turn on the screen saver.
xset s on

# Start the window manager:
exec twm
```

▲ The full text of a sample **.xinitrc** file. Normally, you only want to customize the commands at the end.

# Working with Shell Windows

Despite all the fuss over the X Window System's value as a graphical user interface for UNIX, we find the most frequently used X program to be **xterm**, and close variants such as **dtterm** on CDE systems or **winterm** on Silicon Graphics systems.

Most users still need to enter UNIX commands at a command shell prompt, mainly because X tools simply aren't advanced enough to completely hide the command prompt and make the shells obsolete. Luckily, we're already well-versed on the UNIX shells. The **xterm** program manages the interface to X so that all of your old text-based programs, such as the **vi** text editor or the **elm** electronic mailer, as well as UNIX commands work just fine inside **xterm**, as shown in the upper-left figure on the facing page.

The **dtterm** program, is a lot like an enhanced **xterm**, except that you get menus from which to chose fonts and other settings. For the most part, **dtterm** acts like **xterm**.

It seems odd to use a graphical windowing system merely for command-line windows, but **xterm** and other shell windows provide more than a simple command line.

You can control the window's size, location, font and font size, as well as the foreground and background colors.

You can have multiple shell windows on screen at the same time — and copy and paste between them. (Select text with the left mouse button. Paste with the middle button (X assumes that you're using a three-button mouse). You don't need to copy data to a clipboard, simply copy and paste.) The last two figures on the facing page demonstrate how to copy and paste between **xterm** windows.

Most shell windows provide a handy scrollbar to review previous commands or the long output of complex programs.

If you like the standard 80-column by 25-line text display, then you'll like an 80-column by 46-line text display even more, particularly if you can have two of these side by side.

## Starting xterm

You can start an **xterm** window (normally from another **xterm**) with the following command:

```
$ xterm &
```

Normally, you'll start the **xterm** in the background, so that you can continue to work in your current terminal. You may want to arrange your X startup configuration to launch more than one **xterm** window — all in the background, by editing your **.xinitrc** file. The **-sb** command-line option starts **xterm** with a scroll bar, an option you almost always want to use. The **–ls** option (login shell) tells **xterm** to read in the **.profile** or **.login** file when starting its shell.

To start **dtterm**, use the **dtterm** command:

```
$ dtterm &
```

**CROSS-REFERENCE**

The previous section on configuring X and the **.xinitrc** file covers how to set up your **.xinitrc** file.

**FIND IT ONLINE**

See **/sunsite.unc.edu/pub/Linux/X11/terms/** for a directory of other shell window programs, including source code.

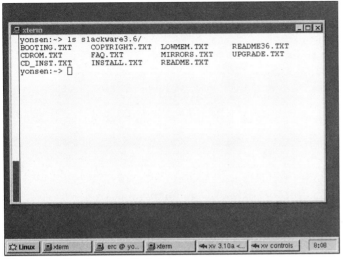

■ *Viewing the **xterm** shell window.*

```
yonsen:~> ls slackware3.6/
BOOTING.TXT      COPYRIGHT.TXT   LOWMEM.TXT      README36.TXT
CDROM.TXT        FAQ.TXT         MIRRORS.TXT     UPGRADE.TXT
CD_INST.TXT      INSTALL.TXT     README.TXT
yonsen:~>
```

■ *Viewing the **dtterm** Common Desktop Environment shell window.*

```
Df-0_0_1_tar.gz
File-Tail-0_81_tar.gz
Filesys-Statvfs_Df-0_51_tar.gz
HTML-Parser-2_22_tar.gz
Logfile-0_202_tar.gz
Net-LDAPapi-1_42_tar.gz
Net-SNMP-1_10_tar.gz
Net-Telnet-3_01_tar.gz
Period-1.20
Period-1_20_tar.gz
SNMP-1_8b3_tar.gz
SNMP-Monitor-0_1007_tar.gz
Time_HiRes_01_19_tar.gz
URI-1.00
URI-1_00_tar.gz
$
$
$
$
```

■ *Select text in an **xterm** window by dragging with the left mouse button held down. The selected text is highlighted.*

```
if [ -f $userresources ]; then
    xrdb -merge $userresources
fi

if [ -f $usermodmap ]; then
    xmodmap $usermodmap
fi


# Start our initial X clients.
xterm -ls -geom 80x35+52+116 -iconic &
xterm -ls -geom 80x22+272+0   &
xterm -ls -geom 80x22+272+370 &

# Turn on the screen saver.
xset s on

# Start the window manager:
exec fvwm95
```

■ *Paste the selected data using the middle mouse button.*

```
yonsen:~> xterm -ls -geom 80x35+52+116 -iconic &
```

# Passing X Command-Line Parameters

Most X programs accept a standard set of command-line parameters. The two most important are the **–display** and **–geometry** parameters.

The **–display** parameter names the X server to display on. As stated before, X applications can run on one system and display their windows on an entirely different system. For a user perspective, the key to this is the **–display** parameter. The basic format is as follows:

```
-display hostname:server.screen
```

The *hostname* is the network name of the system to connect to — the system with the X server. The *server* value is a number that identifies which X server on the *hostname* you want. In most cases, there is only one X server on a given machine, so this number is almost always 0. (Many parts of UNIX start counting with zero instead of one.) The *screen* value is also a number and identifies which screen — usually a physical monitor — to display on. The vast majority of X servers have a single monitor, so again, this number is almost always 0. For example:

```
$ xclock -display yonsen:0.0
```

This command runs **xclock**, connecting to the only X server (and only screen) on machine **yonsen**. Security settings may prevent the **–display** option from working. Consult the **xhost** online-manual entry for more information on this.

The **–geometry** parameter parameter tells an application the desired size and location of its main window. Therefore, you supply the window's width and height, as well as the coordinate location of the upper left corner, in pixels — except for **xterm**. (In X, the screen coordinates start at 0,0 at the top left. The X values increase horizontally across the display, and the Y values increase vertically down the display.) The basic format is *Width • Height +X+Y*.

So, to display an **xclock** window that is 100 pixels wide, 150 pixels high, and located 120 pixels from the left and 300 pixels down from the top, you could use a **-geometry** option of the following:

```
$ xclock –geometry 100x150+120+300
```

You can also omit the size or location, if you are only interested in one part or the other. For example:

```
$ xclock –geometry +120+300
$ xclock –geometry 100x150
```

Table 7-1 lists the most common X command-line parameters. Not every application supports every option. Check the online-manual entries for verification.

---

**TAKE NOTE**

▶ **XTERM USES ROWS AND COLUMNS**

One of the few exceptions to the **–geometry** rule is **xterm**, which uses rows and columns — the number of text character cells — instead of pixels when determining the size. Thus, to display an **xterm** window that is 80 columns across and 32 rows high, you would use a command like the following:

```
$ xterm –geometry 80x32
```

---

**CROSS REFERENCE**

Chapter 5 covers shells.

**FIND IT ONLINE**

For sets of icon bitmaps, see **sunsite.unc.edu/pub/ Linux/X11/icons/**.

## Table 7-1: COMMON X COMMAND-LINE PARAMETERS

| Parameter | Meaning |
| --- | --- |
| **-background** *color* | Sets window background *color*. The **showrgb** command lists available colors. |
| **-bd** *color* | Sets window border *color*. The **showrgb** command lists available colors. |
| **-bg** *color* | Sets window background *color*. The **showrgb** command lists available colors. |
| **-bordercolor** *color* | Sets window border *color*. The **showrgb** command lists available colors. |
| **-borderwidth** *border_width* | Sets window border width, in pixels. |
| **-bw** *border_width* | Sets window border width, in pixels. |
| **-display** *display_name* | Name the display (X server) to connect to. |
| **-fg** *color* | Sets foreground *color*. The **showrgb** command lists available colors. |
| **-fn** *fontname* | Sets font. |
| **-font** *fontname* | Sets font. |
| **-foreground** *color* | Sets foreground *color*. The **showrgb** command lists available colors. |
| **-geometry** *Width · Height +X +Y* | Sets window size and location. |
| **-geometry** *Width · Height* | Sets window size. |
| **-geometry** *+X +Y* | Sets location of upper left corner of window. |
| **-geom** *Width · Height +X +Y* | Sets window size and location. This short name is not supported by many Open Look applications. |
| **-geom** *Width · Height* | Sets window size. This short name is not supported by many Open Look applications. |
| **-geom** *+X +Y* | Sets location of upper left corner of window. This short name is not supported by many Open Look applications. |
| **-iconic** | Starts program as an icon. |
| **-name** *name* | Sets application *name* for grabbing resource values. |
| **-reverse** | Turns on reverse video. |
| **-rv** | Turns on reverse video. |
| **-title** *title* | Sets window title. |
| **-xnllanguage** *language[terr][.code]* | Sets language and optionally territory and codeset for current locale. |
| **-xrm** *resource_command* | Sets the given resource, just like in a resource file. |

# Using the Mouse

Like most other graphical interfaces, such as Windows and MacOS systems, the X Window System requires a mouse. While it is possible to do some things within X strictly from the keyboard, generally speaking you need the mouse to accomplish anything substantial.

The mouse allows you to directly control a pointer on the screen. This pointer is your agent as your move between windows, icons, dialog boxes, pull-down menus, and other screen elements.

Unlike Windows, which uses two-button mice (by default) or the MacOS with its one-button mouse, X assumes that you're using a three-button mouse. X can support up to five buttons. (Yes, there are mice with five or more buttons, but they tend to be limited to the CAD/CAM field.) Internally, X refers to the three mouse buttons as Button1, Button2, and Button3. For a two-button mouse, you can often emulate the missing third button by pressing both buttons at once. For the purposes of this discussion, we refer to the left, middle, and right mouse buttons, assuming that your mouse uses the standard X configuration (which is geared for the right-handed computer user).

Using the mouse to move around the screen real estate isn't a big deal, particularly if you've already done some work on a computer running Windows, OS/2, or the Macintosh operating system.

You can control some of the mouse motion using the **xset** command, which sets X server parameters.

The **xset q** command queries the current settings, shown on the facing page. The **m** option for **xset** allows you to speed up the mouse when moving fast, but still allows for a fine grain of control when you move the mouse more slowly. The basic syntax is:

```
xset m acceleration threshold
```

The *acceleration* controls how much faster (or slower) the mouse should go when moving fast. The *threshold* sets the number of pixels the mouse must move quickly before the acceleration kicks in. For example, an *acceleration* of 2 (or 2/1) with a *threshold* of 40 means that if you move the mouse 40 pixels quickly, then the mouse will start moving twice as fast:

```
$ xset m 2 40
```

This type of control works best on larger screens. With the acceleration turned on, you can move the mouse to the far end of the screen with little motion, so long as you move fast.

Left-handed people, or users not comfortable with the default mouse configurations, can change the mouse buttons through an X client called **xmodmap**. You can swap the first and third mouse buttons to make your mouse work better by using the following command:

```
$ xmodmap -e "pointer = 3 2 1"
```

Except for this instance, **xmodmap** can get complicated very quickly. See the online-manual entry for details of what **xmodmap** can do.

**CROSS-REFERENCE**
You may want to pipe the output of the **xset** command to the **more** command, covered in Chapter 2.

**FIND IT ONLINE**
Logitech, a maker of three-button (and other) mice, is available at **www.logitech.com**.

## Mouse Actions

X allows you to perform many distinct acts with the mouse — probably more than you thought possible. Roughly speaking, X mouse actions can be divided into four groups:

▶ **Click**: Press a mouse button and then release it. The act should be fluid; that is, you shouldn't pause too long between pressing the mouse button and then releasing it. Two clicks in a row represents a double-click.

▶ **Drag**: Position the pointer over an onscreen object (such as a window or an icon), press the left mouse button, and then move the mouse while continuing to hold down the mouse button. As you move the mouse, the window or icon (or an outline representing the window or icon, depending on your system configuration) will move on the screen. When the window or icon reaches the desired destination point, let go of the mouse button.

▶ **Press**: Simply put, you press down the mouse button. At times you'll want to release the mouse button immediately; at other times you'll want to keep the button pressed while you drag a window or choose from a menu.

▶ **Release**: Of course, this is when you let go of the mouse button.

**Listing 7-2: USING THE XSET COMMAND TO QUERY THE CURRENT SETTINGS**

```
$ xset q
Keyboard Control:
   auto repeat:  on  key click percent:  0
   LED mask: 00000000
   auto repeat delay:  500     repeat rate: 5
   auto repeating keys:  00ffffffdffffbbf
                         fa9ffffffffdffdff
                         7f00000000000000
                         0000000000000000
   bell percent:  50  bell pitch: 400  bell
duration: 100
Pointer Control:
   acceleration:  2/1     threshold:  4
Screen Saver:
   prefer blanking:yes allow exposures:yes
   timeout:  600    cycle:  600
Colors:
   default colormap:  0x26    BlackPixel: 0
WhitePixel: 1
Font Path:
   /usr/X11R6/lib/X11/fonts/misc/,
   /usr/X11R6/lib/X11/fonts/Type1/,
   /usr/X11R6/lib/X11/fonts/Speedo/,
   /usr/X11R6/lib/X11/fonts/75dpi/,
   /usr/X11R6/lib/X11/fonts/100dpi/
Bug Mode: compatibility mode is disabled
DPMS (Energy Star):
   Standby: 1200    Suspend: 900    Off: 1800
   DPMS is Disabled
```

▲ *This is an example of using the* **xset** *command to query the current settings on a PC running X emulation software.*

# Setting X Fonts

Most X applications that use fonts will accept a command line parameter to set the font name. Usually, you can use **–fn fontname** or **–font fontname** to set the font.

When you use one of these options, you need to get the name of a valid font. The **xlsfonts** program lists the fonts available on your system. If your system is fully configured, you'll see a listing of hundreds of fonts. Here's a sampling:

```
$ xlsfonts
-adobe-courier-medium-o-normal—12-
120-75-75-m-70-iso8859-1
-adobe-helvetica-bold-r-normal—14-
140-75-75-p-82-iso8859-1
-adobe-times-bold-i-normal—14-140-
75-75-p-77-iso8859-1
-b&h-lucida-bold-r-normal—sans-14-
140-75-75-p-92-iso8859-1
```

Many of these font names tend to be quite long, making it hard to type them correctly. Because of this, we usually copy the name of the font we want with the mouse and then paste the name on the command line. You can see a font using the **xfd** command:

```
$ xfd —fn fontname
```

You can also interactively select a font using the **xfontsel** program, shown in the second figure.

Shell windows are a special case. When picking fonts, you want to ensure that you get a fixed-width font rather than a proportional font. Most of this book is set using a proportional font. The code examples, though, use a fixed-width font.

To select a fixed-width font, look for a single letter near the end of the font name, which will be a **p** (proportional), **m** (monospaced) or **c** (character cell, also fixed width). For example, the following font is a proportional font:

```
-adobe-times-bold-i-normal—14-140-75-75-p-
77-iso8859-1
```

You want an **m** or a **c**. A good font for regular use in a shell window is:

```
-adobe-courier-medium-r-normal—
12-120-75-75-m-70-iso8859-1
```

We find this font much better looking than the small font named **fixed**, the default **xterm** font.

When setting a font for a shell window, use the **–fn** parameter. For example:

```
$ xterm -fn fontname &
$ dtterm -fn fontname &
$ winterm -fn fontname &
```

In each case, *fontname* is the valid name of an X font installed on your system. Use **xlsfonts** to get a list of the available fonts.

## TAKE NOTE

### ▶ WATCH OUT FOR DASHES

Most font names start with a dash, -, the same character most UNIX applications use to signify a command line parameter. Because of this, you should use double quotes around the font names.

## CROSS-REFERENCE

Chapter 1 covers running commands in the background.

## FIND IT ONLINE

For more on X font names, see **www.pconline.com/ ~erc/xfonts.htm**.

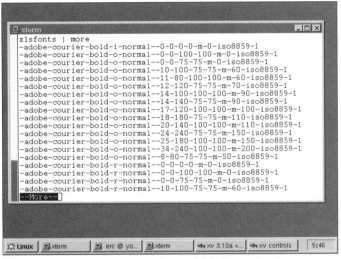

The **xlsfonts** command lists the available fonts. Pipe the output to more.

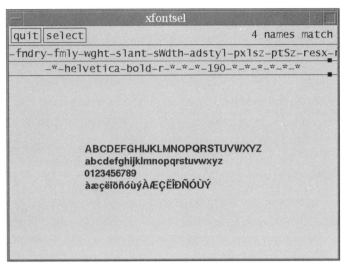

The **xfontsel** program helps you select fonts. Select one of the items near the top of the window, in the line starting with **fndry** and then choose the values you want from the pull-down menu. When you're done, click **select** to place your choice in the X copy and paste buffer.

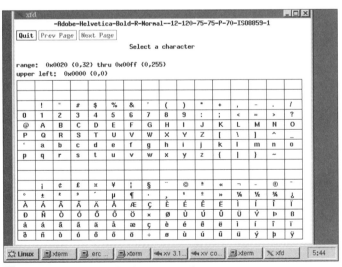

The **xfd** command displays a given font.

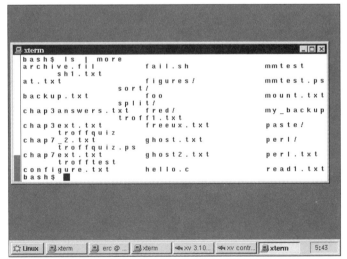

This weird display is what you'll see if you accidentally use a variable-width font with an **xterm** window. Don't do this.

# Basic X Applications

Along with **xterm**, some other basic X applications include the clock programs **xclock** and **oclock**, the calculator **xcalc**, the clipboard holder **xclipboard**, and the text editor, **xedit**. These are part of the standard X Window System release. Many UNIX vendors add additional programs.

The **xclipboard** program acts as a holding area for selected text. You can use it to maintain a number of entries of selected text at one time — normally, X only allows one text selection at any given time. With **xclipboard**, you can save multiple selections.

The **xedit** program forms a very primitive text editor. You can use it if you don't want to learn **vi** or **emacs**, but it's not really meant for daily usage.

Systems with Open Windows include many applications, including the text-editing program called **textedit**, shown in the second figure on the facing page. This program is much better than **xedit**, but then, most editors are.

Common Desktop Environment systems include a text editor called **dtpad**, an icon editor called **dticon**, an enhanced terminal window called **dtterm**, an electronic mail program called **dtmail**, a calendar and scheduling program called **dtcm**, and more. The CDE style manager, **dtstyle**, appears in the third figure on the facing page. This program allows you to control the screen background, window colors, and other aspects of the Common Desktop Environment. You can launch most of the CDE applications from the CDE front panel.

In addition to the applications that come with your system, you can purchase many commercial applications that run under X. Of course, UNIX is justly famous for its freeware and you can find zillions of available X applications, including the TkDesk file manager, shown in the last figure on the facing page.

One problem that may plague your system is the inability to find the X programs in your command path. If you get a "command not found" error when you run any X command, this is probably the case.

The default location for X Window binary executables is in **/usr/bin/X11**, which is a directory that isn't in your normal command path — unless your system administrator or workstation vendor took care of this detail for you. On Linux, X applications normally reside in **/usr/X11R6/bin**. Make sure your PATH environment variable includes the directories where your X programs reside. With OpenWindows, the default location for X programs is in **/usr/openwin/bin**. The Common Desktop Environment applications usually are located in **/usr/dt/bin**.

## TAKE NOTE

### FINDING OUT WHAT'S AVAILABLE

Look in **/usr/bin/X11** for most X applications. You're likely to find a few surprises. You can find graphical demos (so-called "eye candy"), handy utility programs, screen capture applications, and perhaps a graphical editor or two. The X applications on your system depend on which version of UNIX you run.

## CROSS-REFERENCE

Chapter 4 covers environment variables. Chapter 8 covers e-mail. Chapter 14 describes how to compile UNIX freeware.

## FIND IT ONLINE

The TkDesk file manager is available at **people.mainz.netsurf.de/~bolik/tkdesk/**.

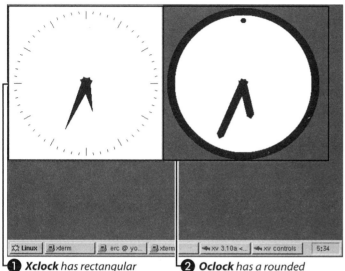

**❶ Xclock** has rectangular borders.

**❷ Oclock** has a rounded window.

**❶** Tear-off menus using a push pin metaphor are a major feature of Open Look interfaces.

**❷** Rounded-corner buttons are another distinctive feature of Open Look applications.

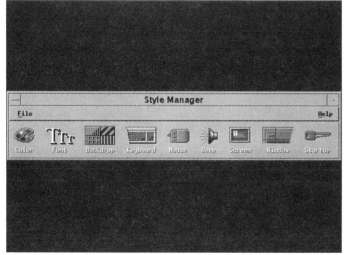

**■** You can control the look of the desktop with the **dtstyle** style manager, part of the Common Desktop Environment.

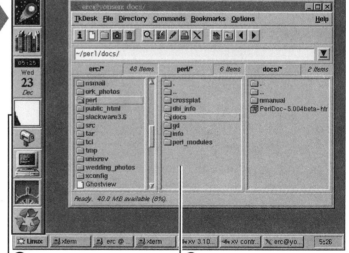

**❶** The **tkdesk** file manager includes an application bar along the left-hand side of the screen to quickly launch applications.

**❷** A file manager window similar to Windows Explorer appears.

# Personal Workbook

## Q&A

**1** Name three ways to start X.

_____

_____

_____

**2** You have a workstation running X and a large file and application server running X applications that you display on your workstation. In X terms, which is the client and which is the server?

_____

_____

_____

**3** The X display is too bright. What can you do to make windows appear darker?

_____

_____

_____

**4** How do you select text in an **xterm** window and paste the text into another window?

_____

_____

**5** How can you list the available fonts?

_____

_____

_____

**6** How can you visually select a font?

_____

_____

_____

**7** What don't you want in a font used for a shell window such as **xterm**?

_____

_____

_____

**8** What can you use to display the time on your screen?

_____

_____

_____

**ANSWERS: PAGE 348**

## EXTRA PRACTICE

1 Determine which window manager you are running.

2 Change your window manager from the default click-to-type keyboard focus policy to the focus-follows-mouse policy.

3 Track down the X applications on your system. Look in **/usr/bin/X11**, **/usr/openwin/bin**, and **/usr/dt/bin**.

4 Practice with the **–geometry** command-line parameter. Try making very large windows, very small windows, and position windows about the screen to see the effects. The **xclock** program is a good application to use for practice.

## REAL-WORLD APPLICATIONS

✔ When you log in every morning, X takes a long time to start up, so you go get a cup of coffee during this time. To make matters worse, often when you get back to your desk, you need to launch extra **xterm** windows before you can really get started. Modify your X startup to launch two extra **xterm** windows.

✔ Your X display is hard to read because the colors don't work well under the office lighting. Experiment with colors and then configure your X startup applications to use a more effective color arrangement.

✔ The XDM login window displays a really dorky message. You have an important demonstration in a few minutes and the first thing people will see is the message. Change the XDM login greeting to something more professional-looking.

## Visual Quiz

This figure shows an **xterm** window in the middle of a display. One of the great advantages of X over normal text-based terminals is that you can display many shell windows at once. How would you move the window over to the left to open up space on this display?

_____

_____

_____

_____

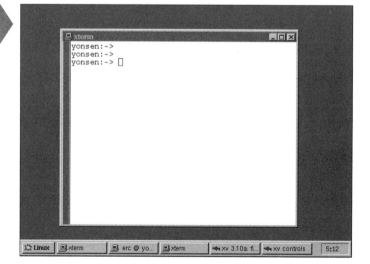

# PART

# II

# Hello, Neighbor!

After your extensive introduction to UNIX basics, you're now ready to take this operating system for a spin and tackle some real-world tasks. The next three chapters cover an area where UNIX is unique — networking capability. UNIX was designed from the beginning to be a networked operating system, and anyone connected to a UNIX network has a powerful set of networking tools at their disposal.

Chapter 8 teaches the basics of electronic mail and how to send mail both to local network users as well as the users of the global Internet. Chapter 9 covers the Internet in detail, showing you how to use Netscape Navigator to cruise the World Wide Web, read your mail, and check out the Usenet newsgroups. The Internet is built upon the same networking protocols that power the UNIX operating system, and one could persuasively argue that the Internet would not have been possible without the technology of UNIX to power it. Navigator has become ubiquitous in the UNIX world, and chances are high that it will be your Web browser of choice when working with the Internet.

The last section takes a look at UNIX networking and how you can use it to your advantage. If you mastered the Internet in Chapter 9, dealing with networking in Chapter 10 will be easy — just think globally and act locally.

# CHAPTER 8

**MASTER THESE SKILLS**

▶ Introducing Various Mail Tools

▶ Opening Your Mail

▶ Responding to Mail

▶ Managing Your Mail

▶ Working with Attachments

# Electronic Mail

From businesses to home users, e-mail connects the world and UNIX provides a large part of the Internet infrastructure that sends mail.

While it originally started as plain text, e-mail has advanced into images, sound clips, and even videos. E-mail software, in turn, has advanced from the primitive **mail** program to glitzy graphical interfaces on programs such as Netscape Navigator and the Common Desktop Environment mail tool, **dtmail**.

One thing that connects all these tools together is a reliance on e-mail standards. The reason you find so many e-mail software packages is because standards give developers all over the world access to the same playing field.

To send an e-mail message to a person, you need that person's e-mail address. Following standards, e-mail addresses have two parts: a domain and a user name. The domain tells the e-mail software which area of the Internet should get the message, such as a university, corporation, or Internet Service Provider. These domains work in a hierarchical fashion. For example, Sun, a large player in the UNIX market, has a domain of sun.com. The .com part specifies that Sun is a corporation with a domain registered in the USA. The sun part names the subdomain that Sun maintains.

The user names the person who should receive the message, usually by way of a login or account name.

In e-mail addresses, the user name comes first, and then an at sign, @, and then the domain. For example,

```
efoster-johnson@bigfun.com
```

In this case, the user name is **efoster-johnson** (using the first initial and last name is a very common scheme used by companies for e-mail addresses. So is first name, a period, and the last name, such as **eric.foster-johnson**.) In this example, the domain is the fictitious company **bigfun.com** (really the *bigfun* domain within the *com* domain).

An older form of e-mail address uses the bang character, !, to separate each system that separates your system from the e-mail recipient, with the user name at the end. For example:

```
uunet!concubine!kevin
```

# Introducing Various Mail Tools

To read e-mail, you need a mail program, often abbreviated in typical computerese i.e., computer terminology as an MUA or Mail User Agent. In true UNIX fashion, you have a great deal of choice when picking an e-mail program.

UNIX mail programs come in two main flavors: graphical tools that sport an X Window user interface, and text-only tools that can work from a dumb terminal or telnet session.

## Graphical Mail Tools

Graphical mail tools, of course, are more fun than simple text-only tools. With the X Window System in place, you can get a number of e-mail programs that run in the graphical environment. Netscape Communicator is one of the most popular, especially since it's now free. Netscape runs on most versions of UNIX, including Linux. While Netscape is known mainly for its Web browsing capabilities, it also includes a handy e-mail package, shown in the first figure on the facing page.

If your system includes the Common Desktop Environment, or CDE, included with most Sun, DEC, Hewlett-Packard, and IBM workstations, you should have a program called **dtmail**. You can launch **dtmail** from the mail icon on the CDE front panel, shown in the third figure on the facing page.

In addition to **dtmail** and Netscape, you can pick from a number of freely-available mail tools. One of the best is called Ratatosk, named after a squirrel in Norse mythology, and shown in the last figure on the facing page. Ratatosk is often abbreviated as tkrat, since it uses Tcl/Tk, a UNIX scripting language.

For all their apparent differences, these graphical e-mail tools actually work quite similarly. In most cases, you see a scrolled list of all your messages. Each message will have some form of indicator to remind you whether you read the message or not.

When you create new messages, you tend to get a separate composition window, like the one shown in the upper-right figure on the opposite page.

All of the tools listed here provide the means to organize e-mail messages into separate folders, the topic of the fourth task in this chapter.

The main limitations of these tools are that they require an X Window session to run. If you aren't running X, you can't run these tools.

In that case, you probably want to use a text-based e-mail tool. If all else fails, all UNIX systems should have a program called **mail, Mail,** or **mailx**, all of which provide a command-line interface to e-mail. Flip the page to read about text-based tools.

*Continued*

---

**TAKE NOTE**

▶ **X MARKS THE SPOT**
All the graphical mail tools require you to run the X Window System.

---

**CROSS-REFERENCE**
Chapter 9 covers the World Wide Web.

**FIND IT ONLINE**
Netscape Ratatosk is available from **www.dtek. chalmers.se/~maf/ratatosk/**.

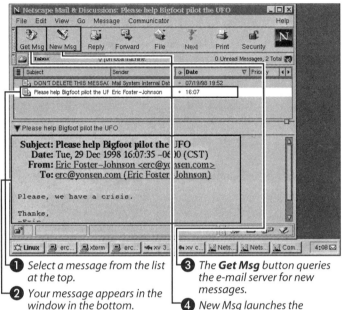

① *Select a message from the list at the top.*

② *Your message appears in the window in the bottom.*

③ *The **Get Msg** button queries the e-mail server for new messages.*

④ *New Msg launches the Compose window, from which you can create new messages.*

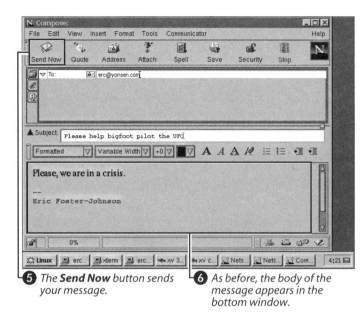

⑤ *The **Send Now** button sends your message.*

⑥ *As before, the body of the message appears in the bottom window.*

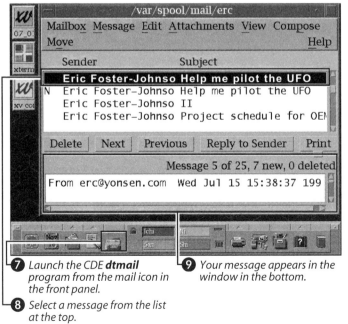

⑦ *Launch the CDE **dtmail** program from the mail icon in the front panel.*

⑧ *Select a message from the list at the top.*

⑨ *Your message appears in the window in the bottom.*

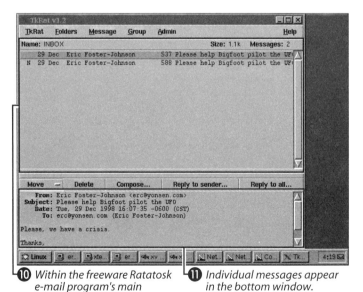

⑩ *Within the freeware Ratatosk e-mail program's main window, a list of messages appears in the top window, like other graphical e-mail tools.*

⑪ *Individual messages appear in the bottom window.*

# Introducing Various Mail Tools
*Continued*

## Text-Based Tools

In addition to the X Window-based graphical tools, UNIX supports a number of text-only tools. These tools are quite handy, especially if you don't have an X Window display running. You can run the text-based tools from a dial-in terminal or a **telnet** session. Even on an X Window display, you can run a text-based mail tool in a shell window, such as that provided by **xterm**.

The **mail** program, a text-based mail tool, has been an important part of UNIX almost since the very beginning. As UNIX evolved, so has **mail**—to an extent. The actual electronic-mail mechanisms are similar to the original **mail** mechanisms; changes mainly concern how a user interacts with a **mail** program. A sample session with **mail** appears on the facing page in the first two figures.

The **mail** program presents a simple command-line interface to electronic mail. You can send messages, read messages, delete messages, and save messages to files from within **mail**. As with many UNIX command-line interfaces, you enter **Ctrl-D**—the UNIX end of file marker—to end input. Because of this, **mail** often works better if you compose messages with a text editor and then use input redirection when sending the message. The main advantage to **mail** is that it should be available on all UNIX systems in some form or another.

In addition to **mail**, a number of friendlier text-based mail tools can make your life much easier. When **elm**, shown in the upper-right figure on the

facing page, starts up, it quickly presents a window of all your incoming messages. The program is surprisingly fast. You can select the message to read using the arrow keys. Pressing **Enter** displays the message. Because of its speed and efficiency, **elm** has proven to be our favorite tool. It's very fast and you can be quite productive with it, even though it doesn't sport a fancy user interface.

Another text-based e-mail tool is called **pine**, continuing the tree-based naming scheme. The main claim to fame of **pine**, shown in the three figures on the facing page, is that **pine** was designed for newcomers to UNIX and makes every effort to help the nonexpert user. The **elm** mailer, in contrast, doesn't present as much helpful information and expects the user to know more.

### TAKE NOTE

▶ **MAIL BY ANY OTHER NAME**

If the **mail** program isn't available on your system, check for **mailx** or **Mail**.

▶ **DIFFERING VERSIONS OF MAIL**

The procedures described here may not appear exactly the same on your system, as there are a number of close variants to **mail**, which vary in how they present information to the user. Most of our examples are based on the BSD **mail** program and the SVR4 **mailx** program (which are virtually identical). Still, the commands and concepts we present here should be applicable to almost every electronic-mail situation you might encounter.

### CROSS-REFERENCE
Chapter 10 covers networking.

### FIND IT ONLINE
Information on **elm** is available at **www.myxa. com/elm.html**.

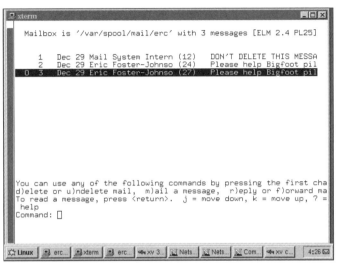

*When **elm** starts up, it lists your current messages.*

*This is the starting screen of the **pine** mail tool, which is known for its friendliness.*

*Here is the main **pine** window showing a menu of choices, including HELP.*

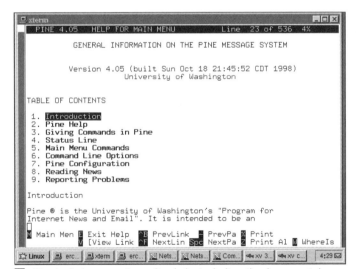

*Pine includes extensive online help, including the document shown here, which you can display with the HELP menu choice or the ? command.*

# Opening Your Mail

As we learned in Chapter 1, UNIX informs you of incoming mail when you log in the system. You see a message which looks something like this:

```
You have mail.
```

Unless you read your mail at this point, this message will reappear periodically, as the shell is automatically set up to remind you of unread mail.

To view this mail, use the **mail** command:

```
$ mail
Mail version 4.0. Type ? for help.
2 messages:
2 reichard@mr.net  Sat Aug 30 2:45 11/274
 "Stuff"
1 eric Thu Aug 21 21:25 11/274 "Hello"
```

The **mail** program responds with a list of your mail messages, listed in the order that they were received by your system, newest mail first. The first field lists the sender of the message, the second through fifth fields denote the time and date the message was received, the sixth field records the number of lines in the message and the size of the message (in bytes), and the final field indicates the subject of the message, such as "Stuff" or "Hello" — heavy subjects indeed.

Press **Enter** to read the first message on the list. If it's a long message, the entire message will scroll by. If you want to stop scrolling the message, type **Ctrl-S**; to start it again, type **Ctrl-Q**. As you can tell, **mail** does not present a fancy interface at all.

Your electronic mail can come from two sources: your own system and from other systems. Mail from other systems, sent on the Internet, uses the domain-style addressing discussed at the beginning of this chapter. Mail from your own system uses the same login names as described in Chapter 1; these names are contained in the **/etc/passwd** file.

The **mail** command forms a primitive means to handle your e-mail. Its main advantage is that it should be available on all UNIX systems. That's about all **mail** has going for it. Most users select another tool. Your system administrator should be able to help you select from among the tools installed. (Many sites, of course, follow a strict model and mandate a particular tool.)

The facing page shows how to read mail from a friendlier tool: **pine**.

## TAKE NOTE

### ▶ WHERE IS YOUR MAIL STORED?

Your incoming mail messages are usually contained in the file **/usr/mail/yourname**, **/usr/spool/mail/yourname**, or **/usr/spool/mqueue/yourname**. The mail server on your system places the messages there.

### ▶ CONFIGURING YOUR MAIL TOOL

You may need to configure your e-mail tool to specify where to get mail from, a mail server or from your local hard disk. See your system administrator for the specification for your system.

**CROSS-REFERENCE**

Chapter 7 covers the X Window System, used by graphical mail tools such as Netscape.

**FIND IT ONLINE**

For more information on **pine**, see the Pine Information Center at **www.washington.edu/pine/**.

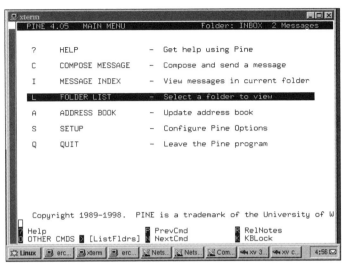

In **pine**, select FOLDER LIST from the main menu.

Select the folder you want to view. In most cases, this will be the INBOX, where your incoming messages appear.

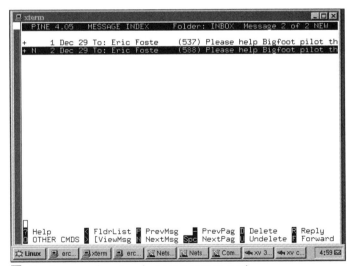

Use the arrow keys to select a message to read.

The **V** command views the selected message.

# Responding to Mail

It's very easy to create mail. To create a short message at the keyboard, simply combine **mail** with the e-mail address of the recipient. Make sure you type the e-mail address very carefully, otherwise your message will bounce back. Your message should follow this style:

```
$ mail reichard@mr.net
Subject: test
This, too, is a test.
```

As always, end input from the keyboard by typing **Ctrl-D**. Some e-mail programs also accept a single period on its own line to terminate the message, instead of **Ctrl-D**.

Sending an existing file as the text of an electronic-mail message is almost as simple. After creating an ASCII file using **vi** or **emacs**, save the file and then redirect it as input on the command line:

```
$ mail reichard@mr.net < note
```

In this case, **note** is the name of the file.

The Berkeley UNIX **mailx** program allows you to call up a text editor from within **mailx**, by using the ~**v** command. You must start this command on its own line:

```
% mailx kevin
~v
```

Unless you've configured your system differently, the default text editor will be **vi**. Edit your message using the **vi** commands and then exit **vi** with the **ZZ** (save and exit) command. Back in the **mailx** program, a single period on a line of its own ends the message. Other tools like **elm** also call up **vi** to enter messages.

The facing page shows an alternate approach using the **dtmail** mail tool to send a message. Select **New Message** from the Compose menu to call up the **dtmail** compose window. You can also launch **dtmail** with a composition window using the –**c** command-line parameter:

```
$ dtmail –c &
```

This provides a much friendlier interface than the **mail** program, as does Netscape.

## TAKE NOTE

### ▶ E-MAIL TIPS

Typing in e-mail addresses is a time-consuming and error-prone process. Messages with bad e-mail addresses tend to *bounce back* to you with an error message. But, this process of bouncing back may take a number of days. Sometimes you never even know whether or not the recipient actually received your message. So, it's a good idea to respond to all messages — except for junk mail — letting the sender know that you received the original message.

### ▶ SAVE E-MAIL ADDRESSES

You can avoid typing in e-mail addresses by storing commonly-used e-mail addresses in an address book. Some e-mail software supports this feature and some do not.

**CROSS-REFERENCE**

Chapter 11 covers the **vi** text editor.

**FIND IT ONLINE**

Netscape Communicator is available from **www.netscape.com/**.

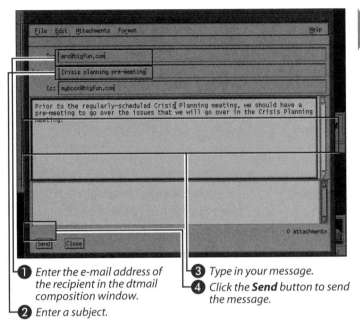

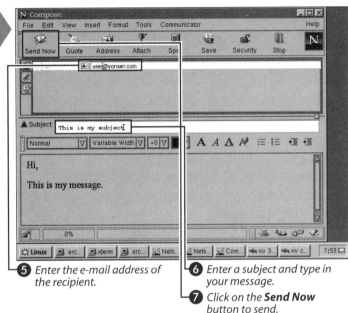

**1** *Enter the e-mail address of the recipient in the dtmail composition window.*

**2** *Enter a subject.*

**3** *Type in your message.*

**4** *Click the* **Send** *button to send the message.*

**5** *Enter the e-mail address of the recipient.*

**6** *Enter a subject and type in your message.*

**7** *Click on the* **Send Now** *button to send.*

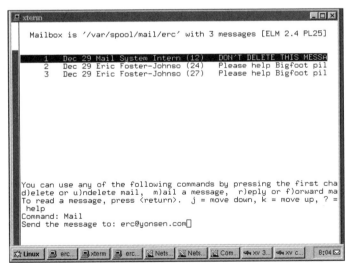

■ *The* **m** *command tells* **elm** *to send a message. Enter the recipient's e-mail address and press Enter.*

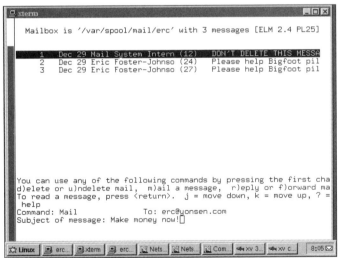

■ *Enter the subject for the message and press Enter. Enter the message in the editor, usually* **vi**. *When done, choose* **s** *to send.*

# Managing Your Mail

Mail is really easy to send. This typically means that you will get a lot of messages. When you start getting lots of e-mail messages, the hard part becomes managing the information. The best way to handle a message, of course, is to delete it. You only want to do this if you are sure you're done with the message, though.

With the **mail** program, a question prompt appears after you read a message. It asks what you'd like to do with the current message. Use the **d** command to delete the current message:

```
? d
```

If the message is important, you can save it to a file. Use the **s** command to do this:

```
? s
```

If you don't specify a filename, the message is saved to the file **$HOME/mbox**. If you don't get many messages, it's no big deal to save them all to the same file. But if you get a lot of messages on a wide variety of topics, it's a good idea to introduce some organization to your mail habits.

Let's say you're working on a project with user **erc**, and you want to keep all of his mail messages in the same file. You do so with the **s** command at the **?** prompt:

```
? s erc.mail
```

In this case, **erc.mail** is the name of the file containing his mail messages. When you do this the first

time, the **mail** program creates a file named **erc.mail**. Subsequent uses will append mail messages to the existing **erc.mail** file.

To read this file, use **mail** with the **-f** option:

```
$ mail -f erc.mail
```

If you work on many projects, you can use folders to organize your e-mail. Supported by Netscape, **dtmail, elm, pine,** and other packages, you can save a message to a *folder*—a named repository of messages. In our work, we use hundreds of folders. We have folders for projects, company policies, memos, and also fun messages that we get now and then. The facing page demonstrates how to use folders from **elm** and **pine**.

## TAKE NOTE

### DON'T ASSUME YOUR MESSAGES ARE PRIVATE

Since mail messages normally appear in unencrypted text files, anyone with super user privileges, such as your system administrator, can read your mail. Even if you delete a message, the original text may have been backed up to tape. In fact, U.S. government investigators have used recovered messages in criminal investigations.

To bring the matter closer to home, few businesses have any policy at all regarding the privacy of electronic-mail communications. So, when in doubt, assume that your boss can read your mail.

---

## CROSS-REFERENCE

Chapter 2 covers a plethora of file-management commands.

## FIND IT ONLINE

For more on the CDE **dtmail** program, see **www.opengroup.org/**.

## Table 8-1: A SELECTION OF COMMANDS IN THE MAIL PROGRAM

| Command | Result |
|---------|--------|
| **Enter** | Prints next message. |
| **-** | Prints previous message. |
| **d** | Deletes current message. |
| **d**N | Deletes message number N. |
| **dp** | Deletes current message and goes to the next message. |
| **dq** | Deletes current message and quits. |
| **u** N | Restores message N. |
| **s** *filename* | Saves message to *filename*. If *filename* is not specified, message is saved to **$HOME/mbox**. |

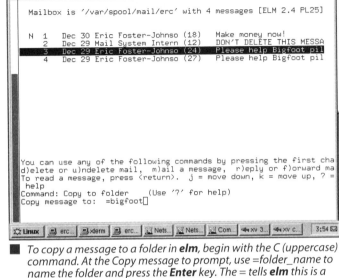

To copy a message to a folder in **elm**, begin with the C (uppercase) command. At the Copy message to prompt, use =folder_name to name the folder and press the **Enter** key. The = tells **elm** this is a folder, not a file.

To save a message to a folder in **pine**, select the message you want to save to a folder. Press O for other commands. The menu at the bottom of the screen changes to show more commands. Select S to save.

Type in the folder name and press **Enter**. The message will be moved to the folder.

# Working with Attachments

ail standards dictate that all messages should consist entirely of text. This allows for easier message transmission between disparate systems. But, this is not realistic when you need to send items such as images via e-mail. Various e-mail programs include different ways to attach such files to e-mail messages. Each scheme includes a different means to encode binary files as text-only e-mail attachments.

After years of ad hoc methods, the Internet powers that be came up with MIME, short for Multipurpose Internet Mail Extensions, a standard for attaching binary files to text-only e-mail messages. MIME defines a way to encode binary files as text (called **base64**). Most UNIX mail programs work with MIME, but many PC-only packages still work with only proprietary formats for attachments.

While most UNIX mail tools support MIME, **mail** won't handle attachments itself. If you use command-line mail readers such as **mail**, you need to run another program to create the MIME format attachment. Unfortunately, most such programs require you to know intimate details of MIME. It's almost always better to run a mail program that can handle MIME attachments, such as Netscape Communicator.

A tool such as **pine** prompts you through all the steps for selecting a file and attaching it.

The **uuencode** command provides an older way to convert binary files to printable text. A number of PC e-mail packages that don't support MIME support uuencode instead. Thus, if your recipient cannot handle MIME attachments, you may be able to encode the file using the **uuencode** command and then manually insert the data into a mail message. The syntax for **uuencode** is:

```
$ uuencode file_to_encode name_in_file >\
encoded_file
```

The *file_to_encode* is the name of the binary file you want to send. The *name_in_file* is the name **uuencode** will place inside the file so that when the file is decoded, it will have that name. The result is the *encoded_file*.

Next, take the output *encoded_file* and place it in the message. You can use input redirection to send the file to the **mail** command:

```
$ mail reichard@mr.net < encoded_file
```

You can decode a file encoded by **uuencode** using the **uudecode** command:

```
$ uudecode encoded_file
```

The name of the file created will come from inside the *encoded_file*. Look for a line that looks like:

```
begin 644 filename
```

### TAKE NOTE

#### ▶ BINARY FILES TEND TO BE LARGE

You can really choke up an e-mail server if you send a multimegabyte attachment. Sound, image, and video files tend to be very large, so you need to be careful.

### CROSS-REFERENCE

Text formatting is covered in Chapter 12.

### FIND IT ONLINE

More information on MIME is available at **www.oac.uci.edu/indiv/ehood/MIME/ MIME.html**.

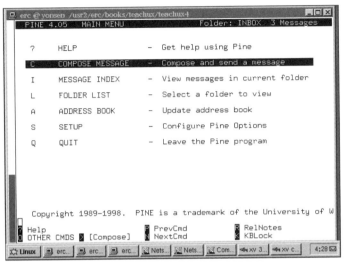

To create a MIME attachment in **pine**, select COMPOSE MESSAGE from the main menu and press **Enter**.

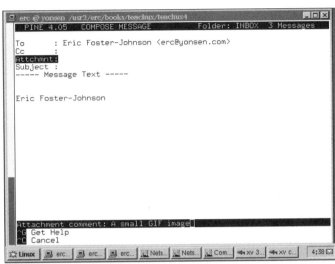

Highlight Attchmnt (short for attachment). Press **Ctrl-J**. You will see the menu at the bottom of the screen change.

Press **Ctrl-T** to get a list of files. Use the arrow keys to highlight the file you want to attach. Press S (short for select) when you have selected the file you want to attach.

At the Attchmnt prompt, type in a comment that helps describe the attachment and press the Enter key. This comment may help your recipient decode the message.

# Personal Workbook

## Q&A

**1** If all else fails and you don't have any friendly e-mail tools, what program should still be available to send and receive e-mail?

_____

_____

_____

**2** To send a message to a person, you need one crucial piece of information to identify that person. What is it?

_____

_____

_____

**3** If you're not running X, and still hate primitive mail tools, name two programs you could try.

_____

_____

_____

**4** How can you send a file using the **mail** program?

_____

_____

_____

**5** If you have too many mail messages in your in box, but want to keep the messages, what can you do?

_____

_____

_____

**6** How do you list your current messages in **pine**?

_____

_____

_____

**7** How do you send a message with **dtmail**?

_____

_____

_____

**8** What is an attachment? What problems can people face with attachments?

_____

_____

_____

ANSWERS: PAGE 349

## EXTRA PRACTICE

1. Send a word processor document as an attachment.

2. Send an e-mail message to yourself and look at the mail header information. What can this tell you about the message?

3. Look at the online-manual entry for your mail tool.

4. See if your system has **elm** or **pine** installed. If so, try out a new mail tool.

5. Save a message to a file with the **mail** program.

6. Download Netscape Communicator to try out its e-mail software.

## REAL-WORLD APPLICATIONS

✔ You need to send an e-mail message to a person named Magnus Magnuson who works for a corporation named Spacely Sprockets. You don't know his e-mail address but you really need to send a message. Since Magnus is a user in a commercial enterprise, can you guess some potential e-mail addresses he could have?

✔ You don't really trust the way your mail tool stores your incoming messages. Go through your messages and save the most important ones to files on disk, so you can make your own backup.

✔ You have a hard time typing in e-mail addresses because they tend to be complicated and long. Set up an address book to store your most frequently used e-mail addresses.

## Visual Quiz

How would you begin to send an e-mail message from the **pine** screen shown here?

_____

_____

_____

_____

_____

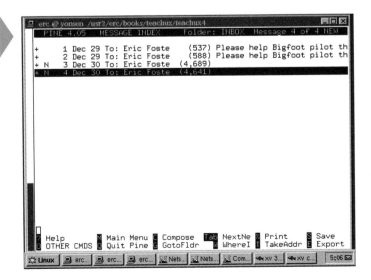

# CHAPTER 9

**MASTER THESE SKILLS**

▶ Surfing the World Wide Web

▶ Catching the URLy Bird

▶ Accessing the Web

▶ Tracing Your Steps

▶ Managing Your Bookmarks

▶ Security and the Internet

▶ Accessing the Usenet

▶ Using Other Web Protocols

# The Internet, World Wide Web, and Netscape Navigator

This is not an exaggeration. The Internet is the result of a natural evolution in networking that began with the UNIX operating system and built upon UNIX standards. The main networking protocol used in the UNIX operating system — TCP/IP — is also the main networking protocol used on the Internet.

Today, most UNIX systems feature some sort of connectivity to the Internet, whether it's a limited connection for electronic mail or a fuller connection for access to the World Wide Web and Usenet newsgroups. Any limits on this connectivity don't come from UNIX itself — after all, any operating system that supports TCP/IP can support the Internet. Those limits come from system administrators who match the offerings of the Internet with the needs of their users. Most UNIX systems now feature some sort of Web browser, most likely the seemingly ubiquitous Netscape Navigator, part of the Netscape Communicator package, as users and corporations are now making Internet access a mandatory part of the computing experience.

The simple reason for this: The Internet and the World Wide Web are incredibly efficient and exciting ways of distributing information. The potential of the Web has been barely scratched, and when all is said and done, the Web (or, more likely, its descendants) will profoundly alter publishing and communications as we know them. We're already seeing the essential nature of the Internet in our daily lives, as more schools, businesses, and households become connected to the Internet.

Such grandiose statements, of course, are a dime a dozen in the computer world (and, to be honest, we usually scoff at such statements ourselves). But the World Wide Web is a case where the hype is warranted — both because of the makeup of the Web itself and the economics of using the Web.

Today, the Web is used both for internal computing purposes and for the public Internet. Many corporations are now junking their legacy systems in favor of intranets, where Internet standards are applied to internal networks. For the purposes of this chapter, it doesn't matter whether you're using Netscape Navigator on an intranet or the Internet — you'll still be browsing Web pages and gathering information.

# Surfing the World Wide Web

To access the World Wide Web, you need a *Web browser* of some sort. The most famous Web browser is Netscape Navigator, a commercial browser from Netscape Communications. In the UNIX world, Netscape Navigator is the most popular Web browser, as it's available for every UNIX platform. Since Netscape Communications decided to make Netscape Navigator available free of charge, many UNIX vendors have begun including it with their UNIX distributions. Netscape Navigator also comes with most distributions of Linux, including Slackware Linux and Red Hat Linux.

In this chapter, we cover Netscape Navigator as a general-purpose tool for all your Internet usage, beginning with the World Wide Web and ending with discussions of the Usenet and other older Internet protocols.

At its core, the World Wide Web is actually an ingeniously simple beast. A Web browser, such as Netscape Navigator, sends a request over the network to a Web server. The server then honors the request by sending a text file formatted in the HyperText Markup Language (HTML), a file that uses tags to tell the Web browser how to render the text. The text file is then rendered by the local Web browser, which matches the tags to resources on the local machine — for instance, a tag for a title would be rendered in a font and point size set up through the Web browser.

The HTML language also allows graphics and hypertext links to be embedded in the document.

The hyperlinks are set off in a different color within the rendered document. For instance, in the figure on the top left of the opposite page, we see the IDG home page makes reference to CNN Interactive and IDG.net. The actual address that would be used by the Internet is **www.idg.com/www/idg/sections.nsf/IMS98/HTML/index.html?OpenDocument**. You don't need to enter any of this by hand; instead, you can just use your mouse and click the link.

Netscape Navigator is one component of Netscape Communicator. The other components are also shown on the opposite page: Netscape Composer (an HTML editor); Netscape Mail (used for electronic mail); Netscape Mail & Discussions (used for reading postings on the Usenet).

## TAKE NOTE

### ▶ WORTHY COMPETITORS

Netscape Navigator is not the only Web browser on the market. There are a host of competitors in the UNIX/X Window world, including:

▶ Lynx (a freeware text-only browser) that is common on UNIX and Linux systems.
▶ tkWWW, a freeware Web browser written in Tcl/Tk. You need to track this one down.
▶ Opera, a freeware browser. When this book was written, Linux and Sun Solaris versions were in development but not yet released. You can find more information at **www.operasoftware.com**.
▶ Microsoft Internet Explorer, available in Sun Solaris and HP-UX versions (as of this writing).

**CROSS-REFERENCE**
You can learn more about electronic mail in Chapter 8.

**FIND IT ONLINE**
The Netscape Communications Home Page is at www.netscape.com.

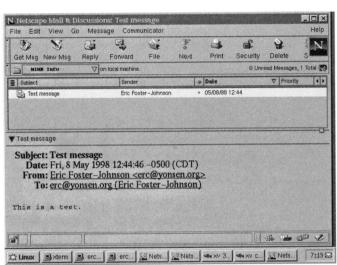

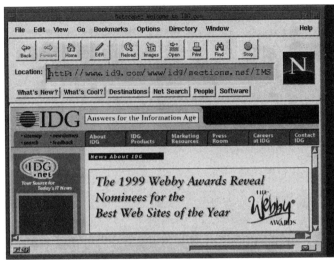

Most companies have their own Web pages. This is the Home Page for IDG, as shown in Netscape Navigator. This home page is known as a portal, leading you to other places on the Internet.

Netscape Mail is used to read and compose electronic mail. A list of all your messages is displayed in the top pane. The actual text of the messages is displayed in the bottom pane.

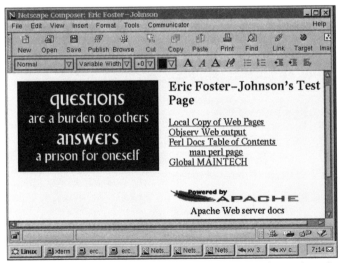

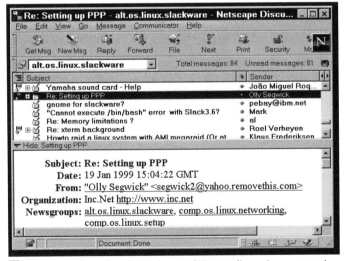

Netscape Composer is used to edit HTML files. It can be used to edit pages grabbed directly from the Internet.

Netscape Discussions is used to read Usenet discussion groups. A list of the Usenet postings is displayed in the top pane. The text of an actual message is displayed in the bottom pane.

# Catching the URLy Bird

You tell a Web browser where to look by entering a *Uniform Resource Locator*, or URL. Pick up a magazine and you will see a URL in almost every advertisement as millions of users have flocked to the Internet as a prime source of information.

URLs are rather simple things: they tell a Web browser where to look for information. The vast majority of URLs begin with **www**, which is short for World Wide Web. After that comes the actual name of the site (such as **kreichard.com**). The URL ends with the type of the site (**com** for commercial, **edu** for educational, **gov** for government, **org** for organization, **mil** for military). In theory, the URL should end with the location of the site, but that convention apparently doesn't appply to U.S.-based sites. However, URLs from non-U.S. sites typically do list the country of origin: **www.netcraft.co.uk** is clearly based in the United Kingdom.

The World Wide Web community has standardized on a number of URL formats:

▶ Web pages transferred via HTTP (HyperText Transfer Protocol). This protocol tells Netscape Navigator to render the page using tags.

▶ Web browsers can also connect directly to FTP (File Transfer Protocol) sites and both upload and download files. A typical URL for this would be **ftp://ftp.cdrom.com**. Here, the URL begins with **ftp://**, not **http://**, and the actual site begins with **ftp**, not **www**. If you knew the exact location of the file at the FTP site, you could enter a fuller URL of **file://ftp.cdrom. com/README.txt**.

▶ A Web browser can also connect to a *Gopher* site. Gopher is an older method of organizing information on the Internet using lists of hyperlinks. While there are few Gophers being started anew these days, there are many useful legacy sites storing information in the Gopher format. A typical Gopher URL would be **gopher://sumex-aim.stanford.edu:70**.

▶ You could use your Web browser to *telnet* to a Telnet site. Telnet is an older, but still quite popular method of connecting via an Internet connection to a larger mainframe or minicomputer and then running a text-based connection.

**CROSS-REFERENCE**

Learn more about using Netscape Navigator to read the Usenet news later in this chapter.

**FIND IT ONLINE**

The mother of all Gophers can be found at **gopher://boombox.micro.umn.edu:70/hh/gopher**.

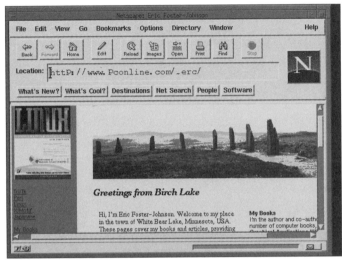

■ The biggest use for a browser is to connect to Web pages. You can tell that a Web page is being requested because the URL begins with **http://**.

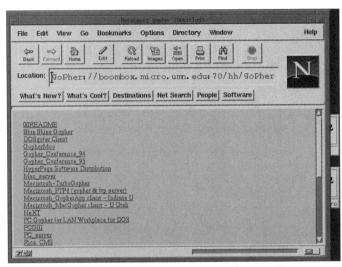

■ In addition to accessing HyperText data via the HyperText Transport Protocol, a Web browser can also connect via other protocols. Here, Netscape Navigator is used to connect to an older Gopher site. Note that the information is displayed in a straight set — the hallmark of a Gopher site.

■ You can also use Netscape Navigator to download files. Here, Netscape Navigator is used to connect to an FTP site, although the details are hidden from you. To download a file, click a filename.

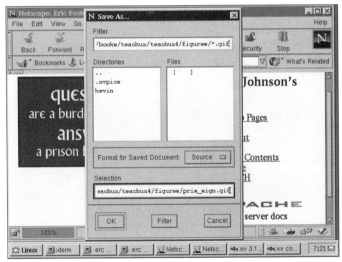

■ When you try to download a file, Netscape Navigator asks you what you want to do with the file. Most of us will want to save the file to disk.

# Accessing the Web

Now that you know what a URL is, it's time to use that knowledge and do some actual Web browsing.

In the middle menu at the top of a Netscape Navigator window, you'll see the Go To entry field. Go ahead and enter the following URL: **www.pconline.com/~erc/xfonts.htm**. This will load a Web page on X Window fonts, an often tricky area of UNIX graphics. This page will undoubtedly look different than the one shown on the opposite page in the upper-left corner. This is a fairly typical index page to a Web site, acting as a front door to the other various offerings of the Web site and to sites beyond.

As you move your pointer around this Web page, notice that it changes shape based on its position over the page. Although the exact shape varies from operating system to operating system, most of the time a pointer located over a link looks like a hand, with a finger extended. This tells you that the pointer is positioned over a link, which is either a link to a resource on the current Web site or to another Web site.

The exact URL of the link will be shown at the bottom of the screen, as is the case with the top-right figure on the opposite page. In this case, the pointer was positioned over the text Programming X at the top of the page, with the link being **www.pconline. com/~erc/xprog.htm**. Select this link and Netscape should load this file.

As you can see from the URL in the Location: field, it's a lot easier to follow Web pages via links and a pointer than entering long URLs into a text-entry field.

---

**TAKE NOTE**

### A SUPPORTING CAST

UNIX users have one disadvantage over Windows and Mac users: a lack of supporting applications for handling some multimedia files. For instance, the Linux implementation of Netscape Navigator doesn't have default applications for many multimedia file types, including .AU and RealAudio audio files. You will probably need to spend some time configuring your UNIX system for Internet multimedia, using the Preferences dialog box from the Edit menu. This dialog box is shown on the opposite page, in the bottom-right corner. You can find UNIX players for MP3 and .wav sounds, along with MPEG, QuickTime, and Windows AVI movies.

---

**CROSS-REFERENCE**

Learn more about URLs and how to keep track of them in the task, "Tracing Your Steps."

**FIND IT ONLINE**

RealPlayer is an essential multimedia tool and can be found at **www.realaudio.com**.

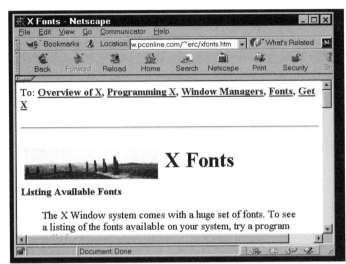

■ *You can enter a new URL in the Go To field. Enter the following:* ***http://www.pconline.com/~erc/xfonts.htm***. *A Web page like this one will load.*

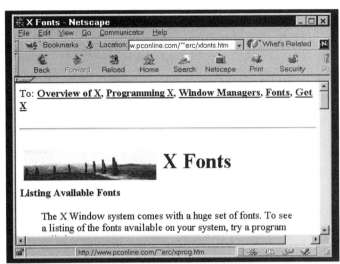

■ *This page looks remarkably like the previous one. The one difference is that the field at the bottom of this window contains link information.*

■ *This is the end result of the Programming X link.*

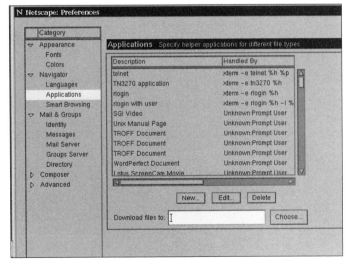

■ *Every file sent across the World Wide Web has a MIME file type. Netscape Navigator can be configured to load another application to handle specific file types. Unfortunately, most UNIX versions of Navigator lack the tools for handing multimedia file types.*

# Tracing Your Steps

In the course of a typical Web session, you'll visit between 10 and 100 Web sites, according to many Web-usage studies. You may be shocked by that number, but the seductive qualities of the World Wide Web encourages jumping from site to site in search of that ultimate data nugget.

Netscape Navigator keeps track of these Web-site visits via its History function. You can access lists of recently visited sites in two ways: You can pull down a listing of the most recently visited sites next to the Location field, or you can select History from the Communicator and see a complete listing of recently visited sites. Pulling down the shorter listing is the easiest way to access a site you've visited in the current session, but this list shows only a URL and no other information about the Web site. An actual menu is shown on the opposite page, in the top-left corner. (You can also scroll through your recently accessed sites with the Back menu button.)

Of the two listings, the History menu selection yields the more detailed and longer entries, as it lists every single Web page visited, even multiple pages within one site. (You can see a typical set of entries in the upper-right figure on the opposite page.) The information tracked in the History menu includes when a page was first and last accessed, how many times you've visited the Web page, and when this Web page expires from the history listings. By default, the entries in the History file are stored for nine days, per the settings shown in the dialog box in the top-right corner of the opposite page.

If you're rather proud of your recent Web sessions and want to save them for posterity, you could save your history list to a file, from where you could bring it up time and time again. To save the history list to file, select Save As from the File menu and then choose a filename and location for the history file.

## TAKE NOTE

### CACHE AS CACHE CAN

When you choose a Web page from your history listings, chances are pretty good that you'll be reloading the page from your *cache*. Navigator sets aside RAM and disk space to store frequently accessed Web pages. When you select a Web page from a history listing, you're probably loading the cached copy and not a copy via the Internet. To reload from the Internet and not from the cache, select Reload and hold down the **Shift** key at the same time. The cache settings — which you can edit — can be seen on the opposite page, in the bottom-right corner.

**CROSS-REFERENCE**
The history menu is the equivalent of a shell's history feature, as seen in Chapter 5.

**FIND IT ONLINE**
You can't have too much history, as you can see at the History Channel Web site: **www.historychannel.com**.

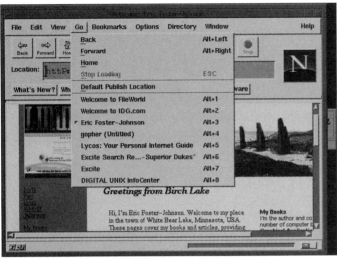

By calling up the short history list, you can access your recently visited pages. Select the page you want to revisit.

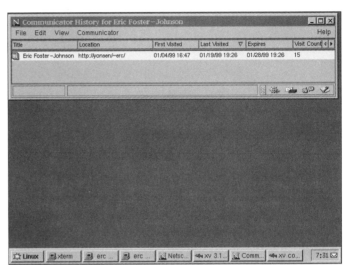

You can also access recently visited pages by selecting History from the Communicator menu. You can sort them by any number of criteria; the default is by when the page was last visited. Clicking a page loads that URL into Netscape Navigator.

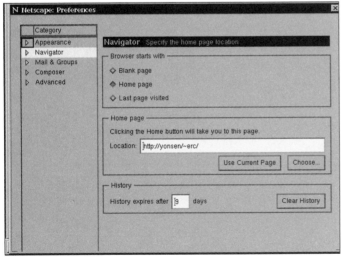

The Netscape Preferences dialog box allows you to set how long entries are stored in the history file. If you're running low on memory, you can clear the history entries.

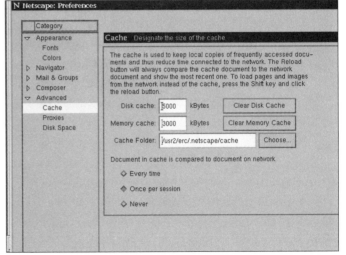

Netscape Navigator also stores copies of frequently accessed documents. By default, Navigator sets aside both RAM and hard-disk space for the cache. When you choose a document from the history list, you're probably reloading from the cache.

# Managing Your Bookmarks

Typing a URL every time you want to connect to a Web site can be rather tedious, so Netscape Navigator includes *bookmarks* for keeping track of frequently accessed Web sites.

Bookmarks are stored in a file and are accessible any time you're using Netscape Navigator. They save you the time of typing in tediously long URLs and also give you a chance to structure your Web-hopping into easily selectable categories.

There are two ways to access bookmarks on the default Netscape Navigator window. First, you can select the Bookmarks icon, shown in the top-left figure on the opposite page, which displays a pull-down menu of all your bookmarks. Secondly, you can directly access your bookmarks via your Personal Toolbar. You can set up your own categories by editing your bookmarks file.

To edit your bookmarks, select Edit Bookmarks from the Communicator menu's Bookmarks choice. A dialog box like the one shown in the upper-right figure on the opposite page appears, from which you can add, delete, or rearrange bookmarks. You can also organize bookmarks into folders.

If you're a persistent surfer and accumulate a wide range of bookmarks, you may find it difficult to keep track of them. Instead of manually checking each bookmark to see whether it has recently changed, you can update them from the same Edit Bookmarks dialog box. Select Update Bookmarks from the View menu, and the dialog box shown in the bottom-left corner of the opposite page appears. You can select to update all your bookmarks or only a selection. After the bookmarks are updated, Web pages with new content are noted with a check mark.

The Edit Bookmark dialog box also allows you to actually edit your bookmarks. When you add a bookmark to your bookmarks file, it uses the default title page for the Web page. You can edit this information to give the page a title that you'll instantly recognize. In addition, you can add a short description about the Web page — which is handy when your bookmarks file has hundreds or thousands of entries. You can also use this dialog box to track down aliases for the original bookmark.

## TAKE NOTE

### ▶ MOVING BOOKMARKS

You can move your bookmarks from computer to computer or even from user to user. Netscape Navigator stores bookmarks in the HTML file format, which means that copying bookmarks is a simple matter of copying a file named `bookmark.htm` in the `Netscape`-subdirectory tree (the exact location differs based on the Navigator version, but you should look for a subdirectory called `Defaults`).

### ▶ USING BOOKMARKS AS A HOME PAGE

You can choose a file as your default home page, instead of the Netscape Home Page. Many users select their Bookmarks file as their home page, which is loaded every time that Netscape Navigator is launched.

**CROSS-REFERENCE**
Bookmarks appear in a hierarchical fashion, much like files and directories discussed in Chapter 2.

**FIND IT ONLINE**
Many Web pages feature bookmarks for easy browsing. For instance, Year 2000 Bookmarks can be found at **pw1.netcom.com/~ggirod/bookmark.html**.

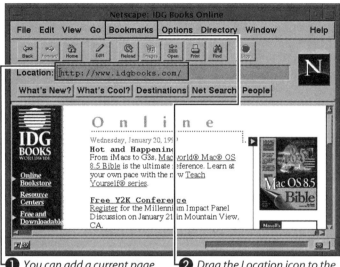

**1** *You can add a current page to your bookmarks at any time. Select the current URL by placing the pointer over the Location icon.*

**2** *Drag the Location icon to the Bookmarks icon, and the current URL is now stored in your bookmarks file.*

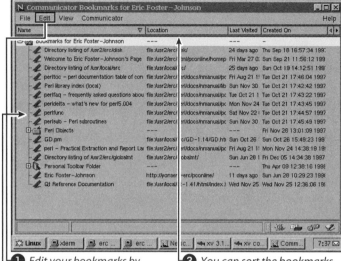

**1** *Edit your bookmarks by selecting Edit Bookmarks from the Communicator menu.*

**2** *The resulting dialog box lists your bookmarks.*

**3** *You can sort the bookmarks using the name, location, last visited, and created-on fields.*

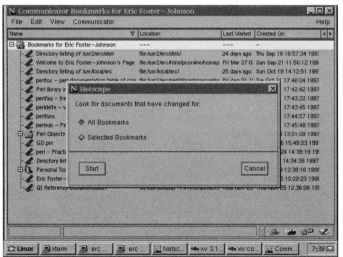

■ *You can update your bookmarks to see which have changed. The resulting dialog box is shown after selecting Update Bookmarks from the View menu. You can choose to update all bookmarks or selected bookmarks.*

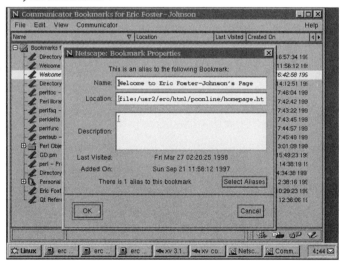

■ *Information is stored about every bookmark. This information includes the name of the bookmark and its location. You can use this dialog box to set up aliases for this bookmark.*

# Security and the Internet

Polls of World Wide Web users show a consistent fear regarding the level of security associated with Internet transactions. The act of sending a credit-card number via the Internet causes normally confident users to break out in a cold sweat. Of course, if you're a credit-card thief, trying to sniff out an individual credit-card number on the World Wide Web is like searching for a needle in a haystack — a thief would have better success dumpster diving outside a bank.

Still, perception is important when it comes to making a buck, which is why vendors and customers both clamor for secure transactions. Netscape Navigator comes with a number of tools to make sure that your online transactions remain secure.

The most important tool for secure transactions is the Secure Sockets Layer, or SSL. This protocol defines to what extent communications are encrypted. Almost every online merchant of any repute accepts secure orders made with SSL encryption. The dialog box for setting SSL is shown in the top-left corner of the opposite page.

To make sure that your transactions are secure on both ends, you should acquire a digital certificate, which verifies to another computer on the Internet that you are authentic. Many authorities issue certificates, but one that's perfect for Web users is VeriSign's Digital ID (**www.verisign.com**), which is used to uniquely identify both your Web transactions

and electronic mail. You can set which certificates you want to accept, as shown in the bottom-left figure on the opposite page.

When a transaction is secure, a closed lock with a yellow background appears, as shown in the bottom-right figure on the opposite page.

You can also encrypt and secure your electronic mail. Once you obtain a digital certificate, you can encrypt entire messages or sign mail messages with secure signatures. Secure MIME (S/MIME) can also ensure that your electronic-mail messages are secure.

## TAKE NOTE

### ▶ READY, SET, GO

A secure protocol that will play a part in your secure-computing future is Secure Electronic Transaction, or SET. Developed by MasterCard and Visa with the assistance of computer-industry leaders (Hewlett-Packard, IBM, Microsoft, Netscape Communications), SET has the approval of the U.S. Treasury Department as the tool of choice for secure transactions.

Proponents say that SET is the most secure way to protect online transactions. Critics say that SET is bloated, slow, and difficult to implement. So far the critics have been on the mark: Vendors and Web-server developers have been quick to implement SSL, but slow to adopt SET. Still, it's likely that SET will pop up sometime in your computing future if you plan on any online transactions.

**CROSS-REFERENCE**

Chapter 2 discusses some of the security tools associated with UNIX.

**FIND IT ONLINE**

A good primer on World Wide Web security, maintained by Lincoln Stein, can be found at **www.w3.org/ Security/Faq/www-security-faq.html**.

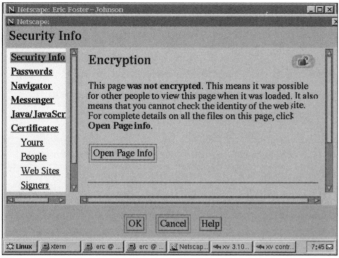

The Security Settings dialog box controls many aspects of Web security. You can control how much information is presented about encrypted sites. You can set which level of SSL is enabled.

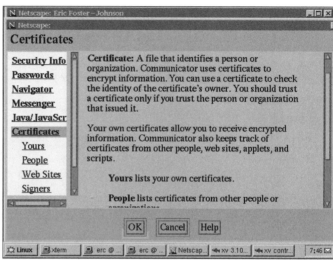

Encrypting electronic mail is a matter of enabling the proper controls. You need to acquire a certificate. You can choose Secure MIME and different levels of message encryption.

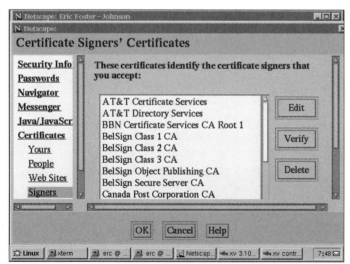

Netscape Navigator controls which certificate signers can be accepted.

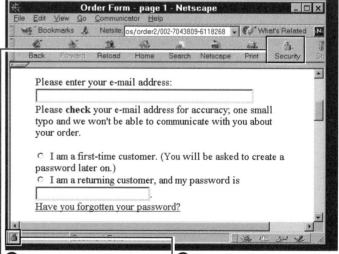

❶ Netscape Navigator tells you in two ways that a connection is secure. First, near the top of the window, you'll see a yellow shading around the security button.

❷ Second, at the bottom left of the window, the lock will be locked.

# Accessing the Usenet

etscape Navigator can be used to read discussions carried both on intranets and in the public Usenet. These discussions are devoted to specific topics (such as Slackware Linux, shown in the top-left corner of the opposite page) and are *threaded*, which means the discussion software tracks what messages are sent in reply to other messages. The message shown in the top-left corner is actually a reply to another message, and the figure in the top-right corner shows the messages in the thread.

Your corporation may have internal discussions on a wide variety of topics, but most Netscape Navigator users will use the Discussions feature to read Usenet news. There are thousands of Usenet groups, ranging from the aforementioned Slackware Linux newsgroup (**alt.os.linux.slackware**) to newsgroups devoted to musicians (such as **alt.fan.elvis-costello**) to newsgroups about hobbies such as folk dancing (such as **rec.folk-dancing**). With thousands of newsgroups, you should find some large or small community that shares the same interests as you. And if you can't find such a group, you can always opt to start your own newsgroup, which isn't that difficult.

There are two ways to find interesting Usenet newsgroups. You can use Netscape to browse a listing of all newsgroups carried by your Internet Service Provider (ISP), as shown on the opposite page in the top-right corner. Or you can use Netscape search capabilities to look for a newsgroup, as shown on the opposite page in the bottom-left corner.

Because there are thousands and thousands of newsgroups, it seems impossible to find what you need. You can narrow down your browsing with some intelligent guesses. If you're looking for a newsgroup devoted to computing topics, you can begin looking at the newsgroups beginning with **comp**. Similarly, scientific newsgroups begin with **sci**, alternative newsgroups begin with **alt**, and regional newsgroups begin with the name of the region (Minnesota-oriented groups begin with **mn**.)

Searching for a specific newsgroup makes more sense. You can enter a word and see if it appears in the list of newsgroups carried by your ISP.

## TAKE NOTE

### ► USENET BASICS

The Usenet has been around for longer than most of the Internet. It's an unruly playing field, an aggressively egalitarian field where most of the newsgroups are open to anyone with a connection to the Internet. (Some of the more specialized newsgroups are *moderated*, which means that postings must first be cleared with a moderator.) Generally speaking, there's a high entertainment value to the Usenet. But you must also take what you read with a grain of salt.

### ► OTHER USENET TOOLS

Most versions of UNIX feature some other tools for reading Usenet news, run from the command line. Check out Appendix B for a list of other UNIX texts, which cover tools such as **inn** in more detail.

**CROSS-REFERENCE**
Some newsgroups are distributed via electronic mail, which was covered in Chapter 8.

**FIND IT ONLINE**
You can also access Usenet newsgroups from the World Wide Web at **www.dejanews.com**.

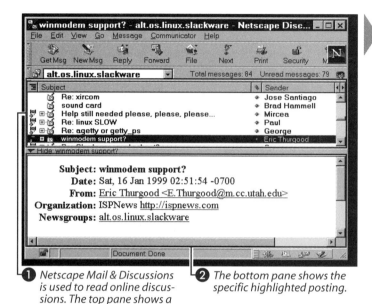

**❶** *Netscape Mail & Discussions is used to read online discussions. The top pane shows a listing of the Usenet postings.*

**❷** *The bottom pane shows the specific highlighted posting.*

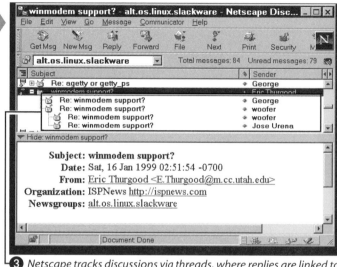

**❸** *Netscape tracks discussions via threads, where replies are linked to an original posting. Here are replies to the original posting.*

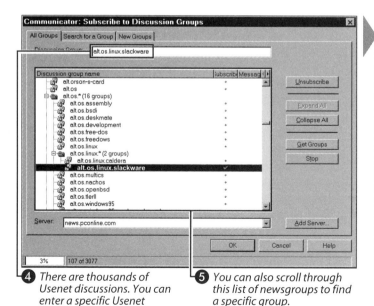

**❹** *There are thousands of Usenet discussions. You can enter a specific Usenet newsgroup in this field.*

**❺** *You can also scroll through this list of newsgroups to find a specific group.*

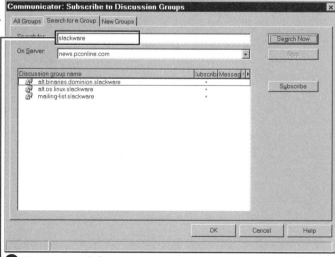

**❻** *You can search for a newsgroup by entering a word in this field and Netscape will match it against a list of newsgroups.*

# Using Other Web Protocols

Those Internet users who are new to the World Wide Web may not know that there are a number of Internet services available that were relatively widely used long before the World Wide Web exploded on the scene.

The most common Internet protocol that you'll encounter outside of the Web and mail is *FTP*, short for *File Transfer Protocol*. The name describes perfectly the purpose of the protocol — transferring files to and from other computers on the Internet. There are special servers on the Internet, called *FTP sites*, that do nothing but store files that are to be downloaded by other users. FTP still plays an important role in the UNIX world, and if you're in a technical field (programmer, system analyst, system integrator) you will probably be spending some time downloading and uploading files from an FTP site.

You can actually use **ftp** from the UNIX command line, either under an X session or working in terminal mode. The top-left figure on the opposite page shows the beginnings of a typical FTP session: you run the **ftp** command, specify an FTP site (in this case, **ftp.netscape.com**), and then login the site (see Take Note for more information on that).

When you're connected, you can browse the contents of the site using standard UNIX commands. To list the contents of the current directory, use the **ls** command (as shown in the lower-left corner on the opposite page). To move from one subdirectory to another, use the **cd** command. To actually transfer a file, use the **get** or **mget** commands. (We suggest checking out a text listed in Appendix B for more information on the **ftp** command.)

You can also use Netscape Navigator to access a Web site, using **ftp://** at the beginning of the URL. To connect to the Netscape FTP site, you'd use a URL of **ftp://ftp.netscape.com**. The results of this are shown on the opposite page, in the bottom-left corner. To transfer a file, simply click the filename.

Finally, there are other Internet protocols that you may use. Gopher is an older menu-driver protocol still used in academia for storing documents and program files in folders. As you can see from the figure in the bottom right-on corner of the opposite page, Gopher uses menus as links to other menus and documents. Sometimes, telnet is also used to open a connection to another computer; like **ftp**, the **telnet** command can be run from the command line to connect to another telnet-enabled host on the Internet.

## TAKE NOTE

### PASSWORDS AND FTP

When you connect to an FTP site, you are asked for your name. If this is a public site, you can enter **anonymous** as your name, with a password consisting of your e-mail address. This process, known as *anonymous FTP*, gives you access to the public portions of the FTP site. There are some FTP sites — most notably, corporate FTP sites or Web sites — requiring you to have an account on the site (complete with unique username and password) in order to access the site.

## CROSS REFERENCE

Chapter 10 covers more on FTP.

## FIND IT ONLINE

You can find a lot of useful freely available software at **ftp.gnu.org**.

■ Begin your FTP session by running the **ftp** command at the command line. When the **ftp** prompt appears, enter the name of the FTP site. You're then asked for your username and password.

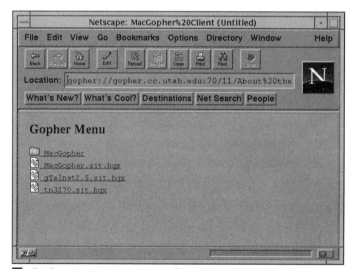

■ Many standard UNIX commands are used in an ftp session. The **ls** command is used to list the contents of the current directory.

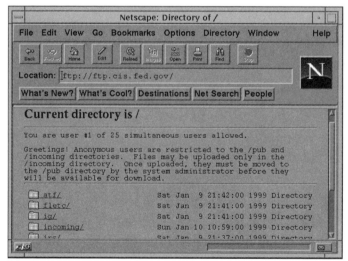

■ You can use Netscape Navigator to connect to an FTP site. Navigator will list the contents of the current directory by default. To download a file, you select it as you would any other hypertext link.

■ Gopher uses menus as an interface to a Gopher site. By clicking a link, you are either taken to another Gopher menu or prompted to download a file.

# Personal Workbook

## Q&A

**1** Which Web browser is typically found on a UNIX system?

_____

_____

_____

**2** What are the major URL formats?

_____

_____

_____

**3** Why does a pointer change over various parts of a Web page?

_____

_____

_____

**4** When you choose a Web page from your history listings, from where will you most likely reload the page?

_____

_____

_____

**5** What are the two ways to view Web sites you've recently visited?

_____

_____

_____

**6** How can you access your bookmarks?

_____

_____

_____

**7** What's the significance of a Usenet newsgroup being threaded?

_____

_____

_____

**8** What does FTP stand for?

_____

_____

**ANSWERS: PAGE 350**

## EXTRA PRACTICE

1. Use your existing Web browser to locate and download another Web browser.

2. Use your Web browser to track down the latest Linux news at **www.slashdot.org**.

3. Connect to the **www.kreichard.com** Web site and send mail to the authors.

4. Send electronic mail to Bill Clinton.

5. Discover the significance behind the name Gopher.

6. Search for a Usenet discussion group devoted to Bob Mould.

## REAL-WORLD APPLICATIONS

✓ You've been asked by your boss to do some opposition research into your competitor, Spacely Sprockets. Use the tools of the Internet to find more about Spacely Sprockets, including prominent employees.

✓ Track down the latest version of Netscape Navigator and install it on your computer.

✓ A customer writes to you in regard to a new offering from your company. Compose a response to the original mail, making sure to quote the original so the recipient will know exactly what prompted your mail.

✓ You've been asked by your boss to compile information about all the favors of UNIX on the market — including freely available versions. Use the Usenet to locate this information.

## Visual Quiz

What Web browser is this? What Web site is loaded in this browser?

_____

_____

_____

_____

_____

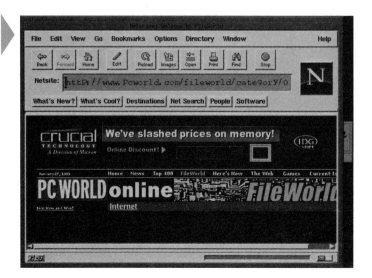

# CHAPTER 10

**MASTER THESE SKILLS**

▶ Accessing File Systems with RFS and NFS

▶ Transferring Files with FTP

▶ Gathering Information with finger and ping

▶ Logging on Remotely with Telnet

▶ Remote Computing with rcp, rsh, and rlogin

▶ Using UUCP

# Extending Your Reach with Networking

Networking allows your UNIX system to stretch beyond the borders of a single computer system. You can access resources from all over the world.

One of the prime reasons for networking systems is to allow you to share resources. You can share file servers, printers, and so on. Once connected, you can log onto remote systems and run commands on those systems. You can find out information on other users, sometimes even users based in other countries.

UNIX systems work well at networking and the main reason for this is standards. UNIX systems follow Internet standards, which are used to make the entire Internet and also used on most UNIX Local Area Networks — or LANs. Even if your site has no connection to the outside world, chances are your UNIX systems use Internet protocols and commands to communicate with each other.

Most UNIX networking runs on top of a family of protocols called TCP/IP, or Transmission Control Protocol/Internet Protocol. These protocols allow UNIX and non-UNIX computers to communicate efficiently, and enable networks to be interconnected, forming even larger networks.

The main things you need to configure on each UNIX system are the host name and Internet — or IP — address. Each UNIX system sports the name you or your administrator chooses. Under the hood, UNIX networking, along with all TCP/IP networking, uses the IP address for actual communication. An IP address includes four one-byte numbers usually formatted as follows: 192.63.42.1.

Most UNIX network commands will accept the IP address or a host name. In most cases, the host name is easier to remember.

On the Internet, domain names extend host names. Domain names identify the owner of the address by listing it in a hierarchical format, and serve to conceptually break up the huge Internet into smaller, more digestible chunks. These domain names are the same as the domain names used in e-mail addresses. Usually, you use a machine (host) name along with a domain name, such as www.idgbooks.com (which actually is a machine named www in the idgbooks.com domain).

# Accessing File Systems with RFS and NFS

Networks allow systems to share resources, and one of the most vital resources is disk space. Consequently, one of the greatest benefits of UNIX networking lies in network shared file systems.

The end result is called a *distributed file system*, and it allows all machines on a network to act as if they are one large disk residing in the same location, even though they may be located miles away. For the user, the resources on a remote machine appear to be as local as the next room; no conscious effort is required on the part of the user to access a remote machine. Shared file systems can allow you to log in to any UNIX system on your organization's network and see the same home directory on all systems. This makes your life easier because you don't have to remember which system you used for storing which files.

## NFS

Originally developed by Sun Microsystems, NFS, the Network File System, is available on just about every UNIX system and is the most-used file-sharing mechanism.

After a server advertises its file system for use by clients, the client then mounts the file system for its own use. For instance, Machine A may want to access files from Machine B regarding company finances, which are located in B's **/usr/data/finances** directory. A directory on Machine A must be specified for mounting the files; this is called the *mount point*. The files from **/usr/data/finances** will appear on Machine A just as if they were physically located on Machine A's hard-disk system. Note that it is very common for the mount point to be at a different location on the second machine. For example, Machine B's **/usr/data/finances** directory may appear as **/b/corp_data/finances** on Machine A. The location of the mount point directory is up to the system administrator.

As another example, you may want to share applications between systems by mounting **/usr/local** — where locally-installed applications should be stored — from a central server. Each remote file system, just like each local file system, gets mounted under the root directory, /, or a subdirectory.

*Continued*

## Mounting a Remote File System

To mount a remote file system, you need to use the mount command as in the following:

**$ mount hostname:exported_path\
local_mount_point**

The **hostname** names the machine where the disk is physically located. The **exported_path** is the directory on the machine **hostname** that is exported. The **local_mount_point** names the directory on your system where the files should be mounted. The facing page shows you how to mount a remote file system.

You often can't tell the difference between local and remote file systems. To see if your system mounts any other file systems, use the **df** command, as shown on the facing page.

**CROSS-REFERENCE**

Chapter 2 covers many file-related commands.

**FIND IT ONLINE**

Sun, the inventor of NFS, includes NFS software with its Solaris version of UNIX at **www.sun.com/solaris/**.

## Listing 10-1: RUNNING DF

```
$ df
Filesystem          1024-blocks        Used
Available  Capacity  Mounted on
/dev/hda1              1811645        419670
1295207      24%   /
/dev/hda2               499652        427811
46037        90%   /usr2
yonsen:/usr/home/erc 3352868       2157867
859714       72%   /mnt/usr/home/erc
$
```

▲ *The df command shows all the file systems mounted, and tells you which file systems are mounted over the network. In this case, /mnt/usr/home/erc is mounted from the /usr/home/erc directory on machine yonsen.*

## Listing 10-2: MOUNTING OFTEN REQUIRES ROOT ACCESS

```
$ mount bigserver:/usr/local /usr/local
mount: only root can do that
$ su
Password:
# mount bigserver:/usr/local /usr/local
mount: bigserver:/usr/local
    write-protected, mounting read-only
# exit
$
```

▲ *This demonstrates mounting the /usr/local directory, where locally-installed programs are stored, from system bigserver onto the local system, also in /usr/local. At sites with many UNIX systems, it's common to share directories, such as /usr/local, between systems from the same vendor running the same version of UNIX.*

## Listing 10-3: MOUNTING AN NFS DRIVE

```
# mount -t nfs \
    nicollet:/usr/home/erc \
    /mnt/usr/home/erc
```

▲ *Here is an example of mounting a user home directory from system nicollet to /mnt/usr/home/erc on the local system, specifying the type (-t) as nfs. As an NFS, or Network File System, the disk is located on another system but it appears to this system as if the files were local.*

## Listing 10-4: LS SHOWS REMOTE FILES THE SAME

```
$ ls /
bin/     proc/
boot/    root/
cdrom/    sbin/
dev/     shlib/
etc/     tmp/
home/     usr/
lib/     usr2/
lost+found  var/
mnt/     unix
$
$ ls /mnt
usr
$
```

▲ *The ls command and other UNIX utilities won't show any difference between remotely-mounted files or files stored on the local hard disk. Files mounted from remote systems will appear just as local files do. UNIX commands will work the same on these files, but you may experience delays due to network traffic.*

# Accessing File Systems with RFS and NFS *Continued*

## Exporting File Systems

Before you can mount a file system, though, the remote system — which has the disk physically connected — must export that file system. With NFS, you typically specify the file systems you want to export in a file named **/etc/exports**. In this file, you name file systems to export and you can control how the file systems are exported, such as read only so that users on other systems cannot modify the files.

## RFS and AFS

In addition to NFS, some systems run other distributed file systems, including Remote File Sharing (RFS), originally developed by AT&T and AFS and the Andrew File System, developed as part of the larger Andrew project.

Economics played an important role in the development of RFS. Additional storage space could be added to a UNIX system without having to install new, expensive computers; when hardware was priced much more than it is today, this was a prime concern to data-processing departments on limited budgets. Similarly, expensive peripherals such as modems and printers could be shared across different systems — at least under RFS.

The Andrew File System, though, was designed as a truly global file system. All file systems are mounted under the AFS root directory, **/afs**. This means *all* file systems that you mount from all over the world. Different organizations manage AFS cells — essentially

mounted file systems. You access files then, by using **/afs**/*cell_name*/*file_path*. These paths work on any AFS system world wide — depending on user access permissions of course.

## Sharing Files with Windows

Windows systems can also share files with UNIX systems — with the right software. Basically, two main approaches exist:

▶ Make the Windows systems interact in the way that UNIX systems expect.
▶ Make the UNIX systems interact in the way that Windows systems expect.

A number of vendors sell Windows suites of NFS software. With this, your Windows systems can mount UNIX systems as well as allowing UNIX systems to mount Windows disks. This solution involves a cost per Windows PC.

An alternative is to make the UNIX systems talk on the network the way Windows systems expect. This approach has the advantage in that organizations typically have fewer UNIX systems than Windows systems, so you will have less work to do to install the software.

A freeware package called Samba allows UNIX systems to act as Windows files and print servers, using the Windows SMB — server message block — protocol. Windows systems should work with the protocol without modification.

---

**CROSS-REFERENCE**
Chapter 2 covers many file-related commands.

**FIND IT ONLINE**
You can purchase NFS for Windows from Hummingbird Communications, at **www.hummingbird.com**.

## TAKE NOTE

### MOUNTING FILE SYSTEMS AUTOMATICALLY

A tool called automount can mount file systems automatically when any program tries to access a directory on the remote file system. This is often used to mount user home directories on any system on a network.

### Listing 10-5: SHOWING /ETC/EXPORTS

```
$ more /etc/exports
/usr -ro -access=software
/usr/local.mnt -root=0 -ro
/usr/home -rw
$
```

▲ *The /etc/exports file lists the file systems you wish to export to other systems on your network. As this example shows, this system exports /usr, /usr/local.mnt, and /usr/home via NFS. The /usr and /usr/local.mnt directories are exported as read only (-ro), so users on other systems cannot modify those files, while /usr/home is exported read-write (-rw). We can assume from this example that the /etc/exports file we're seeing comes from one of the most important UNIX servers on this network, as it serves up /usr, location of most system software and /usr/home, commonly used for user home directories.*

### Listing 10-6: BEFORE AUTOMATICALLY MOUNTING DIRECTORIES

```
$ ls /usr/home
$
```

▲ *With the automount tool, directories don't get mounted until you try to use them. In this case, the ls command shows no subdirectories of /usr/home, which holds user home directories on this system.*

### Listing 10-7: AUTOMATICALLY MOUNTING DIRECTORIES

```
$ ls -1 /usr/home/erc
Dtmail
Mail
NEdit
XTerm
bin
dialogs
docs
foo.pl
pattern.pl
public_html
tmp
tools
$
$ ls /usr/home
erc
```

▲ *When you try to access an automounted directory, /usr/home/erc as shown here, the files suddenly appear — as if by magic — as automount mounts the directory. In the previous listing, there were no subdirectories under /usr/home. The ls command, though, tries to access files under /usr/home, which the automounter provides.*

### Listing 10-8: CHECKING /USR/HOME AGAIN

```
$ ls -1 /usr/home
erc
$ ls -1 /usr/home/fred
Mail
XTerm
bin
$ ls /usr/home
erc     fred
$
```

▲ *Now, when we use ls on /usr/home, there are some entries for the directories we've accessed. At first, we see only the erc directory, which comes from the commands in the previous listing. After accessing /usr/home/fred, we now see two directories underneath /usr/home, erc and fred. Again, the automounter makes the directories appear as needed.*

# Transferring Files with FTP

Most networked UNIX systems support the File Transfer Protocol, or FTP, for exchanging files with other systems. The handiest use of FTP is the **ftp** command, which connects you to any other computer on your network running the **ftp** response program, called **inetd**, which in turn, launches the FTP-handling program, usually named **ftpd**. (The **inetd** program responds to most incoming network requests.)

If your system is connected to the Internet, you can use **ftp** to access files from other Internet computers worldwide. These machines you network with may or may not be running the UNIX operating system; this operating-system independence is what makes **ftp** so widely used.

When you start **ftp**, you get an **ftp**> prompt. This means that **ftp** awaits your commands. To get a list of available commands, type a question mark (**?**) or **help** at the prompt.

In most cases, the following simple commands should work. To open a connection to a remote machine, use the **open** command at the **ftp**> prompt:

```
ftp> open hostname
```

You can also pass the name of a machine to connect to on the original **ftp** command line.

In most cases, you are prompted for a user name and a password. Once authenticated, you can then transfer files — the whole point of **ftp**.

You can use **ftp** for sending and receiving files on your local network, or across the Internet.

The **get** command retrieves a remote file and copies it to your system. As you download the file, you won't be able to enter any keystrokes because there is no prompt. After the file has been transferred successfully, you are told the transfer is completed.

To upload a file to the remote system, use the **put** command:

```
ftp> put filename
```

Again, this may take a long time, especially on a dial-up connection. Be patient. Again, the **ftp**> prompt appears when the command is complete.

To see what files are available on the remote system, use the **dir** command. To change to a different remote directory, use the **cd** command. To change directories on your local system, instead of on the remote system, use the **lcd** command. Once you're through with your file needs, close the connection and quit **ftp** with the **quit** command.

*Continued*

## TAKE NOTE

### USING FTP FROM WEB BROWSERS

The ability to grab files via **ftp** is built into Internet Web browsers, such as Netscape Navigator.

### FTP ON WINDOWS

Windows also supports the **ftp** command, which you can run from an MS-DOS shell window and use to exchange files with UNIX systems. The Windows version of **ftp**, **ftp.exe**, works almost the same as its UNIX brethren.

**CROSS-REFERENCE**

The **cd** command is covered in Chapter 2.

**FIND IT ONLINE**

You can FTP many interesting things from **ftp.cdrom.com**.

## Table 10-1: COMMON FTP COMMANDS

| Command | Result |
| --- | --- |
| ascii | Uses ASCII as the file-transfer type. |
| bell | Rings the bell when file transfer is complete. |
| binary | Uses binary as the file-transfer type. |
| bye | Terminates **ftp** session. |
| cd *directory* | Changes directory on the remote machine. |
| close | Ends **ftp** connection to remote computer, but keeps local **ftp** program running. |
| delete *filename* | Deletes filename on remote computer. |
| dir | Lists the files in the current directory on the remote machine. |
| get *filename* | Gets filename from the remote machine. |
| get *filename1 filename2* | Gets filename1 from the remote machine and saves it locally as filename2. |
| help | Lists available commands. |
| lcd *directory* | Changes directory on your system, the local system. |
| mget *filename* | Gets multiple files from the remote machine. You can use wildcards, such as *.txt for the *filename*. |
| mput *filename* | Copies multiple local files to the remote machine. You can use wildcards, such as *.txt for the *filename*. |
| open *hostname* | Opens a connection to *hostname*. |
| prompt | Toggles the current state of whether you will be prompted when getting multiple files or not. |

## Listing 10-9: THE CD COMMAND WITHIN FTP

```
$ ftp yonsen
Connected to yousen.bigfun.com.
220 yonsen.bigfun.com FTP server
(Linux) ready.
Name (yonsen:erc): erc
331 Password required for erc.
Password:
230 User erc logged in.
Remote system type is UNIX.
Using binary mode to transfer files.
ftp> cd /usr/local/src/perl5.004_04/t/io
ftp> dir
200 PORT command successful.
150 Opening ASCII mode data connection
for /bin/ls
(192.63.42.1,7385).
total 16
-r-xr-xr-x 1 erc system 1249 Mar 20
1997 argv.t
-r-xr-xr-x 1 erc system  732 Mar 20
1997 dup.t
-r-xr-xr-x 1 erc system 4237 Apr 10
1997 fs.t
-r-xr-xr-x 1 erc system 2101 May  1
1997 pipe.t
-r-xr-xr-x 1 erc system  459 Oct 18
1994 print.t
-r-xr-xr-x 1 erc system  265 Nov 18
1996 read.t
-r-xr-xr-x 1 erc system 1199 Apr  4
1997 tell.t
226 Transfer complete.
ftp>
```

▲ *The* **cd** *command changes directory on the remote machine. The* **dir** *command lists the files in a directory.*

215

When you get files from other machines on the Internet, you usually use anonymous **ftp**. *Anonymous ftp* is a public service provided by many Internet sites. The term anonymous refers to the username you provide when you log in. This allows anyone to download files from these public Internet machines. In all other respects, anonymous **ftp** is the same as regular **ftp**.

As with **ftp** and sites within your local network, you need to provide the name of the machine you want to download from, or the machine's IP address. At the login prompt, use **anonymous** as a login name.

You are then asked for a password. Most systems require you to supply your electronic-mail address, while others require **guest**. Use either. Next, you are presented with an **ftp>** prompt.

The remote system has been set up to give you limited access. That means that your maneuverability is limited. A very common location for public files is in the **/pub** directory. You can use **cd** to change to **/pub** and then use the **dir** command to list the files and directories available. Some systems provide gigabytes of files, so you probably want to know what you intend to download in advance.

When downloading software from anonymous FTP sites, you almost always want to use the binary transfer mode. (You can also use an ASCII transfer mode, which maps carriage returns and line feeds to the native format on your system; only use this if you're sure the file is all text.)

Most larger files are stored in compressed form so they take less time to transfer. These compressed files end with **.Z, .z, .tgz,** or **gz,** so they are instantly recognizable.

If you've downloaded a compressed binary file, you will have to uncompress it (and perhaps unarchive it) at the command line using **uncompress, unpack, tar,** or **gzip**. How do you know which one to use? See the table on the opposite page.

If you have the **gunzip** command, you can use this to uncompress files ending in **.Z, .z, .tgz,** and **.gz,** making **gunzip** one of the handiest commands. If your system doesn't feature **gzip**, go ahead and bug your system administrator, as it's freely available over the Internet and through books and CD-ROMs that feature UNIX freeware.

## TAKE NOTE

### GZIP -D IS THE SAME AS GUNZIP

You don't necessarily need the **gunzip** command on your system to make use of **gzip**. The following commands do the same thing:
▶ $ gzip -d file.gz
▶ $ gunzip file.gz

### USING FTP FROM WEB BROWSERS

You can access most FTP servers from a Web browser such as Netscape Navigator. To do so, create a URL in the form of **ftp://ftp_hostname/ directory_to_access**. For example, **ftp:// sunsite.unc.ed /pub/**.

**CROSS-REFERENCE**
The **tar** command is covered in depth in Chapter 16.

**FIND IT ONLINE**
The **gzip** and **gunzip** programs are located at ftp.gnu.org/pub/gnu/.

## Table 10-2: WHAT TO DO WITH DOWNLOADED FILES

| File-name Extension | Command to Run | Type of File |
| --- | --- | --- |
| *filename*.Z | $ uncompress *filename*.Z | Compressed |
| *filename*.z | $ unpack *filename*.z | Packed |
| *filename*.gz | $ gunzip *filename*.gz | Gzipped |
| *filename*.tgz | $ gunzip *filename*.tgz | Gzipped tar archive |
| *filename*.tar | $ tar xvf *filename*.tar | Tar archive |

### Listing 10-10: USING ANONYMOUS FTP

```
$ ftp sunsite.unc.edu
Connected to sunsite.unc.edu.
220-Welcome to the SunSITE USA ftp archives!
220-
220-You can access this archive via http with the same URL.
220-
220-example:    ftp://sunsite.unc.edu/pub/Linux/ becomes
220-            http://sunsite.unc.edu/pub/Linux/
220-
220-For more information about services offered by SunSITE,
220-go to http://sunsite.unc.edu.
220-
220-WE'RE BACK TO USING WUFTPD.
220-
220-Have any suggestions or questions?
220- Email ftpkeeper@sunsite.unc.edu.
220 helios.oit.unc.edu FTP server (Version wu-2.4.2-academ
220 [BETA-13](6) Thu Jul 17 16:22:52 EDT 1997) ready.
Name (sunsite.unc.edu:erc): anonymous
331 Guest login ok, send your complete e-mail address as password.
Password:
230 Guest login ok, access restrictions apply.
Remote system type is UNIX.
Using binary mode to transfer files.
ftp>
```

▲ *When you log on to a public ftp site, you typically use anonymous as your user name and provide your e-mail address as a password.*

# Gathering Information with finger and ping

When you're working on a network, one of the things you may want to do is find out who else is on the network and what they are doing. You may also want to find out why certain networking commands fail.

The **finger** and **rwho** commands can help figure out who's on the network.

The **finger** command fingers a user on the network and provides information about that user.

The basic syntax follows:

```
$ finger username
```

If you want information about a user not on your UNIX system, you can use the following syntax:

```
$ finger username@hostname
```

The **finger** command looks for two files in your home directory, a **.plan** and a **.project** file, both of which you may use to provide information on what you are working on. You can place anything you want in these files, but remember, lots of people may see the contents. If **finger** can't find the **.plan** file, it displays *No Plan*.

While **finger** provides information about a user on the network, **rwho** lists users.

It seems that network failures interrupt work far too often. When a network command fails, or strange things start to happen — or commands just seem to take far too long — you can sit and curse or try to find out why. There's a simple command you can run that will help determine if the network connection to a remote machine is alive. The **ping** command sends out messages to a remote system. The name **ping** comes from the sound of sonar systems on submarines (or bats). When the remote system receives the messages, it should echo those messages back. If a message doesn't bounce back, you know the network connection to the remote machine is not alive. At this point, it's time to call in your system administrator.

Working with **ping** is extremely simple. Just type **ping** and the name of the system you want information on. For example:

```
$ ping www.idgbooks.com
```

You should see a number of lines of output, showing the amount of packets sent and received. The toughest thing about **ping** is that it normally won't exit. You need to type Ctrl-C to stop **ping**.

In addition to using **ping** with a system name, you can also use **ping** with an Internet or IP address, such as the following:

```
$ ping 206.175.162.15
```

## TAKE NOTE

### SECURITY ISSUES

Many systems on the Internet refuse **finger** requests because of the amount of information given out. For example, when trying to finger the super user at the IDG Books Worldwide Web site, we got the following response:

```
$ finger root@www.idgbooks.com
[www.idgbooks.com]
connect: Connection refused
```

## CROSS-REFERENCE

Find out all about the @ in e-mail addresses in Chapter 8.

## FIND IT ONLINE

Search for other computer books at the IDG Books Worldwide home page, located at **www.idgbooks.com**.

## Listing 10-11: USING FINGER ON A LOCAL SYSTEM

```
$ finger eric
Login name: eric
In real life: Eric Foster-Johnson
Directory: /usr/home/eric
Shell: /usr/local/bin/tcsh
On since Jul 17 16:20:10
    on ttyp4 from modem6.bigfun.com
Project: This is my project.
Plan:
I do too have a plan.
Yes, I really do.
So, there.
```

▲ *Running finger on a local system to see information about a user named **eric**. You can tell eric's shell (**tcsh**), home directory (**/usr/home/eric**), and other information.*

## Listing 10-12: RUNNING FINGER ON A REMOTE USER

```
$ finger ericfj@yonsen.bigfun.com
[yonsen.bigfun.com]
Login name: erc
In real life: Eric Foster-Johnson
Directory: /usr/home/erc
Shell: /usr/local/bin/tcsh
On since Jul 27 09:34:11
    on ttypc from mryuk
On since Jul 27 09:34:11
    46 minutes Idle Time
    on ttypd from mryuk
On since Jul 27 09:34:11
    30 minutes Idle Time
    on ttype from mryuk
No Plan.
```

▲ *Running **finger** on a remote Internet user named **erc**, logged in on system yonsen.bigfun.com (not a real system). Some Internet Service Providers do not allow you to run finger on their members.*

## Listing 10-13: USING RWHO TO SEE WHO IS ON THE NETWORK

```
$ rwho
ericfj    system1:ttyp4    Jul 17 16:20 :01
ericfj    system1:ttyp5    Jul 17 16:20 :23
fred gamera:barney:barney  Jul 14 14:37
fred gamera:ttyp1          Jul 14 14:37 :44
barney system1:ttyp0       Jul 17 11:37 :45
barney system1:ttyp8       Jul 17 11:37 :44
barney system1:ttyp9       Jul 17 11:37 :21
```

▲ *The **rwho** command tells you who is on the network and the systems they are logged in from.*

## Listing 10-14: CHECKING A CONNECTION WITH PING

```
$ ping www.idgbooks.com
PING www.idgbooks.com(206.175.162.15):
 56 data bytes
64 bytes from 206.175.162.15:icmp_seq=0
 ttl=236 time=230 ms
64 bytes from 206.175.162.15:icmp_seq=1
 ttl=238 time=170 ms

—www.idgbooks.com PING Statistics—
4 packets transmitted,4 packets received,
 0% packet loss
round-trip (ms) min/avg/max =169/188/230 ms
```

▲ *Using **ping** to verify that a network connection is working. Type **Ctrl-C** to exit **ping**.*

## Listing 10-15: A PING FAILURE

```
$ ping nicollet
PING nicollet (192.63.42.91): 56 data bytes

efoster-johnson.globalmt.com PINGStatistics
73 packets transmitted, 0 packets received,
 100% packet loss
```

▲ *The **ping** just hangs. You need to type **Ctrl-C** to exit.*

# Logging on Remotely with Telnet

The **telnet** command allows you to log onto a remote machine. When you connect to a remote machine, you are prompted for your user name and password. Once authenticated, a shell prompt appears—you're in. With **telnet**, the terminal connection acts much as if you logged in directly to an ASCII terminal. You can enter commands and interact with the remote system. If you run the X Window System, you can use **telnet** to log into a machine and then run X applications on that machine while displaying the windows on the workstation on your desk.

The prime advantage of **telnet** is that it allows you to work on other systems without being physically located near those systems. This is especially helpful if your organization has systems in multiple locations, such as in Minnesota and Ohio.

The **telnet** command works much the same as **rlogin**, a tool covered in the following task, allowing you to connect directly to a remote machine. Because the **telnet** command is considered part of the toolkit used by Internet surfer, it has actually grown in popularity over the years.

With **telnet**, you only need to know the hostname or IP address of the machine you're connecting to, such as sunsite.unc.edu, as illustrated by the following:

```
$ telnet sunsite.unc.edu
```

To log in, you need a valid user name and password on that system. Thus, most people use **telnet** to log onto systems on their local network. Internet service providers often allow you to log in through a dial-in account using **telnet** from a Windows PC and dialup networking.

## TAKE NOTE

### REMEMBER YOU'RE WORKING ON A REMOTE MACHINE

When you use **telnet** to log into a remote machine, you run a shell on that system, and have the configuration and setup that's stored in your shell startup files (such as **.profile** or **.login**) on that system. This fact is easy to forget, especially if you depend on command aliases or other aspects of your local system's configuration.

### YOU MUST HAVE A VALID USER ACCOUNT

Logging in with **telnet** is very similar to other forms of logging in. You must have a valid user name and password on the remote system.

### TELNET FROM WINDOWS

Windows includes a **telnet** application that works pretty much like the UNIX version. This is very useful if you have a Windows system on you desk and want to log into UNIX systems on the network. From the Start menu, choose Run and then type in **telnet** to launch this program. There are also more enhanced **telnet** programs for Windows available on the Internet. There are even versions of **telnet** for Windows CE handheld devices.

**CROSS-REFERENCE**

Chapter 7 covers the X Window System.

**FIND IT ONLINE**

A number of Windows **telnet** programs are available from a listing at **www.winfiles.com**.

## Listing 10-16: RUNNING TELNET ON THE INTERNET

```
$ telnet sunsite.unc.edu
Trying 152.2.254.81...
Connected to sunsite.unc.edu.
Escape character is '^]'.

SunOS 5.6

***** Welcome to SunSITE.unc.edu *****

To access SunSITE's public logins,
  telnet to public.sunsite.unc.edu
To login to SunSITE as a user, telnet to
login.sunsite.unc.edu

login:
```

▲ *You can use **telnet** to connect to public sites on the Internet, but you must have an account to log in.*

## Listing 10-17: THE TELNET PROMPT

```
$ telnet
telnet>
telnet> open yonsen
Trying 192.63.42.121...
Connected to yonsen.
Escape character is '^]'.
Warning: This session is not using secure
authentication.

OSF/1 (yonsen) (ttyp2)

login: erc
Password:
Last login: Tue Jul 21 16:04:15 from
  nicollet.
$
```

▲ *If you don't provide the name of a machine or an IP address on the command line, you can use the open command within the **telnet** application.*

## Listing 10-18: RUNNING TELNET ON A LOCAL NETWORK

```
$ telnet yonsen
Trying 192.63.42.121...
Connected to yonsen.
Escape character is '^]'.

Digital UNIX (yonsen) (ttyp6)

login: erc
Password:
Last login: Tue Jul 21 16:04:15 from
  nicollet.
$ uname -a
OSF1 yonsen.bigfun.com V4.0 878 alpha
$
$ df
Filesystem    1024-blocks   Used      Available
  Capacity    Mounted on
/dev/rz0a         492047     67458       375384
  16%           /
/proc                       0   0           0
  100%          /proc
/dev/rz0g       23787320  16278403  5130185
  77%           /usr
$ who
barney    console    Oct   7 16:06
fred      ttypd      Oct   7 10:47
erc       ttyp0      Oct   7 20:51
$
$ exit
logout
Connection closed by foreign host.
```

▲ *Most users run **telnet** to log in to systems on their organization's network.*

# Remote Computing with rcp, rsh, and rlogin

In addition to **telnet** and **ftp** — mainstays of remote computing — UNIX systems provide another set of commands including **rcp**, a remote copy program, **rsh**, a remote shell, and **rlogin**, a remote login program that acts much like **telnet**. Together, these are called the r utilities.

The **rcp** command copies files between systems. It looks and acts much like **cp**, but you can work with other systems. The basic syntax is the same as for **cp**:

```
$ rcp sourcefile destinationfile
```

To name remote files, use the *hostname:filename* syntax, separating the hostname from the filename on the remote machine with a colon. You can also copy files from a remote system to another remote system using **rcp**. For **rcp** to work, you must have a valid user name — the same user name — on the remote and local systems.

The **rsh** command runs a shell on the remote machine to execute a command you pass on the **rsh** command line. Any data from standard input on your local machine will get passed as standard input to the command on the remote machine. Any output from the remote machine gets passed as standard output on the local machine. Together, this makes it appear as if the remote command actually computes on your local system.

If you don't pass any command to **rsh**, it logs you in as if you used **rlogin**.

The **rlogin** command logs you into a remote machine. As such, **rlogin** works much like **telnet**, although it uses a different protocol. Your terminal type, set in the TERM variable, will get passed to the remote machine.

## TAKE NOTE

### ▶ SECURITY ISSUES

With these r tools (**rcp**, **rsh**, **rlogin**), you can place a file named **.rhosts** into your home directory. Inside the **.rhosts** file, you can place pairs of the names of systems and users from which you want to allow access to your local system. If you are logged into one of those systems, and connect to your original system, **rlogin** won't ask you for a password. An entry in the **.rhosts** file is sufficient. (The target system must be able to resolve your system's host name, too.) Futhermore, you can set up a system-wide file in **/etc/hosts.equiv** that lists locally-trusted hosts. As you'd suspect, this opens up a large hole in security. If a malicious user gains access to your account, that user can create a **.rhosts** file and gain even more access. Furthermore, that user could take advantage of any **.rhosts** files you've set up on systems on your network. Because of this, think carefully about using an **.rhosts** file.

### ▶ RSH MAY BE REMSH

On some systems, the **rsh** command is a restricted shell, not a remote shell. In those cases, the **rsh** command described on this page is normally named **remsh**.

**CROSS-REFERENCE**
Chapter 4 covers the TERM variable.

**FIND IT ONLINE**
The r commands originated with BSD UNIX. See **www.freebsd.org** for more information.

### Listing 10-19: COPYING A REMOTE FILE TO THE LOCAL MACHINE

```
$ rcp yonsen:/usr/home/erc/report.txt
```

▲ Copies remote file **/usr/home/erc/report.txt** from machine yonsen to the local directory.

### Listing 10-20: COPYING A LOCAL FILE TO A REMOTE MACHINE

```
$ rcp report.txt nicollet:/u/erc/reports
```

▲ Copies local file **report.txt** to the **/u/erc/reports** directory on machine nicollet.

### Listing 10-21: USING RLOGIN WITH A DIFFERENT USER NAME

```
$ rlogin -l fred yonsen
Password:
Last login: Tue Apr 21 15:10:51 from
 nicollet

Digital UNIX V3.2G (Rev. 62); Thu Feb 12
17:48:48 CST 1998
Digital UNIX V3.2G Worksystem Software
 (Rev. 62)

Eric Foster-Johnson's Business Box
 (nicollet)

$ whoami
fred
$ exit
logout
rlogin: connection closed.
```

▲ The **-l** option tells **rlogin** to log you in as a different user, in this case as user **fred**.

### Listing 10-22: RUNNING A COMMAND ON A REMOTE MACHINE WITH RSH

```
$ rsh yonsen "who"
erc        tty1       Aug 1 10:30
erc        ttyp2      Aug 1 10:30(:0.0)
erc        ttyp1      Aug 1 10:30(:0.0)
erc        ttyp0      Aug 1 10:30(:0.0)
fred       ttyp5      Aug 1  8:30(nicollet:0.0)
fred       ttyp7      Aug 1  8:31(nicollet:0.0)
fred       ttyp9      Aug 1  8:32(nicollet:0.0)
```

▲ Running the **who** command on remote system yonsen.

### Listing 10-23: RUNNING RSH WITH NO COMMAND

```
$ rsh yonsen
Password:
Last login: Wed Oct  7 16:06:41 on console

No directory!
Logging in with home = "/".
Digital UNIX V4.0D  (Rev. 878); Thu Jun 11
 15:36:29 CDT 1998
$ echo $SHELL
/bin/ksh
$ whoami
erc
$ exit
rlogin: connection closed.
```

▲ Running **rsh** without a command gets you a shell.

# Using UUCP

The **uucp** command, short for UNIX-to-UNIX Copy Program, copies files from one machine to another over a serial link, such as a modem connection. At first glance, in this age of Internet and the Information Superhighway, you may think that this is incredibly retro technology. And, conceptually, it is. It was invented long ago to support the Usenet, which provided e-mail and network news services, both of which are now mostly carried on the Internet.

Realistically, however, the **uucp** command has its widest application in the corporate world, where networked computers are very common. In these situations the corporate systems may not be tied to the outside world, only connected to other corporate systems. In these cases the **uucp** command is a handy way of transferring a file from your system to the corporate headquarters in Sioux City, Iowa.

The **uucp** command works much like **cp**, except that **uucp** works between systems. Like **cp**, the basic **uucp** command line follows:

```
$ uucp sourcefile destinationfile
```

The tricky part comes when you want to copy a file from a local system to a remote system or vice versa. As with the **rcp** command, you need to specify the hostname of remote systems. Unlike **rcp**, **uucp** uses a ! to separate the hostname from the filename (**rcp** uses :). (If the exclamation mark looks familiar, it should; remember, the old Usenet method of electronic-mail addressing makes heavy use of exclamation marks.)

The **uucp** command can also be used to grab files from another machine, as long as you have the proper permissions, as shown on the facing page.

Due to permissions, the **/usr/spool/uucppublic** directory is a common destination for **uucp** commands. Typically, this is the only directory open to remote systems using **uucp**.

The **uucp** command can be very frustrating, especially since it normally works in batch mode and your files may get transferred hours later. You can tell **uucp** to send you a receipt via electronic mail when the file transfer is completed with the **-m** option.

However, if you don't receive the confirming electronic mail, then you can assume that the transfer failed. To help find out why, look at the **uucp** log file with the **uulog** command.

You'll then need to read through the arcane information and try to make some sense of it. Successful file transfers will end with REMOTE REQUESTED or OK. An error like ACCESS DENIED helps track down why the transfer failed.

Sharp readers will note that the C shell will choke on the exclamation mark, as it represents a history command. To counter this, C shell users must structure their **uucp** commands differently. To tell the C shell that the exclamation mark is part of the **uucp** command, you need to precede it with a backslash (\):

```
% uucp chap10.txt \
   spike\!/usr/spool/uucppublic/chap10.txt
```

**CROSS-REFERENCE**
E-mail is covered in Chapter 8.

**FIND IT ONLINE**
Linux systems can run the UUCP commands. See **www.linux.org** for more on Linux.

## UUCP Background

UNIX can use several different methods of transmitting information between systems. Originally, UNIX-to-UNIX Copy Program (**uucp**) was written to communicate between systems via ordinary telephone lines. Today, these connections can take place between those same telephone lines via modem (at all speeds, from 2400 bits per second to nearly 56 kilobits per second), direct wiring, a local-area network, or a wide-area network connected via dedicated phone lines. Although the connection mechanisms have changed, the basic UUCP system has not, and remains mechanism-independent, which makes your life much simpler. As a user, you don't need to know the specifics of the connection mechanism; all you need to know is how to access the utilities that make communications possible.

There's no one, great program that oversees UNIX connections to the outside world. Much like everything else in the UNIX world, the communications utilities are quite small and serve limited purposes by themselves; only when strung together do they actually make up a powerful communications system.

Why connect to the outside world? Some companies directly link far-flung offices via dedicated phone lines to ensure instantaneous communications between employees. Others connect via modem over phone lines to the UUCP Network, a series of UNIX computers that pass along electronic mail and files all around the world.

In a rather confusing situation, *UUCP* refers both to a specific command (**uucp**) and a series of related commands (most of which begin with uu), including **uustat**, **uulog**, **uuname**, and **uux**. In this chapter **uucp** will refer to the specific **uucp** command, while **UUCP** will refer to the general command set.

### Listing 10-24: LIST AVAILABLE MACHINES WITH UUNAME

```
$ uuname
geisha
spike
khan
kirk
picard
```

▲ Before you use **uucp**, you need to know which machines are connected to yours. The **uuname** command does just this.

### Listing 10-25: COPYING A LOCAL FILE TO A REMOTE SYSTEM WITH UUCP

```
$ uucp chap10.txt \
spike!/usr/spool/uucppublic/chap10.txt
```

▲ Copies **chap10.txt** to the **/usr/spool/uucppublic/** directory on the machine named **spike**.

### Listing 10-26: COPYING A REMOTE FILE TO THE LOCAL SYSTEM WITH UUCP

```
$ uucp \
spike!/usr/spool/uucppublic/chap10.txt\
/usr/spool/uucppublic
```

▲ Reverses the previous example and copies **/usr/spool/uucppublic/chap10.txt** from the machine named **spike** to the **/usr/spool/uucppublic** directory on the local system.

### Listing 10-27: SENDING AN EMAIL MESSAGE WHEN DONE COPYING

```
$ uucp -m chap10.txt \
spike!/usr/spool/uucppublic/chap10.txt
```

▲ You can tell **uucp** to send you a receipt via electronic mail when the file transfer is completed with the **-m** option. If you don't receive the confirming electronic mail, then you can assume that the transfer failed.

# Personal Workbook

## Q&A

1. What do you call the address that every system on a TCP/IP network has?

   _____
   _____
   _____

2. Which command do you use to access remote disks transparently from your local system?

   _____
   _____
   _____

3. What can you use to share files with Windows systems?

   _____
   _____
   _____

4. Which two commands allow you to log in to a remote system?

   _____
   _____
   _____

5. Which command allows you to copy files between systems?

   _____
   _____
   _____

6. If you don't have a connection to the Internet, you can still transfer files between systems using what command?

   _____
   _____
   _____

7. How can you log on to remote UNIX systems from Windows?

   _____
   _____
   _____

8. If the **uccp** command fails to make a connection, what can you use to look at the **uucp** logs?

   _____
   _____

ANSWERS: PAGE 350

## EXTRA PRACTICE

1. Use **telnet** to log into another machine on your organization's network.

2. Use the **df** command to see what file systems are mounted on your system. Find out where the file systems originate.

3. See if your site allows **rsh** to run commands on remote systems. This is often turned off for security reasons.

4. Use the **ftp** command to transfer files between systems. Use **rcp** for the same task and compare the two.

5. Use the **ping** command to see if your system can connect to systems on the Internet such as **www.idgbooks.com**.

## REAL-WORLD APPLICATIONS

✔ The company's Web pages on the Internet don't work well with Internet Explorer. A colleague has fixed the Web pages but needs help uploading the changed files to the Web server machine. Use **ftp** to upload these Web pages (files ending in .html) to the Web server system. Your colleague has the machine name, as well as a valid user name and password on the Internet server machine.

✔ Use the **ftp** program to download the **gzip** source code from **ftp.gnu.org/pub/gnu/**.

✔ You find you are frequently logging in to another system on your network and the constant typing of passwords is getting on your nerves. Set up a **.rhosts** file so you can use **rlogin** without entering passwords. Consult with your system administrator first on security issues.

## Visual Quiz

From this anonymous **ftp** session, how would you download the patch program?

_____

_____

_____

_____

_____

_____

```
erc @ yonsen  /usr2/erc/books/teachux/teachux4                    _ □ X
$ ftp metalab.unc.edu
Connected to metalab.unc.edu.
220-          Welcome to UNC's MetaLab ftp archives!
220-          (at the site formerly known as sunsite.unc.edu)
220- Name (metalab.unc.edu:erc): anonymous
331 Guest login ok, send your complete e-mail address as password.
Password:
230 Guest login ok, access restrictions apply.
Remote system type is UNIX.
Using binary mode to transfer files.
ftp> cd /pub/Linux/devel
250 CWD command successful.
ftp> dir
200 PORT command successful.
150 Opening ASCII mode data connection for /bin/ls.
total 1734
-rw-rw-r--  1 347  1002       90 Jun 09  1998 README
-rw-rw-r--  1 347  1002   123258 Jul 12  1996 autoconf-2.10.bin.tgz
-rw-rw-r--  1 347  1002     1140 Jul 12  1996 autoconf-2.10.lsm
-rw-rw-r--  1 347  1002   380539 Jul 12  1996 autoconf-2.10.src.tgz
-rw-rw-r--  1 347  1002      604 Nov 30  1993 patch-2.1-bin.lsm
-rw-rw-r--  1 347  1002    79300 Nov 30  1993 patch-2.1-bin.tar.gz
-rw-rw-r--  1 347  1002    71541 Feb 13  1994 patch-2.1.tar.gz
226 Transfer complete.
ftp> []
```
```
☆ Linux   ▦ erc...  ▦ erc...  ▦ erc...  ◫ Nets...  ◫ Nets...  ◫ Com...  ◀ xv 3...  ◀ xv c...  2:30 ▣
```

# PART

# III

# Working with UNIX Tools

Now that you've been exposed to UNIX's capabilities, it's time for you to put your knowledge into action.

Chapter 11 covers text editing in UNIX, which means the creation of ASCII text files with tools such as **vi** and **emacs**. You can use this text internally — such as programming or shell-script files — or you can send the files to text processors such as **troff** for further processing, as described in Chapter 12.

While other operating systems focus on large tools that do many things at once, UNIX generally sticks to the mantra that each tool should do one thing and do it well. Chapter 12 shows the benefits and drawbacks of this approach.

Chapter 13 covers shell programming basics, including changing shells and executing scripts. Chapter 14 introduces basic C programming tools; in no time at all you'll be a fully functional C programmer, whether you want to be or not. Chapter 15 goes over assorted administrative topics, including system backup, setup procedures, and dealing with emergencies. Finally, chapter 16 explains advanced and additional UNIX tools such as **awk** and **Perl**. The UNIX **cron** facility runs programs (often shell scripts) at periodic intervals. This is very useful for scheduling backups and running tasks such as reports.

# CHAPTER 11

# Text Editing

**W**ithout a doubt, the most common tasks in your day-to-day work are creating and editing text. If you think about it, most of your computing needs are filled by text editors. Letters and memos are written with an editor. Reports are created via the editor. Lists acting as informal databases are created with an editor.

UNIX features several text editors: **vi**, **ed**, and **emacs** are the most common. Their features overlap (indeed, **vi** is actually an extended version of **ed**), and the editor you decide to use regularly (and you will need to use one regularly) will be as much a matter of taste and availability as of features. Not every editor is available on every system: **emacs**, while available for free from a variety of sources, is generally not part of a standard UNIX system. This chapter covers the **vi** and **emacs** editors in a tutorial format, guiding you through the creation and editing of a document.

There are many advanced features to **vi** and **emacs** that we won't even hint at. Our philosophy is to present you with enough information to get you going; the rest is up to you, through perusing the online-manual pages or by consulting other advanced books (which we list in Appendix A).

# Creating a Document with vi

When it was first introduced, **vi,** which stands for visual editor, was considered a great leap forward. (Indeed, when compared to **ed**, an older single-line editor, it was a great leap forward.) Virtually every UNIX system ships with **vi**, making it one of the most ubiquitous pieces of software in the UNIX world. It is used to create and edit ASCII files, which can be used in a variety of situations — creating shell scripts and mail messages, or editing UNIX system files, such as the **.profile** and **.login** files.

If you're used to word processors in the DOS or Macintosh worlds, there are aspects to **vi** that you'll find annoying and primitive, but there are other aspects that you'll find reassuring and familiar. Like most word processors, **vi** is a full-screen editor; instead of having to edit a file one line at a time (as **ed** does), **vi** allows you to load a file and view it one screen at a time. (This capability was quite advanced for its day, so don't snicker.) It does not support any document formatting (such as bold or italic), spell checking, or any preview of the printed page. On the plus side, **vi** is extremely fast when scrolling through large documents, and some of the features it lacks can be found in other standard UNIX utilities (such as the aforementioned spell checking).

You can run **vi** in full screen at a terminal or in an X Window. In the figures on the opposite page, we're running **vi** in an X Window, but running X is not a requirement for running **vi**.

You can start **vi** in two ways — without a file loaded:

```
$ vi
```

or with a file loaded:

```
$ vi filename
```

where *filename* is the name of the file to be created or edited. (Both options are shown on the opposite page.) Command-line options are also available, as listed in Table 11-1 on the opposite page. If you start **vi** without a file (as is the case on the opposite page, in the top-left figure), are presented with a mostly blank screen, with a cursor in the upper-left corner and a series of tilde (~), or null, characters running down the left side of the screen. The null characters tell us that there is nothing on the page (paradoxical, isn't it?).

## TAKE NOTE

### FREE VI

The freely available version of **vi** for Linux and FreeBSD is **elvis**. However, this is more a conceptual and legal distinction than a practical distinction; using **vi** at a command line will summon the **elvis** editor. Apart form one rarely used command, **vi** and **elvis** are virtually identical.

**CROSS-REFERENCE**
Learn about text processing in Chapter 2.

**FIND IT ONLINE**
Further information about the **elvis** text editor can be found at **ftp.cs.pdx.edu/pub/elvis/README.html**.

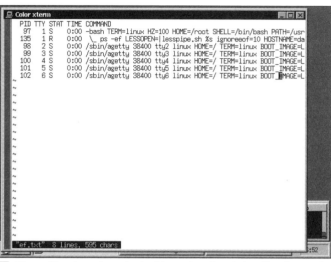

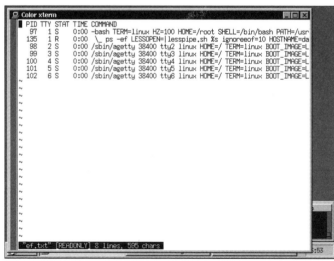

This is **vi** without a file loaded. Notice the series of tilde characters, telling us that there's nothing yet to be edited. At the bottom of the screen there's a status line, showing your place in the file and the size of the file. Here, it tells us we have an empty buffer.

Here, **vi** has been launched with an already existing file. The text is loaded and awaiting editing.

It can also be launched in read-only mode using the **-R** option. You can tell the status is read-only from the status line at the bottom of the screen. If you were to try and edit this file, you'd generate an error message.

## Table 11-1: COMMON VI COMMAND-LINE OPTIONS

| Option | Result |
| --- | --- |
| **-L** | Starts **vi** and recovers a file lost during a system crash. Can be used in conjunction with the **-r** option, described below. (Make sure you type an uppercase **L** and not a lowercase **l** [ell]. Using **-l** would tell **vi** that it's editing a Lisp file, which would change the appearance of your ASCII text.) |
| **-r** | Recovers an open file after a crash. |
| **-R** | Reads a file, but does not allow you to change the file. |

# Applying vi Modes

Working in **vi** is a matter of working in two modes: *insert* and *command*. When you start **vi**, you're automatically placed in command mode. Here, all your keystrokes are interpreted as commands. This is the point when **vi** trips up beginners: It won't accept much in the way of keyboard input, and there's precious little feedback to the user.

Since you have no text yet, working in command mode would be rather fruitless. (You would also generate a series of beeps, signifying error messages.) Your first step, then, will be switching to insert mode. In this mode you can enter text and stop **vi** from sending those annoying beeps your way. Switch to insert mode by typing **i**; this places you at the beginning of the onscreen page. (Lowercase **i** is not the only way to enter insert mode — the other options are listed in Table 11-2 on the opposite page. The other options are for entering text in an already-existing screen with text.) At this point you can begin entering text. Go ahead and type in the text shown in the top-left figure on the opposite page, *exactly* as shown.

Notice that **vi** doesn't wrap words when you get to the edge of the screen (unlike the previous example). If you want a line to end, you have to hit the **Enter** (or **Return**) key yourself. For the purposes of this tutorial, it doesn't matter one way or the other.

After typing in your text, return to command mode; do so by hitting your **Escape** (**Esc**) key. (If at any time you're not sure if you're in command mode,

go ahead and hit the **Escape** key a few times. All you do is generate a beep; you won't do anything to your current file.) Again, **vi** gives you no indication about what mode it is in. As you can tell, **vi** is a very minimalist text editor.

If you want **vi** to tell you when it's in insert mode, type:

```
:set smd
```

while in command mode. This tells **vi** to display INPUT on the bottom-right corner of the screen when in insert mode, as shown in the left-hand figure on the opposite page.

## Searching in vi

While in command mode, you can perform various, minimal, editing chores. As you've already seen, most of the commands in command mode are preceded by a colon (:). In this case, use **vi**'s search capability to find the first instance of **system**. The careful proofreaders in the audience will note that we were inconsistent in our capitalization of **System**. In command mode, type:

```
/system
```

and then press **Enter**.

Surprise! **Vi** *does* provide some minimal feedback, as you can see at the bottom of the screen, in the right-hand figure on the opposite page. This is called the *status line* and provides what little feedback **vi** features.

**CROSS-REFERENCE**
For a review of file and directory basics, see Chapter 2.

**FIND IT ONLINE**
You can find an online tutorial about **vi** at www.csl.mtu.edu/~yzhao/hu333/vi.html.

■ *Notice **vi** is working in insert mode, as seen in the status line.*

■ *Here are the results of a search for the word **system**.*

| Table 11-2: VI INSERT-MODE COMMANDS | |
|---|---|
| **Command** | **Result** |
| **Enter** | Inserts new line immediately following current character. |
| **i** | Inserts before current character. |
| **I** | Inserts at the beginning of the current line. (Uppercase i.) |
| **a** | Appends to the right of the current character. |
| **A** | Appends at the end of the current line. |
| **o** | Inserts new line immediately following current line. |
| **O** | Inserts new line immediately before current line. |

| Table 11-3: VI COMMAND-MODE COMMANDS | |
|---|---|
| **Command** | **Result** |
| **Esc** | Exits insert mode and enters command mode. |
| **Enter** | Moves the cursor to the beginning of the next line. |
| **/string** | Searches forward for the first instance of *string*. |
| **?string** | Searches backward for the first instance of *string*. |

# Editing Text in vi

In the previous task we searched for the word **system** because we incorrectly capitalized it in our example text. When the search was complete, the pointer ended up over the **s** in **system**. Logically, you would think that changing the **s** to **S** would be a matter of just typing **S**, as is the case with every other word processor under the sun. But no. Here, the process is somewhat convoluted:

- ► First you must delete the current character and then insert the new character. Do this by typing **x**, which erases the character under the pointer. (To delete the character to the left of the pointer, type **X**. As always in UNIX, case counts.)
- ► Switch to insert mode by typing **i**.
- ► Type **S** to create the word **System**.

As we said, **vi** is much better suited for scrolling and writing than it is for editing.

Another method of changing our **s** to **S** (we'll let you decide if it's any easier) would be through the use of **vi**'s **r** command, which changes the character under a cursor to a character that you specify. In our case, we want to position the cursor over the **s** and then type **rS** to replace the current character with an uppercase **S**. To change case, you can also position the cursor over the letter you want to change and type the tilde (~) character in command mode. This should change an uppercase letter to a lowercase and vice versa.

Other deletion commands are listed in Table 11-4.

## Cutting and Pasting Text

The editing capabilities of **vi** include rudimentary cut-and-paste capabilities. It's a three-step process: cut (or yank), position, and paste.

You can yank by the character, by the word, or by the sentence. (Table 11-5 lists all the available yank options.) After you yank text, it's then stored in a portion of your UNIX system's memory. After you decide where you want to put the yanked text by placing the pointer at the insertion point, you can use one of two methods to paste the text:

- ► If you want to paste the yank to the right of the pointer, type **p**.
- ► If you want to paste the yank to the left of the pointer, type **P**.

### TAKE NOTE

► **EXPANDING COMMANDS WITH NUMBERS**

Any of the text-manipulation commands in this chapter — deletions, cursor movements, yankings, and so on — can be expanded by adding a number to the command, indicating that the command is to repeated the number of times you specify. For instance, adding a number to the basic **y** command would yank that number of characters.

**CROSS-REFERENCE**
Chapter 16 covers advanced UNIX tools.

**FIND IT ONLINE**
The complete **vi** reference area can be found at **www.math.fu-berlin.de/~guckes/vi/.**

■ *You can use the **:d** command to delete a specific number of lines. Begin by placing the pointer at the beginning of the lines you want to delete. Next, go to command mode by pressing the **Escape** key.*

■ *To delete a line, use the **:d** command. The number used will determine how many lines are cut. Here, you can see the results of cutting a line of text.*

## Table 11-4: VI DELETION COMMANDS

| Command | Result |
| --- | --- |
| **x** | Deletes character under cursor. |
| **d** | Deletes the current line. |
| **D** | Deletes to the end of the current line. |
| **:x** | Deletes character under cursor. |
| **:X** | Deletes character to the left of the cursor. |
| **:D** | Deletes current line. |
| **:D$** | Deletes to the end of the current line. |
| **:U** | Undoes deletion. |

## Table 11-5: A FEW YANKING OPTIONS IN VI

| Command | Result |
| --- | --- |
| **y** | Yanks current character. |
| **yn** | Yanks $n$ number of characters, where $n$ is a number. |
| **yw** | Yanks current word. |
| **yy** | Yanks current line. |
| **nyy** | Yanks $n$ lines of text, where $n$ is a number. |
| **y$** | Yanks to the end of the line. |
| **y)** | Yanks to the end of the sentence. |
| **y}** | Yanks to the end of the paragraph. |
| **Y** | Yanks the current line. |

# Scrolling Through and Saving Files

In the 1970s, not every keyboard featured arrow keys. If you remember keyboards of the 1970s, you will probably feel right at home using **vi**. Because we're not enthralled with a return to the 1970s, we're not going to exhaustively cover all of the strange convolutions **vi** goes to in order to move the cursor around a screen without any cursor keys (or a mouse, for that matter). If your keyboard lacks cursor keys—which would make you a true dinosaur in the UNIX world—refer to your system's documentation for a full listing of the **vi** cursor controls.

You should remember a few things when moving through documents:

▶ Cursor keys can be used in both command and insert modes.
▶ The left and right cursor keys move only to the beginning and end of current lines and will not move the cursor to the surrounding lines. To move between lines, use the **Up** and **Down** keys.

You may also be able to use a pointer if you have a mouse installed on your computer. Depending on your version of UNIX and **vi**, you can move your pointer via the mouse. Also, depending on your version of UNIX and **vi**, you may be able to use the pointer to scroll between different parts of the same page when working under the X Window System. In this instance, you're not actually using **vi** to scroll in the document; you're using the capabilities of **xterm** to scroll in the document. The **elvis** version of **vi** that comes with all Linux distributions and FreeBSD is adept at this form of scrolling.

Other useful cursor and scrolling commands are listed in Table 11-6.

## Saving a File

Saving a file is a simple process. You can save a file and continue working in **vi** or you can simultaneously quit **vi** and save the file. Both methods are explained in the two figures on the opposite page.

Other file-saving options are listed in Table 11-7.

### File Management and vi

When you load a file in **vi**, you really are loading a copy of the file into your computer's RAM (or, as referred to in UNIX parlance, the *buffer*). The original file does not change unless *you* specify a change, either through saving a newer version of the file, deleting the file, or saving an entirely new file to the same filename.

For example, if you made many changes in a file and weren't happy with the results, you could start over by quitting **vi** without saving the file and reloading the original version. If you were to accidentally make many cuts to your original file, you could discard the edited version and reload the original.

**CROSS-REFERENCE**
Learn about **xterm** and the X Window System in Chapter 7.

**FIND IT ONLINE**
If you're really yearning for the 1970s, check out **205.250.133.10/osteamnov8t6/**.

■ To save a file and continue working with **vi**, begin by entering command mode by pressing the **Escape** key. Next, enter a command of **:w test**, with **test** being the name of the file. Notice **vi** is still running, with the file named test still in the edit buffer.

■ When you save a file, **vi** tells you how long the file is (in lines) and size (in characters).

## Table 11-6: SOME USEFUL VI CURSOR AND SCROLLING COMMANDS

| Command | Result |
|---------|--------|
| 0 | Moves the cursor to the beginning of the current line. |
| $ | Moves the cursor to the end of the current line. |
| w | Moves the cursor to the beginning of the next word. |
| *n*G | Moves the cursor to the beginning of line *n* (where *n* is a numeral). |
| G | Moves the cursor to the last line of the file. |
| *n*\| | Moves the cursor to the beginning of column *n* (where *n* is a numeral). |
| Ctrl-B | Scrolls the screen up one full page. (Think back.) |
| Ctrl-F | Scrolls the screen down one full page. (Think forward.) |

## Table 11-7: OPTIONS FOR SAVING A FILE IN VI

| Command | Result |
|---------|--------|
| :q | Quits **vi** after a file is saved. If a file has not been saved, **vi**, quite gallantly, refuses to quit. |
| :q! | Quits **vi** without saving the file. |
| :w | Saves the file. If the file has not been saved previously and you try to save without specifying a filename, **vi** will warn you. |
| :w *filename* | Saves the file to the name *filename*. If you want to save an existing file to a new filename, use this command with a new filename. However, note that you are still editing the file under the original filename. |
| :x | Saves file and quits **vi**. |
| ZZ | Saves file and quits **vi**. |
| :wq | Saves file and quits **vi**, same as **ZZ**. |

# Creating a Document with emacs

The Wordstar of UNIX, **emacs** is a popular, though not necessarily easy to use, text editor. **Emacs** does not ship with every version of UNIX. It is not shipped as part of the generic System V Release 4 distribution, although several vendors have seen fit to ship **emacs** on their UNIX systems.

The first version of **emacs** (though not for a UNIX system) was written by Richard Stallman, whom some of you might recognize as the leader of the Free Software Foundation. Several versions of **emacs** are floating around out there, including one distributed by the Free Software Foundation. We're not going to cover each version here; instead, we try to use a most-common-denominator approach to this discussion, and use a recent version, 20.1, as our example.

**Emacs** can be run both in terminal mode and under the X Window System. For our purposes, we illustrate **emacs** when run under X, but the commands and procedures described here (except for the use of a mouse) will apply to both modes.

To load **emacs**, use the following command line at a system prompt (either in terminal mode or in an **xterm** window):

```
$ emacs
```

The result is shown in the upper-left corner of the opposite page.

If you want to start **emacs** with a file loaded, do so by including the name of the file as an argument:

```
$ emacs filename
```

The result is shown at the upper-right corner of the opposite page. There are some command-line arguments to **emacs**, which are discussed in Table 11-8.

Unlike **vi** or **ed**, **emacs** works in only one mode, so you don't need to worry about hitting the **Esc** key to enter a command. Go ahead and enter the text shown in the bottom-left figure on the opposite page, mistakes and all. You'll be editing this text in the next few tasks. Also, note that **emacs** does not wrap text to fit text within the confines of a display (although this can be changed), so you have to hit the **Enter** or **Return** key at the end of every line. Do so when typing in this text.

## Your Mileage May Vary

If some of the keystrokes we mention here don't work on your system, don't worry — it could be that your version of **emacs** is slightly different to the ones we were using to prepare this chapter. Because we're using the most-common-denominator approach here, we would *strongly* suggest that you consult more advanced texts before relying on **emacs** as your only text editor.

Also, the screens shown in this section have a menu bar near the top. Your version of **emacs** may or may not have this menu bar.

**CROSS-REFERENCE**

To find more information concerning **emacs**, see Appendix B.

**FIND IT ONLINE**

A separate group manages a version of **emacs** running on X, **xemacs: www.xemacs.org.**

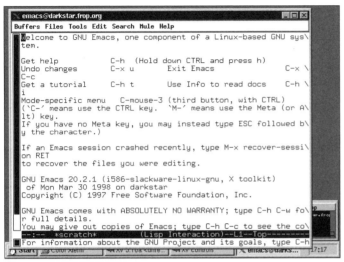

You can launch **emacs** without a file loaded. Doing so yields a screen like this one, explaining some basic **emacs** facts. You could go ahead and type away in this display.

You can also launch **emacs** with a file loaded. To do so, include a filename on the command line. With the file loaded, you can begin typing.

**Emacs** looks like other graphical applications. A pull-down menu accesses commands. Here we choose to display a calendar. Commands can also be entered at the bottom of the screen.

## Table 11-8: EMACS COMMAND-LINE OPTIONS

| Command | Result |
| --- | --- |
| - -no-init-file | Loads **emacs** without your customized initialization file. |
| - -user=*user* | Loads another user's initialization file. |
| +*num file* | Loads *file* and then places the cursor on line number *num*. |

# Navigating emacs

arlier we described emacs as being the Wordstar of UNIX text editing. Why? Like DOS's Wordstar, **emacs** relies heavily on commands issued from the keyboard in conjunction with the **Control** (**Ctrl**) and **Meta** keys. Like Wordstar, **emacs** enables you to do most of your work from the keyboard; touch typists should love **emacs**. And like Wordstar, many of the commands may be obscure and hard to remember.

You always have access to **emacs** commands through pull-down menus, which list the available commands.

## Cursor Commands

Like **vi**, **emacs** features a ton of commands designed to navigate you around the screen, a throwback to the days when many users did not have cursor keys on their keyboards. As with our discussion of **vi**, we're not going to discuss all of the obscure cursor commands. Instead, we list the more useful cursor commands in Table 11-9. Execution of these commands can sometimes be inconsistent, as outlined in the previous section. These commands should be tried only if your regular navigational commands, such as **Page Up**, **Page Down**, and the various cursor keys, don't respond.

## Using the Mouse

If your UNIX system supports a mouse (either in terminal mode or X Window), then **emacs** will recognize it. You can use the mouse to scroll through a document and make selections from a pull-down menu. Be warned that the menus aren't quite as handy as you think. Go ahead and pull down the File menu. Select Open File.

If you have previously worked with Windows or the Mac or even other X Window applications such as Netscape Navigator, you expect a command to be implemented when you select it from the menu. Not so with **emacs** — its creators have stubbornly avoided following other graphical conventions and have stayed with the quirky practice of using the menus to load files in a special area at the bottom of the document.

With the command loaded at the bottom of the document, you can run the command directly or else you can enter additional information (for instance, when loading a file, this is where you can specify the file to be loaded).

### CROSS-REFERENCE

Learn more about Netscape Navigator in Chapter 9.

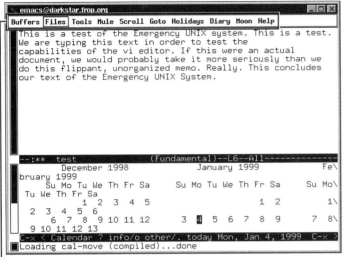

❶ *Access pull-down menus with the mouse or use a keyboard combination. Clicking a menu will pull it down.*

■ *After selecting an item from the pull-down menu, the command is loaded at the bottom of the screen. In this example, we're opening a directory. Press* **Enter** *to run the command. You can also enter additional information, such as a directory name, before running the command.*

■ *If you want to open an existing file, select Open Files from the File menu. The command is then loaded in the bottom of the window. Press* **Enter** *to actually run the command. A listing of files appears. You can select one of these files or change to a different subdirectory.*

## Table 11-9: EMACS COMMAND-LINE OPTIONS

| Command | Result |
| --- | --- |
| **Ctrl-L** | Moves current cursor line to the middle of the screen. |
| **Ctrl-V** | Moves forward one screen. |
| **Meta-V** | Moves backward one screen. |
| **Meta-<** | Moves to the beginning of the file. |
| **Meta->** | Moves to the end of the file. |

# Editing Text in emacs

Most users can use the keyboard **Backspace** and **Delete** keys to delete text. **Emacs** does provide for keyboard equivalents should your system not support **Backspace** or **Delete** keys. With **emacs**, you can map any function to any key, although this process should only be attempted by advanced users. (Why? Because it's easy to incorrectly change the key function and then really screw up your system.) Other deletion commands are listed in Table 11-10.

## Searching and Replacing

To search for a specific string within **emacs**, use the **Ctrl-S** command to invoke **emacs**' search command. (If you're at the end of a file and want to search backwards, use the **Ctrl-R** command.) A prompt appears at the bottom of the screen, as shown in the figure in the top left of the opposite page. Enter your search string to initiate the search.

Note that this provides an incremental search. That is, as you type in the word or phrase to search for, **emacs** is already looking for the text string. This can be good or bad, depending on your needs—many find it easy to enter an entire string and search for the exact string.

## Copying and Moving Text

If you plan on copying and moving a lot of text, you'll find that **emacs**' capabilities in this area are more advanced than **vi**'s. **Emacs** allows you to highlight a section of text for copying and deleting purposes. To mark a section of text, move your cursor to the beginning of the section and drag the mouse to the end of the text. (This is a vast improvement over older versions of **emacs**, where you needed to "mark" the text before moving it.)

To cut the highlighted text, type **Ctrl-w** or select Cut from the Edit menu. To retrieve it from the kill buffer, we position our cursor over the **R** in **Really** and type **Ctrl-y**. The process is explained in the figures on the opposite page.

---

**TAKE NOTE**

▶ **SAVING A FILE**

Saving a file in **emacs** is a simple process: type **Ctrl-x Ctrl-s**. Emacs asks you for the name of the file. If you want to save a file and quit **emacs** simultaneously, you would use the following command sequence: **Ctrl-x Ctrl-c**.

▶ **KILLING TEXT**

Killing text moves the text to a section of memory devoted to storage of deleted text, called a *kill buffer*. You don't need to set up a kill buffer, in fact, you don't need to do anything at all to the kill buffer, except to know that it exists. In our example of cutting and pasting, we are deleting a marked section of text and placing it in the kill buffer.

---

**CROSS-REFERENCE**

A kill buffer is not related to the **kill** command, which you learned about in Chapter 6.

**FIND IT ONLINE**

Information about the many modes of **emacs** can be found at **www.cs.indiana.edu/elisp/major-modes. html**.

■ *Use the **Ctrl-S** command to search for text. The prompt shown at the bottom of this window is used to enter the search string.*

■ *To cut and paste, position the cursor at the beginning of the text to be cut, then drag your mouse to the end of the text. The text to be cut is now marked. Cut the text by typing **Ctrl-W**. The text is now transferred to the kill buffer.*

■ *Decide where you want to paste the previously cut text and move your cursor to that point. To paste the text, type **Ctrl-y** or choose Select ⇨ Paste from the Edit menu.*

### Table 11-10: EMACS DELETION COMMANDS

| Command | Result |
| --- | --- |
| **Delete** | Deletes the character to the left of the cursor. |
| **Ctrl-D** | Deletes character under the cursor. |
| **Ctrl-K** | Deletes all characters to the end of the line. |
| **Meta-D** | Deletes forward to the end of the next word. |
| **Meta-Delete** | Deletes backward to the beginning of the previous word. |

# Help in emacs

**E**macs, amazingly enough, contains a help system that may or may not be of use to you. (We are amazed because help features — other than **man** pages — are extremely rare in the UNIX world.) It's worth a try if you get stuck, anyway.

Depending on your version of **emacs**, type one of the following commands to summon help:

```
Ctrl-H
F1
Esc-?
Meta-?
Meta-x
```

Unfortunately, we've found that different versions of **emacs** treat the help system differently, although **Ctrl-H** is the most common means to enter help. To get a topic of all the help subjects, we find using the Help menu is your best bet, as shown in the upper-left corner of the opposite page.

The **Info** mode of **emacs**, as shown in the top right of the opposite page, is a hypertext-based system that covers all GNU commands and software packages. As hypertext, it allows you to move down layer by layer from general commands and concepts to more specific information.

For instance: The Info section of the Help command brings up a general listing of all the GNU commands and packages. Scroll down the list and find the entry for **emacs** to get to the **emacs**-specific information, as shown in the bottom-left corner of the opposite page.

Once you start descending the different levels, the information becomes more pertinent. At some point you'll make it to a listing of commands and a short two-word description of that they do. If you select either the command or the description, you'll be taken to a more detailed summary of both the command and the functionality. This information can be quite valuable as you try to do more advanced formatting in **emacs**, such as setting up text in multiple columns.

Several other useful information sources exist within **emacs**. The Help menu brings you a Frequently Asked Questions (FAQ) list, which brings some order to tidbits of information about **emacs**. (You can see it in the bottom-right corner of the opposite page.) Information about differences between versions of **emacs**, focusing on the version installed on your system, can also be accessed from the Help menu.

## TAKE NOTE

### NO MAN PAGES?

Unlike virtually every other UNIX application, **emacs** does not rely on online-manual pages for describing its functionality. Why not? A case of Not Invented Here, perhaps. The Free Software Foundation — creators of **emacs** — has always pushed for their own **info** format for online help, but the rest of the UNIX world has basically stayed with the older **man** format. Why? Because the **info** format requires the use of **emacs** to browse documentation, and the UNIX world is too fragmented to put such control in the hands of one organization.

## CROSS-REFERENCE

See Appendix B for more information on Linux and the FSF.

## FIND IT ONLINE

The complete **emacs** manual can be found at **www.delorie.com/gnu/docs/emacs/emacs_toc.html**.

■ *The Help menu features a variety of tools.*

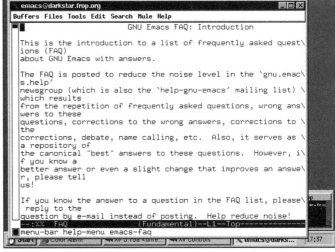

■ *The info mode provides a general overview of all GNU commands. You need to find **emacs** in the list of **info** topics.*

■ *Once you find **emacs**, the **emacs**-specific sections of information becomes available.*

■ *Also included in **emacs** is a handy FAQ, also accessible from the Help menu.*

# Other Text-Editing Tools

**V**i, **emacs**, and **ed** aren't the only tools used to edit and create text on UNIX systems. Here, you learn about a few tools that you may or may not find very useful.

For instance, unless your spelling is perfect, you could benefit from a spelling checker. The UNIX operating system ships with a spelling checker built-in, accessed by (surprise!) the **spell** command. Like everything in the UNIX operating system, the **spell** command is deceptively simple, but requires a little bit of work to be truly useful. To use **spell**, type the following at the command prompt

```
$ spell filename
```

where *filename* is the name of the file to be checked. The **spell** command lists one "misspelled" word at a time after the command prompt.

We say "misspelled" because the **spell** command is really of limited usage. Many beginning computer users make the mistake of relying on their spelling checker to ferret out all errors in a file. A spelling checker will find the obviously misspelled words, but it won't find all the errors in a file. For example, **spell** won't tell you to use *hear* instead of *here* in the following sentence: "It was hard to here the band." It will always trip on proper names, since they are not usually found in the dictionary. Because the dictionary is rather small by spelling-checker standards — about 30,000 words in the last version we examined

extensively — **spell** trips on properly spelled, yet justifiably obscure words. And even though **spell** finds misspelled words, it doesn't suggest correct spellings.

If there are only a few misspelled words in a file, printing them to your screen isn't a big deal. However, with larger files chockfull of potential errors, you need smoother mechanisms for dealing with the errors. That's why we generally send the output of **spell** to a file or directly to a printer. To send the errors to a file, use the following:

```
$ spell test > errors
```

(We chose errors for its descriptive quality. You can choose whatever filename your heart desires.)

The **emacs** text editor has its own spelling checker, as we show in the bottom-left figure on the opposite page. This is a vast improvement on the **spell** command, since it suggests the correct spellings of words. To summon it, use the Edit menu.

---

## TAKE NOTE

### ▶ CHECKING FOR WORD COUNTS

The **wc** command counts how many words are in a file. You use it on the command line in conjunction with a filename, as shown in the figure in the bottom-right corner of the opposite page. You could also specify more than one file for word counting.

---

**CROSS-REFERENCE**
Netscape Navigator, described in Chapter 9, has a very good spelling checker built in.

**FIND IT ONLINE**
View the National Spelling Bee's Web site: **www.spellingbee.com**.

## Listing 11-1: RUNNING THE SPELL COMMAND

```
$ spell test
onorganized
unorganizd
teste
probleme
potatoe
Quayle
```

▲ *When running the **spell** command from the command line, you usually include a filename, in this case, test. The result is a list of misspellings.*

■ *The **spell** command doesn't make any changes to your original file, such as highlighting the misspellings, nor does it suggest correct spellings, so you need to make changes by hand.*

■ *Emacs features its own spelling checker. It's more interactive, showing you a file containing a misspelling. It also suggests the correct spelling of a particular word.*

■ *The **wc** command does only one thing: count the number of words in a file. Here we've used the command to count the number of lines, words, and characters in the file test.*

# Introducing Other Text Editors

You may or may not have other text editors installed on your system. While **vi** and **emacs** will fill the needs of most users, you may want to check out one of these alternatives.

The most common alternative is **xedit**, a basic text editor that ships with the X Window System. (It's no surprise that **xedit** runs only under X and not in terminal mode.) **Xedit** is very basic: It allows you to load, save, and search through text files. To load **xedit**, use the following command line:

```
$ xedit
```

You could also launch **xedit** with a file loaded if you specify the file on the command line.

As you can see from the figure at the top-left of the opposite page, the **xedit** command is rather spartan — three buttons to provide the basic functions, as well as a file buffer with a file already loaded (the infamous **test** file).

## Using Pico

A text editor more commonly used as a programmer's editor is **pico**, which can be found in many UNIX systems and most Linux systems. It is very straightforward: you launch it with or without a file, type in your text, and then save your work. To launch **pico**, use the following command line:

```
$ pico
```

You could also launch **pico** with a file loaded if you specify the file on the command line.

---

**TAKE NOTE**

### COMMERCIAL ALTERNATIVES

As Linux has become more prevalent in the workplace, commercial vendors have rushed to enter the marketplace. The leading commercial word processor for Linux is WordPerfect from Corel, a company that's quite committed to the Linux market. The current version of WordPerfect for Linux (at the time of this writing) is version 8. It's shown in the bottom-right corner of the opposite page. A free download of the product is available from **linux.corel.com/linux8/download.htm**

Applixware is another popular commercial Linux text editor. It is actually a collection of office tools including a word processor, spreadsheet, graphics (drawing) tool, and a mail tool. See the company's site for more information: **www.applix.com/ appware/linux/index.htm.**

For an extensive, frequently updated list of Linux word processing packages, as well as other useful Linux utilities, check out **www.linuxapps.com.**

---

**CROSS-REFERENCE**

Programmers, as explained in Chapter 16, usually use **pico** as their editor.

**FIND IT ONLINE**

An introduction to **pico** can be found at **www.usd.edu/ trio/tut/pico/.**

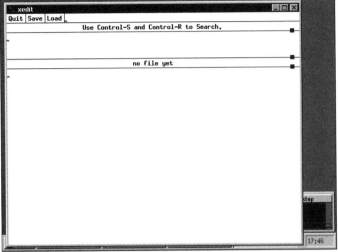

■ *The **xedit** command brings up a text processor.*

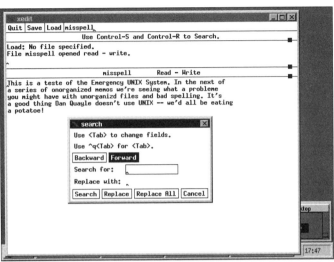

■ *To search for text in the open file, use **Ctrl-S**, which brings up this dialog box.*

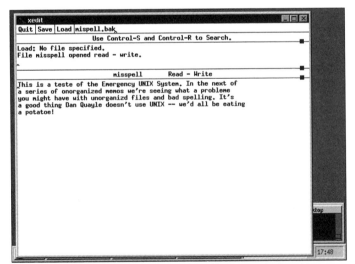

■ *To save the file, enter the name of the file next to the Load button. Next, press the Save button.*

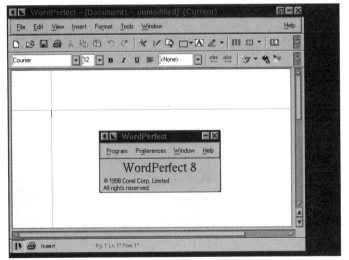

■ *WordPerfect is the leading commercial word processor for the Linux market.*

# Personal Workbook

## Q&A

**1** Where would you use a text editor?

_____

_____

_____

**2** Can you do any spell checking using the **vi** command?

_____

_____

_____

**3** Does **vi** support any fonts?

_____

_____

_____

**4** What's the name of a popular **vi** clone?

_____

_____

_____

**5** Is **emacs** available on every UNIX computer system?

_____

_____

_____

**6** What sort of documentation is included with **emacs**?

_____

_____

_____

**7** How do you search for text in **emacs**?

_____

_____

_____

**8** How do you count the number of words in a file?

_____

_____

_____

**ANSWERS: PAGE 351**

## EXTRA PRACTICE

1. Try using a different text editor.

2. Discover how many text editors are actually installed on your system.

3. Use **emacs** to create a two-column document.

4. Use **vi** to create a new document from scratch and save it to a different directory.

5. Find the portion of the **emacs** documentation where it describes how to switch between its many modes.

6. Read the online-manual page for the **vi** command.

## REAL-WORLD APPLICATIONS

✔ You want to check the spelling of an important letter before mailing it off. Check the spelling using the **emacs** text editor.

✔ You're under a tight word deadline in preparing an article, and you need to know how many words are in your first draft. Use the **wc** command to check the number of words in the first draft.

✔ While writing a long memo, you realize that you've used the wrong name for the potential customer throughout. Use the search capability in **emacs** to find all instances of the mistake.

## Visual Quiz

Four separate sections exist to this **emacs** window. What are they?

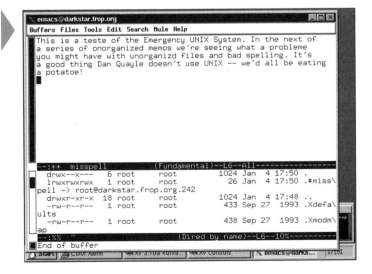

_____

_____

_____

_____

_____

# CHAPTER 12

MASTER
THESE
SKILLS

▶ Introducing troff

▶ Using the Memorandum Macros

▶ Using GhostScript and GhostView

# Text Processing

In this chapter we extend the concept of text editing by discussing text processing and manipulation using the powerful **troff** tool.

The traditional UNIX world makes a distinction between text editors and text processors. On a base level, both appear to do the same thing: create and print text files. The similarity ends there, however, as a text editor is geared more for internal use (creating script files, program files, electronic-mail messages), while a text processor introduces formatting features that spiff up documents intended for the outside world. A text editor allows you to designate characters as bold or italic (depending on the capabilities of your printer), but a text processor actually carries out these commands.

Once the most popular publishing software in the world, **troff** and its predecessors are essential tools for any UNIX user who wants to create professional-looking documents without paying extra for a professional package such as WordPerfect or FrameMaker. These tools come with most versions of UNIX, although some-times they're split out into a package called the Documenter's Workbench.

To understand **troff**, it's important to review its history. The product we call **troff** began life in 1964 as **runoff** and ported to UNIX in the form of **roff**, used to supply simple formatting to documents printed on a line printer. In 1973 **ntroff** was created to add more formatting capabilities. In the same year, **ntroff** was extended to support a typesetting machine and renamed **troff**. Finally, **troff** was revised to support virtually every printer and renamed **ditroff** (for device-independent **troff**). Today, we refer to it as **troff** almost exclusively, even though it's most likely that we're actually using **ditroff**.

In this day of graphical-user interfaces and WYSIWYG (what-you-see-is-what-you-get) computing, **troff** is a throwback to days of yore when you had to visualize your final output and then provide commands to the system on how to achieve this final output. Today, we can highlight text and change its formatting from bold to italic through a simple menu choice, if we're using a word processor that supports a WYSIWYG mode.

# Introducing troff

With **troff**, you don't have a WYSI-WYG publishing system. Instead, you mark up the text with special commands using a plain text editor and then use the **troff** command to produce the final output, which is usually printed.

The best way to explain **troff** is to look at before-and-after examples, as shown on the facing page. The original text file is a standard memo, with several formatting commands that begin with a backslash (\) or a period (.). **Troff** then takes this text file and produces the end result that appears on the facing page.

To try out **troff**, run the example file, **trofftest**, through **troff**. When you run **troff** you must specify the destination of its output; the default output is the screen. You can also redirect the troff output to a file. The text is justified; that is, the spaces between words are increased to allow the text to be stretched across the entire line. We usually prefer that our text be ragged right, spacing the words equally and eliminating any stretched lines. To accomplish this, use the **.ad** command.

In the output, notice that **troff** doesn't just print the text as it appears in the example **trofftest** file. Instead, **troff** will fill out each line of text based on its internal rules. To stop this, use **.nf**, which stands for no fill.

If your system has a printer connected, go ahead and print the result of the **troff** command. Redirect the output to the printer, usually run by the **lp** or **lpr** commands.

In some cases you may need to specify the printer. This specification will depend on your particular hardware configuration; for more information, talk to your system administrator or see the online manual page for **troff**.

The **\f** command changes fonts to bold (**\fB**) and back to regular (**\fR**) — called roman in typesetting. The **\s** command changes the size of the characters, in points. (Point size refers to the height of characters, based on a measurement used in the typesetting and graphics worlds.)

*Continued*

## TAKE NOTE

### ► A TROFF UNDER ANY OTHER NAME

When we refer to **troff**, you may actually use a closely related command such as **ntroff**, **troff**, **ditroff**, or **groff** (the free GNU version found on Linux). **Troff** can be used with laser printers or typesetters; **ditroff** can be used with just about any output device; **psroff** supports only PostScript printers. However, these rules aren't written in stone — most systems, we find, feature **ditroff** under the **troff** name. Check the online-manual pages for all the possible commands to see what's included on your system.

### ► DOT COMMANDS MUST APPEAR ON THEIR OWN LINE

Dot commands must appear on their own line, but backslash commands can appear anywhere in the text.

**CROSS-REFERENCE**
Chapter 2 covers the **lp** and **lpr** printing commands.

**FIND IT ONLINE**
The WYSIWYG Applix Office suite of applications is available at **www.applix.com**.

## Listing 12-1: THE TROFFTEST EXAMPLE FILE

```
\s24
.ce
THE ANDROMEDA CHALLENGE

\s12Our main competitor in the
software-development field,
Andromeda Systems, has come out
with a new X Window word
processor named \fIAlphaBet\fR. It
poses several problems
for us, including:

.in 2
* Andromeda will certainly price this
product \fBvery\fR competitively. We will
more than likely be forced to follow
suit. There go the year-end bonuses.

* Its packaging will be slicker than ours.

*Quite honestly, it's a better product than
anything we have on the market. To make up
this market gap, we recommend putting much
more money into marketing and away from
basic research.

\s20
.ce
Prepared by Kevin and Eric, marketing.
```

▲ The **trofftest** file in a text editor. Enter the text as shown.

## Listing 12-2: POSTSCRIPT OUTPUT FROM TROFF

```
$ more trofftest.ps
%!PS-Adobe-3.0
%%Creator: groff version 1.11
%%Pages: 1
%%PageOrder: Ascend
%%Orientation: Portrait
%%EndComments
%%BeginProlog
/setpacking where{
pop
currentpacking
true setpacking
}if
/grops 120 dict dup begin
/SC 32 def
—More—(6%)
```

▲ PostScript is a text-based format. This example shows some of the output of the **troff** command.

## Listing 12-3: REDIRECTING THE OUTPUT FROM TROFF

```
$ troff trofftest> test.tr
```

▲ You normally want to redirect the output of **troff**, in this case, to a file.

## Listing 12-4: SENDING TROFF OUTPUT TO THE PRINTER

```
$ troff -printer test | lp
```

▲ Sending the output of **troff** to a printer. Your system may use **lpr** instead of **lp** for printing.

## Listing 12-5: USING GROFF

```
$ groff —Tps trofftest > trofftest.ps
```

▲ Using the freeware **groff** program to format PostScript output.

# Introducing troff
*Continued*

## troff and Online Manuals

Originally, **troff** produced output for dot-matrix line printers. The text was all the same size and each character took up exactly the same amount of space. Because of this, you'll see a lot of **troff** output formatted for 80-character lines of text. When printing to the screen, you can use the **nroff** command instead. The **nroff** command acts like **troff**, but formats for text output.

For example, online manual pages are formatted using **troff**. In fact, if you have a manual file, in the **man** format, you can use **troff -man** to format the output. With **nroff**, use the **nroff -man** command to format for the screen. (The **man** command does something similar.)

While **troff** works well for formatting fixed-width 80-column text, most users want something more. In the UNIX world, that something else is usually PostScript.

## troff and PostScript

The PostScript page-description language has become the *de facto* printer style for UNIX. While other printer formats — especially Hewlett-Packard's PCL page-description language — are popular on Windows PCs, PostScript rules the UNIX world.

PostScript files, whether they be graphics- or text-based documents, are exceptionally portable (they can be read by virtually every kind of computer), and PostScript printers are common business tools.

Printing a **troff** document on a PostScript printer is a somewhat involved process; it concerns running a document first through **troff** and then through **dpost**, which translates **troff's** output to PostScript. (Your system may use a program such as **psroff** or **groff** instead.) For instance, let's say we wanted to run our earlier test file, **trofftest**, through **troff**, with a PostScript printer as the file destination. The command line would include **troff** with a type (-T) of post — short for PostScript. The output would get piped to the **dpost** utility and then the output of **dpost** would get piped to **lp** for printing, as shown on the facing page.

Notice that we still need to tell **troff** it is formatting PostScript output, even though we send the **troff** output to **dpost**.

**TAKE NOTE**

► **GHOSTSCRIPT CAN HELP VISUALIZE TROFF OUTPUT**

A tool called GhostScript, covered later in this chapter, can help you display the output on your screen.

**CROSS-REFERENCE**

Chapter 1 covers the **man** command.

**FIND IT ONLINE**

You can find out more about PostScript from the Adobe Web site at **www.adobe.com/print/main.html**.

## Commercial Packages

Professionals — editors, technical writers, documentation specialists — may not want to rely on the admittedly crude troff-based tools. Commercial text-processing software that we can recommend includes:

▶ WordPerfect for UNIX, from Corel.
▶ Applixware, an office suite of applications from Applix.
▶ Adobe's FrameMaker, the most popular electronic-publishing and documentation package on the market.

### Listing 12-6: USING THE MAN MACROS TO NROFF

```
$ nroff -man filename
```

▲ *The* **-man** *option to* **nroff** *formats online-manual entries. Replace filename with the name of a file in* **man** *page format.*

### Listing 12-7: DEALING WITH LOTS OF OUTPUT

```
$ nroff -man filename | more
```

▲ *Because the output of* **nroff** *moves by too quickly, you normally want to pipe its output to more. The* **man** *command works similarly to* **nroff – man** *with the output piped to* **more**. *(The* **man** *command does a little more than this, though.)*

### Listing 12-8: SENDING OUTPUT TO A POSTSCRIPT PRINTER

```
$ troff -Tpost trofftest | dpost | lp
```

▲ *A command to produce PostScript output sent to a printer via the* **lp** *command.*

### Table 12-1: USEFUL TROFF COMMANDS

| Command | Result |
|---------|--------|
| .ad | Turns off text justification. |
| .bp | Page break. |
| .ce *n* | Centers next *n* lines. If no number is specified, only the following line will be centered. |
| .fi | Tells **troff** to fill the lines of text. |
| .ft *n* | Changes font to *n*. |
| \f*n* | Changes font to *n*. |
| .in *n* | Indents the following lines by *n* spaces. |
| .ls *n* | Sets the line spacing on a document; .ls 2 would change the spacing to double-spaced. The default is single-spaced. |
| .na | Turns on text justification. |
| .nf | Tells **troff** not to fill the lines of text. |
| .pl *n* | Sets the number of lines on the page to *n*. The default is 66 lines to a page. Note that laser printers usually have a smaller number of lines per page. |
| .po *ni* | Sets the left margin; .po 1i would set the left margin to 1 inch. It's essential that you set this, because the default has text appearing all the way to the left of the page. (We use inch for our example; centimeters could be specified by using c instead of i.) |
| .ps *n* | Changes the point size to *n*. |
| \S*n* | Changes the point size to *n*. |
| .sp *n* | Sets the number of lines to skip by *n*. To skip a specific amount, use *ni* for inches or *nc* for centimeters. |

# Using the Memorandum Macros

While you can use **troff** as a document publishing system, **troff** can be quite tedious, especially for marking up your text. Furthermore, most of us don't want to go to the trouble of providing specifics to an output device every time we create a document — especially if the document is 500 pages long and serves as the main reference manual for your company's software product. And you certainly don't want to be forced to remember the 80 or so **troff** commands.

Luckily, someone went to the trouble of creating memorandum macros (mm) that can be used to create stylized business letters, resumes, and reports. We won't go into great detail about these macros, as not every system will contain them.

To see if your system supports the memorandum macros, type **mm** at the command prompt. If your system supports the memorandum macros, a short message appears explaining all their available options. If your system does not support the memorandum macros, an error message appears. This test doesn't work for all systems, though.

If your system does feature the memorandum macros and you want to learn them, consult your documentation or read the online-manual pages for mm, which will list the formatting codes for the mm macros. To use these, you enter the mm codes in your document using a text editor. You can freely mix mm macros with **troff** commands, as the mm macros expand to **troff** commands. When you run **troff**, though, you must use the **-mm** option to tell **troff** to load the mm macros.

In addition to the mm macros, there's another set for formatting manuscripts, the ms macros. These macros are intended for articles, theses, and books.

A common set of macros also exists for creating UNIX-style manual pages, mentioned previously. We don't find the online-manual pages very informative for a new user, but they can be lifesavers for experienced users.

## TAKE NOTE

### FORMATTING EQUATIONS

**Eqn** is used to typeset equations through its own set of dot commands. You normally pass a file through **eqn** first, then pipe the output of **eqn** to **troff**. What **eqn** does is intercept **eqn** commands that typeset equations and translates those relatively simple commands into the detailed commands needed by **troff** to actually format the output. So, **eqn** takes as input a file that contains **eqn** and **troff** commands. **Eqn** then converts all **eqn** commands into **troff** commands and sends the converted file as its output.

### FORMATTING TABLES

Another common utility, called **tbl**, typesets tables. Again, **tbl** acts as a filter that operates on its own dot commands and passes the rest of the commands on to **troff**.

**CROSS-REFERENCE**

Chapter 1 covers the **man** command.

**FIND IT ONLINE**

Information on **groff**, a free clone of **troff**, is available at **www.gnu.org/software/grg/grg.html**.

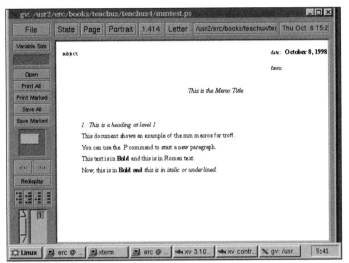

■ *Here is the output of the mmtest example file.*

## Listing 12-9: CHECKING THE DOCUMENTATION ON THE MEMORANDUM MACROS

```
$ man mm
```

▲ *The **man mm** command should list the formatting codes for the memorandum macros.*

## Listing 12-10: RUNNING THE EQN EQUATION PROCESSOR

```
$ eqn testfile.tr | troff | lp
```

▲ *The **eqn** preprocessor formats equations.*

## Listing 12-11: RUNNING THE TBL TABLE PROCESSOR

```
$ tbl testfile.tr | troff | lp
```

▲ *The **tbl** preprocessor formats tables.*

## Listing 12-12: COMBINING EQN AND TBL WITH TROFF

```
$ tbl testfile.tr | eqn¦troff | lp
```

▲ *You can combine multiple preprocessors with **troff**.*

## Listing 12-13: USING THE MEMORANDUM MACROS

```
$ cat mmtest
.MT "This is the Memo Title"
.P

.H 1 "This is a heading at level 1"
.P
This document shows an example of
the mm macros for troff.
.P
You can use the .P command to
start a new paragraph.
.P
This text is in
.BR "Bold" " and this is in Roman text."
.P
Now, this is in
.BI "Bold and " "this is in italic or
underlined."

$ troff -mm mmtest
```

▲ *Use the **–mm** command-line option to tell **troff** to use the mm memorandum macros.*

# Using GhostScript and GhostView

While you can use **troff** as a document publishing system, it isn't the friendliest tool around. One of the main problems lies in visualizing the output. Editing a text file and adding primitive **troff** commands, and only later seeing the output, makes it harder to create documents. If you only work in a text editor, then how can you see what the document will look like? More modern tools typically offer a What-You-See-Is-What-You-Get or WYSIWYG approach instead, and provide direct visualization of the output. You can certainly buy WYSIWYG tools for UNIX from a number of vendors. If you are using **troff**, though, you can run GhostScript and GhostView to display **troff** output.

GhostScript is the generic name for a family of tools that allow you to display PostScript documents under the X Window System on UNIX. GhostScript can also print PostScript documents to non-PostScript printers. This is most useful in the PC UNIX realm, especially for Linux, where GhostScript normally comes with Linux distributions.

In the realm of larger UNIX systems, most printers support PostScript, a commercial product owned by Adobe. But low-end PCs often use laser or ink jet printers that typically don't support PostScript. (Most support Hewlett-Packard's PCL page-description language instead.)

If you run the X Window System, you can use the **GhostView** program. The basic command is simple:

```
$ ghostview filename.ps
```

In place of **filename.ps**, use the name of a PostScript file you have. You'll see the **ghostview** interface, as shown on the facing page.

On the left side of the main window, a number of menus appear. From the File menu, you can reload the PostScript file, which is useful if you're working with **troff** and want to view each small change to your document. You can also print it, which is the topic of the next task. From the Page menu, you can go to the next or previous pages. You can also do this from the scrolled listing of pages next to the menus. The Magstep menu allows you to magnify the image, which is often useful as text that is large enough to read on a printer may appear tiny on the **ghostview** window. The Orientation menu controls the orientation, such as Landscape or Portrait, for the display. The Media menu allows you to control the output page size. The default is usually Letter.

*Continued*

## TAKE NOTE

### ▶ UPGRADING TO THE COMMERCIAL VERSION

GhostScript comes in both free and commercial versions. The commercial version, as you'd expect, supports more features and more printers. If you make heavy use of GhostScript, you'll probably want to upgrade to the commercial version. See **www.ghostscript.com** for details.

## CROSS-REFERENCE
Chapter 7 covers the X Window System.

## FIND IT ONLINE
For more on GhostScript, see **www.cs.wisc.edu/~ghost/**.

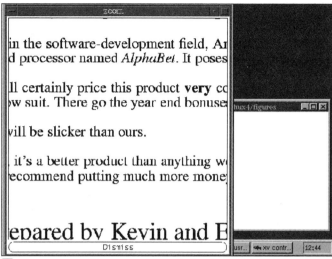

The main ghostview window.

You can magnify an area of the window by clicking the left mouse button.

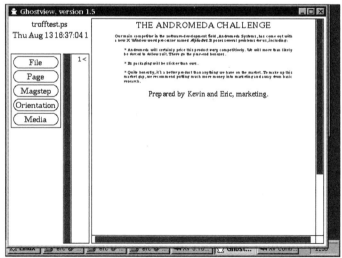

You can change the overall magnification, called a magstep, from the interface.

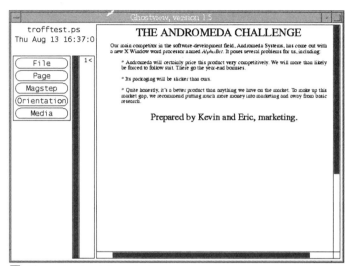

You can also change the orientation from Portrait to Landscape to Upside-down to Seascape (upside-down landscape). This example was created with the –forceorientation and –upsidedown command-line options.

# Using GhostScript and GhostView *Continued*

## Printing with GhostScript

On low-end systems, such as PCs, you may not have a PostScript printer. If you have a printer, it's likely that you have an inkjet or laser printer that supports the Hewlett-Packard page-description language, PCL. Since much of UNIX printing is oriented towards PostScript, this can be a problem. If you are faced with this problem, read on.

You can use GhostScript as your means to print PostScript files. GhostScript, through the **gs** command, supports a large number of printers and other output devices, including fax formats, bitmap formats, and screen-based output.

GhostScript is actually a PostScript interpreter. PostScript itself is really a programming language — contrary to what you'd expect. PostScript just happens to provide graphic commands that you need to describe almost any page layout.

Because of its great flexibility, PostScript has dominated the UNIX printing market for some time. In the PC realm, though, a wide variety of formats exist. Furthermore, the expense — in both RAM and processing power — hampered the adoption of PostScript in the PC world.

To use GhostScript, you can start with the **gs** command. When **gs** starts up, it will present you with a prompt, **GS>**. At this prompt, you can enter PostScript commands, as well as special commands unique to GhostScript. Enter **quit** to exit the program. PostScript is a programming language, but it works backwards from what you'd normally expect.

The command to display a PostScript file is **run**, and you need to pass the name of the file to **run**. But, instead of a command such as **run *filename.ps***, you work backwards:

```
GS> (trofftest.ps) run
```

When working with **gs**, you can shortcut a lot of commands by entering the filename and output device on the command line. For example, the following tells **gs** to format for an HP DeskJet printer:

```
$ gs -sDEVICE=deskjet filename.ps
```

You can set the paper size with an option such as **-sPAPERSIZE=a4**, to use A4-sized paper.

The table on the facing page lists some of the more common devices GhostScript supports. You can use the **gs -h** command to get a full listing. In addition to printers, **gs** also supports a number of graphic formats for output, including the BMP (Windows), PCX, PBM (portable bitmap), and quite a few FAX formats.

You can find even more detailed information in the GhostScript documentation, typically installed in **/usr/local/lib/ghostscript** or **/usr/lib/ghostscript**. Linux systems will likely use the latter directory.

> ### TAKE NOTE
>
> #### ▶ GHOSTSCRIPT SHELL SCRIPTS
> GhostScript comes with a few shell scripts that can be quite useful. These include **unix-lpr.sh**, which acts as a front end to the **lpr** command to print PostScript documents, and **lprsetup.sh**, which helps set up the **unix-lpr.sh** script.

**CROSS-REFERENCE**
Chapter 14 covers programming.

**FIND IT ONLINE**
For more on GhostScript, see **www.cs.wisc.edu/ ~ghost/ghostscript/index.html**.

## Table 12-2: COMMON PRINTERS SUPPORTED BY GHOSTSCRIPT

| Name | Printer |
|------|---------|
| cdj500 | HP DeskJet 500C and 540C |
| cdj550 | HP DeskJet 550C and 560C |
| declj250 | DEC LJ250 |
| deskjet | HP DeskJet |
| djet500 | Hp DeskJet 500 |
| epson | Epson (and Epson compatible) dot-matrix printers |
| iwhi | Apple Imagewriter (high-resolution mode) |
| iwlo | Apple Imagewriter (low-resolution mode) |
| la50 | DEC LA50 printer |
| la70 | DEC LA70 printer |
| laserjet | HP LaserJet |
| paintjet | HP PaintJet |
| pjxl300 | HP PaintJet XL300 and DeskJet 1200C |
| pjtest | HP PaintJet |
| pjxltest | HP PaintJet XL |
| sparc | SPARCprinter |

### Listing 12-14: STARTING GS TO RENDER IN LASERJET PRINTER FORMAT

```
$ gs -sDEVICE=laserjet
Aladdin Ghostscript 3.33 (4/10/1995)
Copyright (C) 1995 Aladdin Enterprises,
Menlo Park, CA. All rights reserved.
This software comes with NO WARRANTY:
see the file COPYING for details.
GS>
```

▲ *You can start **gs** and pass the type of a printer as the output device, in this case, an HP LaserJet printer.*

### Listing 12-15: RENDERING A POSTSCRIPT FILE FROM GS

```
GS> (trofftest.ps) run
Loading NimbusRomNo9L-Medi font from
/usr/lib/ghostscript/fonts/n021004l.pfb...
1750128 434100 1300076 16437 0 done.
Loading NimbusRomNo9L-ReguItal font from
/usr/lib/ghostscript/fonts/n021023l.pfb...
1790280 458529 1300076 17131 0 done.
Loading NimbusRomNo9L-Regu font from
/usr/lib/ghostscript/fonts/n021003l.pfb...
1830432 498908 1300076 18540 0 done.
>showpage, press <return> to continue<<
```

▲ *To display a PostScript file, use the **run** command. Remember, PostScript works backwards from most command languages.*

### Listing 12-16: RENDERING A POSTSCRIPT FILE TO THE SCREEN

```
$ gs -sDEVICE=x11 trofftest.ps
Aladdin Ghostscript 3.33 (4/10/1995)
Copyright (C) 1995 Aladdin Enterprises,
Menlo Park, CA.  All rights reserved.
This software comes with NO WARRANTY:
see the file COPYING for details.
Loading NimbusRomNo9L-Medi font from
/usr/share/ghostscript/fonts/n021004l.pfb...
1750128 433367 1300076 16435 0 done.
Loading NimbusRomNo9L-ReguItal font from
/usr/share/ghostscript/fonts/n021023l.pfb...
1790280 457804 1300076 17133 0 done.
Loading NimbusRomNo9L-Regu font from
/usr/share/ghostscript/fonts/n021003l.pfb...
1830432 498183 1300076 18544 0 done.
>showpage, press <return> to continue<<

GS>
```

▲ *If you pass the name of a file on the **gs** command line, **gs** will render the PostScript image, to the screen.*

# Personal Workbook

## Q&A

**1** Are there any What-You-See-Is-What-You-Get, or WYSIWYG, word processors or document publishing systems for UNIX?

_____

_____

_____

**2** Is **troff** a What-You-See-Is-What-You-Get (WYSIWYG) document system?

_____

_____

_____

**3** What other application do you need to make any use of **troff**?

_____

_____

_____

**4** What type of files do you pass to **troff** as input?

_____

_____

_____

**5** What is the **troff** command for centering text?

_____

_____

_____

**6** What is the command-line option to tell **troff** to use the memorandum macros?

_____

_____

_____

**7** What is the command-line option to tell **troff** to use the online-manual macros?

_____

_____

_____

**8** What commands can you use to display or print PostScript documents on nonPostScript devices?

_____

_____

_____

ANSWERS: PAGE 351

## EXTRA PRACTICE

**1** Which text formatting commands do you have available on your system? **Troff**? **Nroff**? **Groff**?

**2** To help show off your UNIX experience, format your resume using **troff**.

**3** To prevent your resume appearing on a shared printer, format your resume with extra pages in front and back to help hide it.

**4** Check whether or not your system supports the mm memorandum macros.

**5** Determine the GhostScript name for the printer driver that matches your printer.

**6** Look up the online manuals for the **troff** command.

## REAL-WORLD APPLICATIONS

✔ You have an online manual file for a new tool that you must get to work and you really need the documentation. Unfortunately, you don't have permissions to install the manual file in any of the standard locations, so the **man** command doesn't recognize it. View the file on your screen with the **nroff** command.

✔ Print this same file using the **troff** command.

✔ You don't have a PostScript printer but you just received a PostScript document that you need to print. Use the GhostScript commands to print this document.

✔ Use GhostScript to view the file on your screen.

## Visual Quiz

This image shows the output of running **troff** on a file of **troff** commands. Try to create a file of those commands.

_____

_____

_____

_____

_____

_____

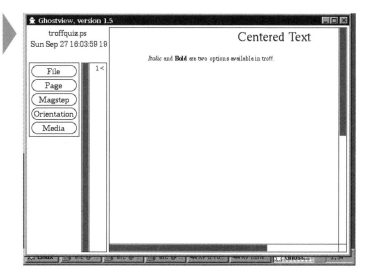

# CHAPTER 13

**MASTER THESE SKILLS**

# Shell Programming Basics

UNIX commands involve a lot of typing. If you're not a typist and don't want to remember the strange UNIX syntax for commands, you may want to bundle a number of commands together into what is called a *shell script*.

Shell scripts contain a series of commands for a UNIX shell, such as the Bourne shell, **sh**, or C shell, **csh**. These scripts are stored in files and act much like DOS batch files. As you execute a shell script, each command in the text file is passed to the shell to execute, one at a time. When all the commands in the file are executed, or if an error occurs, the script ends.

These shell scripts can execute UNIX commands and can also use built-in functions provided by the shell. Like most UNIX commands, these built-in functions tend to the cryptic side. We don't expect you to be a programmer, but as you use UNIX, you'll soon find that small shell scripts provide additional functionality that you may want but traditional UNIX commands lack. A shell script can be either a powerful tool or a cryptic mess. In this chapter, we provide a gentle introduction to shell scripting to help you avoid creating shell scripts that fall into the latter category. By the end of this chapter, you should be ready to create your own mini-commands using the shell.

Most users run **sh**, **csh**, **bash**, or the Korn shell, **ksh**, as their command-line interpreter. (The Korn shell and Bash are both enhanced Bourne shells, at least in most respects, as covered in Chapters 4 and 5.) You can program the shell that you're running right now, but our examples use the Bourne shell, **sh**.

Although few users actually choose to work in the Bourne shell, virtually all shell scripts are written for that shell, mainly because it is the most widely available. Virtually all UNIX systems provide the Bourne shell, which is not true for the other shells.

Furthermore, some people have a number of issues with using the C shell in particular for writing shell scripts. We're not here to try to convince you which shell scripting language is better. As we mentioned, we cover Bourne shell scripts because that's what most UNIX shell scripts are written in. Use your own judgement in choosing which shell to use for scripts.

# Running Scripts

**W**riting shell scripts isn't that hard. In fact, by the end of this chapter, you'll be ready to write a number of your own scripts. A shell script is nothing more than a text file that contains a series of commands, just as you'd type in at the shell prompt. Each line in the text file is interpreted as another UNIX command. That's it. (Well, not really. There's a nicety called syntax built into the shells to aid in writing shell scripts.)

Shell scripts are stored in UNIX text files, so use your favorite text editor, such as **vi** or **emacs**, to create a new file, say **example1**. In this file, enter the text shown in the first listing on the facing page.

There are two lines in the first shell script. Because shell scripts are really shell commands stored in a text file, to see what any command does simply type it in at the prompt, as shown on the facing page.

When **echo** runs, it prints out all its command-line parameters. You can combine all the text into one parameter, using quotation marks, or combine some of the parameters.

If you don't want to output a newline at the end of the text, you can pass the **-n** option to **echo**.

The second command is the **ls** command, which prints out a list of the files in your current directory. As you can tell, we're not breaking any new computational ground here with this first shell script.

Now that we know what the shell script should do, it's time to run it. You can run the shell script in one of two ways. The first is to pass the script as a parameter to the shell program, **sh**, on the command line. The second method involves making the script executable, which we cover later in this chapter.

To ask a shell to run a script, use the shell command, **sh**. The facing page shows a sample run of this command. The actual filenames you see depend on what you have stored in the current directory.

## TAKE NOTE

### SHELL DIFFERENCES

In simple scripts like those presented here, there's no difference between running the script from the Bourne shell, **sh**, or from another shell, such as **ksh** or **csh**.

### USE THE RIGHT HAMMER FOR THE JOB

UNIX provides many tools for creating your own commands. You can use shell, Perl, or awk scripts, or you can write programs in C, C++, or Java, along with a host of other programming options available in UNIX. Which tool works best for you depends on your experience with various tools and your inclinations. Use the tools you feel most comfortable with.

**CROSS-REFERENCE**

Chapter 16 covers Perl and AWK scripts.

**FIND IT ONLINE**

Find out more about the Korn shell, **ksh**, at **www.kornshell.com**.

## Listing 13-1: A FIRST SCRIPT

```
echo This is my first shell script.
ls -1
```

▲ The **example1** shell script. You can enter this with a text editor.

## Listing 13-2: RUNNING THE FIRST EXAMPLE SCRIPT

```
$ echo This is my first shell script.
This is my first shell script.
```

▲ The **echo** command echoes back (prints out) the text you pass to it.

## Listing 13-3: USING ECHO WITHOUT A NEWLINE

```
$ echo -n "Without newline"
Without newline$
```

▲ With the **-n** option, **echo** doesn't print a newline. When entered at the command line, this can result in confusing output.

## Listing 13-4: THE ECHON SCRIPT

```
$ cat echon
echo -n "This "
echo -n "all appears "
echo -n "on "
echo -n "one "
echo "line."
$ sh echon
This all appears on one line.
```

▲ The **echon** script shows how to use the **-n** option (no newline) with **echo.**

## Listing 13-5: ECHO WITH MORE THAN ONE VARIABLE

```
$ echo "User $USER has home directory
$HOME."
User erc has home directory /usr2/erc.
```

▲ You can combine more than one variable in the data passed to **echo.**

## Listing 13-6: RUNNING THE EXAMPLE1 SCRIPT FROM SH

```
$ sh example1
This is my first shell script.
2001
echon
example1
example2
example3
example4
example5
example6
example7
example8
example9
myls
myls2
report.2001
```

▲ The **example1** script echoes the text This is my first shell script and then lists the files in the current directory.

# Making Scripts Executable

In the examples shown so far, you need to execute the shell script by passing the name of the script file to a shell program such as **sh**. This requires you to know where the script file is located (in the current directory in our examples). UNIX provides the capability, though, to create a true command out of a shell script, so you can just run the script as a command itself. With a true command, you can place the script file in any directory that is in your command path (listed in the PATH environment variable).

To use a shell script as a command, you need to indicate the file is executable. Do this with the **chmod** (change mode) command. First, check the file **example1** to see what the file permissions are, as shown on the facing page.

Next, mark the file as executable with the **chmod** **u**+**x** command. The *u* stands for user (owner) and the +*x* for adding the execute permission. All UNIX commands need to have the execute permission set in order to run.

After marking the file **example1** executable, execute the script and see what it does. The facing page shows the result. Notice that you don't need to type the shell command **sh**.

## Getting the Right Shell to Run Your Script

At the start of this chapter, we suggested you run the Bourne shell, **sh**, for shell programming. The problem is that each shell uses a different syntax (we know that this is stupid, but that's the way things are). What works in one shell may fail in another shell. To tell your shell which of the many shell programs should execute the script, place a special line at the very top of the file.

To use the Bourne shell, insert the following line at the start of your shell scripts:

```
#!/bin/sh
```

The # marks this line as a comment. This provides a safety net: If your shell doesn't understand the #! syntax, it will simply treat the # as the beginning of a comment and ignore the rest of the line. After the #!, you need to place the name of the shell program to execute the script (see Table 13-1). This can be any program at all, but most people use **/bin/sh**. If you use a different shell, be sure to verify its location before creating the #! line.

---

**TAKE NOTE**

▶ **RUN REHASH FROM CSH**

If you're using the C shell, **csh**, you'll need to enter the **rehash** command to rebuild the **csh** internal table of all available commands each time you add a new command to your system.

▶ **FIXED LIMITS ON THE #! SYNTAX**

Some versions of UNIX impose strict limits — usually 32 characters — on the path listed with the #! comment.

---

**CROSS-REFERENCE**
Chapter 2 covers the **chmod** command.

**FIND IT ONLINE**
For an explanation of the $@ syntax, see
**www.perl.com/CPAN-local/doc/FMTEYEWTK/
sh_dollar_at**.

## Table 13-1: SPECIAL COMMENTS TO RUN PARTICULAR SHELLS FROMSCRIPTS

| Comment | Runs |
|---|---|
| #!/usr/local/bin/bash | Bash shell (also stored /usr/bin/bash, especially in Linux) |
| #!/bin/sh | Bourne shell |
| #!/bin/csh | C shell |
| #!/bin/ksh | Korn shell |
| #!/usr/local/bin/tcsh | T C shell (location depends on where you installed tcsh) |
| #!/usr/local/bin/perl | Perl (also stored /usr/bin/perl, especially in Linux) |
| #!/usr/local/bin/wish | Tcl/Tk (also stored in /usr/bin/wish, especially in Linux) |

### Listing 13-7: CHECKING THE EXAMPLE1 FILE

```
$ ls -l example1
-rw-rw-r--    1 erc   bigfun    43 Dec 8 15:42
  example1
```

▲ Before running **chmod**, the **example1** file has read and write permissions, but no execute permissions are set.

### Listing 13-8: USING CHMOD TO MARK A SCRIPT AS EXECUTABLE

```
$ chmod u+x example1
$ ls -l example1
-rwxrw-r--    1 erc   bigfun    43 Dec 8 15:42
  example1
$
```

▲ After running **chmod u+x**, the file **example1** has execute permissions set for the file's owner.

### Listing 13-9: RUNNING A SCRIPT AS A COMMAND

```
$ example1
This is my first shell script.
2001
echon
example1
example2
example3
example4
example5
example6
example7
myls
myls2
report.2001
```

▲ Now that **example1** is marked as an executable file, you can run it without typing the shell command, such as **sh**.

### Listing 13-10: MOVING A SCRIPT FROM THE C SHELL

```
% mv example1 /usr/local/bin
% rehash
% example1
This is my first shell script.
2001
echon
example1
example2
example3
example4
example5
example6
example7
myls
myls2
report.2001
```

▲ With the C shell, you need to run **rehash** each time you add a new command.

# Defining Shell Variables and Getting Input

Variables hold values, whether data read in from the user or a file, data returned by a command, or any sort of data you want to store. You can introduce variables in your Bourne shell scripts using the following syntax, as we first described in Chapter 4:

*VARIABLENAME=VARIABLEVALUE*

Don't put any spaces on either side of the equal sign (=). Variable names must begin with a letter or an underscore character ( _ ). You can use letters, underscores, or numbers for the rest of the variable name.

To later retrieve the value of a variable, place a dollar sign ($) in front of the variable name, as shown following:

```
variable1="Yow, are we having fun yet?"
echo "The variable is $variable1."
```

When you execute these commands, you'll see the following results:

```
The variable is Yow, are we having fun yet?.
```

You can place the output of a command into a variable, using the accent marks discussed in Chapter 4:

```
datetoday=`date`
echo "The date is $datetoday."
```

Again, when you execute these commands inside a shell script, you'll see the following output:

```
The date is Fri Dec 31 15:57:59 CST 2010.
```

We put this all together to create a shell script, which we call **example2**, as shown on the facing page. The **example2** script starts out with some variants of the **echo** command. You'll find the lowly **echo** command one of the most useful commands for your scripts. The **example2** script then goes into setting variables from values, especially a value that results from the **date** command, as discussed previously.

One of the most common uses for variables lies in holding data entered by the user. You can read input from the user into variables with the **read** command.

The **read** command reads in user input and places whatever the user types into a shell variable:

```
$ read variablename
```

This command waits for the user to enter data and then press the **Enter** key. The typed-in data is set into the given variable, which you can use in the rest of your script.

The **example3** script, which prompts the user for data, appears on the facing page. Enter this script, naming it **example3**, and then mark **example3** as executable, using **chmod**. When you run this script, you'll be prompted to enter your first and last name, as shown on the facing page.

Type in the requested data, and press the **Enter** key. The **read** command supports limited command-line editing. You can use the **Backspace** key to delete characters.

## TAKE NOTE

### ▶ PROMPT WITH READ

Before using the **read** command, let the user know you want input by using the **echo** command. Otherwise, the user may never fill in the data expected by **read** and may assume your script crashed.

### CROSS-REFERENCE

Chapter 4 covers shell variables and the **stty erase** command.

### FIND IT ONLINE

You can find out more on UNIX shells at dir.yahoo.com/Computers_and_Internet/Software/Operating_Systems/Unix/Shells/.

## Listing 13-11: THE EXAMPLE2 SCRIPT

```
#!/bin/sh
#
# Example 2 from Chapter 12 of
# Teach Yourself UNIX.
#
# More on echo.
#
echo "You can also use quotation marks."
# Note the space after the quotation
# mark and before second.
echo -n "first message"
echo " second message"
# Use a command with echo.
echo "The current directory is `pwd`."
# Use a variable.
variable1="Yow, are we having fun yet?"
echo "The variable is $variable1."
# Set a variable to a command output
datetoday=`date`
echo "The date is $datetoday."
```

▲ The *example2* shell script introducing variables in scripts.

## Listing 13-12: RUNNING THE EXAMPLE2 SCRIPT

```
$ example2
You can also use quotation marks.
first message second message
The current directory is
/usr2/erc/books/teachux/teachux4.
The variable is Yow, are we having fun
yet?.
The date is Fri Dec 31 14:02:26 CDT 2010.
```

▲ The output of the *example2* script.

## Listing 13-13: STORING A COMMAND IN A VARIABLE

```
$ read command
date
$  datetoday=`$command`
$ echo $datetoday
Wed Oct 13 16:04:38 CDT 2010
$
```

▲ The accent operators enable you to execute a command and place its output into a variable.

## Listing 13-14: THE EXAMPLE3 SCRIPT

```
#!/bin/sh
#
# Example 3 from Chapter 13 of
# Teach Yourself UNIX.
#
# Using read.
#
echo -n "Enter your first name: "
read firstname

echo -n "Enter your last name: "
read lastname
echo "Your name is $firstname $lastname."
```

▲ The *example3* shell script.

## Listing 13-15: RUNNING THE EXAMPLE3 SCRIPT

```
$ example3
Enter your first name: Eric
Enter your last name: Foster-Johnson
Your name is Eric Foster-Johnson.
$ example3
Enter your first name: Santa
Enter your last name: Claus
Your name is Santa Claus.
$
```

▲ The output from two sample sessions with the *example3* script.

# Passing Command-Line Parameters

Most UNIX commands support a plethora of command-line parameters for changing what the command does.

Shell scripts can read up to nine command-line parameters, or arguments, into special variables. Anything more than nine are silently ignored. (You can get around this with $*, as we show on the facing page.) Inside shell scripts, these command-line parameters appear as specially named shell-script variables. The command-line parameters are named $1, $2, $3, and so on up to $9.

A special variable holds the name of the executable script, as invoked by the user. This variable is $0. In the example script file **example1**, the value of $0 would be example1. However, if we executed the file **example1** with a command such as **/u/erc/teachux/example1**, $0 would hold **/u/erc/teachux/example1**.

To see how command-line parameters work, refer to the **example4** script shown on the facing page. As with other shell scripts, you can mark the **example4** script as an executable file with the **chmod** command.

After setting the execute permissions, you can run **example4**, as shown on the facing page.

Inside the **example4** script, note the trick of placing a blank space after the data inside the quotation marks in the **echo -n** command. This old programmer trick makes for better-looking output. The next **echo** command prints more data for the same line. The extra space separates the data from the two commands.

If you pass more than nine command-line parameters, the extra parameters will be ignored. If you pass fewer than nine command-line parameters, the extra variables have a null value.

How can you tell the number of command-line parameters? The special variable $# contains this value. The **example5** script on the facing page shows this variable in action. The $# is very useful for verifying whether the user passed the proper number of expected command-line parameters to your script. If the user doesn't pass all the required parameters, your scripts could use the **echo** command to print out an error message.

There's also a special variable, $*, that contains all the command-line parameters. As mentioned previously, the variable $* can hold more than nine parameters. The **example6** script on the facing page shows how to use this variable.

## TAKE NOTE

▶ **THE C SHELL USES $#ARGV RATHER THAN $#**

The C shell doesn't like the $# variable for the number of command-line parameters, as shown in **example5**. Use $#argv instead.

▶ **THERE'S NO $10**

If you use the special variables for command-line parameters, remember that these variables go from $1 to $9. There's no $10 or higher.

**CROSS-REFERENCE**

See Chapter 4 for more on shell variables.

**FIND IT ONLINE**

For reasons why you may not want to use **csh** for scripting, see **language.perl.com/versus/csh.whynot**.

## Table 13-2: SHELL COMMAND-LINE PARAMETERS

| Variable | Meaning |
| --- | --- |
| $0 | The name of the script, as passed on the command line. |
| $1 | The first command-line parameter. |
| $2 | The second command-line parameter. |
| $3 ... $9 | The third through ninth command-line parameters. |
| $# | The number of command-line parameters. (**$#argv** is the C shell.) |
| $* | All command-line parameters. (You can have more than nine.) |

### Listing 13-16: THE EXAMPLE4 SCRIPT

```
#!/bin/sh
# Example 4 from Chapter 13 of
# Teach Yourself UNIX.
# Command-line parameters.
echo "The first parameter was $1."
echo -n "The full parameters were: "
echo $1 $2 $3 $4 $5 $6 $7 $8 $9
echo "The shell script is $0."
```

▲ The **example4** script prints out the value of command-line parameters passed to the script.

### Listing 13-17: PASSING MORE THAN NINE PARAMETERS

```
$ example4 1 2 3 4 5 6 7 8 9 10 11 12 13
The first parameter was: 1
The parameters were: 1 2 3 4 5 6 7 8 9
The shell script command was: example4
```

▲ If you pass more than nine parameters, the extra parameters are ignored.

### Listing 13-18: PASSING LESS THAN NINE PARAMETERS

```
$ ./example4 1 2 3 4
The first parameter was 1.
The full parameters were 1 2 3 4
The shell script is ./example4.
$
```

▲ If you pass less than nine parameters, the extra shell variables have null values.

### Listing 13-19: THE EXAMPLE5 SCRIPT

```
#!/bin/sh
#
# Example 5 from Chapter 13 of
# Teach Yourself UNIX.
#
# Number of command-line parameters.
#
echo The number of parameters was: $#
```

▲ The **example5** script prints out the number of command-line parameters it received. When you run this script, pass a number of command-line parameters to see the number it prints out.

### Listing 13-20: THE EXAMPLE6 SCRIPT

```
#!/bin/sh
#
# Example 6 from Chapter 13 of
# Teach Yourself UNIX.
#
# All command-line parameters.
#
echo "All the parameters were $*"
```

▲ The **example6** script lists all command-line parameters from the **$\*** variable. When you run this script, pass a number of command-line parameters to see what it prints out.

# Including Commands: Loops and if Statements

One of the main features of programming and shell scripting is really a form of programming called *flow control*. The two most common forms of flow control include loops — executing commands again and again — and the if-then command — running different commands in response to a condition.

You can place commands in a loop to be executed again and again until some condition is met. A **for** loop loops for a given number of times.

For example, to list all the filenames that start with *example* and are followed by a single letter, you could use the **example7** script on the facing page.

You can store these commands in a file named **example7** and mark the file as executable — as with every example so far.

For this simple example, we could have used the **ls** command:

```
$ ls example?
```

In real shell scripts, you'll want to use more than **ls**, though.

In our previous example, we used the **in** statement to list the set of values to iterate over. If you omit the **in** statement, **sh** will loop over all the parameters passed to the command line for the script. In other words, if you omit the **in** statement, the results are the same as if you used $*, for example:

```
for filename
   in $*
do
   echo $filename
done
```

This script forms a very primitive **ls** command.

In addition to the **for** loop, **sh** allows the use of **if** statements to check if something is true.

The **if** statement ends with a **fi** command. (*Fi* is *if* backwards, get it?) **Sh** executes the code between the **then** and **else** if the first condition is true. **Sh** also executes the code between the **else** and the **fi** if the first condition results on a nontrue, or false, value. The **else** part is optional.

Most commands result in a true value, unless an error occurs in the command. This means you can use commands as the condition in an **if** statement. For example, if you make up a nonexistent command, **frazzle**, an **if** condition would return a false value.

```
if (frazzle) then
   echo "frazzle is true."
else
   echo "frazzle is not true."
fi
```

If you run this as a script, you should see the output shown on the facing page. You get an error for the nonexistent command, **frazzle**, and the result of **if (frazzle)** is not true.

## TAKE NOTE

### LOOPS AND IF ARE MULTILINE COMMANDS

As with all shell commands, you can enter **for** and **if** commands at the prompt. When you enter a multiline command, you'll see the line continuation or secondary prompt, usually something like >.

CROSS-REFERENCE

See Chapter 4 for more on shell variables.

FIND IT ONLINE

For a collection of shell scripts, see **www.oaseshareware.org/shell/.**

## Listing 13-21: THE FOR SYNTAX

```
for variable
  in list_of_values
do
  command1
  command1
  command2
  ...
  lastcommand
done
```

▲ *Syntax of for loops in the Bourne shell.*

## Listing 13-22: THE EXAMPLE7 SCRIPT

```
#!/bin/sh
# Example 7 from Chapter 13 of
# Teach Yourself UNIX.
# For loops
for filename
  in example?
do
  echo "Example file is $filename."
done
```

▲ *The **example7** script, showing a for loop.*

## Listing 13-23: THE IF SYNTAX

```
if (condition) then
  command1
  command2
  ...
  lastcommand
else
  else_command1
  else_command2
  ...
  last_else_command
fi
```

▲ *The syntax for the **if** command.*

## Listing 13-24: ENTERING A MULTILINE COMMAND AT THE SHELL PROMPT

```
$ if (frazzle) then
>     echo "frazzle is true."
> else
>     echo "frazzle is not true."
> fi
frazzle: not found
frazzle is not true.
```

▲ *An **if** example entered at the shell prompt. The > markers are the line continuation prompt, waiting the completion of the **if** command.*

## Listing 13-25: C SHELL IF SYNTAX

```
if (expression) then
  command1
  command2
  command3
  ...
  lastcommand
else
  command1
  command2
  command3
  ...
  lastcommand
endif
```

▲ *The syntax for the C shell **if** command.*

## Listing 13-26: C SHELL FOR EACH SYNTAX

```
foreach variable (list_of_values)
  command1
  command2
  command3
  ...
  lastcommand
end
```

▲ *The syntax of the C shell for each command, similar to the for command in the Bourne shell.*

# The test Command

To gain more flexibility with **if** statements, you can use the Bourne shell **test** command. This command returns true or false depending on the command-line parameters used with **test**. Many of the **test** options pertain to files, as shown in Table 13-3.

All the **test** file options return false if the named file does not exist. There's also an **-eq** command-line parameter to test for equality, as explained in Table 13-4.

You can combine loops, the **if** statement, and the **test** command to create your own version of the UNIX **ls** command. In the example file, named **myls**, each filename passed as a command-line parameter is read in, and then the **if** statement is used to test if the file is readable, writable, or executable. The results are printed out with the filename.

The magic with the **myls** script is that you have to call **myls** with the names of the files that you want it to test. The *for filename do* line places each command-line parameter passed to **myls** in the variable *filename*, one at a time, as if you wrote *for filename in $\* do*. This isn't very intuitive, but it provides an easy means of searching through a directory.

Checking the same files with **ls** reveals that the **myls** script is accurate for the user's permissions.

## A Shorthand for the test Command

There's also a shorthand alternative form for the **test** command. Even though this form looks odd, it is used in many shell scripts, so you need to be aware of

it. Basically, **test** is replaced with a bracket, [. Between the brackets, you place the parameters for **test**, such as *-r $filename*, as shown on the facing page.

In the example, we rewrite our original **myls** script using the shorthand method for the **test** command. We call this one **myls2** (an original name). It appears on the facing page.

You can test for the return status of a command using the **if** statement. Be careful, for UNIX commands return 0 (false) on success and nonzero (true) on failure.

Thus the **cat** command can be used to test for successful completion with the following code:

```
if cat $filename > $dir/report.backup
then
     # Success!
else
# failed....

fi
```

You can also use the more convenient || operator.

### TAKE NOTE

#### PUT THEN ON THE NEXT LINE WITH [

With the short-hand notation for the **test** command, you must put the **then** statement on the next line.

#### DON'T NAME SCRIPTS TEST

Because **test** is a command, you can mess up your system if you name a shell script **test**.

### CROSS-REFERENCE

Chapter 2 covers the **ls** command.

### FIND IT ONLINE

You can find out more on UNIX shells at **dir.yahoo. com/Computers_and_Internet/Software/Operating_ Systems/Unix/Shells/**.

## Table 13-3: THE TEST COMMAND WITH FILES

| Command | Returns |
| --- | --- |
| **test -r** *filename* | True if you have permission to read *filename*. |
| **test -s** *filename* | True if *filename* has at least one character. |
| **test -w** *filename* | True if you have permission to write to *filename*. |
| **test -x** *filename* | True if you have permission to execute *filename*. |

## Table 13-4: USING TEST TO CHECK FOR EQUALITY

| Command | Returns |
| --- | --- |
| **test** *variable1* **-eq** *variable2* | Returns true if the variables are equal. |
| **test** *variable1* **-ne** *variable2* | Returns true if the variables are not equal. |

### Listing 13-27: SHORTHAND FOR THE TEST COMMAND

```
if [ -r $filename ]
then
  command
else
  else_command
fi
```

▲ The shorthand form of the **test** command.

### Listing 13-28: THE MYLS SCRIPT

```
#!/bin/sh
#
# myls from Chapter 13 of
# Teach Yourself UNIX.
#
# Using test.
# This script acts something like ls.
for filename
do
    if (test -r $filename) then
        r="read"
    else
        r=""
    fi
    if (test -w $filename) then
        w="write"
    else
        w=""
    fi
    if (test -x $filename) then
        x="execute"
    else
        x=""
    fi
    echo "$filename has $r $w $x
permissions."
done
```

▲ The **myls** example script uses the test command to list information about filenames passed to it on the command line.

# The case Statement

If you have really complex conditions, the **if** statement tends to break down. For more complex conditions, you probably want to use the odd-looking **case** statement. The **case** statement enables you to test a value against a number of cases, or choices, you know in advance. For example, you can check a variable containing a type of animal against values such as *dog, cat*, and *platypus*.

The syntax for the **case** statement appears on the facing page.

Scripts using the **case** statement can be as confusing as they look. The **case** statement tries to match the word following **case** with one of the values. If a value matches the word, the commands after the value are executed up to the double semicolons (;;). If nothing matches, the commands after the *) are executed, again, up to the double semicolons (;;). The whole statement ends with **esac**, which is *case* backwards.

A special catch-all choice, *), matches any value that the other cases didn't catch. This is useful for capturing bad input or any input your script doesn't expect.

The third listing on the facing page shows the **case** statement in action in the **example8** script. This shell script presents a simple game. The user is prompted to enter the most preferred animal, a dog, cat, or platypus. Based on the input, the script prints out a short message using the **echo** command.

If the user enters an animal that's not expected, the script prints out a message asking the user to enter one of the accepted values: dog, cat, or platypus.

One of the most common uses for the **case** statement lies in detecting the operating system type and then taking different actions based on the operating system. For example, the print command often differs by version of UNIX (**lp** or **lpr**). To determine the type of UNIX, use the **uname** command.

In looking at the examples on the facing page, you can see that the *) choice at the end is very useful for providing the user of your shell script hints about bad input.

**CROSS-REFERENCE**

Chapter 2 covers the **ls** command.

**FIND IT ONLINE**

For more on Linux, see **www.linux.org**.

## Listing 13-29: THE CASE SYNTAX

```
case word
in
value1)
  command1
  ...
  lastcommand
;;
value2)
  command1
  ...
  lastcommand
;;
*)
  command1
  ...
  lastcommand
;;
esac
```

▲ The syntax for the **case** statement.

## Listing 13-30: THE UNAME.SH SCRIPT

```
#!/bin/sh
# Script to determine the version of UNIX.
#
os=`uname -s`
case $os
in
Linux)
    echo "You are using Linux."
;;
SunOS)
    echo "You are using Solaris."
;;
*)
    echo "You are using $os."
;;
esac
# uname.sh
```

▲ Example script using the **uname** command to differentiate between versions of UNIX.

## Listing 13-31: THE EXAMPLE8 SCRIPT

```
#!/bin/sh
#
# Example 8 from Chapter 13 of
# Teach Yourself UNIX.
#
# Using case.
#
echo -n "Which do you like better, "
echo "a dog, cat, or platypus?"
read animal

case $animal
in
    dog)
        echo "You like dogs best."
    ;;
    cat)
        echo "Cats ARE the best."
    ;;
    platypus)
        echo "Why did you pick a platypus?"
    ;;
    *)
    echo -n "Can't you pick one of a dog,"
    echo "cat, or platypus?"
    ;;
esac
```

▲ The **example8** script uses the case statement to create a "choose an animal" game.

283

# Working with Standard Input/Output

**S**hell scripts, like UNIX commands, understand the basic concepts of the standard files: standard input, output, and error. You can redirect the output of a shell script, for example, to a file using the > redirection operator, just as you can for UNIX commands. What's of more use, though, is the fact that you can redirect the input and output of commands you call within your shell scripts.

This capability enables you to make use of temporary files for storing data or for building up files from a number of commands. Inside your shell scripts, you can use any of the shell redirection and pipe operators, <, >, >>, and |, in shell scripts as well as with commands you type in at the command line. For example, you can collect the contents of a number of files and store this data into a backup file using the >> append operator. To append the contents of a file stored in a variable named *$filename* into a file named **report.backup**, you could use the following command:

```
$ cat $filename >> report.backup
```

Running a similar command multiple times would append files to the **report.backup** file. In fact, you could use this as the basis for a script that collects multiple files and then appends these files to the end of a backup file. The **example9** script on the facing page does just that.

The **example9** script loops over all files in the current directory that start with the text *report*. These files are assumed to be reports of some kind. All the files starting with *report* are concatenated and appended to a file named **report.backup** in the backup directory. To make the script more useful, it prompts you to enter the name of the directory for storing the backup file. This enables you to backup different files into different subdirectories. For example, you could backup all reports for the year 2001 into a directory named **2001**. The backup directory must exist, or the script will fail.

When running the **example9** script, the name of a subdirectory, such as 2001, where the backed up data will be stored must be entered in. To verify the script worked, you can use the **ls** command to check that the directory (**2001** in this case) has the backup file, named **report.backup**.

In addition to using redirection operators on their own, you can combine operators in your scripts. For example, you could build up an output file with the > and >> operators. You could then use this file as input to another command using the < operator.

---

**TAKE NOTE**

### BE CAREFUL WITH REDIRECTION

The > operator can easily wipe out files. You may want to check if a file exists before before using > to write to a file. The **test** command can help with this.

---

**CROSS-REFERENCE**
See Chapter 3 for more on **cut**, **paste**, and **join**.

**FIND IT ONLINE**
More information on writing shell scripts is located at **www.ocean.odu.edu/ug/shell_help.html**.

## Listing 13-32: USING OUTPUT REDIRECTION

```
$ date > report.header
$ cat report.header
Tue Oct 13 18:33:17 CDT 1998
```

▲ *Using output redirection.*

## Listing 13-33: USING INPUT REDIRECTION WITH SHELL COMMANDS

```
$ read datetoday  < report.header
$ echo $datetoday
Tue Oct 13 18:33:17 CDT 1998
```

▲ *You can use input redirection with shell commands, as well as in shell scripts. The* **read** *command is especially useful for this.*

## Listing 13-34: APPENDING TO THE OUTPUT

```
$ uname -n
yonsen
$
$ uname -n > report.header
$ cat report.header
Tue Oct 13 18:37:26 CDT 1998
yonsen
```

▲ *Building up a file from multiple commands. You can then use this file as a report header, for example.*

## Listing 13-35: RECREATING THE HEADER FILE EACH TIME

```
$ date > report.header
$ uname -n >> report.header
$ cat report.header
Tue Oct 13 18:42:23 CDT 1998
yonsen
```

▲ *The first command uses the > redirection symbol to clobber any existing file named* **report.header** *and then place the date in the file. This way, you always start fresh. Subsequent commands need to use the append operator, >>, to add to the data already in the file.*

## Listing 13-36: SCRIPT TO BUILD A REPORT HEADER

```
#/bin/sh
# Script to create a report header.
#
# Get name of output file.
if ( test $# -ge 1 ) then
    output_file=$1
else
    output_file=report.header
fi
# Gather data
datetoday=`date`
sys=`uname -s`
hostnm=`uname -n`
# Output the report header.
echo -n "Report for $sys " > $output_file
echo "system $hostnm " >> $output_file
echo "on $datetoday" >> $output_file
```

▲ *This script creates a two-line report header using the system type, name, and current date.*

## Listing 13-37: THE EXAMPLE9 SCRIPT

```
#!/bin/sh
#
# Example 9 from Chapter 13 of
# Teach Yourself UNIX.
#
# Input and output.
#
echo -n "Enter name of backup directory: "
read backupdir
for filename
    in report*
do
  cat $filename >> $backupdir/report.backup
done
```

▲ *A backup script using the >> output redirection to append all filenames that start with report to a file in the given directory.*

# Troubleshooting Shell Scripts

A lot can go wrong with a shell script, but most problems are merely typos. The first step in troubleshooting is always to examine the file with a text editor. Correct any errors. (This is always easier said than done.)

You may have a problem with individual commands in the shell script. In UNIX, each command should return a number to test for success. Commands return zero (0) for success and nonzero for failure. The shell variable $? holds the return value of the last command. You can check this variable to see if all went well, as shown on the facing page. The **example10** file, on the facing page, calls **make**, which is used in building, or making, programs. If you run the **make** command in a subdirectory without a **Makefile**, this will generate an error, as shown on the facing page.

Note that **make** printed out its error message and that the shell script also detected the error from the $? variable, which held a nonzero value (1). You can use $? in your own shell scripts to make them more robust when errors occur.

It's also a good idea to place shell scripts in a directory, along with any executable programs you develop. A common name for this directory is **bin** (most UNIX commands are in directories named **bin**, short for *binary*), and is usually a subdirectory of the home directory. Keeping commands in such a directory indicates two things: (1) A given file is a command (if the file is stored in the **bin** directory), and (2) It's not a good idea to mess with the file (because it is presumably a working command). Make sure this **bin** directory is in your path.

## Tracing the Execution of Shell Scripts

If you still have problems with your shell scripts, you might want to try tracing the scripts. You can use the tracing facility of **sh** to watch each command in a shell script execute. To do this, pass the shell script in question as a command-line parameter to **sh**, along with the *-v* or *-x* option. The **sh -v** command prints out the lines in the shell script as they are read and then executes the script. The more useful **sh -x** command prints out each shell script command as it executes, which should help you narrow down any problems.

Going back to our first example, you can trace the execution of the shell script file **example2** using the *-x* command-line parameter to **sh**, as shown on the facing page.

### TAKE NOTE

#### DON'T NAME SCRIPTS AFTER COMMANDS

Don't name a shell script **ls** if it calls the **ls** command, for example, as this could lead to an infinite loop. If the script is named **ls**, then it may try to re-execute itself over and over.

**CROSS-REFERENCE**

See Chapter 14 for an introduction to **make** and explanation for configuring the necessary **Makefile**.

**FIND IT ONLINE**

You can access a Web page covering Stupid Shell Tricks at www.cs.virginia.edu/~bah6f/funnies/unixcmds.html.

## Listing 13-38: RUNNING THE SCRIPT WITH SH -V

```
$ sh -v example2
#!/bin/sh
# Example 2 from Chapter 13
# of Teach Yourself UNIX.
# More on echo.
echo "You can also use quotation marks."
You can also use quotation marks.
# Note the space after the quotation
# mark and before second.
echo -n "first message"
first messageecho " second message"
 second message
# Use a command with echo.
echo "The current directory is `pwd`."
pwd
The current directory is
/usr2/erc/books/teachux/teachux4.
# Use a variable.
variable1="Yow, are we having fun yet?"
echo "The variable is $variable1."
The variable is Yow, are we having fun yet?
# Set a variable to a command output
datetoday=`date`
date
echo "The date is $datetoday."
The date is Fri Dec 31 14:02:26 CDT 2010.
```

▲ *Using the -v option to sh with the example2 script, presented earlier. Notice how the script's output is merged with the output of the -v option.*

## Listing 13-39: THE EXAMPLE10 SCRIPT THAT CREATES AN ERROR

```
#!/bin/sh
make
echo "The result of the command was $?"
# example10
```

▲ *A script to display the results of running a command — in this case make — from within the shell script.*

## Listing 13-40: RUNNING THE SCRIPT AND CREATING AN ERROR

```
$ example10
Make: No arguments or
   description file.  Stop.
The result of the command was 1
```

▲ *Running the example10 script in a directory without a file named Makefile will result in an error. The make command returns a 1, indicating an error, instead of 0, which indicates no errors occurred.*

## Listing 13-41: RUNNING THE EXAMPLE2 SCRIPT WITH SH -X

```
$ sh -x example2
+ echo You can also use quotation
marks with echo.
You can also use quotation marks with echo.
+ echo -n first message
first message+ echo  second message
 second message
++ pwd
+ echo The current directory is
/usr2/erc/books/teachux/teachux4.
The current directory is
/usr2/erc/books/teachux/teachux4.
+ variable1=Yow, are we having fun yet?
+ echo The variable is Yow,
are we having fun yet?.
The variable is Yow, are
we having fun yet?.
++ date
+ datetoday=Fri Dec 31 14:02:26 CDT 2010
+ echo The date is Fri Dec 31
14:02:26 CDT 2010.
The date is Fri Dec 31 14:02:26 CDT 2010.
```

▲ *Tracing a shell script in action with the -x parameter.*

# Personal Workbook

## Q&A

**1** The **echo** command normally prints a newline at the end of the text it prints. How can you prevent **echo** from printing this newline?

_____

_____

**2** With the **if** statement, what value is considered true and what false?

_____

_____

_____

**3** When running a command, what return value means success and what means failure?

_____

_____

_____

**4** How do you mark a file with executable permissions?

_____

_____

_____

**5** How can a script handle more than nine command-line parameters?

_____

_____

_____

**6** How can you do this from the C shell?

_____

_____

_____

**7** How can you read a value into a shell variable?

_____

_____

_____

**8** If a shell script doesn't work the way you want, what option can you use to trace the execution of the script?

_____

_____

_____

ANSWERS: PAGE 352

## EXTRA PRACTICE

❶ Discuss which tools are better — creating shell aliases for commands, writing shell scripts, or programming?

❷ Look up the online manual entry for **sh** and concentrate on the sections relevant to writing shell scripts.

❸ Look up the **http://language.perl.com/versus/csh.whynot** document on the Web to see some reasons why you may want to avoid using the C shell for shell scripts.

❹ When marking a file with executable permissions, all the examples in this chapter mark the permissions only for the user, or owner, of the file. Look up the options to mark a script as executable by any user.

## REAL-WORLD APPLICATIONS

✔ Your systems are running out of disk space at various times of the day. Create a script that will append to a log file the current time, the system name, who is logged on, and the current available disk space. Run this script periodically to determine who is the disk space culprit.

✔ Automate a common task you perform every day by creating a shell script.

✔ A former colleague created a shell script prior to leaving the company. Now the script no longer works. Discuss some techniques you'd use to try to debug the script.

## Visual Quiz

Create a script that can make output similar to that shown here.

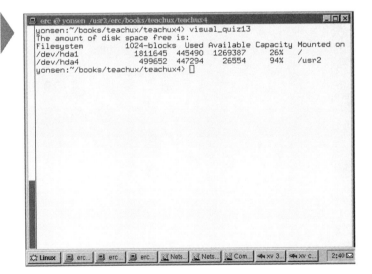

_____

_____

_____

_____

_____

_____

# CHAPTER 14

# C/C++ Programming Tools

UNIX sports a long history as a programming environment. From the very beginning, you could write programs in UNIX in what was then considered a high-level programming language, C. In fact, most of UNIX was written in C (and still is for that matter). In the early days of UNIX (the beginning of the 1970s), this was quite an accomplishment. Previously, most operating systems were written in the assembly code for a particular processor. Because of this, the task of getting an operating system to work on different computer hardware proved extremely tough.

By writing UNIX mostly in C, the designers of UNIX created a very portable operating system. This is due to the ease with which the C language can be made to run on new computer platforms. Making UNIX work on another platform—a process called *porting*—was a much smaller task than porting other operating systems. Soon, UNIX ran on a variety of platforms.

In many respects, this is a good thing, as you can run UNIX on everything from very small computers (as we write this, efforts are underway to port Linux to the Palm Pilot handheld computer) to extremely powerful supercomputers, and everything in between.

Many software developers find UNIX to be a better platform for software development than other systems, even if the final products won't run on UNIX at all.

This chapter covers the basics of UNIX tools for C and C++ programming. Even if you program in other languages, such as Java, you'll still find the techniques in this chapter useful. UNIX is strongly tied to its roots in the C language, and the C programming tools, such as compilers, linkers, and so on, are part of any programming on UNIX. Languages as diverse as Perl and Java still show many influences from C, especially in how they access the underlying operating system.

Furthermore, most UNIX freeware comes as source code, typically written in C. Thus, even if you have no intention of ever programming, you still need to know the basics of compiling C programs.

# Speaking the Languages

UNIX supports more computer languages than you'd ever think possible, including Ada, APL, BASIC, COBOL, C, Java, Modula-2, Eiffel, Objective-C, Fortran, Pascal, Perl, Tcl, and C++.

The most common programming language used on UNIX, though, is the C programming language. C and UNIX share the same team of inventors at Bell Labs, and the evolution of both C and UNIX are tightly intermixed. All the UNIX system facilities, from disks to networking, are accessed by a set of code libraries written in C. Although quite a few other languages run on UNIX, the underlying code necessary to access the system is really written in C. For example, the Perl scripting language has a run-time engine — called **perl** — that is written in C. Java, too, has a C-based run-time engine — **java**.

Because of the tight connection between C and UNIX, you'll find a plethora of C programming tools on most UNIX platforms.

## Programs Start as Text

It may seem odd, but virtually every program — no matter the programming language — starts life as a text file, which is called *source code*. The text file contains programming statements that tell the computer what to do. A separate tool called a *compiler* converts the text file, which the programmer wrote, into object, or machine, code for your programming platform. Next, *object modules* (files of object code) are linked together to make an executable program, a

brand new UNIX command. Once the process is successfully completed, you can execute this program like any other command you type at the command line. Being able to create your own commands is handy. However, you can often write shell scripts, as we described in the last chapter, that do essentially the same thing. So, from the plethora of UNIX tools, you need to choose what is the appropriate tool for any given task.

Even if you never write C programs, though, it is important to know about the process of compiling and linking C programs because the vast majority of UNIX freeware comes in source-code format, which you must compile to be useful.

Some languages are interpreted — that is, they require a special program, known as an *interpreter*, to read in the text file and execute the instructions. Shell scripts are interpreted.

For compiled languages such as C, the compiler usually produces *object code*, binary data in the native processor machine code. A separate process called *linking* then combines the object code for a program with standard built-in libraries and outputs an executable program, a new command that you can run.

---

**TAKE NOTE**

▶ **FILENAME EXTENSIONS**
Unlike Windows, UNIX doesn't depend on filename extensions. Even so, most programs use certain extensions, as listed in Tables 14-1 and 14-2.

---

**CROSS-REFERENCE**
Shell scripts are covered in Chapter 13.

**FIND IT ONLINE**
For information on **nedit**, a text editor that provides a Windows-like look and feel, see **www-pat.fnal.gov/ nirvana/nedit.html**.

## Table 14-1: C AND C++ FILENAME EXTENSIONS

| Extension | DOS/Windows Equivalent | Common Usage |
|---|---|---|
| .c | .c | C source code |
| .h | .h | C or C++ include file |
| .hxx | .hxx | C++ include file |
| .o | obj | Object module (compiled from a C or C++ source file) |
| .s | .asm | Assembly code |
| .a | .lib | Library archive of compiled object files (.o files) |
| a.out | .exe | Executable (no one uses the a.out name) |
| .C | .cpp | C++ source code (note uppercase C) |
| .cc | .cpp | C++ source code |
| .cpp | .cpp | C++ source code or temporary file used by C preprocessor |
| .cxx | .cpp | C++ source code |
| .c++ | .cpp | C++ source code |
| .sl | .dll | Shared (dynamic) library |
| .so | .dll | Shared (dynamic) library |

## Table 14-2: FILENAME EXTENSIONS USED FOR OTHER PROGRAMMING LANGUAGES

| Extension | DOS/Windows Equivalent | Common Usage |
|---|---|---|
| .cgi | .cgi | Common Gateway Interface script for Web forms, typically Perl |
| .class | .class | Compiled Java byte codes |
| .f | .for | Fortran program |
| .for | .for | Fortran program code |
| .gz | .zip | File compressed with gzip |
| .jar | .jar | Java archive |
| .java | .java | Java source code |
| .ph | .ph | Perl-formatted C include files |
| .pl | .pl | Perl source code |
| .pm | .pm | Perl module source code |
| .py | .py | Python source code |
| .sh | .bat | Shell script |
| .tar | NA | Tar archive |
| .tcl | .tcl | Tcl/Tk source code |
| .tk | .tk | Tcl/Tk source code |
| .Z | .zip | File compressed with **compress** |

# Learning the C Compiler

Most C programs are stored in one or more files that end with *.c*, like **inventory.c** or **checkin.c**. When you compile a C file, the C compiler, **cc**, creates an object file (in the machine code of the processor your system uses). Object files usually end with *.o*. The linker (called *linkage editor* in UNIX parlance), **ld**, then links the *.o* files together to make an executable program. For a typical program, you will have a number of *.o* files that need to be linked together. Along with the *.o* files from your source code, C programs link to a number of prebuilt libraries of functions. UNIX comes with a variety of libraries for everything from math to X Window graphics.

When building an executable program, the default name is **a.out**, although few really use **a.out** for their program names. Instead, programs end up with names like **ls**, **cp**, or **mv**.

## The cc Command

The **cc** command executes the C compiler, which can compile and link C programs to form executable commands. The myriad options to **cc** control exactly what the compiler does. We won't cover all of the many **cc** options; instead, we'll introduce the most important ones and let you read the online manual for **cc** for the rest. (Each version of UNIX tends to provide different options for **cc**; we cover the most used options that should be common to all versions of **cc**.) Use the following command to read the manual pages for **cc**: $ man cc

We must warn you that you'll see a lot of output for this command.

## Getting a C Compiler

Many modern UNIX systems don't come with the tools you need to write your own programs. In this case, you're out of luck unless you can somehow acquire those tools. For many of us stuck in these circumstances (C compilers typically cost thousands of dollars on UNIX systems), there's a nice alternative. The Free Software Foundation folks, creators of **emacs**, have also created a nifty free C compiler. (It also compiles C++ and Objective C, if you're interested.) This compiler, called **gcc** (for GNU C Compiler), is available over the Internet (see Chapter 10 for more on the Internet). The GNU C compiler is available in source-code form, which leaves you with a chicken-and-egg problem: You need a C compiler, the **cc** program, to compile the source to this C compiler. So, you'll need to get both the binary version for your hardware platform as well as the source code.

*Continued*

**TAKE NOTE**

**NOT ALL SYSTEMS HAVE COMPILERS**
It used to be that every version of UNIX shipped with at least a C compiler. Nowadays, this is no longer the case for many popular versions of UNIX, such as Solaris from Sun Microsystems.

**CROSS-REFERENCE**
The **emacs** text editor is covered in Chapter 11.

**FIND IT ONLINE**
The GNU C compiler is available from **prep.ai.mit.edu**.

## Table 14-3: COMMON COMMAND-LINE PARAMETERS FOR CC

| Parameter | Meaning |
| --- | --- |
| **-Idirectory** | Searches the given directory for include files, as well as */usr/include*. |
| **-c** *filename.c* | Compiles the file *filename.c* and build the object module *filename.o*. Do not create an executable command. |
| **-o** *progname* | Names the executable program *progname*. The default name is **a.out**. |
| **-g** | Compiles with debugging information. |
| **-O** | Optimizes the program for best performance. |

### Listing 14-1: COMPILING A HELLO WORLD PROGRAM

```
$ cc -o hello hello.c
```

▲ *The standard way to compile a simple C program stored in one file. The **-o** option names the output executable — **hello** in this case.*

### Listing 14-2: LOOKING FOR INCLUDE FILES IN MULTIPLE DIRECTORIES

```
$ cc -I/usr/X11R6/include -I../tcl -o
hello\hello.c
```

▲ *Telling the C compiler to look in both **/usr/X11R6**/include and ../**tcl** for include files, in addition to the normal locations. You can list as many directories as you like.*

### Listing 14-3: COMPILING WITH DEBUGGING INFORMATION

```
$ cc -g -o hello hello.c
```

▲ *Compiling with debugging information, to aid using a debugger on the output executable.*

### Listing 14-4: COMPILING WITH OPTIMIZATIONS

```
$ cc -O -o hello hello.c
```

▲ *The **-O** (uppercase Oh) option tells the compiler to optimize the output.*

### Listing 14-5: COMPILING WITH LESS OPTIMIZATIONS

```
$ cc -O2 -o hello hello.c
```

▲ *The **-O2** (with uppercase Oh) option tells the compiler to optimize the output, using only the second level of optimization, typically less than **-O**. See the online manual entry for **cc** for more on what levels your system supports.*

### Listing 14-6: COMPILING WITH BOTH DEBUGGING AND OPTIMIZATIONS IS NOT ALLOWED

```
$ cc -g -O -o hello hello.c
cc: Warning: File not optimized;
use -g3 if both optimization and debug
wanted.
```

▲ *With most compilers, you cannot mix and match **-O** (optimize) with **-g** (debugging) command-line parameters.*

### Listing 14-7: MIXING OPTIONS WITH GCC

```
$ gcc -g -O -o hello hello.c
```

▲ *With the GNU C compiler, you can mix the **-O** and **-g** options.*

# Learning the C Compiler

*Continued*

## Libraries

Software development takes a long time and is therefore a very expensive process. To help cut down the time it takes to develop software, most people who program try to reuse source code written previously. UNIX helps support this activity by enabling you to build collections of prebuilt software—called *libraries*.

A library contains of compiled object modules—*.o* files—collected into a library archive file, an *.a* file. You can then link libraries to your programs. Most C libraries (common C libraries are listed in Table 14-4) contain prebuilt C functions. These functions can create windows, calculate square roots, and do most anything. Most C++ libraries include prebuilt C++ classes (more on that later in this chapter).

Most libraries are stored in files ending in *.a*, short for archive files. Library filenames start with *lib*, such as libm.a, the math library, and libX11.a, the X Window library.

Shared libraries have a variety of extensions, depending on your version of UNIX. Shared libraries—called Dynamic Link Libraries on Windows—typically have an *.so* or *.sl* extension. Sometimes, you'll find a version number in the extension, such as **libc.so.5.4.44**.

To link with a standard library, you can use the **-l** (ell) option with the short name of a library—that is, the library name without the *lib* prefix and *.a* suffix. For example, **-lX11** links in the X Window library typically named **libX11.a**. The C compiler will link, by default, the standard C library, usually **libc.a**.

UNIX expects libraries to be located in **/usr/lib** or **/lib**. In many cases, the libraries you want are not located in these directories. In such an instance, you can use the **-L** option to tell the C compiler (really the linker, **ld**, launched by the compiler) where to look for libraries. For example, the X Window System libraries, even though X is standard on most versions of UNIX, are typically located in **/usr/lib/X11** (and often in **/usr/X11R6/lib** on Linux).

You can build your own libraries from compiled *.o* files with the **ar** command. The basic syntax follows:

```
$ ar rv libMyLib.a file1.o file2.o file3.o
```

The **rv** options tell **ar** to replace the named object files in the library with the new versions (**r**) and print out verbose information about the operation (**v**). The library file, **libMyLib.a** in this example, gets updated versions of the three object files passed on the command line. Libraries are really collections of *.o* files bundled into *.a* files. Table 14-5 lists the main **ar** options.

---

### TAKE NOTE

▶ **USE RANLIB IF NECESSARY**

On some versions of UNIX, you must run a program named **ranlib** on a library created by **ar** to update the library's equivalent of a table of contents. Use the **man ranlib** command to verify if this is so for your system.

---

**CROSS-REFERENCE**

Chapter 7 covers the X Window System.

**FIND IT ONLINE**

For more on the X Window System, see
www.opengroup.org/x/.

## Table 14-4: COMMON C LIBRARIES

| Library | Purpose |
| --- | --- |
| libc.a | C library (linked in by default) |
| libcurses.a | Text terminal-based interface library |
| libDtWidget.a | Common Desktop Environment widget (user interface) library |
| libm.a | Math library |
| libX11.a | Low-level X Window library |
| libXm.a | Motif library |
| libXt.a | X (Window) Toolkit Intrinsics library, used by Motif |

## Table 14-5: OPTIONS FOR AR

| Option | Usage |
| --- | --- |
| r | Replaces files in archive with new files |
| s | Updates symbol table |
| t | Prints library table of contents |
| v | Prints out verbose information |

### Listing 14-8: COMPILING WITH CC

```
$ cc -o foo foo.c
$
```

▲ *When compiling, if all goes well, you'll normally just see a prompt after calling the **cc** command.*

### Listing 14-9: LOOKING FOR LIBRARIES IN DIFFERENT LOCATIONS

```
$ cc -o foo foo.c -L/usr/lib/X11 -lX11 -lm
```

▲ *Linking with the X11 and math (m) libraries, telling the linker to look in **/usr/lib/X11** as well as the standard locations.*

### Listing 14-10: LOOKING FOR LIBRARIES IN MULTIPLE LOCATIONS

```
$ cc -o foo foo.c -L/usr/lib/X11 \
    -L/usr/lib/Xm -L/usr/openwin/lib \
    -L../mylibraries -lX11 -lm
```

▲ *You can add as many directories to the library path as you need.*

### Listing 14-11: CREATING A LIBRARY WITH AR

```
$ ar rv libMyLib.a file1.o file2.o file3.o
a - file1.o
a - file2.o
a - file3.o
ar: Warning: creating libMyLib.a
```

▲ *You can create a library file — an .a file — with the **ar** command. The **v** option tells **ar** to print verbose output.*

# Writing a Small C Program

To test your C compiler (and ensure that you have one), you can enter the source code for a program shown on the facing page.

In this program, the text between /* and */ are comments. Like shell scripts, comments are important for describing what your program intends to do. Unlike shell scripts, the C programming language does not recognize the shell script comment marker, #, as starting a comment. If you use # for comments in a C program, you will likely get an error. (C uses # for different purposes — for example, with C preprocessor commands such as #include, so you may get lucky with # comments and create statements the C preprocessor will accept. In any case, don't use # for comments in C programs; use /* to start a comment and */ to end the comment.)

The program in Listing 14-12 is short, and you can probably type it in using **vi** or **emacs** or another text editor, in under one minute. Type in each line one at a time, exactly as presented. If you name the file **hello.c**, you can use the following **vi** command to start editing the file:

```
$ vi hello.c
```

Then, in **vi** (or **emacs**), enter in the program listed on the facing page.

Save the file and quit **vi** (or **emacs**). After you type in this short program, you can go through the following simple steps to create a working executable program from this C file.

The program you typed in was simply a text file. There's nothing in it to make it an executable command. C programs aren't like shell scripts (covered in the last chapter), so we can't simply mark the text file with the execute permission to make it a working program. (Would that it were this easy!) Instead, we need to compile and link the program. Both steps, compiling and linking, are accomplished by the following **cc** command:

```
$ cc -o hello hello.c
```

This command runs the C compiler, **cc**. The *-o* option tells **cc** to build a program named **hello**. You can use any name you like with the *–o* option, such as *hello.exe*. Watch out, though — UNIX uses the filename, *hello.exe* in this case, as the command name. Thus, if you want a command *hello*, you need to pass the name *hello* to the *–o* option to **cc**. The **hello.c** part of the command tells **cc** to compile the file named **hello.c**. The **cc** command compiles and links the program. During this process, the **cc** command executes a number of programs behind the scenes, including **cpp**, the C preprocessor, and **ld**, the UNIX linker, which is used in the final stages to create the executable program **hello**.

Now, you should have an executable program named **hello**. You can execute this program by typing **hello** at the command line.

**CROSS-REFERENCE**

Chapter 13 covers shell scripts, another way to create commands.

**FIND IT ONLINE**

The C programming list of frequently asked questions, or FAQ, is located at **www.faqs.org/faqs/C-faq/faq/**.

## TAKE NOTE

### ▶ WORKING WITH #INCLUDE

C uses include files — also called *headers* — to define functions and data structures for libraries (in this case, the C library, **libc.a**). The #include directive tells the C preprocessor, **cpp**, to find a file named **stdio.h** and insert the file in place of the #include. If you use the angle brackets around an include filename, like <stdio.h>, this means that **cpp** looks for the file in its search path, which defaults to **/usr/include**. You can list other locations to look in with the **-I** option. You can also use quotation marks (") around the filename, instead of < and >.

### ▶ FILENAME EXTENSIONS

On Windows systems, when you build an executable program, it includes a *.exe* extension. Thus, the hello program would have a filename of **hello.exe** on Windows. Even so, on Windows, you just need to type in **hello** to run **hello.exe**. On UNIX, you type in the exact name of the program: **hello**. The file is named **hello**. If you do like the *.exe* extension (and there's nothing wrong with it), you can name your executable program **hello.exe**. In that case, though, you must type in **hello.exe** to run the program. UNIX requires exactness, but gives you the freedom to name your programs anything you want.

### Listing 14-12: THE HELLO.C PROGRAM

```
/*
A first C program.
Written for Teach Yourself UNIX.
*/
#include  <stdio.h>

int main(
    int argc,
    char** argv)

{   /* main */

    printf("This is the famous ");
    printf("hello world program.\n");
    printf("It prints out a message:\n");
    printf("Hello world!\n");

    return 0;
}   /* main */

/* hello.c */
```

▲ *A short C program. This program merely prints the text in the* ***printf*** *statements.*

### Listing 14-13: COMPILING THE HELLO.C PROGRAM

```
$ cc -o hello hello.c
```

▲ *Use the* ***cc*** *command to compile the* ***hello.c*** *program.*

# Writing a Small C++ Program

C++ is an object-oriented language built on top of C. True to its roots in C, the command to compile and link C++ programs is normally **CC**, all uppercase in contrast to the C compiler command, **cc**, which is all lowercase. **CC** takes most of the same parameters as **cc** — again, this differs by platform. The options listed in the Table 14-3 should work with all versions of **CC**.

C++ adds the ability to create classes and objects to the basic C language, hence the ++ in the name C++ (which implies C++ is an incremental improvement to C). The main purpose to C++ is to provide a framework for object-oriented programming.

As with everything else involving computers, people argue over definitions. The main purpose of object-oriented programming is to provide a better way to divide problems and to make programs easier to change. (Programming continues to be a time-consuming, labor-intensive process.) An *object*, though, is usually agreed to be a structured collection of data and *methods*, or functions, that can operate on the data. You want all the functions that operate on the data collected in one place to make it easier to handle changes to the object. (In a normal C program, you may have to track down changes throughout your source code. With object-oriented programming — if you're lucky — you can make a change to just one small area of the software.)

In the object-oriented view, a program is made up of objects. Each object stores the data it needs and provides access to that data through methods. Each object is a member of a class. A *class* defines the layout of an object — the data and methods that each object of the class will have. (Objects are also called *instances* of a class.) The way you divide the problem domain into classes largely determines how well your programs will work and how easy they will be to maintain over the years.

Although **CC** remains the traditional name for the C++ compiler, we've seen some variants on different systems. If you run the GNU suite of compilers, you may have **g++** in place of **CC**. (The **g++** command may even be a script that runs **gcc**, the GNU C and C++ compiler, with special options.) On other systems, commercial compilers may sport different names such as **CXX**.

Although many UNIX systems come with a C compiler, C++ is another story. In most cases this will be an add-on option and will cost money. However, the freeware GNU C compiler also supports C++.

**CROSS-REFERENCE**

Compare the C++ program here with the C program covered under "Writing a Small C Program" earlier in this chapter.

**FIND IT ONLINE**

The C++ programming list of frequently asked questions, or FAQ, is located at **www.faqs.org/faqs/C++-faq/part1/**.

## TAKE NOTE

### INHERITANCE

In addition to classes and objects, another key topic in object-oriented programming is inheritance. Inheritance allows a class to borrow methods and data from other classes. (Borrowing saves time, and so is a virtue in software development.) For example, a *Rectangle* class may inherit from a more general *Shape* class. Other classes derived from the generic Shape class could include *Circle*, *Trapezoid*, and so on.

### POLYMORPHISM

In working with objects, you'll soon discover that you want to apply the same — or very similar — operations to objects from multiple classes. For example, you may want to apply a draw operation to both objects of type *Circle* and objects of type *Rectangle*. To make your code easier to understand, you may want to give both the *Circle* and the *Rectangle* draw operation a simple name like *draw*. Now, drawing a circle is clearly different from drawing a rectangle. The capability to have multiple functions named *draw* that operate differently depending on the class (in other words, these functions are smart enough to know the type of the object involved) is called *polymorphism*.

### CLASSES ARE LIKE STRUCTURES

A C++ class is a lot like a C structure (struct in C), except that a class can contain member functions, which are functions that apply to that class. (In C++, structures can also have member functions, just as classes do. C does not allow this, though.)

### Listing 14-14: THE HELLO.CC C++ PROGRAM

```
//
// Simple C++ example
// program for Chapter 14 of
// Teach Yourself UNIX.
//
#include <iostream.h>


int main(
    int argc,
    char** argv)

{ // main

  cout << "Hello world" << endl;

}  ^// main
```

▲ The **hello.cc** sample C++ program that prints out "Hello world."

### Listing 14-15: COMPILING A C++ PROGRAM

```
$ CC -o hellocpp hello.cc
```

▲ On most systems, the C++ compiler is named **CC**. On Digital UNIX, the C++ compiler is named **cxx**. With GNU C, the C and C++ compiler is named **gcc**. With GNU C, your C++ compiler (often a shell script wrapping the **gcc** command) may be named **g++**.

# Working with the C Compiler

The **cc** command — as well as **CC** — first compiles the program into an object module and then links the object module to create an executable program, the file named **hello** (or **hellocpp** for C++, in our example). The concept of object modules is very important if you have more than one file to compile into your program. Most C and C++ programs require a number of source files, all of which must be compiled and then linked together to form one program. One of the main reasons for separating source code into multiple files is simply sanity: Reading one megabyte of source code in one file is ludicrous. And yes, C programs can get to this size and even much bigger.

To use the long method of compiling and linking, we split the tasks into two steps. First, you compile all the source code files you require to object modules. Second, you link the resulting *.o* files (we get into this a bit later) to your executable program. Because you have a very small C program typed in already (you did type it in, didn't you?), start with that.

To compile **hello.c** into an object module (an *.o* file), use the **-c** option. If successful, you should see a file named **hello.o** in your directory. The *.o* file is called the object file (or object module).

The next step is to link the object files (usually there's more than one) to an executable file. To do this, you pass a *.o* file at the end of the command line, rather than the *.c* file you used previously. You still create the program, **hello**, only this time from a precompiled object module file, **hello.o**. You can place more than one object filename on the command line.

## Working with cc

All C programs are built around the section labeled **main**. The **main** section (called a *function* in C parlance) is executed when the program starts. The **main** function for this example has four C program statements, the **printf** function, which prints out the text between the quotation marks to your screen, and a **return** statement, which in this case, ends the program. As you can tell, this is not a sophisticated program.

Each **\n** character passed to **printf** in the example source code means that a newline character is printed. This starts a new line. If you're used to a Windows machine, you'll note that UNIX uses a newline character where Windows and DOS use a carriage return and then a newline. The backslash, \, is used as a special character in C programs. Usually, a backslash is combined with another character to make a nonprintable character, such as **\n** for a newline or **\a** for a bell.

### TAKE NOTE

#### COMPILING FOR C++ IS SIMILAR TO C

**CC**, the C++ compiler, generally takes similar options to those for **cc**. The options presented here should work fine for both **CC** and **cc**.

**CROSS-REFERENCE**

The **ls** command is covered in Chapter 2.

**FIND IT ONLINE**

For more on the GNU C compiler, which also supports C++, see www.gnu.org/software/gcc/gcc.html.

### Listing 14-16: COMPILING TO AN .O FILE

```
$  cc -c hello.c
```

▲ *Compiling to an object module (file).*

### Listing 14-17: COMPILING AND CHECKING THE OUTPUT

```
$ cc -c hello.c
$ ls -l hello*
-rw-r-r-   1 erc   users    235 Jul 28 21:11
hello.c
-rw-r-r-   1 erc   users    646 Jul 28 21:11
hello.o
$
```

▲ *After you compile a .c file with the -c option, you should see the corresponding .o file, called the object module.*

### Listing 14-18: COMPILING AND LINKING FROM AN OBJECT MODULE

```
$ cc -o hello hello.o
```

▲ *Once you have an object module, you can build the final program.*

### Listing 14-19: LINKING WITH MORE THAN ONE FILE

```
$ cc -o hello hello1.o hello2.o hello3.o
```

▲ *You can link more than one .o file with the cc command. Simply list all the .o files on the command line.*

### Listing 14-20: COMPILING SEPARATE FILES

```
$ cc -c hello1.c
$ cc -c hello2.c
$ cc -c hello3.c
$ cc -o hello hello1.o hello2.o hello3.o
```

▲ *Before you can link .o files, you must compile the .c files to create the .o files in the first place.*

### Listing 14-21: LOOKING FOR INCLUDE FILES IN MULTIPLE DIRECTORIES WHEN COMPILING TO OBJECT MODULES

```
$ cc -I/usr/X11R6/include \
    -I../tcl -c hello1.c
$ cc -I/usr/X11R6/include \
    -I../tcl -c hello2.c
$ cc -I/usr/X11R6/include \
    -I../tcl -c hello3.c
$ cc -o hello hello1.o hello2.o hello3.o
```

▲ *Telling the C compiler to look in both /usr/X11R6/include and ../tcl for include files in addition to the normal locations. You can list as many directories as you like. You need to run commands like this for each .c file. C++ compilers also support the –I option.*

### Listing 14-22: COMPILING WITH DEBUGGING WHEN MAKING OBJECT MODULES

```
$ cc -g -c hello1.c
$ cc -g -c hello2.c
$ cc -g -c hello3.c
$ cc -g -o hello hello1.o hello2.o hello3.o
```

▲ *The -g option tells the compiler to store debugging information inside your program. For the -g option to be useful, you need to compile the individual .c files with the -g option as well.*

# Dealing with Errors

If you entered any of the example programs exactly as we wrote them, you should get no error messages from **cc**. If you made a typo and the **cc** command found any errors, though, you'll see some cryptic error messages that often won't make sense. Even so, each message tells you the line number in which **cc** detected an error. (Note that this line number isn't always accurate — the error may be a number of lines above, but **cc** does give you a starting place from which to look for problems.)

For example, if we add the word *blech* to our sample program, it will generate an error. Just type in **blech** on a line of its own and run **cc** again. You should see something like the output shown on the facing page.

If you get errors like this, go back into **vi** or **emacs** and correct the problem. Make sure your program looks like the example program. You have a more serious problem, though, if you get an error message such as "Command not found."

This means your system cannot find the C compiler. All is not lost, though. You may have a system that provides a different name for the **cc** command. For example, a commercial compiler vendor such as LPI may name their C compiler **lpicc**. If you use the free C compiler from the GNU project, the **cc** command may be named **gcc** instead.

The worst problem is if your system does not come with a C compiler at all. In days past, every UNIX system came with a C compiler. But nowadays many vendors omit the C compiler to cut costs and

to create a version of UNIX that doesn't use up all your hard disk space. If you don't have a C compiler, you won't be able to complete the examples, but you can still follow through the text.

When you write programs with the C language (or with any programming language for that matter), the programs often won't work the first time. Many times this is due to a typo in the program's text files. But sometimes you may find very subtle problems. To aid in tracking down these problems, you can use a UNIX debugger. The debugger is supposed to help you remove the problems, or bugs, from your programs.

To work with a debugger, you must first compile your programs with the **-g** command-line parameter to **cc**. This **-g** option places special debugging information into the executable program. A debugger can then extract this information to help tell you what the program is doing at any particular time.

The most common debugger programs include **sdb**, **adb**, **dbx**, **xdb**, and **gdb**. Each of these debuggers uses its own cryptic syntax, so be sure to check your system's documentation and the online manual pages.

**TAKE NOTE**

**GRAPHICAL FRONT ENDS TO DEBUGGERS**

You may also have some graphical programs that act as front ends to these debuggers, such as **xdbx**, **dbxtool**, or the SunPro debugger (on Sun workstations). Hewlett-Packard's Softbench environment also comes with a graphical debugger, **softdebug**.

**CROSS-REFERENCE**

Chapter 11 covers text editors.

**FIND IT ONLINE**

The DDD debugger, a graphical debugger, is located at www.cs.tu-bs.de/softech/ddd/.

### Listing 14-23: THE HELLO2.C PROGRAM WITH AN ERROR

```
/*
A first C program.
Written for Teach Yourself UNIX.
*/
#include  <stdio.h>

int main(
    int argc,
    char** argv)

{   /* main */

    printf("This is the famous ");
    printf("hello world program.\n");
blech

    printf("It prints out a message:\n");
    printf("Hello world!\n");

    return 0;
}   /* main */
```

▲ *Our modified and incorrect program. The blech statement is an error.*

### Listing 14-24: SHOWING ERRORS FROM THE CC COMMAND

```
$ cc -c hello2.c
"hello.c", line 16: blech undefined
"hello.c", line 16: syntax error
"hello.c", line 16: illegal character: 134
(octal)
"hello.c", line 16: cannot recover from
earlier errors: goodbye!
```

▲ *Compiling the **hello2.c** program with the error. The various C compilers identify errors differently. Errors can also be identified after the line containing the bad blech statement.*

### Listing 14-25: A DIFFERENT ERROR IN THE HELLO3.C PROGRAM

```
/*
A first C program.
Written for Teach Yourself UNIX.
*/
#include  <stdio.h>

int main(
    int argc,
    char** argv)

{   /* main */

    printf("This is the famous ");
    printf("hello world program.\n");
    blech();

    printf("It prints out a message:\n");
    printf("Hello world!\n");

    return 0;
}   /* main */
```

▲ *In the **hello3.c** program, the bad statement — **blech();** — resembles valid C syntax. The problem is that no **blech** function is defined in this program nor in any library.*

### Listing 14-26: SHOWING THE LINK-TIME ERROR

```
$ cc -o hello3 hello3.c
ld:
Unresolved:
blech
```

▲ *When you try to link the **hello3.c** file, you'll see a link-time error from the **ld** program. You won't see a compiler syntax error.*

# Using Programming Tools

In addition to the compilers, UNIX includes a number of tools to help you manage software development. The program called **lint** flags any "lint" it discovers in your programs, "lint" being the places in your C programs where you bend and warp the rules. Even if your code is legal C, you may still have problems, and **lint** tries to warn about potential problems.

The Source Code Control System (SCCS) and Revision Control System (RCS) aim at keeping older versions of your C program text files, in case you make a mistake and want to back out of a change.

Both SCCS and RCS work much the same way. What you do is check in a key file. If you want to edit the file, you must check it out, and only one person at a time can check a file out. When you're done making changes, you check the file back in. If you made a mistake, you can check out an older version of the file. Both SCCS and RCS keep records of every version of the file that you've checked in. To save on disk space, both packages use what are called delta files. That is, for any version of a file, SCCS and RCS only have to keep the changes or differences from the last version. (SCCS and RCS act slightly differently in this regard, but to users, the result is the same.)

SCCS is available on most commercial versions of UNIX. RCS is freeware and can run on virtually all versions of UNIX. We've found RCS generally better for larger projects than SCCS, mostly because RCS better supports the capability to create separate versions of the source code, called *branches*.

## Checking for Performance Bottlenecks

UNIX comes with a number of tools to check your programs for performance bottlenecks. Two of the most common of these tools are **prof** (short for *profiling*) and **gprof**, an extended tool that includes more detailed output.

These profiling tools help you find out what parts of your programs take the most time to execute. To use these tools, you must compile with **cc** using the **-p** option (**prof**) or **-pg** option (**gprof**). Note that many systems have only one (or none) of these tools.

Once you've compiled with **-p** or **-pg**, you can run your program as you normally would. You'll notice the program runs slower than you're used to because the way **prof** and **gprof** monitor the time it takes your program to perform tasks also takes time.

When you're done running your program, use **prof** or **gprof** to compile the data from the run of the program. The end result is a chart showing every function that the program executed, along with the average time each call to a given function took to complete, the total cumulative time spent in that function, and the total number of times the function was called.

**CROSS-REFERENCE**

Chapter 2 covers file permissions used by RCS programs to control access.

**FIND IT ONLINE**

You can download RCS from **www.gnu.org/software/ software.html**.

## TAKE NOTE

▶ **USING DIFF**

The **diff** program forms one of the most used programming tools. This command, with its graphical cousins, enables you to compare files for differences, such as different versions of the same program source code file. This is quite useful as you track a program from its initial version to later versions and need to see the differences.

▶ **ANALYZE FIRST, THEN IMPROVE**

The key point for performance analysis is to always measure performance first and then try to optimize. If you start to optimize before measuring and analyzing the situation, you may end up optimizing a part of your program that really doesn't impact the total system performance (that is, an area that is not the performance bottleneck).

### Listing 14-27: RUNNING LINT

```
$ lint hello.c
"hello.c", line 9: warning: argument argc
     unused in function main
"hello.c", line 10: warning: argument argv
     unused in function main
"stdio.h", line 868 ("llib-lc.c"): warning:
function printf
     return value is always ignored
```

▲ *The **lint** command points out problems in C programs. This example shows the complaints **lint** makes about our simple **hello.c** program. Most versions of **lint** do not support C++, although you can get special C++ **lint** programs.*

### Listing 14-28: RCS REQUIRES AN RCS DIRECTORY

```
$ mkdir RCS
```

▲ *To make use of RCS, you generally need a subdirectory of the current directory named **RCS**. This is where RCS stores information to recreate older versions of the file. You need an **RCS** subdirectory in every directory for which you want to check in and check out files.*

### Listing 14-29: CHECKING IN A FILE FOR THE FIRST TIME

```
$ ci -u hello.c
RCS/hello.c,v  <-  hello.c
enter description, terminated with single
'.' or end of file:
NOTE: This is NOT the log message!
> This is a simple hello world program
> .
initial revision: 1.1
done
```

▲ *The **ci** command checks in a file in RCS. You need a subdirectory named **RCS**. Enter a description and then type a period (.) on a line by itself (after the > prompt) to end the comment. The **-u** option unlocks the file for modification by others.*

### Listing 14-30: CHECKING OUT A FILE WITH RCS

```
$ co -l hello.c
RCS/hello.c,v  ->  hello.c
revision 1.1 (locked)
writable hello.c exists; remove it?
[ny](n): y
done
```

▲ *The **co** command checks out a file in RCS. The **-l** option locks the file so others cannot modify it while you make changes. If you have a writable version of the file in the current directory, the **co** command will prompt you (as shown here) whether you want to overwrite that file.*

# Using make and imake

Any large programming project, which includes just about any commercial software package, involves a large number of program files with complex rules for putting the whole thing together into executable programs. To help manage the complexity of larger software projects, UNIX provides a tool called **make**, which helps build or "make" UNIX programs from the C language text files.

To work with **make**, you write a set of rules that describe the steps necessary to rebuild the program. These rules are most effective for large programs made up of many files.

The rules used by **make** are stored in a special file named **Makefile**. You keep a **Makefile** in each directory where you develop C programs. This **Makefile** requires a rigid syntax, and **make** complains about the slightest variances. In fact, according to UNIX legend, the creator of **make** never knew his tool would catch on so fast, or he would have invented a looser, easier syntax.

The basic **make** syntax is deceptively simple. You start out with a target. The *target* is something that you want to build, such as the **hello** program from the previous example.

To create a target in the **Makefile**, begin with a new line, name the target — what you want to build — and then type in a colon (:), a **Tab**, and a list of the files that the target depends on. Starting on the next line, begin with a **Tab**, and then place the UNIX command used to build the target. You can have multiple commands, each of which should go on its own line, and every command line must start with a **Tab**. The **Tab** is very important. If you use spaces, the **Makefile** won't work. (This rigid syntax is one of the drawbacks of **make**.)

In our example, the target we want to build is the **hello** program. The **hello** program, the target, depends on the object module **hello.o**. We create a new rule — target — and we need a command to build the **hello** program from **hello.o**, **cc -o hello hello.o** in this case.

The **hello.o** file, in turn, depends on the C source file, **hello.c**. So, we need another rule to build **hello.o** from **hello.c**, as well as the command to build **hello.o**, **cc -c hello.c**. The facing page shows this **Makefile**.

The command to build the **hello** program now becomes the following:

```
$ make hello
```

When you use **make**, you need to specify which target in the **Makefile** to build (there can be many), **hello** in this case. If you pass no target, **make** builds the first target it finds. If you run **make** and have no **Makefile**, **make** will generate an error.

*Continued*

**CROSS-REFERENCE**

The book *UNIX Programming Tools* covers **make** in greater depth. See Appendix A.

**FIND IT ONLINE**

A good tutorial on Makefiles is located at **ima.udg. es/~frederic/onMakefiles.html**.

## TAKE NOTE

### STANDARD TARGETS

Over the years, a number of **make** targets have become standardized by convention. These targets include:

**all**: Generally set to be the first target in the **Makefile**, this builds everything in the **Makefile**.

**clean**: This deletes the executable program, **hello** in this case, all object modules (*.o* files), libraries (*.a* files), any core dump files, and other files built by **make**.

**install**: This installs the program in the proper location, often **/usr/local/bin**.

**libs** or **lib**: Usually makes all libraries that may go into a program.

**test**: Builds and runs a test or test suite that verifies the software is properly running.

Of course, there's no magic here. You need to create these targets yourself in your **Makefile**.

### ENHANCED MAKE

The GNU project includes **gmake**, an enhanced version of **make**. The **gmake** command accepts the standard **Makefile** syntax supported by **make**, but also supports a number of enhancements, including a set of wildcard rules. This enables you to state in general how to build any *.c* file in an *.o* file and to include other files of rules within a **Makefile**.

### Table 14-6: MAKE COMMAND-LINE PARAMETERS

| Parameter | Meaning |
|---|---|
| **-f** *filename* | Uses the named *filename* instead of **Makefile** for the rules |
| **-n** | No execute mode — only prints out the commands, but doesn't execute them |
| **-s** | Silent mode — doesn't print out any command that **make** executes |

### Listing 14-31: MAKEFILE SYNTAX

```
what_to_build:  what_it_depends_on
  command1_to_build_it
  command2_to_build_it
  command3_to_build_it
  ...
  lastcommand_to_build_it
```

▲ In the abstract, the **Makefile** rules look like this.

### Listing 14-32: EXAMPLE MAKEFILE

```
#
# Test Makefile
#
# The program hello depends on hello.o.
hello:  hello.o
        cc -o hello hello.o

# The object module hello.o depends
# on hello.c.
hello.o:  hello.c
        cc -c hello.c

# end of Makefile
```

▲ The **Makefile** rule to build the **hello** program. The lines starting with **cc** start with **tab** characters.

# Using make and imake
*Continued*

When using **make**, everything depends on the file modification dates and times. After building the **hello** program, if we try **make** again, it tells us that there's no new work to do.

Why? Because the **hello** program has been built, and nothing has changed that would require **make** to rebuild the program. Now, edit the **hello.c** file again, or use the **touch** command to modify the date/time associated with the file.

When you call **make** again, it knows it now needs to rebuild the **hello** program, because presumably the **hello.c** file has changed since the last time **hello.c** was compiled with **cc**. You've discovered the secret to the rules of **make**. Everything depends on the modification date/time of the files, a very simple but clever idea. The idea is that if the text of the program *.c* file is modified, you better rebuild the program with **cc**. Because most users are impatient, if the *.c* file hasn't been changed, there's simply no reason (at least in our example) to rebuild the program with **cc**. However, because **touch** only updates the date/time associated with the file and doesn't change the internals of the file in any way, we've just fooled **make**. Normally, though, you don't want to fool **make**, you want to use its simple rules to make your life easier.

## imake

When using **make**, you place all the rules to build a program inside one or more **Makefiles**. The problem with this approach is that **make** rules depend on many factors in your system, the compiler you use, the version of UNIX you have, any special programming differences, and so on. If you ever need to compile an application on more than one version of UNIX, you may need to create new **Makefiles** for each new system, a tedious process at best. This is where a tool called **imake** fits in.

The **imake** command builds a **Makefile** tuned to your version of UNIX. You then use the resulting **Makefile** normally.

To build a **Makefile**, **imake** uses a set of rules you store in a file called **Imakefile**, along with configuration data for your system, usually stored in **/usr/lib/X11/config**. The **Imakefile** contains generic rules that describe how to build the program without specifying exact details that may differ between systems. The configuration data helps **imake** expand the rules into a **Makefile** that will work on your system.

## TAKE NOTE

### ▶ IMAKE AND X

You'll find **imake** especially popular with programs for the X Window System, for which installations vary widely. There's simply no way you could write a portable **Makefile** that could work on all such platforms.

### ▶ RUNNING THE XMKMF SHELL SCRIPT

If you have an **Imakefile**, run the **xmkmf** shell script, which backs up the existing **Makefile** to **Makefile.bak**, and then creates a new **Makefile** for your system. After that, type **make**, and the program should build.

**CROSS-REFERENCE**

Chapter 7 covers the X Window System.

**FIND IT ONLINE**

For more on **imake**, see **www.primate.wisc.edu/software/imake-stuff/**.

## Table 14-7: COMMAND-LINE PARAMETERS FOR IMAKE

| Parameter | Meaning |
|---|---|
| **-D**_define_ | Defines the value _define_. |
| **-e** | Specifies that **imake** should build and execute the **Makefile**. The default is to not execute the **Makefile**. |
| **-f** _filename_ | Names the local **Imakefile**, which defaults to **Imakefile**. |
| **-I**_directory_ | Names the directory for the **Imake.tmpl** file, which contains general rules for **imake**. |
| **-s** _filename_ | Names the output file. The default is **Makefile**. |
| **-T**_template_ | Names the master template file. The default is **Imake.tmpl**. |
| **-v** | Turns on verbose mode, which prints out **cpp** (C preprocessor) commands. |

### Listing 14-33: AN IMAKEFILE

```
LOCAL_LIBRARIES1 = $(XAWLIB) $(XMULIB)\
    $(XTOOLLIB) $(EXTENSIONLIB) $(XLIB)
# Debugging flag.
CDEBUGFLAGS = -g
SRCS1 = file1.c file2.c file3.c file4.c
OBJS1 = file1.o file2.o file3.o file4.o
INCLUDE_FILES = include1.h include2.h
PROGRAM = myedit
ComplexProgramTarget_1(myedit,
    $(LOCAL_LIBRARIES1), )
# End of Imakefile
```

▲ A sample **Imakefile** used to build an X Window program named **myedit**.

### Listing 14-34: WORKING WITH MODIFICATION TIMES

```
$ make hello
        cc -c hello.c
        cc -o hello hello.o
$ make hello
`hello' is up to date.
$ touch hello.c
$ make hello
        cc -c hello.c
        cc -o hello hello.o
```

▲ Everything with **make** depends on the file modification dates and times.

### Listing 14-35: RUNNING XMKMF

```
$ xmkmf
mv Makefile Makefile.bak
imake -DUseInstalled -I/usr/lib/X11/config
```

▲ The **xmkmf** script acts as a front end to **imake**.

### Listing 14-36: RUNNING XMKMF AND THEN COMPILING USING MAKE

```
$ xmkmf
mv Makefile Makefile.bak
imake -DUseInstalled -I/usr/lib/X11/config
$ make hello
cc -c hello.c
        cc -o hello hello.o
```

▲ After running **xmkmf**, you can then use **make** normally.

# Building Freeware

Free software, also called open source software, has always been a part of the UNIX community. Many commonly used commands, including the **emacs** text editor, are free applications. The X Window System, used for UNIX graphics, started out as freeware. In addition, the Apache Web server is not only free software, but claimed to be the number one Web server program used on the Internet.

Because of all the free tools available, you may want to download free software and use it on your system. If you're used to Windows or MacOS systems, though, you are in for a few surprises with UNIX freeware.

First, virtually all UNIX freeware comes in source code format (mostly C or C++). The main reason you get source code is because UNIX runs on a wide variety of processor architectures. And, it's unlikely that any one person or organization has all possible processors covered, from low-end PCs to high-end Cray supercomputers. So, you get source code.

Second, you'll rarely find binary — precompiled — versions of the code, except for the larger UNIX distributions. These include Sun Solaris on SPARC and Linux on Intel processor systems.

Third, you'll need a C compiler to build most programs.

Fourth, and most annoyingly, you may have to download other packages in order to build an application. For example, to build MRTG, which monitors network routers, you also need Perl.

Most UNIX freeware comes packaged in a **tar** archive file, which you expand with the **tar** command. To cut down on storage space and download time, many packages are compressed using the **compress** or **gzip** commands.

Once you've downloaded a package and expanded all the files, the next step is figuring out how to build the program. Start by looking for files named **README** or some variant of **README** (such as **README_OR_DIE** or **README.FIRST**). Read this file. The **README** file usually contains the information necessary to build and install the package. Many applications include a file named **INSTALL**, or some variant like **INSTALL.Solaris** and **INSTALL.Linux**. Follow the relevant directions.

To make things flow smoothly, many free applications use a tool called **configure** from the GNU project that helps configure a program for building on your system. If instructed in the **README** or **INSTALL** files, you type in a command like the following:

```
$ ./configure
```

After you use **configure**, you usually run **make**.

---

**TAKE NOTE**

### X WINDOW PROGRAMS USUALLY SUPPORT IMAKE, NOT CONFIGURE

Most X Window programs come with an **Imakefile** described previously. Instead of running configure, you run **imake**.

---

**CROSS-REFERENCE**

Chapter 10 covers **ftp** and downloading files from the Internet, along with the **tar, compress,** and **gunzip** commands.

**FIND IT ONLINE**

For more on open source software, see **www.opensource.org**.

## Table 14-8: SOURCES OF FREE SOFTWARE

| URL | Contains |
|-----|----------|
| **www.gnu.org** | GNU project, home of GNU C, **gmake**, and so on |
| **sunsite.unc.edu/ pub/Linux** | SunSite FTP archive of Linux (and UNIX) software. |
| **www.sunfreeware.com** | Sun Microsystems site for free versions of Solaris |
| **www.cdrom.com** | Home of Walnut Creek CD-ROM, which contains Linux, FreeBSD, and lots of UNIX source code |
| **www.perl.com** | Perl source code, add-on modules, and information |
| **www.scriptics.com** | Tcl/Tk source code, add-on extensions, and information |
| **ftp.linux.org** | Linux |
| **ftp.freebsd.org** | FreeBSD UNIX |
| **ftp.netbsd.org** | NetBSD UNIX |
| **ftp.neosoft.com** | Software written in Tcl/Tk |
| **ftp.x.org** | Sources for the X Window System and X applications and utilities |

## Table 14-9: WHERE TO GET SPECIFIC APPLICATIONS

| URL | Contains |
|-----|----------|
| **ww.apache.org** | Apache Web server, a popular Web server package |
| **www.research.digital. com/SRC/personal/ Sanjay_Ghemawat/ical/ home.html** | Ical calendar software |
| **people.mainz.netsurf.de/ ~bolik/tkdesk** | TkDesk file manager |
| **home.netscape.com** | Netscape Communicator Web browser |
| **www.mozilla.org** | Mozilla, an Open Source version of Netscape Navigator Web browser |
| **samba.anu.edu.au/ samba** | SAMBA, Windows SMB network server software for UNIX |
| **www.PLiG.org/xwinman** | A list of window managers for the X Window System |
| **themes.org** | Free themes for the Enlightenment, AfterStep, and other window manager. |

# Personal Workbook

## Q&A

**1** What is the name of the command that compiles C programs?

_____

_____

**2** What is the typical filename extension for C program files?

_____

_____

_____

**3** What are some of the extensions typically used for C++ programming?

_____

_____

_____

**4** What is the name of the typical command that compiles C++ programs?

_____

_____

_____

**5** What is the name of the command for the GNU C compiler?

_____

_____

_____

**6** Which command builds software libraries?

_____

_____

_____

**7** Which program does the **xmkmf** shell script work with?

_____

_____

_____

**8** What does the **ci** program do?

_____

_____

_____

ANSWERS: PAGE 353

## EXTRA PRACTICE

1. Determine whether or not you have a C compiler installed.

2. If so, look at the online manual pages for the **cc** command.

3. Determine whether you have a C++ compiler installed.

4. Use the online manuals for the **ranlib** command to determine whether you need to run the **ranlib** command on libraries created by the **ar** command.

5. Create a program and compile it.

## REAL-WORLD APPLICATIONS

✔ You've just downloaded a neat-o new text editor program. You've uncompressed the files. How do you go about building the package?

✔ Your boss wants to spend thousands of dollars for Web server software. Check out the free Apache Server package and see if it will meet your company's needs.

✔ You've downloaded a nifty new graphics utility that runs under X, but has little or no documentation. What are the likely commands you'll need to build this program?

✔ Check the Web page for the TkDesk application. This may be very useful for helping Windows users adapt to UNIX.

## Visual Quiz

This image shows a directory listing for a freeware package (the e-mail program TkRataosk, or tkrat for short). Looking at the files, determine what commands you should enter to build this software.

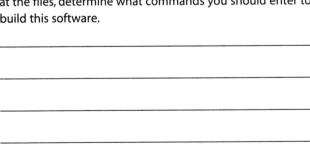

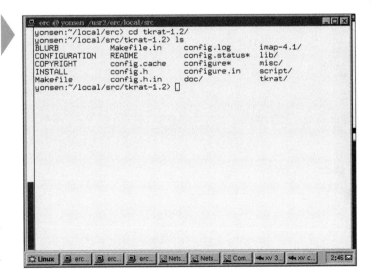

```
erc @ yonsen /usr2/erc/local/src
yonsen:~/local/src> cd tkrat-1.2/
yonsen:~/local/src/tkrat-1.2> ls
BLURB            Makefile.in     config.log      imap-4.1/
CONFIGURATION    README          config.status*  lib/
COPYRIGHT        config.cache    configure*      misc/
INSTALL          config.h        configure.in    script/
Makefile         config.h.in     doc/            tkrat/
yonsen:~/local/src/tkrat-1.2> []
```

CHAPTER **15**

MASTER
THESE
SKILLS

▶ Setting Up a New System

▶ Learning About States

▶ Backing Up Your System

▶ Shutting Down Your System

# System Administration

Not everyone is going to have a system administrator available 24 hours a day. In some situations, system administration happens between other tasks. If you're a workstation user, you're both the end user and the system administrator in many cases—at the very least you're the system administrator assigned to your personal workstation. Quite honestly, some simple acts don't necessarily require the intervention of a system administrator. If you're a new UNIX user with a new UNIX system, it is likely that you won't have a system administrator handy; your wits and your documentation are your only guides. And although we can't speak to the condition of your wits, we can speak to the condition of UNIX documentation—it makes books like this necessary.

In this chapter, we cover some simple, basic system administration to be performed with a new UNIX or Linux machine. If you've not read the preceding chapters and are not at ease performing the basic tasks we have enumerated, we advise you to go back and start reading this book from the beginning; you should know the basics of shell commands, text editors, and command lines before embarking on this chapter. The commands we cover here are available only to system administrators, not to every user. And they may not even be available to you as a system administrator. One of the great strengths of the UNIX operating system is that it's not controlled by one large corporation; customization among vendors is rampant. And many UNIX vendors have been known to greatly customize systems, especially with such simple tasks as basic, new-user installation. Although you should be able to use the procedures described here on your system, we can't guarantee it.

Here, we don't describe heavily involved tasks requiring a ton of time on your part. But the procedures will help you to run your UNIX system more smoothly from day one. And they'll give you a taste of the power you might have should you continue down the path to UNIX gurudom by becoming a full-fledged system administrator.

If you're running Linux, there are some special things you need to do, as a new Linux system starts out with you as the root user—the superuser.

# Setting Up a New System

In this book, we've assumed that you are computing on an existing UNIX system. However, there are cases when you'll need to set up your system from scratch. For instance, you may have the pleasure of setting up a standalone UNIX workstation for your own use. Or, you may have a PC plunked on your desk, with some version of UNIX or Linux waiting for your personal configuration.

Unfortunately, there's no one way to install UNIX software — either the actual operating system or any applications. However, each version of UNIX should come with installation instructions.

During the course of your system installation, you probably will have been asked to supply a password to the root user account. You'll begin your first UNIX session by entering root as the login name and then pressing the Enter key after the password. This logs you on as the root user. (Again, this may be different depending on your particular system configuration.)

Why log on as root, and not with the login names and passwords covered in Chapter 1? Here, we are working under the assumption that your new system doesn't have any login names installed yet. So the login name will be utterly meaningless to the new system.

The root user, or superuser, has access to all parts of the UNIX operating system. There are no files that cannot be read by the superuser, there are no portions of the file system inaccessible to the superuser, and there are no UNIX commands unavailable to the superuser. The superuser controls all aspects of UNIX system usage and configuration — which is why you're logging in as the root user.

As superuser, you're entitled to your own special prompt: #.

Now you need to name your system and set the date. First off, you must name your system in two ways: with a system name and a communications node name. Generally the system name is set to whatever version of UNIX you happen to be running, whereas the communications node name — or host name — is a unique name used to identify your system when communicating with other computer systems. You can set both at the same time using the same command, **setuname**.

The **setuname** command comes with UNIX System V Release 4 systems. On other systems, you can often use the **hostname** command.

You might also need to set the time and date with the **date** command. (You don't need to do this with Linux, because it uses the PC system clock.)

Because you have no restrictions, as the root user you can seriously damage your UNIX system. A simple accident can cause you a lot of grief. So be very careful when you are logged in as the root user.

**CROSS-REFERENCE**
Chapter 2 covers the **date** command from the point of view of users.

**FIND IT ONLINE**
The Computer Emergency Response Team, or CERT, maintains information on security issues at **www.cert.org**.

## TAKE NOTE

### ▶ THE DREADED YEAR 2038

We've all heard about problems dealing with the roll-over to the year 2000. With a relatively recent version of UNIX, you should be OK. In general, UNIX can indeed handle the millennium — whether you believe the 21st century starts in the year 2000 or 2001. But, 2038 is another year to worry about. UNIX bases all dates and times by counting the number of seconds from the start of the epoch — the UNIX epoch in this case, which began on January 1, 1970. Systems that use 32-bit numbers to store these time values roll over in early 2038. If you upgrade to UNIX systems that use 64-bit numbers for times, and recompile all your applications to use the larger-sized numbers to store times, you should be OK.

### ▶ YEAR 2000 AND THE DATE COMMAND

Normally, you pass the last two digits of the year, such as 99, to the **date** command. Depending on the version of UNIX, you can still do that after 1999. Most updated versions of UNIX will treat two-digit years in the range of 00 to 68 as part of the 21st century, (for example, 2015) and two-digit years 69 and above as part of the 20th, (for example, 1999).

Check with the online manuals for the **date** command to see how it handles dates after January 1, 2000.

## Listing 15-1: CHANGING TO THE ROOT USER

```
$ su
Password:
#
```

▲ *You can use the **su** command to change to the root user.*

## Listing 15-2: FAILING TO LOG ON AS ROOT

```
$ su
Password:
Sorry

$
```

▲ *You normally need a password for root to change to the root user. If you don't enter the password properly (or don't know it), you won't be able to use the **su** command to change to the root user.*

## Listing 15-3: RUNNING THE SETUNAME COMMAND

```
# setuname -n attila -s SVR4
#
```

▲ *The **setuname** command sets the system name (-s), usually the version of UNIX you run and here set to SVR4, and the host name (-n), here set to attila.*

## Listing 15-4: SETTING THE DATE

```
# date 0812192699
Wed Aug 12 19:26:00 CDT 1999
#
```

▲ *Here, 08 refers to August, 12 refers to the day of the month, 19 refers to the hour (using 24-hour military notation, of course), 26 refers to the minutes after the hour, and 99 refers to the year.*

## Listing 15-5: REVISED SYNTAX FOR DATE COMMAND

```
# date mmddHHMMccyy
```

▲ *Syntax of the **date** command revised for Year 2000 compliance. Here, mm refers to month, dd refers to date, HH refers to hour (using 24-hour military notation, of course), MM to the minutes after the hour, cc refers to the first two digits of the year (that is, 19 or 20), and yy refers to the last two digits of the year.*

# Learning About States

Most UNIX systems are designed to boot into multiuser state, where other users can log on to the system and the entire file system is accessible. However, this is not always true. We've listed the basic system states—also called *run levels*—in Table 15-1. Most of the time you'll want to work in the multiuser state. (There are additional, advanced system states also available; we've listed the ones you're most likely to use.)

Depending on your needs, you may want to use the system in a different state. As we said earlier, it's most desirable to work in the multiuser state. At some point in the login sequence, you'll be told what state you're in. To change to the administrative state, you can issue a command something like the following:

```
# init 1
```

(Some systems use the command **telinit**, short for tell the init process). Before you change to a single-user state (typically 1 or S), you probably want to warn any other users logged in to the system. In fact, it's a good idea to give users a chance to log off before you unceremoniously cut them off from their work. Usually, the **write** or **wall** commands work for this task.

To change to multiuser state, type the following:

```
# init 2
```

When you change system state with the **init** program, most versions of UNIX will run the commands inside the **/etc/inittab** file for that particular state. Each line in the **inittab** file contains an entry formatted as follows:

*ID:run_level: how_to_run_command:command*

The *ID* names the item. The *run_level* refers to one of the states, such as 3. The *how_to_run_command* section tells init how to run the following command, which can have one of the following values: *respawn* (restart if the command quits), *once* (run command only once), *wait* (wait for command to complete before going on), *boot* (the command is only run at boot time), and *initdefault* (specifies the default state the system should go into at boot time). A few other values may be available to you depending on your version of UNIX.

So, when you enter a command such as **init 1**, UNIX looks in the **/etc/inittab** file and runs the commands associated with the run-level 1.

---

### TAKE NOTE

▶ **YOU NORMALLY WON'T SWITCH RUN STATES**

Unless you need to bring the system down to single-user level or are testing the configuration files, you normally won't need to change UNIX run states.

▶ **RUN STATES OFTEN START X**

The X Display Manager, or XDM, which presents a graphical login screen, is often started from a special run-level, either 4 or 6.

▶ **NOT ALL SYSTEMS SUPPORT STATES**

Not all versions of UNIX support run states. The majority do, though.

---

**CROSS-REFERENCE**
Chapter 7 covers the X Window System and XDM.

**FIND IT ONLINE**
You can find information on Sun's Solaris at **www.sun.com/developers/developers.html**.

## Table 15-1: SYSTEM STATES

| State | Meaning |
|---|---|
| 0 | Shutdown. The machine is off. |
| 1 | Administrative. The full file system is available to the superuser, but other users cannot log on. Background tasks can run. |
| 2 | Multiuser. Other users can log on the system and access the file system. |
| 3 | RFS. If you're mounting file systems from other machines, this state connects your machine to the RFS network and makes it accessible to all users. This state is also multiuser. |
| 4 | Often used to start the X Display Manager and present a graphical logon screen. |
| 5 | Not standardized. |
| 6 | Used to reboot a Slackware Linux system. |
| S | Single-user. The file system is unavailable, other users cannot log on, and only the root file system is available. |

## Listing 15-6: SYNTAX FOR WALL

```
# wall
Your message here
Ctrl-D
#
```

▲ *The basic syntax for the **wall** (write all) command. Use **Ctrl-D** to exit **wall** (technically, to end the input to **wall**).*

## Listing 15-7: RUNNING WALL

```
# wall
WARNING! The system will be shut down
for maintenance in three minutes. Please
save your work and log off.

If you have any questions, please contact
your friendly neighborhood system
administrator at 555-5555.

Ctrl-D

#
```

▲ *Sending a shutdown message with the **wall** command.*

## Listing 15-8: A SOLARIS /ETC/INITTAB FILE

```
is:3:initdefault:
p3:s1234:powerfail:/usr/sbin/shutdown \
-y -i5 \
  -g0 >/dev/console 2<>/dev/console
s0:0:wait:/sbin/rc0  >/dev/console \
  2<>/dev/console \
  </dev/console
s1:1:wait:/usr/sbin/shutdown -y -iS \
  -g0 >/dev/console 2<>/dev/console \
  </dev/console
s2:23:wait:/sbin/rc2  >/dev/console \
  2<>/dev/console </dev/console
s3:3:wait:/sbin/rc3  >/dev/console \
  2<>/dev/console </dev/console
s5:5:wait:/sbin/rc5  >/dev/console \
  2<>/dev/console </dev/console
s6:6:wait:/sbin/rc6    >/dev/console \
  2<>/dev/console </dev/console
```

▲ *Part of an **/etc/inittab** file from Sun Solaris 2.6. Lines ending with a backslash, \, are continued on the next line. Note that states S2 through S6 run an rc script, which determines what runs in that state.*

# Backing Up Your System

We advise that you back up your work as often as possible. There isn't a computer user anywhere who hasn't accidentally erased an important file at one time or another. In many ways, the regular and systematic backup of files is the most important task a system administrator fulfills — a task that you should perform regularly if you lack a system administrator.

Luckily, UNIX features a powerful, yet easy-to-use command for archiving and storage: **tar**.

The **tar** command stands for *tape archiver*, and it started life as a tool for backing up files to a tape drive — still the predominant backup storage device on UNIX systems. Today **tar** can be used to back up any storage device — tape drive, floppy — supported on your UNIX system. Specifics may differ from system to system; our examples cover backups to both tape drives and floppy disks. (We strongly advise you to check your system documentation or **tar**'s online-manual page before embarking on a backup.)

For a glimpse of **tar** in action, let's say you wanted to back up all the files in an important directory — **/usr/erc/data/reports** — to ensure you don't lose any of your work to date. Before using **tar**, make sure that your current directory is **/usr/erc/data/reports**.

Next, back up the files in the directory, using the following command:

```
# tar -cvf ../archive.fil .
```

The **tar** options appear in Table 15-2. The **f** option specifies the output file is named **archive.fil** in the

parent directory. The lone period at the end of the command tells **tar** to back up the current directory.

If, for example, we wanted to back up only those files ending with *c*, we could invoke a wildcard instead of the lone period indicating the current directory.

Because UNIX treats hardware devices as files (remember that abstraction), you can back up your files to a tape by replacing the filename **../archive.fil** with the name for the tape device, usually **/dev/tape**. (Table 15-3 lists the device name for common tape drives. Refer to your system administrator or your system documentation for the device name of your tape drive — assuming of course, you have a tape drive.)

Note that you should insert a blank tape into the tape drive before issuing the **tar** command. (Some tape drives spin the tape heads for a short while after you insert a new tape. Make sure this process is also complete before executing the **tar** command.) In addition to tapes, there are other backup devices such as floppies and ZIP disks. For these types of devices, you often need to mount the floppy or disk before using it.

To restore files from the archive, use **tar** as in the following:

```
# tar -xvf archive.fil
```

The previous command extracts (via the **-x** option) the files stored in a **tar** archive file and places these extracted files into your current directory.

**CROSS-REFERENCE**

Chapter 14 covers using **tar** with files downloaded from the Internet.

**FIND IT ONLINE**

For information on BRU, a commercial backup tool from Enhanced Software Technologies, see **www.estinc.com**.

## TAKE NOTE

### ▶ WHAT FILES SHOULD YOU BACK UP?

What kind of files should you back up regularly? Essentially, your system contains three types of files: system files, configured system files, and data files. System files rarely change and can be reinstalled from the original floppies, CD-ROM, or tape (though, admittedly, not without a little bit of sweat), so you don't need to back up these files often. System files that you've configured and data files, on the other hand, are key to the success of your enterprise, because they are crucial for your UNIX system to run properly. Many of the system files that you will change are located in the **/etc** directory. (As you change system files, you should maintain a log so that you know which files you need to back up.) Data files form the core of your daily computer work. You'll generally want to back up all user accounts.

### ▶ OTHER BACKUP TOOLS

**Tar** is not the only backup tool available in UNIX, though we find it the most widely used. Another backup tool is **cpio**, which has been called the most difficult-to-use UNIX command by many astute observers and users. If you're interested in **cpio**, check your system documentation or the **cpio** online-manual page.

## Table 15-2: OPTIONS FOR TAR

| Command | Result |
|---|---|
| c | Creates a new archive. |
| f *filename* | Sends **tar** output to *filename*; the default ( including no **f** option) sends output to the default tape drive. |
| o | Overwrites file permissions associated with the files in the archive. |
| t | Provides a listing of the contents of the archive. |
| u | Updates files in the archive. If the files do not need updating, no action is taken. |
| v | Outputs verbose information as **tar** works. |
| w | Asks for confirmation before backing up an individual file. |
| x | Extracts files from the backup device. |

## Table 15-3: COMMON TAPE DEVICE NAMES

| Device | Usage |
|---|---|
| /dev/rmt0 | First raw magnetic tape drive. Historical default for **tar**. |
| /dev/tape | Usually a link to the real device file for your tape drive. |
| /dev/dat | Usually a link to a DAT tape drive. |

# Shutting Down Your System

Most UNIX systems — especially servers — run 24 hours a day, seven days a week. Many workstations run on a similar schedule, only rarely being shut down.

However, there are times when you want to turn off your system. You may need to move it; whether you're moving it across the office or across the country, you should turn off your system or be prepared to use a very long extension cord. You may need to attach a new peripheral or remove an existing one. Your office may be getting too hot for computer use; generally, it's good to shut off computer systems when the temperature in a room rises over 85 degrees (Fahrenheit). Or you may be leaving for vacation and don't want to waste electricity running your UNIX workstation when no one will be using it.

Earlier we mentioned the shutdown state of 0. A better way of shutting down your system is through the command **shutdown**. If used correctly, **shutdown** will shut down the system and alert other users that the system is shutting down:

```
# shutdown
```

If for some reason you get an error message when you run these commands, you may want to try specifying the full pathname of the commands.

The **shutdown** command does differ somewhat from system to system. If your system doesn't work in this exact fashion, check your online-manual pages or documentation.

After issuing the **shutdown** command, the system will ask you if you want to send a message before shutting down, and how long to wait before shutting down. It will also confirm that you really want to shut the system down. If you're working by yourself on a UNIX workstation, you don't need to send a message, and you can shut down immediately. If you're working on a multiuser system and want to give the users some warning, you can send a message to them, and you can give them 60 seconds before shutting down (60 seconds is the default; any other period would be specified by you).

With System V UNIX, you can speed up the **shutdown** command using the following command-line parameters:

```
# shutdown -g0 -y
```

The **-g** option specifies the grace period before shutting down, in seconds. The zero (0) means not to wait at all. The **-y** answers yes to the question, "Do you really want to shut down?" If you include this, you won't be prompted to confirm the shutdown operation.

After **shutdown** runs, it displays something like the text shown on the facing page.

To shut down a Linux system, simply press **Ctrl-Alt-Delete**, used ostensibly to shut down the system and reboot it. When the system gets ready to reboot, just turn off the power.

---

**CROSS-REFERENCE**

The task "Learning About States" covers the **wall** (write all) command.

**SHORTCUT**

Shutdown differs by system. Use **man shutdown** to see the options for your system.

## TAKE NOTE

### ▶ AUTOMATIC SHUTDOWNS

Some systems shut down automatically when temperature sensors indicate too high a temperature. Many servers are set up to act in this manner. In these situations, it is better to perform an orderly, if fast, shutdown than to let the system overheat and crash. Also, once the system shuts down, you can turn it off to create less heat. Even in Minnesota — known for its chilly winters — we've faced systems forced to shut down due to high heat. As a general rule, if you feel uncomfortable about the temperature, your computers do, too.

### ▶ POWERFAIL SHUTDOWNS

On critical systems, you'll need to attach some form of reliable power backup, such as a Universal Power Supply, or UPS. Typically, UPS devices maintain a number of minutes of battery backup power. When the electricity goes out, the UPS kicks in and maintains the power for your systems. Most UPS devices include a serial port interface that can signal your system that it has lost power. Any power outage longer than a short blip should result in an automatic shutdown of your system. Just as in overheating conditions, the loss of electrical power can lead to a hard crash of your system, from which recovery may be iffy. Instead, it's better to automatically shut the system down. Many UNIX systems include a powerfail state in **/etc/inittab** to handle this situation.

### Listing 15-9: ALERTING USERS FIRST

```
# wall
WARNING! The system will be shut down
for maintenance in 1 minute. Please save
your work and log off.
Ctrl-D
# shutdown —g60 -y
```

▲ *Giving users a very short period of time to finish their work and get off the system. Grace periods of three to five minutes are more friendly.*

### Listing 15-10: EXAMPLE SHUTDOWN ON LINUX

```
# shutdown —h now
```

▲ *Running the **shutdown** command on Linux halts the system (**-h**) and shuts it down now (with no time delay).*

### Listing 15-11: A FINAL MESSAGE SHOWING SHUTDOWN HAS COMPLETED

```
Safe to Power Off
      -or-
Press Any Key to Reboot
or
Reboot the computer now.
```

▲ *A message you'll often see after shutting down a system.*

# Personal Workbook

## Q&A

**1** What command do you use to get the current time?

_____

_____

_____

**2** What command do you use to set the current time?

_____

_____

_____

**3** What command do you use to set the current date?

_____

_____

_____

**4** What command can you use to send a message to all users currently logged in?

_____

_____

_____

**5** What are some common names for tape drives?

_____

_____

_____

**6** What command is often used to back up files?

_____

_____

_____

**7** What is the "three-fingered salute" that you can use to reboot or shut down most Linux systems?

_____

_____

_____

**8** Can UNIX support floppy and ZIP disks in addition to tapes?

_____

_____

_____

ANSWERS: PAGE 353

## EXTRA PRACTICE

1. Find out the device filenames for any backup or peripheral devices located on your system. Look for common names like **/dev/tape**, **/dev/dat**, and so on.

2. DOS and Windows users often run the time command to set the system time. Find out what the time command does on UNIX. Does it also set the system time?

3. Search for information on the network time protocol on the Internet. Using this service, you can synchronize the clocks on a number of UNIX systems.

4. Ask your users what a good grace period for them would be when you need to shut down the system.

5. Track down where the **shutdown** command is located on your system.

## REAL-WORLD APPLICATIONS

✔ Most of the documentation on the **date** command assumes you enter a two-digit year, such as 99. But what happens for 00 or 01? Look up the documentation for **date** on your system to see how it works in the 21st century.

✔ You've been experiencing sporadic power outages due to storm activity. Quickly save your work and shut down your system.

✔ Alert all other users to the problems with the air conditioning unit that you've discovered and may cause the system to shut down.

✔ Various systems at your site display different times, causing problems for text editors and tools such as **make**. Adjust the time on a number of systems to be the same.

## Visual Quiz

This command sets the system clock to what time?

_____

_____

_____

_____

_____

_____

_____

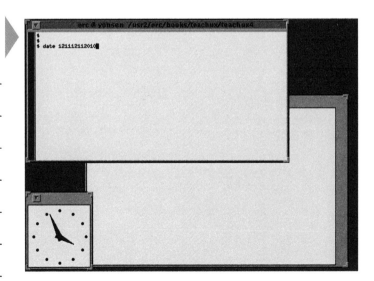

CHAPTER **16**

MASTER
THESE
SKILLS

▶ **Processing Text with Perl**

▶ **Programming with awk**

▶ **Scheduling Tasks with at, batch, and nice**

▶ **Arranging Events with cron**

# Additional and Advanced UNIX Tools

As we've repeated throughout this book, perhaps the greatest strength of the UNIX operating system is that it's a collection of small, useful tools that can be combined to form even more powerful tools. The majority of our discussion, therefore, has centered around tools that are applicable to your needs and skill level as a beginning UNIX user.

You won't be a beginner forever, however. In this chapter we describe what we feel are advanced tools. While we don't expect you to rush out and start programming with Awk tomorrow, there's a pretty good chance you may want to look at it in the future. This chapter deviates from the rest of the book in that it's not strictly based on tutorials (though we will be using some of the commands and tools in tutorial form). Instead, we describe the advanced tools, alerting you to their existence. When you're ready to tackle the use of these tools, we suggest checking out some of the more advanced books described in Appendix A.

UNIX includes a wide variety of tools. One thing you'll notice, though, is that most of these tools still deal with text files in some form or another. Long ago, the designers of UNIX decided that most things are best stored as text and this design decision lives through today.

This chapter covers two text-processing languages: Perl and Awk. Both are quite common on UNIX and both allow you to reformat text in a wide variety of ways. Perl goes further than AWK and supports networking, Web data-entry forms, and a lot more.

In addition, UNIX provides a number of tools to run tasks at specific times, based on time periods, and when the system is reasonably idle. Probably the most commonly used tool in this area is called **cron**. This tool runs commands at particular times, such as running a report (implemented via a UNIX command, of course) on the first and fifteenth of the month. You can also use **cron** to schedule backups for times when users are not likely to be on the system, such as at 3:00 a.m.

# Processing Text with Perl

Perl, which stands for Practical Extraction and Report Language, is a freeware scripting language developed to handle a number of system administration tasks. The whole point of the language is to make it easier for you to extract data from UNIX and output reports on things such as Usenet news, disk usage, and the users on your systems, sorted in order of largest disk usage. From its humble beginnings, Perl is now the tool of choice for handling data entered on interactive Web forms, called Common Gateway Interface, or CGI scripts. As a scripting language, Perl has a lot in common with awk and the C and Korn shell languages.

Perl language scripts are executed by a command named **perl**. Before starting with Perl, you need to verify you have it installed. To test this, enter **perl –v**, as shown on the facing page. If you don't have Perl, you can acquire it over the Internet.

To help get a flavor of Perl, enter in the script on the facing page. Like most UNIX scripting languages, any line with # is ignored from the # onward. To print out data, use the print statement. The \n stands for a newline, or linefeed character, and is typical UNIX parlance.

To run a Perl script, pass the name of the script file to run to the **perl** command, in our case, we named the file **perl1.pl**.

You can run Perl scripts from the perl command, or use the #! syntax described with Bourne shell scripts in Chapter 13. The example script uses the #! syntax to indicate the shell that should run the script. In this case, the shell is really the Perl interpreter, **perl**. In Chapter 13, shell scripts use **/bin/sh**. With the #! syntax, UNIX treats Perl as yet another shell language (although Perl isn't a shell, it is a scripting language).

Like the shell scripts discussed in Chapter 13, you can mark Perl scripts as executable using the **chmod** command. This Perl example assumes you have installed the **perl** command in the **/usr/bin** directory (the default location for **perl**). Another common location is **/usr/local/bin**.

With UNIX, you can use more than one language. Our best recommendation is to look around at the choices and see which one you think best fits your task—there's no one right answer. UNIX gives you a lot of choice but little guidance. Before choosing a language, you probably want to try out Perl, Awk, Bash, C, or Korn shell scripts and perhaps even C, C++, or Java.

Perl tends to be good at tasks that revolve around reporting system information, working with Web pages, or dealing with text.

*Continued*

**CROSS-REFERENCE**
Chapter 5 covers the C and Korn shells. The Programming with AWK task covers Awk scripting.

**FIND IT ONLINE**
You can download Perl add-on modules from **www.perl.com/CPAN-local/modules/00modlist.long.html**.

## TAKE NOTE

### ▶ ACQUIRING PERL

The source code for Perl is free. You need a C compiler to compile Perl and create the interpreter, **perl**. You can acquire the Perl source code from the Internet, or a number of books such as *Perl Modules* and *Cross-Platform Perl*, both published by IDG Books Worldwide. See Appendix A for more information.

### ▶ PERL RUNS ON MANY PLATFORMS

Perl runs on just about every system under the sun, including Windows, BeOS, and MacOS systems. Most Perl commands run the same on all systems, but platform differences do exist. Virtually all UNIX systems run Perl.

### ▶ PERL FOR CGI SCRIPTS

Data-entry forms on the Web, and Web search engines, often use Perl to process the data entered via the Web. Perl works really well for processing text files and specialized add-on modules support writing CGI scripts, the Common Gateway Interface scripts used to handle Web forms.

### ▶ ADD-ON MODULES ABOUND

One of the biggest strengths of Perl is the wide variety of Perl add-on modules. You can find add-on modules to support most networking protocols, from FTP (File Transfer Protocol) to SMTP (Simple Mail Transfer Protocol) to LDAP (Lightweight Directory Access Protocol). Special modules allow Perl to interface with database systems such as Oracle and Informix. Other modules work with the Apache Web server. These modules are available on CPAN, the Comprehensive Perl Archive Network, a collection of FTP sites worldwide that all mirror and organize the same Perl add-on modules.

## Listing 16-1: CHECKING FOR PERL

```
$ perl -v
This is perl, version 5.004_04 built for
i586-linux

Copyright 1987-1997, Larry Wall

Perl may be copied only under the terms
of either the Artistic License or the
GNU General Public License, which may
be found in the Perl 5.0 source kit.
```

▲ The **perl** command is the main **Perl** scripting interpreter. The **-v** option lists the version number. This is a useful test to check for the presence of Perl.

## Listing 16-2: THE PERL1.PL SCRIPT

```
#!/usr/bin/perl
# My first Perl script.

print "This is my first Perl script.\n";

print "I'm now ready for a new career.\n";

# End of perl1.pl script.
```

▲ The first Perl script, **perl1.pl**. Note that if your system has Perl installed in **/usr/local/bin** or another location, you will need to change the first line. The **print** command prints out text.

## Listing 16-3: RUNNING THE PERL1.PL SCRIPT

```
$ perl perl1.pl
This is my first Perl script.
I'm now ready for a new career.
```

▲ Running the **perl1.pl** script with the **perl** command.

# Processing Text with Perl
*Continued*

## Prompting For Data

You can prompt for data in Perl by setting a variable to hold the value <STDIN>. This means that perl reads from standard input — usually the keyboard. See the first script on the facing page for an example of this.

From the **perl2.pl** example, you'll note that Perl seems more difficult than the Bourne shell for getting input from users (which uses the **read** command).

Where Perl excels, though, is in arrays, UNIX process control, and text string handling. Perl offers a large set of array operations, which allow you to have a set of data treated as one unit, for example:

```
(1,2,3,4,5,6)
```

The above array has the values 1 through 6. You can also intermix text and numeric values, as shown following:

```
(1,2, 3, "Text")
```

You can assign this array to a variable and then access any element in the array.

In Perl, variables that begin with a $ are individual values (called scalars), while variables that begin with @ are arrays. The **perl3.pl** example script on the facing page shows how to set array values.

A great strength of Perl is its associative arrays — also called *hashes* — where you can use a key value for an array index and associate this with a data value. For example, you can have a Perl array for a first name, last name, and street address, as shown on the facing page in the **perl4.pl** script.

Associative arrays form a very powerful feature and can be used effectively in a lot of system administration tasks. The reason this type of array is so powerful is that each element has a key name, such as *firstname* or *address*, as well as a value, such as *Tony* or *No. 10 Downing Street*. By allowing you to associate keys with values, you can store a lot of data elements more easily than regular variables (scalars) or regular arrays, that index based on the position in the array (first, second, third and so on) rather than by the key value.

In addition to associative arrays, Perl has a lot of commands available to format text to enable you to create reports (the original reason for Perl's existence). Perl is intimately tied in with UNIX and provides a number of shortcuts for common UNIX activities, such as accessing the password file, as shown in the **perl5.pl** script on the facing page. The **getpwnam** function allows you to access entries in the **/etc/passwd** file from within Perl scripts.

### TAKE NOTE

#### FINDING OUT MORE

There's a lot more to Perl, which fills zillions of books on the subject. If you're interested in learning more about Perl, see Appendix A.

**CROSS-REFERENCE**

Chapter 1 describes the **/etc/passwd** file. It also covers the standard input, output, and error file descriptors.

**FIND IT ONLINE**

You can download the source code for Perl from **www.perl.com**.

## Listing 16-4: THE PERL2.PL EXAMPLE SCRIPT

```perl
#! /usr/bin/perl
# Prompting for input in Perl.
print "What is your first name: ";
$first_name = <STDIN>;
# Remove trailing linefeed.
chomp($first_name);
printf "What is your last name: ";
$last_name = <STDIN>;
chomp($last_name);
# Separate output with a blank line.
print "\n";
print "Your name is $first_name
$last_name.\n";
print "Thank you for responding.\n";
```

▲ *A script that reads from standard input into a variable that holds a single value — called a scalar variable in Perl. The* **chomp** *command removes any trailing new-line characters from the input.*

## Listing 16-5: SETTING AN ARRAY TO HOLD MIXED DATA

```perl
@array = (1,2, 3, "Text");
```

▲ *This example shows how to set an array in Perl with mixed data. The array variable named @array gets set with four elements, one text and the rest numeric.*

## Listing 16-6: THE PERL3.PL ARRAY SCRIPT

```perl
#!/usr/bin/perl
# An array example in Perl.
# Set an array to all numeric data.
@array1 = (1,2,3,4,5,6);
print "@array1\n";
# Set an array to mixed numeric
# and textual data.
@array2 = (1,2, 3, "Text");
print "@array2\n";
```

▲ *An example showing how to set array values.*

## Listing 16-7: THE PERL4.PL ASSOCIATIVE ARRAY SCRIPT

```perl
#!/usr/bin/perl
# Associative arrays in Perl.
# tony is an associative array.
$tony{"firstname"} = "Tony";
$tony{"address"} = "No. 10 Downing Street";
print $tony{"firstname"};
print "'s address is ";
print $tony{"address"};
print "\n";
```

▲ *An associative array — or hash — example.*

## Listing 16-8: THE PERL5.PL SCRIPT TO ACCESS THE PASSWORD FILE

```perl
#!/usr/bin/perl
# Get Eric's password entry and print it.
@erc_entry = getpwnam("erc");
($username, $realname, $homedir) =
@erc_entry[0,6,7];
print "User $realname has\n";
print "\t a home directory of $homedir\n";
print "\t and a username of $username.\n";
```

▲ *The* **perl5.pl** *script accesses the password file.*

# Programming with AWK

Developed by three Bell Labs researchers (Alfred *Aho*, Peter *Weinberger*, and Brian *Kernighan* — hence the acronym *AWK*), AWK manipulates structured text files, where information is stored in columnar form and information is separated by consistent characters (such as tabs, spaces, or other characters), through editing, sorting, and searching.

Let's think back to Chapter 3, when we discussed UNIX tools that allowed you to edit and manipulate similarly structured files. We used a data file named workers; we use it again in the examples on the facing page.

Let's sink into the trap of abstraction for a minute and compare our example file output to a two-dimensional graph. Each row across is called a record, which in turn is made up of vertical fields or columns, almost like a database. AWK allows us to manipulate the data in the file by either row or column, which makes it more powerful and useful than the tools described in Chapter 3.

AWK programs are executed by the **awk** command. Using the **awk** command is not a complicated process. The structure of the **awk** command looks like this:

```
$ awk [option] 'pattern action'
```

(The only options available with **awk** are **-F**, which allows you to specify a field separator other than the default of white space, and **-f**, which allows you to specify a filename full of AWK commands instead of

placing a complex pattern and action on the UNIX command line.) Here we should define our terms. A *pattern* can be an ASCII string, a numeral, a combination of numerals, or a wildcard, while *action* refers to an instruction we provide. So, essentially, AWK works by having us tell it to search for a particular pattern and on finding the pattern, doing something with it, such as printing the pattern to another file.

The simplest AWK program merely prints out all lines in the file, as shown on the facing page in Listing 16-9.

Continuing this example, if we wanted to pull all records that began with the string *Geisha*, we'd use the following:

```
$ awk '$1 ~ /Geisha/ print $0' workers
```

Here's what the command means, part by part:

- ▶ *$1*: Tells AWK to use the first column for the basis of further action. Awk will perform an action on a file based on either records or fields; a number beginning with a *$* tells AWK to work on a specific field. In this case *$1* refers to the first field.
- ▶ *~*: Tells AWK to match the following string.
- ▶ */Geisha/* : Is the string to search for.
- ▶ *print $0*: Tells AWK to print out the entire record containing the matched string. Using the $ sign with the character 0, tells AWK to use all of the fields possible.
- ▶ *workers*: Is the file to use.

*Continued*

**CROSS-REFERENCE**

Chapter 14 covers the C programming language.

**FIND IT ONLINE**

You can find documentation on **awk** at www.softlab.ntua.gr/cgi-bin/man-cgi.

# AWK Relational Operators

Not every action needs to be the result of matching a specific pattern, of course. In AWK, the tilde (~) acts as a relational operator, which sets forth a condition for AWK to use. There are a number of other relational operators available to AWK users that allow AWK to compare two patterns. (The relational operators are based on algebraic notation.) It supports the same relational operators as found in the C programming language; listed in Table 16-1.

We could increase the sophistication of AWK searches in a number of ways. First, we could incorporate the use of compound searches, which uses three logical operators:

▶ &&, which works in the same way as the logical AND
▶ ||, which works in the same way as the logical OR
▶ !, which returns anything NOT equaling the original

For example, let's say we wanted to know how many workers had a value in the fifth field that is greater than or equal to 10, you would use a command such as the following:

```
awk '$5 >= 10  print $0  ' workers
```

Now we start to see the power of AWK. AWK provides a great ability to parse text files and extract records.

While these examples are obviously contrived, you can use AWK to help pull out all entries that share certain postal (ZIP) codes, or all employees who have a salary in a certain range. We're just scratching the surface here.

## Table 16-1: AWK RELATIONAL OPERATORS

| Operator | Meaning/Usage |
|---|---|
| < | Less than. <br> $1 < "Eric" returns every pattern with an ASCII value less than "Eric." |
| <= | Less than or equal to. <br> $1 <= "Eric." |
| == | Equals. <br> $1 == "Eric" returns every instance of "Eric." |
| != | Does not equal. <br> $1 != "Eric" returns every field not containing the string "Eric." |
| >= | Greater than or equal to. <br> $1 >= "Eric" returns every field equal to or greater than "Eric." |
| > | Greater than. <br> $1 > "Eric" returns every field greater than "Eric." |

## Listing 16-9: A SIMPLE AWK COMMAND

```
$ awk ' print ' workers
Eric     286     555-6674     erc       8
Geisha   280     555-4221     geisha   10
Kevin    279     555-1112     kevin     2
Tom      284     555-2121     spike    12
```

▲ *One of the simplest AWK programs just prints out all records in the file.*

# Programming with AWK

*Continued*

As with other UNIX commands, **awk** can be used in pipes, and its output can be directed to other files or directly to the printer. For example, if we were looking through a large file and expecting many matches to a particular string (such as salary ranges or employment starting dates), we might want to direct that output to a file or to a printer.

For example, to use **awk** with the UNIX **sort** utility, we can sort the output of the example that extracted all records between Eric and Kevin. (Note that this is sorting on the leading number.)

AWK also provides some summary abilities as well. The **NR** symbol in an **awk** command returns the number of records, for example.

We can combine this with **awk's** ability to total fields in an AWK program.

## awk Programs

You're not limited to what fits on the command line with **awk**. You can also store a series of **awk** commands in a file and then use **awk** to execute the file, creating a program, as shown on the facing page.

You can combine this with the **awk BEGIN**, **END**, and **NR** commands to make a more complex **awk** program. When working with this, it's good to remember that **awk** applies each **awk** command to every record; that is, every line of text, in the input file. A program such as {**print**}, prints each and every line in the input file.

The **awk BEGIN** command lists what to do before reading the first line of text. The awk.2 example program on the facing page, **awk.2**, shows a **BEGIN** command that prints out the text "Workers for Spacely's Sprockets" before printing each line in the workers file.

Similarly, the **END** statement lists commands to execute after data is read. Here's where the **NR** command, number of records (or lines), comes in handy, as shown on the facing page.

The awk.3 example program uses cleaner formatting for the **END** statements. It makes no difference to the output if we place the entire **END** command on one line.

---

**TAKE NOTE**

### ▶ FOR MORE ON AWK

This brief explanation covers AWK in the simplest terms. For example, AWK includes most of the trappings of a full programming language, including loops, variables, string operations, numeric operations, and the creation and manipulation of arrays. If you're interested in a useful programming language that can be mastered relatively quickly, we recommend further reading on AWK; our recommendations can be found in Appendix A.

---

**CROSS-REFERENCE**
Chapter 13 covers shell programming basics.

**FIND IT ONLINE**
For information on gawk, GNU AWK, see **www.gnu.org**.

## Listing 16-10: USING AWK WITH OTHER UNIX COMMANDS

```
$ awk '$1 ~ /Eric/,/Kevin/ { print $2, $1
}'\
  workers | sort
279 Kevin
280 Geisha
286 Eric
```

▲ *Using **awk** with sort to sort by the leading number.*

## Listing 16-11: USING THE END DIRECTIVE

```
$ awk 'END {  print "There are", NR,\
"workers" } ' workers
There are 4 workers
```

▲ *With this **END** code and **NR**, we have a count of the number of records.*

## Listing 16-12: THE AWK.1 EXAMPLE PROGRAM

```
{ print }
```

▲ *This simple program prints out all records in the file. Save this in a file named **awk.1**.*

## Listing 16-13: RUNNING THE AWK.1 EXAMPLE PROGRAM

```
$ awk -f awk.1 workers
Eric     286      555-6674      erc      8
Geisha   280      555-4221      geisha   10
Kevin    279      555-1112      kevin    2
Tom      284      555-2121      spike    12
```

▲ *Running our first simple **awk** program.*

## Listing 16-14: THE AWK.2 EXAMPLE PROGRAM

```
BEGIN { print "Workers for Spacely's
Sprockets"; print "" }
{ print }
```

▲ *The **BEGIN** command lists what to do before reading the first line of text.*

## Listing 16-15: THE AWK.3 EXAMPLE PROGRAM

```
BEGIN  { print "Workers for Spacely's
Sprockets"; print "" }

{ print }

END { print "There are",
     NR,
     "employees left after the latest wave
of
     layoffs." }
```

▲ *The **awk.3** program adds in an **END** command as well as a **BEGIN** command.*

# Scheduling Tasks with at, batch, and nice

The **at** command runs a command at a particular time. Using **at** is simple, you specify a time for execution, followed by the command line.

**At** is very flexible about defining the time when the command is to be run; you can use a time like *11am*, or you can use a more precise number based on military time.

After you hit the **Enter** (or **Return**) key, you'll be placed on the following line, without a prompt. As you recall, this is the UNIX method of asking you for additional input. This is where you provide the commands that **at** is to execute; end each command by pressing the **Enter** (or **Return**) key. When you're through, type **Ctrl-D**.

The system's response is a single line of information that confirms when the command (designated by the system with a job ID of many digits) will be run. This job ID is very valuable information. Should you need to see a list of pending job IDs, use **at** with the **-l** option. If you want to cancel a pending command scheduled with **at**, use **at** with the **-r** (remove) option.

The **batch** command runs commands in the background when the system load is low.

As with **at**, you enter commands and type **Ctrl-D** to signify the end of input. Next, **batch** will run your commands at a later time, depending on the system load. If your commands require some sort of confirmation message or output delivered to you, the message will be conveyed as a mail message; you won't find messages popping up on your screen while you're in the middle of some other action.

Elsewhere in this book, we have discussed running programs in the background using the ampersand (&). There are some fundamental differences between background tasks and **batch**:

- ▶ Commands issued to **batch** are accorded even less priority than commands run in the background.
- ▶ With **batch**, commands will continue to execute even if you log off the system (shades of **nohup**!). Background tasks are killed if you log off the system.
- ▶ Background tasks will interrupt you should your background command specify some kind of output or confirmation. Batch does not; as we noted, confirmation or output is sent as a mail message.

The **nice** command runs a command at a low priority, to be nice to other users. The facing page shows its syntax. For example, if you're performing an extremely complicated sort with many files, you may want to launch the sort using **nice** before that typical two-hour lunch.

### TAKE NOTE

▶ **NOT EVERY USER CAN RUN AT**

System administrators have the power to deny users — usually beginners — access to **at**. If you try to use **at** and are denied permission, check with your system administrator.

**CROSS-REFERENCE**

The **nohup** command is covered in Chapter 1.

**FIND IT ONLINE**

You can find documentation on **at** at **www.softlab.ntua.gr/cgi-bin/man-cgi**.

## Listing 16-16: RUNNING AT

```
$ at 11am
ls
df
who
whoami
Ctrl-D
Job 1 will be executed using /bin/sh
```

▲ After typing *at* and a time, press **Enter** and then type in all the commands you want to run. Type **Ctrl-D** to terminate the list of commands. The **at** command then responds with the job ID for that *at* command.

## Listing 16-17: GETTING OUTPUT FROM COMMANDS RUN BY AT

```
From erc@yonsen.com Thu Oct29 19:00:07 1998
Date: Thu, 29 Oct 1998 19:00:07 -0600
From: Eric Foster-Johnson <erc@yonsen.com>
To: erc@yonsen.com
Content-Length: 791
Subject:Output from your job c0000100e759dc
report.1999
report.2000
report.date
report.header
report1
report4
Filesystem      1024-blocks  Used Available
Capacity Mounted on
/dev/hda1       1811645    888823    826054
52%      /
/dev/hda4       499652     409317    64531
86%      /usr2
erc       tty1     Oct 29 18:54
erc
```

▶ If any command run by *at* produces output, *at* will mail the output to you. Notice that the output of the commands, **ls**, **df**, **who**, and **whoami**, is placed one after another. This makes it hard to understand the output.

## Listing 16-18: LISTING AVAILABLE AT JOBS

```
$ at -l
Date                  Owner   Queue   Job#
19:00:00 10/29/98     erc     c       1
```

▲ The **-l** option tells **at** to list the queued jobs.

## Listing 16-19: SYNTAX FOR REMOVING AT JOBS

```
$ at -r job-ID
```

▲ Remove an *at* job with the **–r** option. Some systems provide an **atrm** command instead of the **–r** option to *at*.

## Listing 16-20: RUNNING THE BATCH COMMAND

```
$ batch
df
Job 5 will be executed using /bin/sh
```

▲ Use the **batch** command to run commands when the system load is low.

## Listing 16-21: SYNTAX FOR NICE

```
$ nice command filename
```

▲ Syntax for the **nice** command.

# Arranging Events with cron

System administrators have all the fun — or used to, anyway — as evidenced by the **cron** command, which started life as a tool allowing the system administrator to schedule regular tasks unattended. These tasks were stored in a file called **crontab**, usually found in the **/usr/lib** directory. Some versions of UNIX, either pre-System V or Berkeley, still allow **cron** privileges to the system administrator. However, if you're using a newer version of UNIX, you have access to cron.

Why use **cron**? You may want to back up your data to tape drive weekly or even daily. You may want to send yourself a mail message to remind you of important noncomputer chores. Or you may want to send electronic mail to other UNIX systems late at night when the long-distance rates are lower.

There are two parts to **cron:** The **crontab** file and the actual **cron** command. We cover both.

The **crontab** file contains the tasks that are to be performed regularly. You have your own personal **crontab** file stored in the **/usr/lib/crontab** directory. The **crontab** file installation, as well as the structure of the actual file, can be a tad confusing.

You can use **vi** or **emacs** to create a **crontab** file. However, you can't save the file directly in the **/usr/lib/crontab** directory; instead, you must save it under a different name and use the **crontab** command to install it.

There are six fields to a **crontab** file, each separated by a space. The first five fields specify exactly when the command is to be run; the sixth field is the command itself.

Let's say that you want to run a command every morning at 8:30 a.m. The structure of the **crontab** line should look something like this:

30 8 * * * *command*

The exact values associated with the five fields are listed in Table 16-2.

After creating our **crontab** file (which must be saved under a filename of anything but crontab; in this case, let's call it **ourfile**), we can then install it, using the **crontab** command.

This command then takes **ourfile**, copies it, and saves the copy under our username in the **/usr/lib/crontab** directory, with a filename of **/usr/lib/crontab/username**. If we want to make changes to our **cron** configuration, we must edit our original file (which still exists — remember, **crontab** only makes a copy) and then reinstall it using **crontab**. If we want to totally remove the file, we must use the **crontab** command with the **-r** option.

To prevent mischief or some unintended damage, we are allowed access to only our own **crontab** file.

The **crontab -l** command lists out the **crontab** entry for your username.

Run the **crontab** command to alert **cron** to the new tasks you'd like run periodically. You should never have to run the **cron** command itself, as this gets started when a UNIX system boots.

---

**CROSS-REFERENCE**

The previous section on Scheduling Tasks covers the **at** command.

**FIND IT ONLINE**

For more on **crontab**, see **nerc-online.com/support/ www/crontab.html**.

## TAKE NOTE

### WHEN CREATING CRONTAB FILES

▶ Asterisks (*) are used to specify when commands are to be run in every instance of the value of the field. An asterisk in the third field means to run the command every day of every month, an asterisk in the fourth field means to run the command every month, an asterisk in the fifth field means to run the command every day of every week.

▶ For days of the week, the week begins with a 0 for Sunday and ends with a 6 for Saturday. (Computer people are famous for starting to count with 0.)

▶ Times are specified in 24-hour time. Thus, specify 10 p.m. as 22.

▶ You can specify ranges, instead of specific days and times. For instance, to perform a command only on the 15th and 30th days of the month, use 15,30 in the third field. (Watch out for February.) Or you can specify that a command be run only in the fall months by using 10-12 in the fourth field. You can combine these two methods: Running a command in spring and summer means using 4-6,10-12 in the fourth field.

### LACK OF ACCESS TO CRON

If you're not using System V UNIX, you won't have access to the cron command unless you're a system administrator with superuser capabilities. Also, system administrators have the power to deny users access to cron. If you're using a newer version of UNIX and still are denied access to cron, consult your system administrator.

### Table 16-2: FIELDS IN A CRONTAB LINE

| Field | Meaning |
|-------|---------|
| 1 | Minutes after the hour. |
| 2 | Hour, in 24-hour format. |
| 3 | Day of the month. |
| 4 | Month. |
| 5 | Day of the week. |

### Listing 16-22: INSTALLING YOUR CRONTAB COMMANDS

```
$ crontab ourfile
```

▲ The **crontab** command alerts cron that you have new periodic commands to run. Pass **crontab** the name of the file that you created (in this case, **ourfile**). Inside the file **ourfile**, you must follow the precise syntax described in this task, or cron will not properly run your commands.

### Listing 16-23: RUNNING A COMMAND ONLY ON MONDAYS

```
15 3 * * 1 sh /u/erc/my_backup
```

▲ If you only wanted to back up on Mondays, you could use this **crontab** entry. Again, we've left the time to execute the script at the arbitrary time of 3:15 a.m.

### Listing 16-24: RUNNING BACKUPS ON THE FIRST AND 15TH

```
15 3 1,15 * * sh /u/erc/my_backup
```

▲ If you wanted to only perform backups on the first and fifteenth of each month, you could use this **crontab** entry.

# Personal Workbook

## Q&A

**1** What command or commands allow you to run tasks at a particular time?

_____

_____

_____

**2** What's the difference between commands run with **batch** and commands run in the background?

_____

_____

_____

**3** How could you schedule a command to run at 3 p.m.?

_____

_____

_____

**4** What do you use to tell the **batch** command that you have finished entering commands?

_____

_____

_____

**5** What do you use to tell the at command that you have finished entering commands?

_____

_____

_____

**6** What command can you use to eliminate the commands you have scheduled with **cron**?

_____

_____

_____

**7** Should you run the **cron** command directly?

_____

_____

_____

**8** What command do you use to schedule tasks with cron?

_____

_____

_____

ANSWERS: PAGE 354

## EXTRA PRACTICE

**1** Determine whether or not your system has Perl installed.

**2** Check the version of Perl. You want at least Perl 5.004 or higher.

**3** Look up the online manual page for **perlfunc**, which describes the main functions available for Perl scripts.

**4** Discuss the differences between Perl and AWK. Which tool seems to be better for you?

**5** Verify whether or not you have permission to run the **at** command.

**6** Discuss the **at** and **cron** commands. Which do you think will work better for your needs?

## REAL-WORLD APPLICATIONS

✔ You're running an office pool for betting on football games. Set up a database in a text file and then create a script using AWK so that anyone can find out their standing in the pool or find out those with earnings in a particular range.

✔ Set up a backup script to run every night at 2:25 a.m., a time determined to be a low-usage time for your site.

✔ You downloaded a number of Perl scripts from the Internet to monitor your systems. But, none of the scripts work. Looking at a few of the scripts, the very first line seems to point to a place where your version of Perl is not installed. Correct the first line of these scripts (first you need to know where Perl is installed on your system).

## Visual Quiz

This crontab entry sets up a command, **sh /u/erc/ my_backup**, to run at particular times. When will this command run?

_____

_____

_____

_____

_____

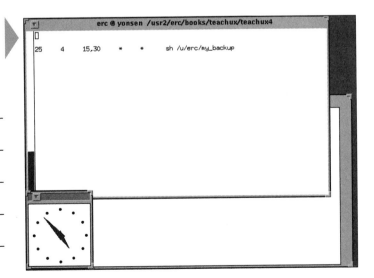

```
                    erc @ yonsen  /usr2/erc/books/teachux/teachux4

25      4      15,30      *      *        sh /u/erc/my_backup
```

# Appendix A: Personal Workbook
# Answers

## Chapter 1

see page 4

**1** **Why is an account important in your UNIX usage?**

**A:** This is how UNIX works; every user must have an account.

**2** **What two important pieces of information do you need to enter when you login a UNIX system?**

**A:** Your name and a password.

**3** **What are the three standard elements of a command line?**

**A:** Command, option, and argument.

**4** **In standard input/output, where does input come from?**

**A:** The keyboard.

**5** **In standard input/output, where does output go?**

**A:** To the screen.

**6** **In a pipe, what are you redirecting from a command? And where is it being redirected?**

**A:** Standard output and standard input.

**7** **What's the difference between running commands in the foreground and in the background?**

**A:** In the foreground you do not get a terminal prompt. In the background you do, and thus can run another command.

**8** **How do you log off a UNIX system?**

**A:** Type **exit**.

### Visual Quiz

**Q:** Here are four separate applications. Can you name them?

**A:** They are, **xterm**, **xclock**, **xlogo**, and **xmag**.

## Chapter 2

see page 38

**1** **Is a filename of boss report a valid filename under UNIX?**

**A:** No.

**2** **What kind of file typically has a filename extension of .txt?**

**A:** Text (ASCII) files.

**3** **What's the difference between an ordinary file and a link?**

**A:** An ordinary file is in a fixed place in the file system, while a link is a reference to another file.

**4** **What command is used to return the name of your current working directory?**

**A:** The **pwd** command.

# Appendix A: Personal Workbook Answers

**⑤ What command is used to change your current directory?**

**A:** The **cd** command.

**⑥ What command is used to delete a directory?**

**A:** The **rm** command.

**⑦ What character do you add to a command line to run a command in the background?**

**A:** The **&** (ampersand) character.

**⑧ What command do you use to send a file to the printer?**

**A:** **The lp** or **lpr** command.

## Visual Quiz

**Q:** This window displays the contents of an average directory. Using the information in this chapter, which UNIX variant is being used?

**A:** Linux.

## Chapter 3

see page 78

**❶ Which command searches for text in files?**

**A:** The **grep** command.

**❷ How could you find all occurrences of Bob Marley and Peter Tosh in a text file?**

**A:** Use the following command: egrep "Bob Marley|Peter Tosh" *file_to_search*

**❸ How would you search a text file for all instances of *Spacely* or *spacely*?**

**A:** Use the following command: grep -i Spacely *file_to_search*

**④ How would you sort a file numerically rather than alphabetically?**

**A:** Use the **–n** option to the **sort** command.

**⑤ How do you store the output of sort in a file?**

**A:** To store the output in the same file, use a command like: `sort –o filename filename` Otherwise, you can simply use output redirection: `sort filename > output_file`

**⑥ How would you split a file into chunks that are each no larger than 60 KB?**

**A:** Use the following command: `split –b 60k filename`

**⑦ How would you compare two sorted files to find out which lines are contained in both files and which are unique to a particular file?**

**A:** Use the **comm** command: `comm AL_Central.sort NL_Central.sort`

**⑧ Which command should you use to view text messages that may be hidden inside a program?**

**A:** Use the **strings** command. You could also use **od**.

## Visual Quiz

**Q:** What full command line would you use to place the contents of each line of file2 onto the end of each line of file1 and have the output as shown for file3?

**A:** Use paste -d: file1 file2 > file3.

## Chapter 4

see page 98

**❶ How can you view the value held in a shell variable?**

**A:** You can use a number of methods. Two of the easiest include:
```
echo $VARIABLE
env | grep VARIABLE
```

**2** **What is the EDITOR environment variable for?**

**A:** It holds the command you want to use as a text editor. Normally this is either **vi** or **emacs**.

**3** **What does the PS1 environment variable hold?**

**A:** The main prompt for **sh**, **ksh**, and **bash**.

**4** **What startup files set up the environment for C shell users?**

**A:** The C shell uses **.login** and **.cshrc**.

**5** **Which command should you use to set variables in the C shell? How about the Korn shell?**

**A:** C shell: setenv VARIABLE VALUE
Korn shell: VARIABLE=VALUE export VARIABLE

**6** **What is held in the PATH variable?**

**A:** A list of directories that the shell searches for commands.

**7** **What does the TERM environment variable signify?**

**A:** The type of terminal you are using, for example vt100 for a VT-100 compatible terminal.

**8** **How can you run two or more commands from the same command line?**

**A:** Use a semicolon: $ cal; ls

## Visual Quiz

**Q:** **From the files listed here, guess which shell this user runs.**

**A:** From the presence of the **.profile** file, it's likely this user runs the Bash or Korn shells.

# Chapter 5

see page 114

**1** **How can you find out what shell you are running?**

**A:** Try the following command: echo  $SHELL

**2** **You're working with data files with very, very long filenames. What can you use to avoid so much typing when you work with these files?**

**A:** Command-line completion is a big win in such cases. You can also use shell aliases and shell scripts.

**3** **Does the C shell support vi or emacs command-line editing?**

**A:** No, but a related shell, **tcsh**, does.

**4** **How do you turn on the vi command-line editing mode in the Korn shell?**

**A:** Use the following command: set —o vi

**5** **Which shell allows you to create graphical applications?**

**A:** The dtksh shell.

**6** **How do you control the number of commands stored in the command history in the C shell? In the Korn shell?**

**A:** C shell: Use a command like set history=32.
Korn shell: Set the **HISTSIZE** environment variable: HISTSIZE=32.

**7** **How do you turn on filename completion in the C shell?**

**A:** Use the following command: set filec

**8** **How do you re-execute the last command in the Korn shell? In the C shell?**

**A:** Korn shell: r
C shell: !!

# Appendix A: Personal Workbook Answers

## Visual Quiz

**Q:** Which shell is shown here? How can you tell?

**A:** This is probably the **tcsh shell**; the **bindkey** command gives it away.

## Chapter 6

see page 134

**1** How do you generate a short list of processes on your system?

**A:** With the **ps** command.

**2** How do you generate a long list of processes on your system?

**A:** With the **–a** option to the **ps** command.

**3** How do you generate a long list of processes on the entire UNIX network?

**A:** With the **–ef** option to the **ps** command.

**4** How do you kill a process?

**A:** With the **kill** command.

**5** How do you kill a process that refuses to be killed?

**A:** With the **kill –9** command line.

**6** Why are real-time processes important?

**A:** Because they are used when programs are run in real time and you need a way to manage them.

**7** How do you stop a process when using the job shell?

**A:** With the **stop** command.

**8** How do you relaunch the same process when using the job shell?

**A:** With the **fg** or **bg** command.

## Visual Quiz

**Q:** Find the process that launches the shell in this listing.

**A:** PID 97, -**bash** command.

## Chapter 7

see page 144

**1** Name three ways to start X.

**A:** Three ways to start X include XDM (and **dtlogin**, used in CDE systems), **xinit** and **startx**. There are other means, but these are the main ones.

**2** You have a workstation running X and a large file and application server running X applications that you display on your workstation. In X terms, which is the client and which is the server?

**A:** The workstation is the X server; the file server runs the X clients.

**3** The X display is too bright. What can you do to make windows appear darker?

**A:** The **–rv** option to most X commands reverses black and white. The **–background** and **–foreground** options can change colors.

**4** How do you select text in an xterm window and paste the text into another window?

**A:** By default, dragging the mouse while pressing the left mouse button selects text. Clicking the middle mouse button pastes text.

**5** How can you list the available fonts?

**A:** Use the following command: `xlsfonts`

**6** How can you visually select a font?

**A:** Use the following command: `xfontsel`

**7** **What don't you want in a font used for a shell window like xterm?**

**A:** Proportional fonts are really bad for xterm, which expects a fixed-width font.

**8** **What can you use to display the time on your screen?**

**A:** Use the following commands: **xclock**, **oclock**, **clock**, and countless other clock programs. The CDE front panel also has a clock.

## Visual Quiz

**Q:** **How would you move the window over to the left to open up space on this display?**

**A:** Select the title bar by pressing and holding the left mouse button. Move the mouse (with either an outline of the window or the window itself) to the desired location and release the mouse button.

## Chapter 8

see page 172

**1** **If all else fails and you don't have any nice e-mail tools, what program should still be available to send and receive e-mail?**

**A:** The **mail** program.

**2** **To send a message to a person, you need one crucial piece of information to identify that person. What is it?**

**A:** You need the recipient's e-mail address.

**3** **If you're not running X, and still hate primitive mail tools, name two programs you could try.**

**A:** You can try **elm** and **pine**.

**4** **How can you send a file using the mail program?**

**A:** You can use input redirection to send a file with **mail**, for example: `mail reichard@mr.net < note`

**5** **If you have too many mail messages in your in box, but still want to keep the messages, what can you do?**

**A:** Move some of the messages to mail folders. You can use folders to help organize your work.

**6** **How do you list your current messages in pine?**

**A:** In **pine**, select FOLDER INDEX from the main menu to see your current messages.

**7** **How do you send a message with dtmail?**

**A:** From the Compose menu, select New Message, then fill in the data in the compose window and click the Send button when you're done.

**8** **What is an attachment? What problems can people face with attachments?**

**A:** An attachment is a file sent along with — attached to — an e-mail message. Typically, attachments are binary files, such as spreadsheet documents, images, and so on.

## Visual Quiz

**Q:** **How would you begin to send an e-mail message from the pine screen shown here?**

**A:** Type C for Compose.

# Appendix A: Personal-Workbook Answers

## Chapter 9

see page 188

**1** **Which Web browser is typically found on a UNIX system?**

**A:** Netscape Navigator.

**2** **What are the major URL formats?**

**A:** HTTP, mailto:, FTP, news.

**3** **Why does a pointer change over various parts of a Web page?**

**A:** Because the page contains links to other Web pages.

**4** **When you choose a Web page from your history listings, from where will you most likely reload the page?**

**A:** Chances are pretty good that you'll reload the page from your *cache*.

**5** **What are the two ways to view Web sites you've recently visited?**

**A:** Through the History dialog box and from the Location pull-down menu.

**6** **How can you access your bookmarks?**

**A:** From the Bookmarks icon or the Communicator menu.

**7** **What's the significance of a Usenet newsgroup being threaded?**

**A:** Answers to postings are associated with the original posting.

**8** **What does *FTP* stand for?**

**A:** File Transfer Protocol.

## Visual Quiz

**Q:** **What Web browser is this? And what Web site is loaded in this browser?**

**A:** Navigator, with the IDG Books Online Home Page.

## Chapter 10

see page 208

**1** **What do you call the address that every system on a TCP/IP network has?**

**A:** An IP or Internet Protocol address.

**2** **Which command do you use to access remote disks transparently from your local system?**

**A:** The **mount** command mounts disks.

**3** **What can you use to share files with Windows systems?**

**A:** Windows systems can run file-sharing software such as NFS. UNIX systems can support Windows file-sharing protocols with Samba. There are a number of other solutions, including passing floppy disks back and forth (the so-called sneaker net).

**4** **Which two commands allow you to log in to a remote system?**

**A:** Use **rlogin** and **telnet**.

**5** **What command allows you to copy files between systems?**

**A:** You can use **ftp** or **rcp** (also **uucp**).

**6** **If you don't have a connection to the Internet, you can still transfer files between systems using what command?**

**A:** Try using **uucp**.

**7** How can you log on to remote UNIX systems from Windows?

**A:** Windows comes with a telnet client, telnet.exe.

**8** If the uccp command fails to make a connection, what can you use to look at the uucp logs?

**A:** Use the **uulog** command.

## Visual Quiz

**Q:** From this anonymous ftp session, how would you download the patch program?

**A:**
```
ftp> binary
ftp> get patch-2.1.tar.gz
```

## Chapter 11

see page 230

**1** Where would you use a text editor?

**A:** In any situation where any writing — of letters, of memos, of program code — is necessary.

**2** Can you do any spell checking using the vi command?

**A:** No.

**3** Does vi support any fonts?

**A:** No.

**4** What's the name of a popular vi clone?

**A:** Elvis.

**5** Is emacs available on every UNIX computer system?

**A:** No.

**6** What sort of documentation is included with emacs?

**A:** Lots! Online documentation in the form of **info** files and FAQs.

**7** How do you search for text in emacs?

**A:** Use the **Ctrl-S** command to search for text.

**8** How do you count the number of words in a file?

**A:** Use the **wc** command.

## Visual Quiz

**Q:** There are four separate sections to this emacs window. What are they?

**A:** File, directory listing, file information, and toolbar.

## Chapter 12

see page 254

**1** Are there any What-You-See-Is-What-You-Get, or WYSIWYG word processors or document publishing systems for UNIX?

**A:** Yes. Programs include Adobe FrameMaker, Applix Words, and Corel WordPerfect.

**2** Is troff a What-You-See-Is-What-You-Get, or WYSIWYG document system?

**A:** No.

**3** What other application do you need to make any use of troff?

**A:** A text editor.

**4** What type of files do you pass to troff as input?

**A:** Text files.

**5** What is the troff command for centering text?

**A:** Use the **.ce** command.

**6** What is the command-line option to tell troff to use the memorandum macros?

**A:** Use the **–mm** option.

**7** What is the command-line option to tell troff to use the online manual macros?

**A:** Use the **–man** option.

**8** What commands can you use to display or print PostScript documents on non-PostScript devices?

**A:** You can use the **ghostview** and **gs** commands.

## Visual Quiz

**Q: Using troff commands try to create output like this.**

**A:** Here's the file we used:

```
\s24
.ce
Centered Text
\s12
\fIItalic\fR and \fBBold\fR are two
options available in troff.
```

# Chapter 13

see page 268

**1** The echo command normally prints a new line at the end of the text it prints. How can you prevent echo from printing this new line?

**A:** Use the **–n** option to **echo**.

**2** With the if statement, what value is considered true and what false?

**A:** The **if** statement normally considers 0 to be false and non-zero (typically 1) to be true.

**3** When running a command, what return value means success and what failure?

**A:** When running a command, success is 0 and failure a non-zero value.

**4** How do you mark a file with executable permissions?

**A:** Use the **chmod** command, such as: chmod a+x *filename*

**5** How can a script handle more than nine command-line parameters?

**A:** You can use the special variable $*, which contains all the command-line parameters.

**6** How can you do this from the C shell?

**A:** The C shell also supports the $*. (The C shell doesn't support $#, which is the number of parameters in the Bourne shell; instead the C shell uses $#argv.)

**7** How can you read a value into a shell variable?

**A:** Use the **read** command: read *variablename*

**8** If a shell script doesn't work the way you want, what option can you use to trace the execution of the script?

**A:** The **sh -v** command prints out the lines in the shell script as they are read and then executes the script. The more useful **sh -x** command prints out each shell script command as it executes, which should help you narrow down any problems.

## Visual Quiz

**Q: Create a script that can make output similar to that shown here.**

**A:** Here's the script we used:

```
#!/bin/sh
echo "The amount of disk space free is:"
df
```

## Chapter 14

see page 290

**①** **What is the name of the command that compiles C programs?**

**A:** Use the **cc** command.

**②** **What is the typical filename extension for C program files?**

**A:** C programs typically use a .c extension.

**③** **What are some of the extensions typically used for C++ programming?**

**A:** C++ programs typically use .cc, .C, or .cxx extensions.

**④** **What is the name of the typical command that compiles C++ programs?**

**A:** The traditional C++ compiler command is CC, but this name is not used on all systems.

**⑤** **What is the name of the command for the GNU C compiler?**

**A:** The GNU C compiler is **gcc**.

**⑥** **Which command builds software libraries?**

**A:** Use the **ar** command to build libraries.

**⑦** **Which program does the xmkmf shell script work with?**

**A:** The **xmkmf** script is a front end to the **imake** program.

**⑧** **What does the ci program do?**

**A:** The **ci** program checks a file into the RCS repository.

## Visual Quiz

**Q:** **This image shows a directory listing for a freeware package (the e-mail program TkRataosk, or tkrat for short). Looking at the files, can you guess what command you would likely run to set up to build this software?**

**A:** After reading the **README** and **INSTALL** files, note the script named **configure** in the directory. You need to run this script to configure the source code for your system.

## Chapter 15

see page 316

**①** **What command do you use to get the current time?**

**A:** Use the **date** command.

**②** **What command do you use to set the current time?**

**A:** Use the **date** command to set the time. Note that usually only the superuser can set the time.

**③** **What command do you use to set the current date?**

**A:** The **date** command sets the date and time (unlike DOS, which has separate commands).

**④** **What command can you use to send a message to all users currently logged in?**

**A:** Use the **wall** or **write** commands.

**⑤** **What are some common names for tape drives?**

**A:** Common names for tape drives include **/dev/rmt0**, **/dev/tape**, and **/dev/dat**.

**⑥** **What command is often used to back up files?**

**A:** Many use the **tar** command for backups. The **cpio** command is also used, along with **dd** and a host of commercial products.

**7** **What is the "three-fingered salute" that you can use to reboot or shut down most Linux systems?**

**A:** Press and hold the **Ctrl**, **Alt** and **Delete** keys at the same time.

**8** **Can UNIX support floppy and ZIP disks in addition to tapes?**

**A:** Yes, UNIX supports quite a few different kinds of devices.

## Visual Quiz

**Q:** **This command sets the system clock to what time?**

**A:** Sat Dec 11 12:11:00 p.m., A.D. 2010.

# Chapter 16

see page 328

**1** **What command or commands allow you to run tasks at a particular time?**

**A:** The **at** and **cron** commands run tasks at a particular time.

**2** **What's the difference between commands run with batch and commands run in the background?**

**A:** There are some fundamental differences between background tasks and **batch**:

▶ Commands issued to **batch** are accorded even less priority than commands run in the background.

▶ With **batch**, commands will continue to execute even if you log off the system (shades of **nohup**!). Background tasks are killed if you log off the system.

▶ Background will interrupt you should your background command specify some kind of output or confirmation. **Batch** does not; as we noted, confirmation or output is sent as a mail message.

**3** **How could you schedule a command to run at 3 p.m.?**

**A:** You could use the **at** command as follows:
at 3pm
You could also set up a **crontab** entry for the **cron** command, but note that **cron** runs commands periodically, so you may end up running the command every day at 3 p.m.

**4** **What do you use to tell the batch command that you are done entering commands?**

**A:** Type **Ctrl-D**, the UNIX end-of-file marker.

**5** **What do you use to tell the at command that you are done entering commands?**

**A:** Type **Ctrl-D**, the UNIX end-of-file marker.

**6** **What command can you use to eliminate the commands you have scheduled with cron?**

**A:** Use the **crontab –r** command.

**7** **Should you run the cron command directly?**

**A:** Generally, you don't want to run the **cron** command directly. Instead, you run **crontab** to alert **cron** to the tasks you'd like to run periodically.

**8** **What command do you use to schedule tasks with cron?**

**A:** Use the **crontab** command.

## Visual Quiz

**Q:** **When will this command get run?**

**A:** 4:25 a.m. on the 15th and 30th of each month with at least 30 days. Note that February has less than 30 days.

# Appendix B:
# Learning More About UNIX

## Books

Obviously, this book serves as a brief introduction to a very complex operating system. To learn more about the UNIX operating system, we highly recommend the following as part of your core reading list:

▶ *UNIX in Plain English, Third Edition*. Kevin Reichard and Eric Foster-Johnson. MIS:Press, 1998. Designed as a companion for *Teach Yourself UNIX, UNIX in Plain English* is a quick reference for the UNIX command set. Each major command is covered on its own page, and entries are cross-referenced by type and with DOS commands.

▶ *UNIX System V Release 4: An Introduction for New and Experienced Users*. Kenneth Rosen, Richard Rosinski, and James Farber. Osborne McGraw-Hill, 1995. Weighing in at a little over four pounds and close to 1,200 pages, *UNIX System V Release 4* is the most thorough documentation of SVR4 in one volume. It should be — the three authors all work for AT&T and have been working with UNIX for years.

▶ *UNIX Fundamentals: The Basics, Second Edition*. Kevin Reichard. MIS:Press, 1997. This covers the basics of UNIX on a far more introductory level than the book you're holding. If you're still confused about some aspects of UNIX, you may want to take a step back and read this book.

Over the last few years a number of specialized UNIX books have cropped up. For the **vi** text editor, you could try:

▶ *The Ultimate Guide to the Vi and Ex Text Editors*. Hewlett-Packard Company, Benjamin Cummings, 1990.

For more than you ever wanted to learn about **nroff**, **troff**, and an entire family of related programs, check out:

▶ *Text Processing and Typesetting with UNIX*. David Barron and Mike Rees. Addison-Wesley, 1987.

For more on the Internet, read:

▶ *The Whole Internet User's Guide and Catalog*, Third Edition. Ed Krol. O'Reilly & Associates, 1997.

If you need to know more about the X Window System, check out:

▶ *Using X*. Eric F. Johnson and Kevin Reichard. MIS:Press, 1992.
▶ *The UNIX System Administrator's Guide to X*. Eric F. Johnson and Kevin Reichard. M&T Books, 1994.

# Appendix B: Learning More About UNIX

To learn more about Linux, check out:

- *Linux Configuration and Installation, Fourth Edition.* Patrick Volkerding, Kevin Reichard, and Eric Foster-Johnson. MIS:Press, 1998.
- *Linux in Plain English*, Patrick Volkerding and Kevin Reichard. MIS:Press, 1997.

To find out more about programming C and C++ applications, as discussed in Chapter 14, look at:

- *C in Plain English.* Brian Overland. MIS:Press, 1995.
- *Teach Yourself C++.* Al Stevens. MIS:Press, 1997.
- *UNIX Programming Tools.* Eric Foster-Johnson. M&T Books, 1997.

You can find out more about the Perl scripting language discussed in Chapter 16 by looking up the following books:

- *Programming Perl.* Larry Wall, Tom Christiansen and Randal Schwartz. O'Reilly and Assoc., 1996.
- *Learning Perl.* Randal Schwartz and Tom Christiansen. O'Reilly and Assoc., 1997.
- *Cross-Platform Perl.* Eric F. Johnson. M&T Books, 1996.
- *Perl Modules.* Eric Foster-Johnson. M&T Books, 1998.

If you're not only learning UNIX as a user, but also find yourself a reluctant system administrator, we recommend:

- *UNIX System V Release 4 Administration, Second Edition.* David Fielder, Bruce Hunter, and Ben Smith. Hayden Books, 1991.
- *UNIX Administration Guide for System V.* Rebecca Thomas and Rik Farrow. Prentice Hall, 1989.

Another text we find useful is:

- *!%@:: A Dictionary of Electronic Mail Addressing and Networks.* Donnalyn Frey and Rick Adams. O'Reilly and Assoc., 1989.

## Usenet Newsgroups

In Chapter 10 we covered the Internet and the Usenet quite extensively. The Usenet, specifically, features many newsgroups geared for UNIX users of all sorts. We present an introductory list in Table A-1.

| Table A-1: USENET NEWSGROUPS COVERING UNIX | |
|---|---|
| **Newsgroup** | **Purpose** |
| comp.unix.admin | Administering a UNIX-based system. |
| comp.unix.advocacy | Arguments for and against UNIX. |
| comp.unix.aix | A discussion of IBM's AIX. |
| comp.unix.bsd | A discussion of the Berkeley Software Distribution UNIX. |
| comp.unix.dos-under-unix | Running MS-DOS under UNIX. |
| comp.unix.misc | Miscellaneous UNIX topics. |
| comp.unix.programmer | Q&A for people programming in UNIX. |
| comp.unix.questions | Discussion of UNIX geared for beginners. |
| comp.unix.shell | Programming UNIX shells. |
| comp.unix.sys5.r4 | Discussion of System V Release 4. |
| comp.lang.perl.announce | Announcements relevant for Perl users. |
| comp.lang.perl.misc | The main Perl newsgroup. |
| comp.os.linux.announce | One of many comp.os.linux.* newsgroups; includes announcements for Linux users. |
| comp.windows.x.announce | Announcements about the X Window System. |

# Appendix B: Learning More About UNIX

## User Groups

We've learned a lot by attending our local meetings of UNIX Users of Minnesota and you certainly could learn a lot by attending a meeting of your local UNIX user group. Most groups follow the same format: Meetings for beginners, followed by general meetings with guest speakers and Q&A sessions.

Unfortunately, there's no centralized list of UNIX user groups. We recommend checking out a local computer publication for a listing of local user groups. Readers in larger cities can look for their local editions of *Computer User* or *Computer Currents*.

# Appendix C:
# Basic UNIX Commands

UNIX is made up of literally thousands of commands and variations. In the course of the summary, we did not have the chance to cover every command and variation. Here we have the chance to cover the major commands in some detail. As always, this doesn't cover every possible command. We do differentiate between the various shells: The default is the Bourne shell, while **csh** refers to the C shell, and **ksh** refers to the Korn shell. Unless noted otherwise, a command should work with every shell. Should you require additional information about these commands (or those we fail to list), refer to the online manual pages or your system's documentation.

This is a truncated listing; a full listing of UNIX commands and their many options fill entire books. If you're looking for a complete reference to the UNIX command set, check out *UNIX in Plain English* (see Appendix B for details).

## alias

### Description

Displays and sets command aliases. Alias by itself will give a summary of current aliases.

### Syntax

alias *name=cmd* (**csh** and **ksh**)
alias *name=cmd* (**ksh**)

## at

### Description

Performs specified commands at given times, as long as the commands require no additional input from you. For instance, you may want to print a series of long documents at midnight, so you don't need to tie up the laser printer for hours when other people may need it. You can use the **at** command to print at midnight, as long as you make sure the paper tray is filled before leaving work.

### Syntax

at *time*
at *options job-ids*

### Options

-l        Lists current job.
-r        Removes specified job.

# Appendix C: Basic UNIX Commands

**time**  Obviously, the time when the commands should run. Unless you specify otherwise (with a.m. or p.m. as a suffix), the system assumes military time.

# banner

## Description
Displays up to ten characters in large letters using asterisks (*) or number signs (#), depending on your system. For instance, the command **banner kevin** would display the following on your screen:

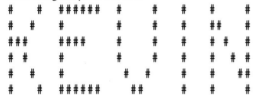

## Syntax
banner *text*

# bg

## Description
Resumes a suspended job.

## Syntax
bg *PID*

# cal

## Description
Displays the current month in calendar form.

## Syntax
cal *month year*
cal *year*

## Options
**month**  Specifies month to display.
**year**  Specifies year to display.

# cancel

## Description
Cancels pending printer jobs. You can either specify the job ID or printer to be canceled.

## Syntax
cancel *ID*
cancel *printer*

# cat

## Description
Combines or displays files.

## Syntax
cat *options filename*

## Options
**-u**  Output is unbuffered.
**-v**  Prints nonprinting characters.

# cc

## Description
Compiles C language programs.

## Syntax

cc *options filename link options*

## Options

| | |
|---|---|
| **-c** *filename* | Specify the name of the file to compile, to generate an .o file. |
| **-g** | Generate debugging information. |
| **-o** *filename* | Specify the name of the executable file to generate. |
| **-O** | Optimize while compiling. |
| **-l***library* | Links the given *library*, e.g., -lX11. |

# cd

## Description

Change current directory to a new directory.

## Syntax

cd *directory*

# chgrp

## Description

Changes a file's group ID, which is used for the group access permissions.

## Syntax

chgrp *groupname filename*

# chmod

## Description

Changes the access permissions on a given file. The mode is an octal number in the following format:

| Number | Meaning |
|---|---|
| 400 | Owner has read permission. |
| 200 | Owner has write permission. |
| 100 | Owner has execute permission. |
| 040 | Group has read permission. |
| 020 | Group has write permission. |
| 010 | Group has execute permission. |
| 004 | World has read permission. |
| 002 | World has write permission. |
| 001 | World has execute permission. |

Add together the numbers for the permissions you want. For example, 423 means that you, the user, can read the file, users in your group can write the file, and the rest of the world can write and execute the file.

## Syntax

chmod *mode filename*

# chown

## Description

Changes the ownership of a given file.

## Syntax

chown **owner filename**

## Options

| | |
|---|---|
| **-h** | Changes the ownership of a symbolic link. |

# compress

## Description

Compresses a file (or files), creating *filename.Z*.

## Syntax

compress *filename*

# Appendix C: Basic UNIX Commands

## cp

### Description

Copies the contents of one file into another file.

### Syntax

cp *options filename newfilename*

### Options

-i  Makes sure you don't overwrite existing file.
-p  Retains existing permissions.
-r  Copies entire directory.

## crontab

### Description

Tells the **cron** command to run a set of commands at specified times.

### Syntax

crontab *filename*   Where *filename* is the name of a crontab file.

## csh

### Description

Starts the C shell.

### Syntax

csh

## date

### Description

Displays current date. Or, if you have superuser status, can be used to set the system date and time.

### Syntax

date *options*

### Options

**mmddHHMMMMYY**   Sets month (mm), date (dd), hour (hh), minute (MM), and year (YY).

## diff

### Description

Compares two files.

### Syntax

diff *options filename1 filename2*

### Options

-b  Ignores blanks at the end of lines.
-c  Generates a context diff.
-e  Creates a script for the ed editor to make *filename1* the same as *filename2*.

## du

### Description

Displays how much disk space is used by a directory (and all its subdirectories), in blocks (usually 512 or 1,024 bytes each).

## Syntax

du *options directories*
du *options filenames*

## Options

| | |
|---|---|
| **-a** | Displays all information. |
| **-r** | Reports on files and directories **du** cannot open. |
| **-s** | Silent mode. Displays only totals. |

# echo

## Description

Echoes text to standard output.

## Syntax

echo *text*

# env

## Description

Displays the current user environment variables with their values.

## Syntax

env *options*

## Options

| | |
|---|---|
| **ENV=VALUE** | Sets environment variable (*ENV*) to *VALUE*. |

# exit

## Description

Quits the current session.

## Syntax

exit

# file

## Description

Describes file type of given file.

## Syntax

file *filename*

# find

## Description

Finds a file.

## Syntax

find / -name *filename* -print

## Options

| | |
|---|---|
| **-name** | Searches for the file by its name. |
| **-print** | Prints the results of the search. In most versions of UNIX, this option is mandatory if you want to see the results of your search. |

# grep

## Description

Searches files for a pattern.

## Syntax

grep *options pattern filenames*

# Appendix C: Basic UNIX Commands

## Options

| | |
|---|---|
| **-c** | Only displays the number of lines that match. |
| **-i** | Ignores case. |
| **-l** | Lists only filenames that have matching lines. |
| **-n** | Lists each matching line with its line number. |
| **-v** | Lists lines that don't match. |

## head

### Description

Displays the beginning of a file. The default is ten lines.

### Syntax

head *filename*

### Options

**-n**    Specify the number of lines to display.

## history

### Description

Displays previous command lines. Used with the C and Bash shells.

### Syntax

history

## jobs

### Description

Display all current jobs.

### Syntax

jobs

## kill

### Description

Kills a current process by ID number.

### Syntax

kill *process.id*

## ln

### Description

Links two or more files.

### Syntax

ln *filename1 filename2*

### Options

**-s**    Creates a symbolic link.

## lp

### Description

Sends a print request to a printer. Can be used to print multiple files with one request. On some systems, you may need to use the **lpr** command instead.

### Syntax

lp *filename*

### Options

| | |
|---|---|
| **-c** | Copies the file before sending the request. |
| **-d** | Specifies a printer other than the default printer. |
| **-m** | Sends a message to the user when the file is printed. |

# Appendix C: Basic UNIX Commands

## lpstat

### Description
Returns the status of print requests.

### Syntax
lpstat *options*

### Option
**-d**    Copies the file before sending the request.

## ls

### Description
Lists the contents of the specified directory. If no directory is specified, the contents of the current directory are listed.

### Syntax
ls *names*
where *names* refers to filenames or pathnames.

### Options
**-a**    Lists all contents, including hidden files.

**-d**    Lists only the name of the directory, not the contents.

**-l**    Lists the contents of a directory in long form.

**-m**    Lists the contents across the screen, separated by commas.

**-q**    Lists contents with nonprinting characters represented by a question mark (?).

**-r**    Lists the contents in reverse order.

**-t**    Lists the contents in order of time saved, beginning with the most recent.

**-1**    Lists contents one entry to a line.

## make

### Description
Builds programs from a set of rules stored in a makefile.

### Syntax
make *options targets*

### Options
**-f** *makefile*    Use *makefile* instead of a file named **Makefile** for **make**'s rules.

**-n**    No execute mode. Only print out commands, don't execute them.

**-s**    Silent mode. Don't print out any commands make executes.

## man

### Description
Displays the online-manual page for a command.

### Syntax
man *command*

## mkdir

### Description
Create a new directory.

### Syntax
mkdir *dirname*
where *dirname* refers to the name of the new directory.

### Options
**-m** *mode*    Specifies the mode of the new directory.

# Appendix C: Basic UNIX Commands

## more

### Description

Displays all or parts of a file. Type **q** to quit, **Spacebar** to continue.

### Syntax

more *filename*

### Options

-c      Clears the screen before displaying the file.

## mv

### Description

Moves a file or multiple files into another directory or to a new name in the current directory.

### Syntax

mv *filename directory*
mv *filename newfilename*

### Options

-f      Moves file without checking for confirmation in case of an overwrite.

-i      Prompts users if action would overwrite an existing file.

## nice

### Description

Runs a command nicely, by giving it a very low priority.

### Syntax

nice *options command*
where *command* refers to the command to execute nicely.

### Options

-n      Specifies **n** as the decrement in priority. The default is 10.

## nohup

### Description

Keeps a command running even if you log off the system.

### Syntax

nohup *command*

## page or pg

### Description

Displays a file one page at a time.

### Syntax

pg *filename*

### Options

+*n*      Starts the display at line number *n*.

+/*string*      Searches for the string *string*.

## passwd

### Description

Sets the user's password.

### Syntax

passwd *user*

# pr

## Description
Prints a file or files to the default printer.

## Syntax
pr *filename* | lp

## Options
| | |
|---|---|
| **-d** | Double-spaces the text. |
| **-h** *text* | Prints the header *text* at the beginning of the output. |
| *-l* | Sets the page length. |
| **-w** | Sets the page width. |

# ps

## Description
Returns the status of all current processes.

## Syntax
ps

## Options
| | |
|---|---|
| **-e** | Displays expanded information about all current processes. |
| **-f** | Displays full information about processes. |

# pwd

## Description
Returns the current working directory.

## Syntax
pwd

# rcp

## Description
Copies files to and from remote systems.

## Syntax
rcp *host1:filename host2:filename*

# resume

## Description
Starts a suspended job.

## Syntax
resume *PID*

# rlogin

## Description
Logs in to a remote system.

## Syntax
rlogin *hostname*

## Options
| | |
|---|---|
| **-l** *username* | Remotely login under the new *username*. |

# rm

## Description
Removes files.

## Syntax
rm *filename*

# Appendix C: Basic UNIX Commands

## Options

**-f**      Removes files without verifying action with user.

**-i**      Removes files after verification from user.

# rmdir

## Description

Removes a directory.

## Syntax

rmdir *directory*

# set

## Description

Returns the values of all current environment variables.

## Syntax

set

# setenv

## Description

Sets an environment variable. (Used only with C shell.)

## Syntax

setenv *variable newvariable*

# spell

## Description

Returns incorrectly spelled words in a file.

## Syntax

spell *filename*

## Options

**-b**               Checks for spelling based on British usage.

**+s** *filename*    Creates a sorted file (*filename*) of correctly spelled words.

# stop

## Description

Suspends a currently running process.

## Syntax

stop *PID*

# stty

## Description

Sets your terminal configuration and options.

## Syntax

stty

## Options

**-a**      Displays current options.

# tabs

## Description

Sets the tab settings.

## Syntax

tabs

## Options

| | |
|---|---|
| -*filename* | Inserts tab information in the file **filename**. |
| -*n* | Sets tab every *n* characters. |

# tail

## Description

Displays the final ten lines of a file.

## Syntax

tail *options filename*

## Options

| | |
|---|---|
| -*n* | Specifies the number of lines from the end of the file to be displayed. |

# tar

## Description

Archives files to **tar** files, often on backup tapes.

## Syntax

tar *options filenames*

## Options

| | |
|---|---|
| c | Create a new **tar** archive. |
| f *filename* | Write archive to *filename*, often **/dev/tape**. |
| t | Print out a table of contents |
| v | Verbose mode: Print out status information. |
| x | Extract files from within the **tar** archive. |

# telnet

## Description

Logs in to a remote system.

## Syntax

telnet *hostname*

# uncompress

## Description

Uncompresses a file, usually with a name ending in .Z.

## Syntax

uncompress *filename*

# unset

## Description

Unsets a specified variable.

## Syntax

unset *variablename*

# unsetenv

## Description

Unsets an environment variable. (Used only in the C shell.)

## Syntax

unsetenv *variablename*

# Appendix C: Basic UNIX Commands

## wc

### Description

Counts the number of words, characters, and lines in a text file or files.

### Syntax

wc *options filenames*

### Options

-c      Only print the number of characters.
-l      Only print the number of lines.
-w      Only print the number of words.

## who

### Description

Displays the names and other information about users on the system.

### Syntax

who *options*

### Options

am I      Displays your user account information.

## write

### Description

Sends a text message to another user. Use **Ctrl-D** to exit.

### Syntax

write *username*

# Glossary

## A

**absolute pathname**  The complete name of a file, replete with the total path of directories indicating the file's location on the directory tree. For instance, the absolute pathname of the file **file1** is **/usr/users/kevin/docs/file1**.

**address**  Either the name of a specific machine on a network or the name of the entire UNIX system. Both meanings are used in discussions of electronic mail and communications.

**aging**  Used by the system to determine when passwords or files are old enough to be changed or deleted.

**alias**  A substitute for a command set up by the user, often a short substitute for a longer, frequently used command.

**anonymous ftp**  A remote login that requires no password; used for downloading files from a remote machine. See *ftp*.

**append**  To attach text to the end of an existing text file.

**application**  Software that supplies specific functions to end users; for example, WordPerfect is a word-processing application.

**argument**  Used to modify a command on the command line.

**ASCII (American Standard Code for Information Interchange)**  A standard format used to communicate data between different computer types. An ASCII file created on a UNIX computer is readable on other kinds of computers.

**at**  Command that lets you schedule tasks to be run at a future date.

**AWK**  A programming language geared toward text manipulation.

## B

**BSD (Berkeley Software Distribution)**  A still-popular version of UNIX originated at the University of California-Berkeley that was noted especially for its advanced networking capabilities. Several freely available versions of BSD, such as FreeBSD and NetBSD, are available.

**background**  When programs are run in this mode, the user can perform other tasks and will be notified when the background program is completed. Background commands are notated with an ampersand (&) at the end of the command line.

**backup**  An archived copy of user-specified files, kept as an insurance policy should the original files be damaged or corrupted. The UNIX operating system uses the **tar** and **cpio** commands to create backups.

**batch**  Command that allows you to input many commands to be run unattended in sequence.

**batch processing**  Where the system is given a series of commands (some of which may depend on the output of other commands) and performs these commands without any interaction with the user. Although a throwback to the bygone days of computing, much of what can be done in UNIX can be done with batch processing.

# Glossary

**bc**  Command that turns a $10,000 workstation into the equivalent of a $20 calculator.

**bin**  Directory that contains most of the standard UNIX programs and utilities.

**binary file**  A machine-readable format that usually cannot be read directly by other computers.

**bitmap**  A method of displaying graphics where the machine maps out every specific point (called *pixels*) on a display.

**boot**  Starting the computer and loading the operating system into memory.

**Bourne shell**  A commonly used shell (**sh**) created by Steven Bourne of Bell Labs. The original shell.

**Bourne Again Shell (bash)**  A freely available shell that combines many features of the Bourne and C shells. It's distributed widely with Linux distributions and FreeBSD.

**buffer**  A section of random-access memory (RAM) used to temporarily store data for future use.

**bug**  Errors in software. Sometimes called unanticipated features.

# C

**C**  A programming language created by Dennis Ritchie (Bell Labs) in the 1960s. Most UNIX programming utilizes the C programming language (as well as the C++ language), since most of UNIX is written in C.

**C++**  An enhanced object-oriented version of C written by Bjarne Stroustrup.

**C shell**  A commonly used shell created by Bill Joy and others at the University of California–Berkeley.

**CPU (central processing unit)**  The brains of the computer; usually a processor that performs much of the actual work, including processing data and carrying out instructions.

**cal**  Command that displays a one-month calendar.

**cat**  Command used to concatenate files, though the most common usage may be the simple viewing of files.

**cd**  Command that changes your current directory.

**child process**  A process started by a parent process through a fork. Every UNIX process is a child of another process, except for **init**.

**chmod**  Command used to change file permissions.

**client**  In a distributed file system, a computer that accesses the files and services on a server. In the X Window System, an application that runs on the local machine (as opposed to the server).

**command**  An instruction sent to the shell, which interprets the command and acts upon it.

**command history**  See *history*.

**command line**  One or more commands, arguments, and options strung together to create a command.

**command mode**  In a text editor, the mode where the user supplies commands for saving and editing files.

**command substitution**  Using the output of one command as input for a new command.

**comments**  Text included in script or programming files that is not meant to be acted upon by the computer, but rather used to illuminate commands for someone reading the file.

**compiler**  A program that turns source code into programs that can be executed by the computer. For example, C source-code files must be run through a compiler before being run by the computer as a full program.

**compressed file** A file that has been shrunk by compression software.

**conditional execution** A construction where one action won't be taken unless another action is performed satisfactorily (*if* this, *then* that).

**console** Two meanings: A terminal that is the mother of all terminals, displaying all the system error messages; or, more generally, the terminal used by the system administrator.

**core dump** A very bad thing. If an error occurs that a program can't deal with, the program displays all of the memory content before shutting down.

**cp** Command used to copy a file from one directory to another.

**cpio** Command used to back up files.

**cron** Command used to schedule routine and regular tasks, such as backing up files.

**crontab** The file that contains settings for the **cron** command.

**csh** Command that launches the C shell.

**current directory** Your current location on the file system. The **cd** command is used to change current directories.

**cursor** A symbol used to display the current position on a screen. Older terminals use blinking squares; X Window System users can use just about anything, including (our favorite) a Gumby character.

**DOS (Disk Operating System)** An operating system designed by Microsoft for personal computers and sold under the MS-DOS and PC-DOS names.

**daemon** Despite the title, a good thing. A daemon (pronounced *demon*) is set up to perform a regular, mundane task without any user initialization or supervision. See *cron* for an example of a daemon.

**database management** A structured way of storing information so it can be easily sorted and otherwise managed by the computer.

**date** Command used to print out or change the current date and time.

**debugger** A program that provides information about bugs in software.

**default** A value or state assumed when no other is supplied.

**delimiter** A marker used to distinguish between sections of a command or a database. With UNIX, spaces are used as delimiters between portions of a command line.

**destination** As you might expect, the target for a directed command.

**dev** Directory containing device files.

**device** A physical device attached to the computer system, such as a printer or a modem. UNIX's device drivers allow the system to talk to these devices.

**device file** A file that contains a description of the device so the operating system can properly send data to and from the device.

**device independent** Having the ability to perform a task without regard for a specific computer or peripheral. The text processor **ditroff** is device independent because it will work with many different printers.

**directory** A grouping of files and other directories; analogous to a folder residing in a file cabinet.

**display** The physical part of the computer system used to communicate back and forth with the user.

# Glossary

**distributed file system** A group of two or more physical computers containing files and programs that appears as one contiguous system to the end user. Also refers to the software introduced in System V Release 4 that accomplishes this goal.

**distributed processing** A theory of computing that allows resources to be allocated efficiently on a network; for instance, a PC user could use a more powerful workstation on the network for computational-heavy processing.

**ditroff** A device-independent version of the text processor **troff**.

**domain** Best envisioned as a pyramid, a domain is a group that has control over all groups.

**domain addressing** Electronic-mail addressing scheme that specifies a specific address within a larger domain; if the address name is reichard@mr.net, the domain would be mr.net.

**dot command** Just what the name implies: A command preceded by a dot. Used to tell the shell to execute the commands in a file; also used by **troff** and other text-processing tools to indicate formatting commands.

# E

**echo** A UNIX command used to print standard input to standard output.

**ed** Retro text editor that edits an ASCII file one line at a time.

**edit buffer** A section of RAM used to contain a file while you edit the file with a text editor.

**editor** A program used to edit ASCII files, such as **ed**, **vi**, and **emacs**.

**editing mode** In a text editor, the mode where editing changes (like inserting new text, cutting, pasting, etc.) occur. Also known as *command mode*.

**electronic mail** The ability to send and receive mail from computers on your own network or via the Internet.

**emacs** Full-screen text editor. Widely distributed, though not standard on all UNIX implementations.

**encryption** A method of encoding a file so that it's not readable by other users, used as a security measure.

**end-of-file (EOF) character** The character, surprisingly enough, that indicates the end of a file. The combination **Ctrl-D** is the EOF character in UNIX.

**environment** The sum of all of your shell variables, which are set individually by you and either stored in your **.profile** file or set manually by the user as need be.

**environment file** Specific to the Korn shell, this file also contains environment settings.

**environment variable** An individual shell setting that makes up part of your environment. For instance, you can designate a directory such as your HOME directory as an environment variable.

**eqn** Dot commands used to typeset equations in conjunction with **troff**.

**error message** In a nutshell, a message that tells you something is awry.

**escape key** Character labeled **Esc** on a keyboard and used for a variety of functions.

**etc** Directory containing everything but device files and program files.

**executable file** A program file that runs simply by typing its name on the command line.

**execute permission** A setting for an executable file that denotes who can run the program.

**exit** Quitting a running program; in UNIX, technically you are terminating a process.

**export** To make environment variables available to other users.

**extension** A suffix to a filename that helps identify the data contained in the file. A C source-code file usually ends with a *.c* suffix.

## F

**field** A vertical column of data in a structured data file, with all the entries of the same type. If we were to create a file containing the names, phone numbers, and salary of every employee, with each employee's phone number contained in the second column, we would call that column a field.

**file** A defined set of characters (called *bytes*) referenced by a filename.

**file sharing** The mechanisms (RFS and NFS) used to make files on one system available to users on another system.

**file system** The pyramid-like method used in UNIX to organize files and directories: A root directory (analogous to the top of the pyramid) contains several subdirectories, and these subdirectories in turn may contain further subdirectories. Any directory can hold files.

**filename** The obvious: The name given to a file. Files in the same directory cannot have the same filename, but files in different directories may have the same name.

**filling** An action in a text processor where as much text as possible is crammed onto a line.

**filter** A type of UNIX program that takes input from one file and provides output to the display or another file based on parameters set up by the user.

**find** Command used to find a file.

**finger** Command that provides information about another user locally or on the Internet.

**foreground** Commands that have the full attention of the system and do not return control to the user until the command is completed. In UNIX, the default is to run commands in the foreground.

**fork** When a program starts another program, called a child process.

**ftp** Command used to connect to any other computer on your network running an FTP daemon; when connected, **ftp** can then be used to transfer files to your computer. Can also be used to access files anywhere on the Internet provided you have access to the Internet.

**full pathname** The full description of the location of a file on the directory tree, from the root directory down.

**function key** A key (usually marked as **F1**, **F2**, etc.) that can be defined by the operating system and/or applications to perform any number of functions. The actions attached to the key usually differ from program to program and operating system to operating system.

## G

**gateways** Computers that forward mail, news, or other stuff to other connected machines.

**global** To make changes to all occurrences of a given object; to change every instance of *Word* to *word* in a file with **emacs** would be an example of a global search and replace.

# Glossary

**graphical user interface**  A metaphoric display of a computer system, with icons, windows, and scrollbars. Motif, Open Look, the Macintosh, and Windows are all examples of graphical user interfaces.

**graphical windowing system**  See *graphical user interface*.

**grep**  A UNIX command that searches for user-specified strings in a file or files.

**group**  A defined set of users.

**head**  Command used to display the beginning of a file.

**header**  The beginning area of a file that contains vital statistics about the file. A mail file contains a header that specifies, among other things, the sender of the message and the route it takes.

**header file**  A C-language file used to include system-specific information. Sometimes called *include* files, as they are specified in a source-code file with the include command.

**hidden file**  A file beginning with a dot (**.profile**, for example) that is not returned by the **ls** command unless **ls** is told to return the names of all files in a directory, including hidden files.

**hierarchical file system**  See file system.

**history**  A record of previous commands maintained in your computer's memory by the shell.

**history substitution**  Plucking a command line from a history list and using it again by typing the number assigned to the command.

**home directory**  The directory the user is placed in after logging in. This directory is set in the **.profile** file with the HOME= command.

**hostname**  The name of your UNIX system.

**icon**  A graphical representation of a program or file.

**inbox**  The storage area for electronic mail that has not been read.

**init**  The initial process, which launches when you boot a computer running the UNIX operating system. All processes are children of the **init** process.

**inode**  The location of information about files in the file system.

**input mode**  The mode where a text editor will accept input and includes it in the edited file. The opposite of *editing mode*.

**interactive**  Involves a dialogue of sorts between user and computer; the computer does not perform future tasks until given approval by the user. Most UNIX work can be done with the opposite of interactive computing, batch processing.

**Internet**  The umbrella name for a group of computer networks that distributes newsgroups and electronic mail around the world. Computers with access to the Internet are said to be internetworked.

**Internet address**  The numeric address given to a computer system that allows it to receive Internet news and mail.

**job**  Another name for process or program running.

**job control** Changing the status of a job, such as killing it or resuming a suspended job.

**job shell** A superset of the Bourne shell (**sh**) devoted to job control.

# K

**kernel** The core of the UNIX operating system that interacts directly with the computer.

**keyboard** That big thing with keys used to provide input. If you really looked up the definition of keyboard in a UNIX tutorial, we strongly advise you to take a remedial "Introduction to Computers" class before proceeding with any UNIX usage.

**kill** Command that stops a running process.

**kill buffer** A section of RAM devoted to storage of deleted text, which can then be called back into the text editor for further editing.

**Korn shell** The shell (**ksh**) created by David Korn that improved on the older, popular Bourne shell.

# L

**language** Instructions that are translated into commands a computer can understand. Popular languages include C, BASIC, PASCAL, and FORTRAN.

**library** A set of commonly used C-language functions.

**line editor** A text editor that processes one line at a time, such as **ed**.

**link** Instead of wasting disk space on multiple copies of a commonly used file, one copy of the file is maintained and other filenames are linked to the original file.

**ln** Command used to link files.

**local-area network** A group of personal computers connected via cable to a central computer (the server) that distributes applications and files.

**login** Establish a session on the main UNIX system after providing a login name and a password.

**login name** The truncated, unique name given to all users on a UNIX system.

**logname** See *login name.*

**logoff** Quit a UNIX session, typically by typing **exit**, **logout**, or **Ctrl-D**.

**look and feel** The specific arrangement of elements on a screen (scrollbars, title bars, etc.)

**loop** A state where commands are to be executed again and again until some condition is met.

**lp** Command used to print a file.

**lpstat** Command used to view the current status of print requests.

**ls** Command that lists the files in a directory.

# M

**macros** Short instructions that are expanded by the shell to mean longer, more explicit commands.

**mail** Command used to send and receive mail from other users.

**mailbox** The file area used to store electronic-mail messages.

**make** A UNIX program used to create applications based on system-specific information.

# Glossary

**man** Command that displays online-manual pages.

**man pages** See *online-manual pages.*

**manual macros** Macros used to create formatted online-manual pages.

**memorandum macros (mm)** Macros used in conjunction with **troff** to create stylized business letters, resumes, and reports.

**mesg** Command that lets you block messages from other users created with **talk** or **write**.

**Meta key** A specified key used in conjunction with other keys to create additional key combinations. On a PC keyboard, the **Alt** key is the **Meta** key; on a Sun keyboard, the **Alt** key is not the **Meta** key.

**more** Command used to display a file one page at a time.

**Motif** Created by the Open Software Foundation and now overseen by the Open Group, Motif is a style guide that defines a particular look and feel for programs as well as a set of programming libraries and a window manager (**mwm**). Based on the X Window System.

**mount** Make a file system available to users, either locally or remotely.

**multiprocessing** Running more than one task or process at a time; one of the great strengths of the UNIX operating system.

**multitasking** Running more than one task or process at a time; one of the great strengths of the UNIX operating system.

**multiuser** Allowing more than one user to be active on the system at once; one of the great strengths of the UNIX operating system.

**mv** Command that moves a file from one directory to another.

## N

**NFS (Network File System)** Software developed to create a distributed file system for use with both UNIX and non-UNIX computers.

**networking** Connecting computers via phone line or direct link so that they can share data.

**newline** Character placed at the end of every line in a text file, usually created by pressing the **Return** (or **Enter**) key.

**news** Command that displays text files containing news items.

**news feed** On the Usenet, all the incoming message files from the worldwide newsgroups.

**news readers** Software dedicated to reading Usenet newsgroups.

**newsgroup** On the Usenet, public discussions of various topics.

**nice** Command that allows you to assign a lower priority to a process, thus relieving an overstressed UNIX system.

**noclobber** Condition set where a new file cannot overwrite an existing file with the same line unless the action is approved by the user.

**nroff** Text-processing software, used to output formatting documents on a line printer.

## O

**online-manual page** Technically detailed information about a command, accessed by the **man** command.

**Open Look** Created by Sun Microsystems and AT&T, Open Look is a style guide that defines a particular look and feel for programs, as well as a set of programming libraries and a window manager (**olwm**).

**operating system** Software that controls a computer, acts as an interface for a user, and runs applications. UNIX is an operating system.

**options** Characters that modify the default behavior of a command.

**ordinary file** A text or data file with no special characteristics; the most common file type in the UNIX operating system.

**orphan** A process that runs even though its parent process has been killed.

**owner** The user with the ability to set permissions for a file.

# P

**paging** A memory-management scheme that divides RAM into 4K segments for more efficient shuffling of data to and from RAM and a hard disk.

**parent process** A process that generates another process.

**parsing** Logically dividing a command so that we can divine its meaning.

**partition** A section of a hard disk treated as a separate area by the operating system.

**passwd** Command that allows you to change your password.

**password** A unique set of characters designed to confirm your status as a legitimate user of a system.

**path** A list of directories the system uses to search for executables.

**pathname** A description of where a file resides in the file system. All pathnames flow from the root directory.

**permissions** A security tool that determines who can access a file.

**pipes** A device that allows standard output from one command to be used as standard input for another command.

**pg** Command used to view a file one page at a time.

**PostScript** A system-independent page-description language developed by Adobe Systems.

**process** Essentially, a program running on the computer.

**process identification number (PID)** A unique number assigned to a program so that it can be tracked and managed by the operating system and user.

**profile** A description of a user's environment variables, stored in the **.profile** file.

**program** A set of instructions for the computer to carry out.

**prompt** A character used by the shell to indicate that it is waiting for input. In addition, some programs (like **ftp**) supply their own unique prompt.

**ps** Command that shows what processes are running on your system.

**pwd** Command that prints the working, or current, directory.

# Glossary

## R

**RAM (Random-Access Memory)** A physical area of the computer used for short-term storage of data and programs. When a computer is turned off, the data in RAM disappears.

**RFS (Remote File System)** Software developed to create a distributed file system for use only with the UNIX operating system.

**read** Command reads in user input and places whatever the user types into a shell variable.

**record** A row in a structured data file. If we were to create a file containing the names, phone numbers, and salary of every employee, with each employee's information contained in a single row, we could call that row a record.

**redirection** See *standard input and output.*

**relational operator** A symbol that sets forth a condition in a programming language, such as C or **awk**. These conditions are based on algebraic notation.

**relative pathname** The location of a file in relation to another location in the file system.

**rlogin** Command that allows you to remotely login another computer on your network.

**rm** Command that deletes a record of the file from the file system.

**root directory** The directory in a file system that contains all other directories and subdirectories. Indicated in all pathnames as a slash (/).

**root user** See *superuser.*

## S

**screen editor** A text editor that allows the user to view a document one screen at a time and to edit anywhere on that screen through movement via cursors or the mouse.

**secondary prompt** A character used by the shell to indicate that additional input is needed before a program can run.

**sed** Filtering text editor that requires you supply filenames, operations, and text before running it.

**server** In a distributed file system, a computer that supplies files and services to other computers.

**sh** Command used to switch shells.

**shell** A program that interprets commands from the user into instructions the computer can understand. Popular shells include the Bourne, Korn, Bourne Again, and C shells.

**shell script** A file containing a series of commands for a UNIX shell.

**shutdown** Command used to shutdown a UNIX system before powering down.

**signal** An instruction sent by the operating system to a program, telling it to shutdown or otherwise modify its behavior.

**sort** Command used to sort files.

**SPARCstation** Popular UNIX workstation sold by Sun Microsystems.

**spell** Command that generates a list of words not contained in a dictionary file.

**standard error** The default location for error messages, usually your screen.

**standard input and output**  The path that the data takes: Input usually comes from your keyboard or another program, while output is usually sent to your screen, to a file, or to a printer. When you specify output to anything but the defaults, you are redirecting the input and output.

**state**  See *system state.*

**status line**  A portion of the screen used to provide feedback to the user. Not supported by all UNIX programs.

**stty**  Command that allows you to assign different meanings to a key.

**superuser**  The user who can do just about everything possible within the UNIX operating system.

**swapping**  Using the hard disk as a slower form of RAM when there's no RAM available to run programs or to store data.

**symbolic links**  An advanced form of a linked file that allows links between files located on remote file systems.

**system administrator**  A worker officially assigned to oversee housekeeping details on a UNIX system, including adding new users and scheduling system backups.

**system call**  Actions available to programs only after communicating with the kernel, such as printing files or saving data to disk.

**system state**  The state of the operating system: single user, multiuser, administrative, and more.

# T

**TCP/IP (Transmission Control Protocol/ Internet Protocol)**  Protocols used to link UNIX and non-UNIX computers worldwide via the Internet.

**tail**  Command used to display the final ten lines of a file.

**talk**  Command that lets you send instant messages to other users logged on the system.

**tar**  Command that archives files and data to a backup device, such as a tape drive or floppy disks.

**tbl**  Dot commands used to create tables in conjunction with **troff**.

**telnet**  Command that allows you to remotely login another computer on your network.

**terminal**  Originally used to describe a machine consisting of little more than a keyboard and a screen that relies on the larger system for its computing power; now used to describe any computer used to communicate with a UNIX system.

**test**  Command used to check variables under the Bourne shell.

**text editor**  A UNIX program, like **vi** or **emacs**, used to create ASCII text files.

**text-formatting program**  A program, such as **troff**, that takes a text file created elsewhere and prepares it with formatting commands for output to a printer.

**thrashing**  A condition where the computer is slowed down because the system is writing extensively to and from hard disk when all the RAM is in use.

**tmp**  Directory used by the system for temporary storage of working files.

**troff**  Text-processing program that processes text files for output on a typesetting machine. The original **troff** was upgraded to support all output devices (typesetting machines, laser printers, etc.) and renamed **ditroff**, though most users still refer to **ditroff** generically as **troff**.

# Glossary

## U

**UUCP (UNIX-to-UNIX System Copy)** Program that copies files from one system to another via the Internet, a network, or ordinary telephone lines.

**UUCP Network** A series of UNIX computers that pass along electronic mail and files all around the world. Largely supplanted by the Internet.

**UNIX** The greatest operating system in the whole wide world. You should be commended for your astute and informed selection of such a great operating system.

**Usenet** A loose confederation of computer systems (both UNIX and non-UNIX) that transmits electronic mail and newsgroups.

**userid** See *login name.*

**utility** A very specialized program that performs only a few actions.

## V

**vi** A text editor that ships with virtually every UNIX system.

**virtual memory** See *paging.*

## W

**wc** Command that returns the number of words in a given file.

**who** Command that displays other users logged on the system.

**wildcards** Special characters within a filename that tells the shell to search for all files with similar filenames: *r, for example, would tell the shell to return all files ending with the character *r.*

**window manager** X Window program that defines how other programs actually appear and act on the display.

**word processor** Software that combines the powers of text editors and text processors into single packages.

**workstation** Usually a powerful, networked, single-user computer running the UNIX operating system.

**write** Command that lets you send instant messages to other users logged on the system.

**WYSIWYG (what-you-see-is-what-you-get)** A term describing word processors and electronic-publishing packages that display exactly how a document will look before it is printed.

## X, Y, Z

**X terminal** Computer that runs a local X server, but relies on a machine elsewhere on the network for most of its computing power.

**X Window System** Graphical windowing system created by MIT that can be described as building blocks for fuller user interfaces, like Motif or Open Look. It is not tied to any particular operating system, but it has been popularized with the UNIX operating system.

**xterm** Popular X Window program that provides a command-line interface to the UNIX operating system.

**zombie** Process that is not active, but not yet killed by the parent process.

# Index

## A

# Index

# INDEX

*Continued*

# Index

# Index

# Index

## O

O command/o command, 235
object-oriented programming (OOP), 300–302
    code, 292
    files, 294
Objective-C, 292
oclock, 166, 167
octal dumps, 94
od, viewing files with, 94–95
online manuals, 24, 49, 101, 258
Open Group, 12, 146
open hostname command, 215
Open Look, 150, 153, 161, 167
Open Software Foundation, 12
Open Windows, 166
options, 16
    commands, 21, 27
    variety, 17, 26
or UPS, 325
Oracle, 84, 331
orphans, 138
OS/2, 136
overwriting files, 63

## P

pack command, 43
page breaks, 259
Palm Pilot handheld computer, 291
paper size, 264
parameters, command line, 26, 27, 276–277
parsing
    commands, 110
    pathnames, 50–51
Pascal, 292
passwords, 6, 8, 94, 214, 216, 220
    changing, 18–21
    FTP sites, 204
    root user account, 318
patch utility, 86, 87
paths, 50–51, 63, 102, 118

PCs
    clock, 318
    logging off, 34
    Slackwave Linux, 16
    text files, 44
    UNIX application accessibility, 146
pdksh, 10, 120
Perl, 270, 273, 291–293, 312, 313, 330–333
permissions
    begging, 56–57
    changing, 58, 60–61
    copying remote files, 224–225
    subdirectories, 51
pg command, 73
Pico, 250–251
PID number, 138
pine, 176–178
    attachments, 185
    folders, 182, 183
ping command, 218–219
pipe (|) operators, 30–31, 79, 122, 284, 336
Platypus Society, 282
point size, type, 256
pointing devices, 148
polymorphism, 301
PostScript printers, 256, 258–259, 262, 264
power failures, 325
Practical Extraction and Report Language. *See* Perl
–print option, 71
printers, 45, 255
    GhostScript supported, 265
    PostScript printers, 256, 258–259, 262, 264
    sharing, 209
printing
    current working directory, 47
    error messages, 286
    files, 74–75
    GhostScript, 264–265
    library data, 297
    preview, 232, 262–263
    scripts as executed, 286
    search results, 33, 71
    troff, 256
privacy, e-mail, 182
prof, 306–307

# Index

# T

# Index

## U

## V

## W

# my2cents.idgbooks.com

## Register This Book — And Win!

Visit **http://my2cents.idgbooks.com** to register this book and we'll automatically enter you in our fantastic monthly prize giveaway. It's also your opportunity to give us feedback: let us know what you thought of this book and how you would like to see other topics covered.

## Discover IDG Books Online!

The IDG Books Online Web site is your online resource for tackling technology — at home and at the office. Frequently updated, the IDG Books Online Web site features exclusive software, insider information, online books, and live events!

### 10 Productive & Career-Enhancing Things You Can Do at www.idgbooks.com

- Nab source code for your own programming projects.

- Download software.

- Read Web exclusives: special articles and book excerpts by IDG Books Worldwide authors.

- Take advantage of resources to help you advance your career as a Novell or Microsoft professional.

- Buy IDG Books Worldwide titles or find a convenient bookstore that carries them.

- Register your book and win a prize.

- Chat live online with authors.

- Sign up for regular e-mail updates about our latest books.

- Suggest a book you'd like to read or write.

- Give us your 2¢ about our books and about our Web site.

You say you're not on the Web yet? It's easy to get started with IDG Books' Discover the Internet, available at local retailers everywhere.